W9-BYT-745

"AN ELOQUENT CRY FROM THE LAND OF SILENT PEOPLE, where blacks are assigned by whites to a permanent role of inferiority." —*John Barkham Reviews*

"COMPELLING, CHILLING, AUTHENTIC . . . an emotionally charged explanation of how it felt to grow up under South Africa's system of legalized racism known as apartheid." —*Milwaukee Sentinel*

"Despite the South African government's creation of a virtually impenetrable border between black and white lives, this searing autobiography breaches that boundary, drawing readers into the turmoil, terror, and sad strategems for survival in a black township." —*Foreign Affairs*

"VIVID"—*Library Journal*

"TOLD WITH RELENTLESS HONESTY . . . the reader is given a rare personal glimpse behind the televised protests and boycotts, of the daily fear and hunger which is devastating to both body and soul." —*The Christian Science Monitor*

"A CHILLING, GRUESOME, BRAVE MEMOIR . . . Mathabane provides a straightforward, harrowing account of apartheid as it is practiced." —*Kirkus Reviews*

MARK MATHABANE attended the Columbia University School of Journalism and now lives in High Point, North Carolina. He is a much sought-after lecturer on South Africa, where his family remains.

KAFFIR BOY

The True Story of a Black Youth's
Coming of Age in
Apartheid South Africa

MARK MATHABANE

A PLUME BOOK

NEW AMERICAN LIBRARY

NEW YORK AND SCARBOROUGH, ONTARIO

NAL BOOKS ARE AVAILABLE AT QUANTITY DISCOUNTS WHEN USED TO PROMOTE PRODUCTS OR SERVICES. FOR INFORMATION PLEASE WRITE TO PREMIUM MARKETING DIVISION, NEW AMERICAN LIBRARY, 1633 BROADWAY, NEW YORK, NEW YORK 10019.

SIGNET, SIGNET CLASSIC, MENTOR, ONYX, PLUME, MERIDIAN and NAL BOOKS are published in the United States by New American Library, 1633 Broadway, New York, New York 10019, in Canada by The New American Library of Canada Limited, 81 Mack Avenue, Scarborough, Ontario M1L 1M8

Library of Congress Cataloging-in-Publication Data

Mathabane, Mark.
  Kaffir boy.

  Reprint. Originally published: New York : Macmillan, c1986.
  Includes index.
  1. Mathabane, Mark. 2. Blacks—South Africa—Biography. 3. Apartheid—South Africa. I. Title. DT779.95.M38A34 1987 968'00496024 [B] 86-28521
ISBN 0-452-25943-6

First Plume Printing, March, 1987

9 10 11 12 13 14 15 16 17 18

This book is dedicated to those handful of white South Africans who helped me grow as a human being and a tennis player, and with whom I share the hope of someday seeing a South Africa free of apartheid; and to Stan and Marjory Smith, who believed in me and gave me a new lease on life by providing me with the opportunity to realise my dream.

A very special dedication goes to my family and to millions of my black brothers and sisters who still remain slaves in the prison house of apartheid. To them, for teaching me to fight and to be a survivor, I chant, "*Amandla! Awethu!* (Power is ours!)"; let us not rest until we are free to live in dignity in the land of our birth.

CONTENTS

Preface   ix

Part I: The Road to Alexandra
1

Part II: Passport to Knowledge
121

Part III: Passport to Freedom
213

Index   351

PREFACE

I am always asked to explain what it felt like to grow up black under South Africa's system of legalized racism known as apartheid, and how I escaped from it and ended up in America. This book is the most thorough answer I have heretofore given.

The last thing I ever dreamed of when I was daily battling for survival and for an identity other than that of inferiority and fourth-class citizen, which apartheid foisted on me, was that someday I would attend an American college, edit its newspaper, graduate with honors, practise journalism and write a book.

How could I have dreamed of all this when I was born of illiterate parents who could not afford to pay my way through school, let alone pay the rent for our shack and put enough food on the table; when black people in Alexandra lived under constant police terror and the threat of deportation to impoverished tribal reserves; when at ten I contemplated suicide because I found the burden of living in a ghetto, poverty-stricken and without hope, too heavy to shoulder; when in 1976 I got deeply involved in the Soweto protests, in which hundreds of black students were killed by the police, and thousands fled the country to escape imprisonment and torture?

In *Kaffir Boy* I have re-created, as best as I can remember, all these experiences. I have sought to paint a portrait of my childhood and youth in Alexandra, a black ghetto of Johannesburg, where I was born and lived for eighteen years, with the hope that the rest of the world will finally understand why apartheid cannot be reformed: it has to be abolished.

Much has been written and spoken about the politics of apartheid: the forced removals of black communities from their ancestral lands, the Influx Control and Pass laws that mandate where blacks can live, work, raise families, be buried; the migrant labour system that forces black men to live away from their families eleven months out of a year; the breaking up of black families in the ghettos as the authorities seek to create a so-called white South Africa; the brutal suppression of the black majority as it agitates for equal rights. But what does it all mean in human terms?

When I was growing up in Alexandra it meant hate, bitterness, hunger, pain, terror, violence, fear, dashed hopes and dreams. Today it still means the same for millions of black children who are trapped in the ghettos of South Africa, in a lingering nightmare of a racial system that in many respects resembles Nazism. In the ghettos black children fight for survival from the moment they are born. They take to hating and fearing the police, soldiers and authorities as a baby takes to its mother's breast.

In my childhood these enforcers of white prerogatives and whims represented a sinister force capable of crushing me at will; of making my parents flee in the dead of night to escape arrest under the Pass laws; of marching them naked out of bed because they did not have the permit allowing them to live as husband and wife under the same roof. They turned my father—by repeatedly arresting him and denying him the right to earn a living in a way that gave him dignity—into such a bitter man that, as he fiercely but in vain resisted the emasculation, he hurt those he loved the most.

The movies, with their lurid descriptions of white violence, reinforced this image of white terror and power. Often the products of abject poverty and broken homes, many black children, for whom education is inferior and not compulsory, have been derailed by movies into the dead-end life of crime and violence. It is no wonder that black ghettos have one of the highest murder rates in the world, and South African prisons are among the most packed. It was purely by accident that I did not end up a *tsotsi* (thug, mugger, gangster). It was no coincidence that, until the age of ten, I refused to set foot in the white world.

The turning point came when one day in my eleventh year I accompanied my grandmother to her gardening job and met a white family that did not fit the stereotypes I had grown up with. Most blacks, exposed daily to virulent racism and dehumanized and embittered by it, do not believe that such whites exist. From this family I started receiving "illegal books" like *Treasure Island* and *David Copperfield*, which revealed a different reality and marked the beginning of my revolt against Bantu education's attempts to proscribe the limits of my aspirations and determine my place in South African life.

At thirteen I stumbled across tennis, a sport so "white" most blacks thought I was mad for thinking I could excel in it; others mistook me for an Uncle Tom. Through tennis I learned the important lesson that South Africa's 4.5 million whites are not all racists. As I grew older, and got to understand them more—their fears, longings, hopes, ignorance and mistaken beliefs, and they mine—this lesson became the conviction that whites are in some ways victims of apartheid, too, and that it is the system, not they, that has to be destroyed; just as it was Hitler's regime that had to extirpated, not the German people. Such an attitude helped me survive the nightmare into which my life was plunged by the Soweto protests of 1976. A tennis scholarship to an American college, arranged by the professional tennis player Stan Smith, in 1978, became my passport to freedom.

Kaffir Boy is also about how, in order to escape from the clutches of apartheid, I had to reject the tribal traditions of my ancestors. It was a hard thing to do, for there were many good things in my African heritage, which, had it been left to me to choose freely, I would have preserved and venerated. I, too, had the burning need like human beings everywhere to know where I came from, in order to better understand who I was and where I was going in this world. But apartheid had long adulterated my heritage and traditions, twisted them into tools of oppression and indoctrination. I saw at a young age that apartheid was using tribalism to deny me equal rights, to separate me from my black brothers and sisters, to justify segregation and perpetuate white power and privilege, to render me subservient, docile and, therefore, exploitable. I instinctively understood that in order to forge my own identity, to achieve according to my aspirations and dreams, to see myself the equal of any man, black or white, I had to reject this brand of tribalism, and that in the rejection I ran the risk of losing my heritage. I took the plunge.

Being in America has afforded me the rare opportunity of gaining a proper perspective on my African heritage, of looking at South Africa critically, of understanding what it means to be regarded as a human being, of learning about the nitty-gritty of a democracy and, most important, of using the pen to fight against injustice and racism in my native land.

My family is still in Alexandra, undergoing the same hardships I describe in this book. The youths of my generation have become more militant, the tools of repression have become more numerous and sophisticated and black schools and ghettos have become centers of social protest and bloody conflict with the police and soldiers. South Africa has entered its darkest hour, and all its sons and daughters have a responsibility, a duty, to see to it that truth and justice triumph. I hope to do my part.

I would like to thank Edward T. Chase and Dominick Anfuso, my editors at Macmillan, and Fifi Oscard and Kevin McShane, my agents, for their support and encouragement throughout the writing of this book. I would also like to thank Jeanne Moutoussamy-Ashe and Hajima Ota, whose photographs have been invaluable.

New York, 1986

The word *Kaffir* is of Arabic origin. It means "infidel." In South Africa it is used disparagingly by most whites to refer to blacks. It is the equivalent of the term *nigger*. I was called a "Kaffir" many times.

Except those of my family, Stan and Marjory Smith, Arthur Ashe, Wilfred Horn, Owen and Jennifer Williams, Ray Moore and Agnes and Bremer Hofmeyer, all the names in this book are fictitious, and any resemblance to living persons is coincidental.

I, as a Christian, have always felt that there is one thing above all about "apartheid" or "separate development" that is unforgivable. It seems utterly indifferent to the suffering of individual persons, who lose their land, their homes, their jobs, in pursuit of what surely is the most terrible dream in the world.

—Albert Luthuli, 1960 Nobel Peace Prize winner

"Rise like Lions after slumber
In unvanquishable number—
Shake your chains to earth like
dew
Which in sleep had fallen on you—
Ye are many—they are few."

—Percy Bysshe Shelley, *The Mask of Anarchy*

The limits of tyrants are prescribed by the endurance of those whom they oppress.

—Frederick Douglass

Give me the liberty to know, to utter, and to argue freely according to conscience, above all liberties.

—John Milton

PART ONE

THE ROAD TO ALEXANDRA

1

WARNING
THIS ROAD PASSES THROUGH PROCLAIMED BANTU LOCATIONS, ANY PERSON WHO ENTERS THE LOCATIONS WITHOUT A PERMIT RENDERS HIMSELF LIABLE FOR PROSECUTION FOR CONTRAVENING THE BANTU (URBAN AREAS) CONSOLIDATION ACT 1945, AND THE LOCATION REGULATION ACT OF THE CITY OF JOHANNESBURG.

The above message can be found written on larger-than-life signs staked on every road leading into Alexandra, where I was born and raised, or for that matter, into any other black ghetto of South Africa. It is meant to dissuade white people from entering the black world. As a result, more than 90 percent of white South Africans go through a lifetime without seeing firsthand the inhuman conditions under which blacks have to survive.

Yet the white man of South Africa claims to the rest of the world that he knows what is good for black people and what it takes for a black child to grow up to adulthood. He vaunts aloud that "his blacks" in South Africa are well fed and materially better off under the chains of apartheid than their liberated brothers and sisters in the rest of Africa. But, in truth, these claims and boasts are hollow.

The white man of South Africa certainly does not know me. He certainly does not know the conditions under which I was born and had to live for eighteen years. So my story is intended to show him with words a world he would otherwise not see because of a sign and a conscience racked with guilt and to make him feel what I felt when he contemptuously called me a "Kaffir boy."

At the writing of this book the ghetto of Alexandra had just been saved from extinction by Bishop Desmond Tutu, winner of the 1984 Nobel Peace Prize, and a group of clergymen. When the reprieve came over half of Alexandra had already been destroyed, for the ghetto had been on death row since 1962 when the South African

3

government first decreed that it had to go because it occupied land onto which whites wished to expand.

The remains of Alexandra can be found about ten miles north of Johannesburg. You will not mistake those remains for anything else. They occupy a one-square-mile pit constantly shrouded by a heavy blanket of smog. It is the only such pit in an enclave of spacious, fresh-aired, verdant white suburbs sporting such melodious names as Northcliff, Rosebank, Lower Houghton, Bramley, Killarney and Edenvale.

The Alexandra of my childhood and youth was a shantytown of mostly shacks, a few decent houses, lots of gutters and lots of unpaved, potholed streets with numbers from First to Twenty-third. First Avenue was where Indians—the cream of Alexandra's quarantined society—lived, behind their sell-everything stores and produce stalls, which were the ghetto's main shopping centre. Indians first came to South Africa in 1860, as indentured servants, to work the sugarcane fields of Natal.

Second, Third and Fourth avenues were inhabited mostly by Coloureds, the mulatto race which came into being nine months after white settlers arrived in South Africa in 1652—without women. The rest of Alexandra's streets were filled by black faces, many of them as black as coal, full-blooded Africans. Many of these blacks were as poor as church mice. In South Africa there's a saying that to be black is to be at the end of the line when anything of significance is to be had. So these people were considered and treated as the dregs of society, aliens in the land of their birth. Such labelling and treatment made them an angry and embittered lot.

The Alexandra of my childhood and youth was one of the oldest shantytowns in the Witwatersrand—the area where black miners toil night and day to tear gold from the bowels of the earth so that the white man of South Africa can enjoy one of the highest standards of living in the world. Many of Alexandra's first settlers came from the tribal reserves, where they could no longer eke out a living, to seek work in the city of gold. Work was plentiful in those days: in mines, factories and white people's homes. As a result these black pioneers stayed, some bought plots of land, established families and called Alexandra home, sweet home. Many shed their tribal cloth and embraced Western culture, a way of life over 350 years of white oppression had deluded them into believing was better than their own. And so it was that in the mid-1950s Alexandra boasted a population of over one hundred thousand blacks, Coloureds and Indians—all squeezed into a space of one square mile.

My parents, a generation or so removed from these earliest settlers of Alexandra, had, too, come from the tribal reserves. My father came from what is now the so-called independent homeland of the Vendas in the northwestern corner of the Transvaal. Venda's specious independence (no other country but South Africa recognizes it) was imposed by the Pretoria regime in 1979, thus at the time making three (Transkei and Bophuthatswana were the other two) the number of these archipelagos of poverty, suffering and corruption, where blacks are supposed to exercise their political rights. Since "independence" the Venda people have been under the clutches of the Pretoria-anointed dictator, Patrick Mphephu, who, despite the loss of two elections, continues clinging to power through untempered repression and brutality.

My mother came from Gazankulu, the tribal reserve for the Tsongas in the Northeastern Transvaal. Gazankulu is also being pressured into "independence." My parents met and married in Alexandra. Immediately following marriage they rented a shack in one of the squalid yards of the ghetto. And in that shack I was born, a few months before sixty-nine unarmed black protesters were massacred— many shot in the back as they fled for safety—by South African policemen during a peaceful demonstration against the pass laws in Sharpeville on March 21, 1960. Pass laws regulate the movement of blacks in so-called white South Africa. And it was the pass laws that, in those not so long ago days of my childhood and youth, first awakened me to the realities of life as a Kaffir boy in South Africa. . . .

2 It was early morning of a bitterly cold winter day in 1965. I was lying on a bed of cardboard, under a kitchen table, peering through a large hole in the blanket at the spooky darkness around me. I was wide awake and terrified. All night long I had been having nightmares in which throngs of black people sprawled dead in pools of red blood, surrounded by all sorts of slimy, creeping creatures. These nightmares had plagued me since I turned five two weeks ago. I thought of waking my mother in the next room, but my father's words of warning not to wake her on account of bad dreams stopped me. All was quiet, save for the snores of my sister

Florah—three years old—huddled alongside me, under the same blanket, and the squeaks of rats in the cupboard. From time to time the moon shone eerily through the window. Afraid to go back to sleep lest I have another nightmare, I stayed awake, peering at the quivering blackness through the hole. The darkness seemed alive.

My father woke up and began arguing sharply with my mother in the bedroom. It was five o'clock by the *kikilihoo* (cock's crow), time for him to go to work. He always went to work at this time—and he was angry at my mother for forgetting to prepare his *scufftin* (food for work). Soon he emerged, holding a flickering tallow candle in one hand, and a worn-out Stetson hat in the other. He silently went about preparing his *scufftin* from what was left of yesterday's *pap 'n vleis* (porridge and meat). He wrapped the *scufftin* in sheets of old newspapers, took the family's *waslap* (facecloth) from the window, dampened it with water from a mug and wiped his face. He drank what was left of the water in the mug. Minutes later he was out through the door, on his way to work, but not before I had said to him: "Don't forget our fish and chips, Papa."

"Fish and chips is tomorrow, son. Today is Thursday. Payday is tomorrow."

" 'Bye, 'bye, Papa."

"Go back to sleep."

As soon as he was out through the door my mother, clad only in her skimpy underwear, came into the kitchen, chamber pot in hand. The chamber pot dripped and had a bad smell, like the one which always pervaded the yard whenever our neighbours hung urine-soaked blankets and cardboard on fences to dry under the blazing African sun.

"Where are you going, Mama?"

"To the outhouse."

"Those bad dreams came back, Mama."

"I'll be back soon."

Before she left, she blew out the candle to save it from burning out and took with her a book of matches. I lingered between sleep and wakefulness, anticipating my mother's speedy return. Twenty minutes passed without any sign of her. I grew more afraid of the darkness; I shut my eyes, pulled the blanket over my head and minutes later I was in dreamland. I had been asleep but a short while when my mother came bursting through the door, yelling, in a winded voice, "Get up, Johannes! Get up quickly!" And as she yelled she reached under the table and shook me vigorously.

"Hunh?" I mumbled sleepily, stirring but not waking up, thinking it a dream.

"Get up! Get up!" she yelled again, yanking the torn blanket covering Florah and me, and almost instantly I awoke and heard a door shut with a resounding slam. From then on things became rather entangled for me. Unaware that I was still under the table I jerked upward, and my head banged against the top of the table. I winced but didn't cry; my father had warned me that men and boys never cry, ever. Still only half awake, I began crawling upon my hands and knees from under the table, but the darkness was all around me, and I couldn't see where I was going.

As I was crawling blindly my face rammed into one of the concrete slabs propping one of the table's legs. I let out a scream and drew back momentarily, dazed and smarting. At this point half my mind still told me that I was in a dream, but the hot pain all over my face convinced me otherwise. I resumed groping for a way from under the table, to find out where my mother had suddenly gone, and why she had awakened me. Finally I was out. I leaned myself for a while against the side of the table and waited for the throbbing pain in my head to cease.

Suddenly, as I stood leaning against the table, from outside came a series of dreadful noises. Sirens blared, voices screamed and shouted, wood cracked and windows shattered, children bawled, dogs barked and footsteps pounded. I was bewildered; I had never heard such a racket before. I was instantly seized by a feeling of terror.

"Mama! Where are you?" I screamed, groping about with one hand, the other clutching the table. I did not know whether my mother had gone back out, or was still in the house.

"Over here," a voice suddenly whispered from somewhere behind me. It was my mother's voice, but it sounded so faint I could barely hear it. I turned my head and strained to see where it was coming from and saw nothing but darkness. Where was my mother? Why was it so dark? Why the dreadful noises outside? My imagination ran wild. The pitch-black room seemed alive with the voodoo spirits of my mother's tales, ready to pounce upon me if I as much as took a step from where I was standing.

"Mama! Where are you?" I screamed again, fear mounting inside me.

"I'm over here," the disembodied voice of my mother said from somewhere in the dark.

I swung around and saw a candle coming out of the bedroom. It stopped briefly by the door. It was my mother. In the dim candlelight, her body, crouched like that of an animal cowering in fear, cast an oblong, eerie shadow on the flaking whitewashed wall. She stole over to where I stood transfixed, handed me the flickering candle and told me to keep it down and away from the window.

"What's the matter, Mama?"

"Not so loud," she cautioned, a finger on her lips. Still clad only in her underwear, she hurriedly draped a tattered black shawl, which had been lying on a tin chair nearby, over her shoulders, but the shawl didn't cover much. She reached under the kitchen table and grabbed the torn blanket and draped it in place of the shawl and took the shawl and spread it over the newspapers and cardboard covering Florah.

"What's the matter, Mama?"

"Peri-Urban is here."

"Peri-Urban!" I gasped and stiffened at the name of the dreaded Alexandra Police Squad. To me nothing, short of a white man, was more terrifying; not even a bogeyman. Memories of previous encounters with the police began haunting me. Will the two fat black policemen with *sjamboks** and truncheons burst open the door again? And will the one with the twirled mustache and big hands grit his teeth at me while threatening, "Speak up, boy! or I'll let you taste my *sjambok!*" and thereafter spit in my face and hit me on the head with a truncheon for refusing to tell where my mother and father were hiding? And will the tall, carroty-haired white man in fatigues stand by the doorjamb again, whistling a strange tune and staring fear into Florah and me?

"W-where a-are t-they?" I stammered.

"Outside. Don't be afraid now. They're still in the next neighbourhood. I was in the outhouse when the alarm came." "When the alarm came" meant people leaping over fences in a mad dash to escape the police.

I nodded sheepishly, the sleep now completely gone from my eyes. I was now standing—naked, cold and trembling—in the middle of the room. My mother took the candle from my hand and told me to dress. I reached under the kitchen table for my patched khaki shorts and dressed hurriedly. Meanwhile the pandemonium outside was intensifying with each minute; the raid, it seemed, was gathering

---

* An animal-hide whip used to enforce apartheid.

momentum. Suddenly a gust of wind puffed through the sackcloth covering a hole in the window; the candle flickered but did not go out. I felt something warm soak my groin and trickle down my legs. I tried to stem the flow of urine by pressing my thighs together, but I was too late; a puddle had formed about my feet, and I scattered it with my toes. My mother handed me the candle and headed toward the table in the corner. As she went along she said, without turning to face me, "Take good care of your brother and sister while I'm gone, you hear?"

"Yes, Mama." I knew she had to leave, she had to flee from the police and leave us children alone as she had done so many times before. By now my mother had reached the table, and her big brown eyes darted about its top, searching for something.

"Where's my passbook?" she asked in a frantic voice, her tense body bent low over the table. "Bring the candle over here. Keep it down! Away from the window!" As I hurried the candle, which had now burnt to a stub, over to her, a loud scream leaped out from the dark outside. Alarmed, I stumbled and fell headlong into my mother's arms. As she steadied me she continued asking, "Where's my passbook? Where is it?" I did not know; I could not answer; I could not think; my mind had suddenly gone blank. She grabbed me by the shoulder and shook me, yelling frantically, "Where is it! Where is it! Oh, God. Where is it, child? Where is the book? Hurry, or they'll find me!"

"What book?" I said blankly.

"The little book I showed you and your sister last night, remember," she stared at me anxiously, but my eyes merely widened in confusion. No matter how hard I tried it seemed I could not rid my mind of the sinister force that had suddenly blotted out all memory.

"Remember the little black book with my picture in it. Where is it?" my mother said, again grabbing me and shaking me, begging me to remember. I could not snap out of my amnesia.

The noise outside had risen to a dreadful crescendo. Suddenly several gunshots rang out in quick succession. Shouts of "Follow that Kaffir! He can't get far! He's wounded!" followed the shots. Somehow it all jolted me back to consciousness, and I remembered where my mother's little black book was: under the pallet of cardboard where I had tucked it the night before, hoping to sneak it out the next day and show it to my friends at play—who had already shown me their mothers'—to see whose mother's picture was the most beautiful.

"It's under the table, Mama!" I cried out.

My mother thanked her ancestors. Hurriedly, she circled the table, reached under it, rolled Florah away from the damp cardboard, lifted them up, and underneath, on the earthen floor, she found her little black book. I heaved a great sigh of relief as I watched her tuck it into her bosom.

My sister's naked, frail body, now on the bare floor, shook from the icy cold seeping through a hole under the door. She coughed, then moaned—a prolonged rasping sound; but she did not wake up. My mother quickly straightened out the cardboard and rolled Florah back to sleep and covered her with more newspapers and cardboard. More screams came from outside as more doors and windows were being busted by the police; the vicious barking of dogs escalated, as did the thudding of running feet. Shouts of "Mbambe! Mbambe! (Grab him! Catch him!)" followed the screams of police whistles.

My mother was headed for the bedroom door when a shaft of very bright light flashed through the uncurtained window and fell upon her. Instantly she leaped behind the door and remained hidden behind it. Alarmed, I dropped the candle, spilling the molten wax on my feet; the room was plunged into utter darkness, for the bright light disappeared barely seconds after it had flashed. As I groped about for the candle, the bright light again flashed through the window and flooded the kitchen. This time it stayed. It seemed daylight.

My mother crept from behind the bedroom door and started toward the kitchen door, on tiptoe. As she neared it, my year-old brother, George, who slept with my mother and father on the only bed in the house, started screaming, piercing the tenuous stillness of the house. His screams stopped my mother dead in her tracks; she spun around and said to me, in a whisper, "Go quiet your brother."

"Yes, Mama," I said, but I did not go. I could not go. I seemed rooted to the spot by a terrifying fear of the unknown.

"I'll be gone a short while," my mother, now by the door, whispered. She stealthily opened it a crack, her blanketed body still in a crouch, her head almost touching the floor. She hesitated a moment or two before peering through the opening. The storm of screams that came through the door made me think that the world was somehow coming to an end. Through the opening I saw policemen, with flashlights and what looked like raised cavemen's clubs, move searchingly about several shacks across the street.

"Don't forget to lock the door securely behind me," my mother said as she ran her eyes up and down the street. More gunshots rang out; more screams and more shouts came from somewhere deep in the neighbourhood.

"Don't go, Mama!" I cried. "Please don't go! Don't leave us, please!"

She did not answer, but continued opening the door a little wider and inching her blanketed body, still bent low, slowly forward until she was halfway in and halfway out. Meantime in the bedroom George continued bawling. I hated it when he cried like that, for it heightened, and made more real, my feelings of confusion, terror and helplessness.

"Let him suck thumb," my mother said, now almost out of the house. She was still bent low. She spat on the doorknob twice, a ritual that, she once told me, protected the innocent and kept all evil spirits away, including the police. I felt vaguely reassured seeing her perform the ritual.

"And don't forget now," she said, "don't ever be afraid. I'll be back soon." Those were her last words; and as I watched her disappear behind the shacks, swallowed up by the ominous darkness and ominous sounds, her figure like that of a black-cloaked ghost, she seemed less of the mother I knew and loved, and more of a desperate fugitive fleeing off to her secret lair somewhere in the inky blackness.

I immediately slammed the door shut, bolted it in three places, blew out the candle and then scampered to the bedroom, where my brother was still crying. But as I flung open the bedroom door a new and more dreadful fear gripped me and made me turn and run back to the front door. I suddenly remembered how the police had smashed open the door during a raid one morning even though it had been bolted. I must barricade the door this time, I told myself; that will stop them. I started dragging things from all over the kitchen and piling them up against the door—a barrel half-filled with drinking water, a scuttle half-filled with coal and several tin chairs. Satisfied that the door was now impregnable I then scuttled back to the bedroom and there leaped onto the bed by the latticed window.

"Shut up, you fool!" I yelled at my brother, but he did not quiet. I then uttered the phrase, "There's a white man outside," which to small black children had the same effect as "There's a bogeyman outside," but still he would not stop. I then stuck my thumb into his wide-open mouth, as my mother had told me. But George had other plans for my thumb; he sunk his teeth into it. Howling with pain, I grabbed him by the feet and tossed him over and spanked him on the buttocks.

"Don't ever do that!"

He became hysterical and went into a seizure of screams. His body writhed and his mouth frothed. Again I grabbed his tiny feet and shook him violently, begged him to stop screaming, but still he would not quiet. I screamed at him some more; that made him worse. In desperation I wrenched his ears, pinched him black and blue, but still he continued hollering. In despair I gave up, for the time being, attempts to quiet him. My head spun and did not know what to do.

I glanced at the window; it was getting light outside. I saw two black policemen breaking down a door at the far end of the yard. A half-naked, near-hysterical, jet-black woman was being led out of an outhouse by a fat laughing black policeman who, from time to time, prodded her private parts with a truncheon. The storm of noises had now subsided somewhat, but I could still hear doors and windows being smashed, and dogs barking and children screaming. I jerked George and pinned him against the window, hoping that he would somehow understand why I needed him to shut up; but that did not help, for his eyes were shut, and he continued to scream and writhe. My eyes roved frantically about the semidark room and came to rest on a heavy black blanket hanging limply from the side of the bed. Aha! I quickly grabbed it and pulled it over George's head to muffle his screams. I pinned it tightly with both hands over his small head as he lay writhing. It worked! For though he continued screaming, I could hardly hear him. He struggled and struggled and I pinned the blanket tighter and tighter. It never crossed my mind that my brother might suffocate. As he no longer screamed, I waited, from time to time glancing nervously at the window.

Suddenly I heard the bedroom door open and shut. Startled, I let go of my hold on the blanket and turned by head toward the door only to see Florah, her eyes wild with fear, come rushing in, screaming, her hands over her head. She came over to the bedside and began tugging frantically at the blanket.

"Where's Mama! I want Mama! Where's Mama!"

"Shut up!" I raged. "Go back to sleep before I hit you!"

She did not leave.

"I'm scared," she whimpered. "I want Mama."

"Shut up, you fool!" I screamed at her again. "The white man is outside, and he's going to get you and eat you!" I should not have said that; my sister became hysterical. She flung herself at the bed and tried to claw her way up. Enraged, I slapped her hard across the mouth; she staggered but did not fall. She promptly returned to the bedside and resumed her tugging of the blanket more determinedly. My brother too was now screaming. My head felt hot with confusion and desperation; I did not know what to do; I wished my mother were present; I wished the police were blotted off the surface of the earth.

I could still hear footsteps pounding, children screaming and dogs barking, so I quickly hauled my sister onto the bed, seeing that she was resolved not to return to the kitchen. We coiled together on the narrow bed, the three of us, but because of all the awkward movements everyone was making, the bricks propping the legs of the bed shifted, and it wobbled as if about to collapse. I held my breath, and the bed did not fall. I carefully pulled the blanket tautly over the three of us. Under the blanket I saw nothing but darkness.

But the din outside after a temporary lull surged and made its way through the bolted door, through the barricade, through the kitchen, through the blanket, through the blackness and into my finger-plugged ears, as if the bed were perched in the midst of all the pandemonium. My mind blazed with questions. What was really going on outside? Were the barking dogs police dogs? Who was shooting whom? Were the *Msomi** gangs involved? I had often been told that police dogs ate black people when given the order by white people—were they eating people this time? Suppose my mother had been apprehended, would the police dogs eat her up too? What was happening to my friends?

I ached with curiosity and fear. Should I go to the kitchen window and see what was going on in the streets? My sister had wet the bed, and it felt damp and cold. Childish curiosity finally overcame the fear, and I hopped out of bed and tiptoed to the kitchen window. I had barely reached the bedroom door when I heard my sister whimper.

"Where are you going? I'm scared." I looked over my shoulder and saw Florah on the edge of the bed, her legs dangling over the side, poised to follow.

"Shut up and go back to sleep!"

"I'm coming with you." She dropped her tiny feet to the floor.

"Dare and I'll whip you!"

*Legendary black gangsters of the fifties and early sixties in the mode of the Mafia.

She whined and retracted her body frame under the blanket. I slowly opened the bedroom door, taking care to keep low and away from the shaft of light still streaming through the uncurtained window. I reached the window. What next? A piece of sackcloth covered the bottom half of the window where several panes were missing, the result of a rock hurled from the street one night long ago. My father hadn't replaced the window but used the flap as a watchpost whenever police raided the neighbourhood.

With mounting excitement I raised myself toward the window and reached for the flap. I carefully pushed it to one side as I had seen my father do and then poked my head through; all the time my eyes were on the prowl for danger. My head was halfway in and halfway out when my eyes fell upon two tall black policemen emerging from a shack across the street. They joined two others standing alongside a white man by the entrance gate to one of the yards. The white man had a holstered gun slung low about his waist, as in the movies, and was pacing briskly about, shouting orders and pointing in all different directions. Further on in the yard, another white man, also with a gun, was supervising a group of about ten black policemen as they rounded up half-naked black men and women from the shacks. Children's screams issued from some of the shacks.

The sight had me spellbound. Suddenly the white man by the entrance gate pointed in the direction of our house. Two black policemen jumped and started across the street toward me. They were quickly joined by a third. I gasped with fear. A new terror gripped me and froze me by the window, my head still sticking halfway out. My mind went blank; I shut my eyes; my heart thumped somewhere in my throat. I overheard the three black policemen, as they came across the street, say to each other.

"That's number thirty-seven."

"Yes. But I don't think we'll find any of the *Msomi* gang in there."

"*Umlungu* [the white man] thinks there may be a few hiding in there. If we don't find them, we can still make easy money. The yard is a haven for people without passbooks."

"But I think everybody has fled. Look at those busted doors."

"There's a few over there still shut."

"All right, then, let's go in."

Suddenly there was a tremendous thud, as of something heavy crashing against the floor, and I heard George's screams of pain pierce the air. I opened my eyes momentarily and saw the three black policemen, only a few steps from the door, stop and look at one another. I quickly retracted my head but remained crouched under the window, afraid of going anywhere lest I be seen. I heard the three policemen say to one another:

"You heard that?"

"Yes. It's an infant crying."

"I bet you they left that one alone too."

Suddenly my sister came screaming out of the bedroom, her hands over her head.

"Yowee! Yowee!" she bawled. "Johannes! Come an' see! Come an' see!"

I stared at her, unable to move, not wanting to move.

"It's G-george," she stammered with horror; "B-blood, d-dead, b-blood, d-dead!" her voice trailed into sobs. She rushed over to where I stood and began pulling my hand, imploring me to go see my brother who, she said dramatically, was bleeding to death. My mouth contorted into frantic, inaudible "Go aways" and "shut ups" but she did not leave. I heard someone pounding at the door. In the confusion that followed angry voices said:

"There's no point in going in. I've had enough of hollering infants."

"Me too."

"I bet you there's no one in there but the bloody children."

"You just took the words right out of my mouth."

"Then let's get back to the vans. We still have more streets to comb. This neighbourhood is about dry anyway."

They left. It turned out that George had accidently fallen off the bed and smashed his head against a pile of bricks at the foot of the bed, sustaining a deep cut across the forehead. The gash swelled and bled badly, stopping only after I had swathed his forehead with pieces of rags. The three of us cowered together in silence another three hours until my mother returned from the ditch where she had been hiding.

3 That evening the neighbourhood was gripped by rumors that the Peri-Urban police were going to launch another raid soon, to "clean up" the neighbourhood, so to speak, because the one that morning had been—by police standards—unsuccessful. The back-to-back raids, the rumors went, marked the beginning of the annual "Operation Clean-up Month," a month during which hundreds of black policemen, led by white officers, combed the entire Alexandra ghetto—street by street and yard by yard—searching for people whose passbooks were not in order, gangsters, prostitutes, black families living illegally in the township, shebeen owners and those persons deemed "undesirables" under the Influx Control Law. I did not understand what many of these names meant, though I was told that we and most of our neighbours were counted under them.

That night we went to sleep with the rumors of an imminent police raid hanging over the neighbourhood like a dark cloud.

"We will have to leave before daybreak," I heard my mother say to my father as we prepared to go to sleep. "That way when the raid comes we won't be here." Upon hearing that Florah and I tensed and grew frightened. My mother calmed us.

"Don't believe the rumors, woman," my father said with an air of authority. "There won't be any raid. Weren't the police here just today? People are just scared. They are always scared. They always will be scared."

"But everybody says they're coming," my mother insisted. "It's the start of Operation Clean-up Month, remember?"

"Woman," my father said sternly, "I tell you there won't be any raid. It's just another false rumor."

But a raid was coming. A little after midnight, while everybody was sound asleep and snoring and dreaming, the police invaded the neighbourhood.

"OPEN UP!" Fists banged at the kitchen door. "IT'S PERI-URBAN!"

For a minute I thought I was dreaming because from outside there suddenly erupted the same volcano of noise of a day ago. Dogs barked. People shrieked and shouted and ran. Sirens screamed. Children screamed. Doors and windows smashed. Feet clumped. I tossed and turned as if in a nightmare, but the persistent pounding and kicking at the door, and the muffled voices coming from the bedroom convinced me otherwise.

"OPEN UP OR WE'LL BREAK IT DOWN!" demanded the police more loudly.

I slowly crept out from under the blanket; the sheets of newspaper rustled; I felt a tightening in the pit of my stomach, as if a block of ice were embedded there and were now freezing my guts. My sister stirred and whimpered; I reached under the blanket and told her to hush.

"OPEN UP!"

I lost control of my bladder and quickly soaked the cardboard, the newspapers and the blanket. My sleepy eyes strained to make out objects in the dark, but the darkness was impregnable, ominous; the more I stared into it, the blacker and blacker it became. I felt dizzy. I wanted to scream but my voice was paralyzed. Suddenly flashlights flared through the uncurtained window. Glass shattered somewhere nearby. I yearned to become invisible, to have the ground beneath me open and swallow me until it was all over.

"OPEN UP!" a voice bellowed by the window. "WE KNOW YOU'RE IN THERE!"

I succeeded in reaching the bedroom door, fear all over me. I pasted my ear to the door and heard my mother and father whispering to each other in frantic tones. So they were both still in there. How were they going to escape?

"Mama," I whispered frantically, tapping lightly on the door, "the police are here."

"Johannes, is that you?" my mother whispered back.

"They're here, Mama. What should I do?"

"Don't let them in yet."

"But they're breaking the door down, Mama."

"Don't open yet."

"They're breaking it down, Mama."

Silence.

Should I open the door? The police were smashing it, and if I didn't open it their anger would know no bounds once they got in; I remembered well how they beat me up the last time. But my mother and father were attempting to hide, and if I opened too soon they would be taken away; I remembered well how they were taken away the last time. What should I do?

The pounding and kicking at the door awakened my sister, and she started screaming from under the table. After what seemed like an eternity I unlatched the door. As it swung wide open, with tremendous force, two tall black policemen in stiff brown uniforms rushed in and immediately blinded me with the glare from their flashlights. Before I knew what was happening one of them had kicked me savagely on the side, sending me crashing into a crate in the far corner. I hit the crate with such force that I nearly passed out. With stars in my eyes I grabbed the edges of the crate and tried to rise, but I couldn't; my knees had turned to Jell-O, my eyes were cloudy and my head pounded as if it were being split with an axe. As I tried to gather my senses, another kick sent me back to the floor, flat on my face. As I went down, my jaw struck the blunt side of the blade of an axe jutting from the side of the crate. My head burned with pain. Blood began oozing from my nostrils and lips. Several of my teeth were loose. I started screaming, forgetting all about my father's rule, begging for forgiveness from my assailant for whatever wrong I had done. My bloodied hands reached out and clung to his legs, but he shoved me away. I again lost control of my bladder. My muscles tightened and beads of sweat mingled with blood covered my body. My foggy eyes tried to see where my assailant was and what he was going to do to me next, but I could only make out indistinct shapes and shadows floating like ghosts about the room. Suddenly a crushing, viselike grip clutched my left armpit and jerked me up. I screamed: "Mama!"

"SHUT UP!" the policeman hissed, a hazy shadow of terror towering in front of me. He shook me violently, the glare of his flashlight trained into my eyes, searing them. He jammed me against the brick wall by the ribs, warning me to shut up or else. . . .

"WHAT TOOK YOU SO LONG TO OPEN THE BLOODY DOOR?" he hissed.

"He's had enough, Solly," a deep, surly voice said from somewhere in the room. "He's had enough, let him go."

"DON'T DO IT AGAIN, UNDERSTAND?" my assailant snarled, bringing the flashlight so close to my eyes they seemed to cook. I blinked repeatedly.

"I w-won't d-do i-it a-again." I said with bated breath.

"Where are your parents?" my assailant hissed.

"I d-don't k-know." I felt I had to protect my parents, no matter what.

"You're lying to me, boy!"

"We'll find them, Solly. Let him go. We'll find them."

My assailant let go of me, and I slumped to the floor, spent with fear. I felt the side of my head; it was bruised and swollen, and something pounded like tribal drums inside my ears. My head no longer felt like my head but like a dead weight on my torso. I coughed and spit, and the spittle was all red with blood. My body was wet and slippery with sweat, urine and blood, as if I had been soaked in grease.

Feeling dizzy, I leaned against the crate, disbelieving all that was happening, thinking it all a dream—a bad dream—a nightmare, expecting to awaken any time and find that I was unscathed, that nothing had happened.

The lightheadedness dissolved, and I was able to lift my head up again. I saw the two policemen searching the kitchen, kicking chairs, crates, boxes, tins, pots, dishes, rags, cardboard; searching under the table, behind the cupboard, behind the door, in the corners, everywhere; cursing how shabby the place looked, and how everything was hindering their search. Finding no one in the kitchen they went for the bedroom door, where my sister cowered in screams. My heart fluttered, my skin prickled and the tightness in my throat returned. I felt a thick lump of fear force its way down my tight throat, into my tight stomach, where it settled.

One of the policemen grabbed my sister and shoved her away from the door. My sister screamed hysterically and flailed her arms as her owlish eyes searched wildly about the kitchen. She saw me and rushed toward me, urine streaming down her legs. The policeman who had shoved her away now barred her way with his long arms outspread like the wings of some prehistoric bird. He gritted his gleaming teeth at her.

"Where do you think you're going, you little bastard!"

My sister whirled and dove under the table and curled into a tight knot of screaming, helpless, naked fear; there was nothing I could do to protect her or myself. The policeman went over to the table and shook a truncheon in her face, warning her to shut up or else. But my sister was beside herself with fear and did not let up screaming. The policeman left her and strode across the room to the broken window to glance outside. The second policeman meanwhile was struggling to open the bedroom door; apparently my parents had bolted it from within.

"Open up!" he rapped on the door. "Open up or we'll break it down! We know you're in there!" He then paused, expecting his order to be carried out by whomever he thought was inside. It was not. He again seized the doorknob and twisted it violently, but still it would not open. He started pounding the door with his fist and kicking it with his steel-rimmed boots.

"Hey, you bastard," the policeman peering through the window turned to me and demanded to know who was in the bedroom.

"My brother," I said softly.

"Speak up! And who else?"

"I don't know."

"You're lying to me again, boy," he hissed and started toward me with a raised truncheon. "You're parents are in there, aren't they? No use protecting them, boy, for we'll find them. And when we do," he smiled fiendishly, "you'll get it."

I remained silent, resigning myself to the worst.

"Now will you stop lying to me, boy," he shook the truncheon in my face.

I tried to say something, to trump up an excuse; my mouth opened wide but no words came out. The policeman lifted his truncheon, and I closed my eyes, expecting a blow; it didn't come. The policeman instead told his comrade to "smash the bloody thing." The other policeman was about to do that anyway, for he had taken several steps away from the door. He flung himself at the door, bursting it at the butt-hinges. Streams of perspiration poured down my face. I could scarcely breathe. The policemen had been so thorough in rummaging the kitchen that I had no doubt they would find my parents. There was no way they could possibly have escaped. The window was latticed with iron bars, and there was only the one door.

"There's someone under the bed!" the policeman in the bedroom shouted triumphantly.

"Haul him out!" the policeman by the kitchen window shouted back as he left his station for the bedroom.

"Come out of there, old man! Out, out!"

As he passed me, the policeman who had been standing by the window gave me a wicked look and grinned.

"Hurry up, old man! Come out of there!" the policeman in the bedroom said impatiently "Hurry, hurry, we haven't got all day!"

"I'm coming, nkosi [lord]," my father whimpered. They had found him. My mother was sure to be next. What would happen to us children if they took both my mother and father away?

"Who's in there with him?"

"Where's your wife, old man?"

I inched slowly toward the bedroom door, taking care not to attract the attention of the policemen.

"I said, where's your bloody wife, old man?" the question was repeated.

"She's at work, nkosi," my father said plaintively. He was standing, naked and head bowed, in the middle of the bedroom. To his right was an old, worn-out wardrobe; to his left a trundle bed with a straw twin-size mattress, upon which George lay, bawling; in front of the bed was an old, flecked brown table, against which my father's interrogator leaned, as he flashed his light all over my father, keeping him blinking all the time.

"At this time of the night?" the question came slowly, ringing with incredulity.

"Yes, *nkosi.*"

"What job does she do at two o'clock in the morning?"

"She's a kitchen girl, *nkosi.* She sleeps in. She's a maid in Edenvale."

The interrogator muttered something to himself then said, "Come, let's see your pass."

My father reached for his tattered overalls at the foot of the bed and from the back pocket he removed a small, square, bulky black book and handed it over to the policeman, who hurriedly flipped through it. Stonily, running his eyes up and down my father, he said, "The bloody thing is not in order, you know?"

"Yes, *nkosi,* I know that very much. I didn't pay my poll-tax. I was meaning to do so."

"It's not only your poll-tax, damn it, old man. Many other things are wrong with it. You know that?"

"Yes, *nkosi,*" my father whimpered. "I know that very much. I was meaning to fix them too."

"And I see here that you haven't paid your tribal tax too. Were you meaning to fix that too?" the policeman said sarcastically.

"Yes, *nkosi.*" My father's brow started to sweat.

"And the stamp on page fifteen says you're supposed to have a wife here in the city," the policeman said triumphantly, looking at us children, all the time brandishing the bulky black book in my father's face, "What have you to say to that, heh? How are you going to fix that, heh?"

My father became speechless. He parted his parched lips and tried to say something, but no sound came. He lowered his bony head and buried it in the palms of his gnarled hands; and at that moment he seemed to age a thousand years, a pitiful sight. The policeman playfully prodded my father's penis with a truncheon. I gasped with horror.

"Old man," the policeman said floutingly, throwing his head backward, "you're an old man, aren't you?" My father, only in his mid-thirties, nodded. "You're as ancient as my father, yet your irresponsibility makes me ashamed of saying that. Why isn't your pass in order? Mine is. Anyway, look here, as an old man you ought to be back in the Bantustan. My father is back there and living in peace. What are you still doing in the city but asking for trouble?"

The policeman confirmed my suspicions of his being fresh from a tribal reserve. The authorities preferred his kind as policemen because of their ferociousness and blind obedience to white authority. They harboured a twisted fear and hatred of urban blacks; they knew nothing of black solidarity, relishing only the sense of raw power being a policeman gave them over their own kind.

"I'm working, *nkosi*," my father said. "There are no jobs in the Bantustan."

"No jobs in the Bantustan?" the policeman laughed. "What about raising cattle? Or have you forgotten how to do that since coming to the city?"

My father did not answer; he continued gazing at the floor.

"A lot of things are wrong with your pass, and you can be endorsed* out at any time, you know that?"

"Yes, *nkosi*, I know that very much."

"Then what do you think we should do with you?"

My father forced a fake smile. It was not a spontaneous smile— my father never smiled. It was a begging smile, a passive acceptance of the policeman's authority. After smiling my father again dropped his eyes to the floor. He seemed uncharacteristically powerless and contrite, a far cry from the tough, resolute and absolute ruler of the house I knew him to be, the father whose words were law. I felt sorry for him. The policeman, still brandishing the bulky black book, leaned into my father's ear and whispered something.

The other policeman meantime was still at the doorjamb, revelling at the sight of my father being humiliated. The emotional and physical nakedness of my father somehow made me see him in a different light —he seemed a stranger, a total alien. Watching him made tears surge to my eyes, but I fought desperately to keep them from flowing. I cannot cry, I told myself, I would not cry, I should not cry in front of these black beasts. For the first time in my life I felt hate and anger rage with furious intensity inside me. What I felt was no ordinary hate or anger; it was something much deeper, much darker, frighten-

---

* Deported to tribal reserve.

ing, something even I couldn't understand. As I stood there watching, I could feel that hate and anger being branded into my five-year-old mind, branded to remain until I die.

"Hurry up, old man!" the interrogator said, as my father fidgeted with his overalls, "we haven't got all day. Do you have it or don't you?" he said, trying to wring a bribe out of my father.

"*Nkosi*, I beg you," my father whimpered, drooping his bony shoulders and letting the overalls dangle limply at his side. "I have no money," he sighed.

"Nothing," the policeman cried, astonished; the black policemen were used to getting bribes.

"Nothing, *nkosi*," my father said, slowly running his right hand through his kinky hair. "Not a cent. I have no job. I just applied for a permit to look for a job yesterday."

"Well," frowned the policeman, closing the bulky book in my father's face, "I gave you your chance. You refused it. Now hurry up and put on your clothes and come with us. It's 'Number Four' for you, old man."

"But the little ones—"

"That's none of my bloody business," the policeman cut in sharply. "Tell that to the magistrate. Now hurry up and get dressed!"

My father jumped into his overalls. He was handcuffed.

"Go quiet your brother," he said as he saw me staring at him. I did not go. I watched impassively as they led him through the front door, his head bowed, his hands manacled, his self-esteem drained, his manhood sapped. I wondered where they were taking him, what grievous wrong had he committed deserving of being shackled, what type of fiends the two policemen were. They weren't humans to me, neither were they black. Though I feared them as one would fear monsters, I didn't let fear panic me, for I hated them more than I feared them.

Curious to find out where they were taking my father, and what was going on outside, I followed them, forgetting all about my mother. I ordered my sister, who was crying, "Papa, Papa!" by the door, back into the house. I stepped outside in time to see the two policemen, flanking my father, go up a rocky slope leading out of the yard. I saw more black policemen leading black men and women out of shacks. Some of the prisoners were half-naked, others dressed as they went. Several children, two and three years old, stood in tears outside smashed doors, imploring their mothers and fathers to come back. In the middle of the yard an old man was being shoved by a black policeman for being slow; a woman was being kicked by another black policeman for being stubborn; another woman was being ordered to leave a bawling infant behind. Several red-necked white men in safari suits and fatigues, guns drawn, paced briskly about the entrance gate, shouting orders and supervising the roundup. I avoided them by going around the shacks. I passed on my way to the gate shacks whose windows had been shattered, whose doors had been busted. The interior of some of the shacks were a mess, as if a tornado had hit. I arrived at the gate and found a group of boys in a half-circle on a stoep overlooking the street.

Dawn was starting to break but stars still twinkled faintly in the distant, pale eastern sky. PUTCO buses droned in the distance, carrying loads of black humanity to the white world to work. I joined the group of boys. My eyes wandered up, then down the street. I gasped at what I saw down the street. A huge throng of handcuffed black men and women, numbering in the hundreds, filled the narrow street from side to side. The multitude, murmuring like herds of restless cattle, was being marched by scores of black policemen and a dozen or so white ones, some of whom had fierce police dogs on leashes, toward a row of about ten police vans and trucks parked farther down the street. More handcuffed men and women were still filing out of the yards on either side, swelling the ranks of those already choking the streets. It seemed as if the entire population of Alexandra had been arrested.

As I stood there, openmouthed with fearful anticipation, watching the handcuffed men and women being shoved, jostled, kicked and thrown like bundles into the trucks and vans, along with the dogs, I saw, out of the corner of my eye, a short, pot-bellied black policeman leading a naked black man with bony, stiltlike legs, out of an outhouse in a yard across the street. The naked man pleaded that he be allowed to go and dress, but the fat policeman simply roared with laughter and prodded the naked man in the back with a truncheon, telling him that it was not his fault that he had caught him naked.

"Next time hide with your clothes on, brother," the policeman jeered.

The boys around me giggled at the sight of the naked man being marched down the street, toward the throng of handcuffed men and women, his gnarled hands cupped between his bony legs. I remained silent. A tall black man standing by the gate to one of the yards overlooking the street—one of the few adults left behind, presumably because his papers were in order—saw the naked man and instantly dashed into his house and came out waving a pair of tattered overalls. He hurled them across the *donga*, and they landed in the middle of the street, a few paces from the approaching policeman and his naked captive. Grudgingly, amid shouts of "Hurry up, we haven't got all day," intended to please the group of women prisoners gaping at the scene from a short distance, the policeman allowed the naked man to pick up the overalls. He dressed in the middle of the street.

Meanwhile the truck and vans, now jam-packed with handcuffed men and women and dogs and black policemen, hummed engines and prepared to leave. More handcuffed men and women and policemen and dogs still remained in the streets. Within minutes more vans and trucks came, and the loading was finally completed. The convoy of vans and trucks sped away in a huge cloud of dust, with several of the black policemen dangling from the side and rear doors like rags on a line.

As the group dispersed, some of the boys started talking in soft, subdued tones.

"They've taken my father away."

"They've taken my mother and father."

"They've taken my brother."

"They've taken my sister."

"They've taken my whole family."

"They've taken my aunt and uncle."

"They've taken my mother and left my father after he had given them some money."

Mother! Where was my mother? All along I had been oblivious of her. Remembering that the police did not find her when they searched the house, I ran back home as fast as I could to try and find her. I found my brother and sister still crying, but I ignored them.

"Mama! Where are you?" I shouted, standing in the middle of the bedroom. "They're gone."

No reply.

I repeated the shout. The wardrobe creaked and a voice inside softly asked, "Are they gone?"

Instantly I leaped back; my eyes popped out in fearful astonishment.

"Mama, is that you?" I warily approached the wardrobe.

"Yes, let me out!"

"Mama, are you in there?" I said, to make sure that I had indeed heard her voice. I could not believe she had hidden herself in so small a wardrobe. My sister and I often had trouble fitting in there whenever we played hide-and-seek.

"Yes, let me out!"

"It's locked, Mama. Where's the key?"

My mother told me that my father had it. I told her he was gone. She remained silent for a moment or two and then told me to look for it on the table. I looked; no key. I told her so. She told me to look where my father had been hiding. Flickering candle in hand, I crawled under the bed to the far corner where my father had been hiding but I found no key on the earthen floor. Where was the key? Had my father unwittingly taken it with him? How would I get my mother out? "There's no key where he was, Mama!" I shouted from under the bed.

"Look again!"—pause—"and thoroughly this time!"

Before resuming the search I spat twice on my right palm and parted the spittle with my left forefinger, watching to see where the most spit went. It went to the right. I then uttered the supplication my mother had taught me. "Ancestors! Ancestors! Guide me to whatever I'm looking for, wherever it may lie!" I concentrated my search on the right side of the bed. Still no key. I became frantic.

"There's no key, Mama."

She told me to look everywhere. I began ransacking the house and while overturning the torn straw mattress I found a pair of old, rusted keys in one of the holes. I tried them on the wardrobe lock; they wouldn't even fit. Finally, in exasperation, I went to the kitchen, grabbed a heavy wood axe and went back to the bedroom, determined to chop the wardrobe down and get my mother out.

"Mama, should I chop the door down and let you out?" I said fervently. Florah, standing nearby, shrieked with horror as I lifted the axe.

"NO!" my mother shrieked from inside the wardrobe.

"What should I do then?"

"LOOK AGAIN!"

"Look where? I've looked everywhere."

"LOOK AGAIN UNDER THE BED!"

"I've looked there twice already. There's nothing there."

"LOOK AGAIN CAREFULLY!"

"Please look again, Johannes," my sister begged. "I'll help you look."

"Shut up, you!"

Reluctantly, I leaned the axe against the wardrobe door and crawled back under the bed. "For ancestors' sake," I cried, "where's the key!" I was now convinced that my father had unwittingly taken it with him. If he had, what then? My mother would just have to let me chop down the door. Didn't my father always say I chopped wood like a man?

I don't know what made me look between the bricks propping up one leg of the bed, but in one of the crevices I found a long, glistening key, along with several farthings, which I pocketed. The key slid easily into the lock. I turned it twice to the right, and then the knob; they both turned easily. The door swung open. My mother, clad only in her underwear, wriggled out from the tiny compartment where clothes would have been hanging, had we had any worth hanging. She stretched her numb legs and cracked her neck and back. She then dressed and quieted my brother by letting him suckle. Afterward she went about the task of restoring a semblance of order to the mess the police had created.

My father spent two months doing hard labour on a white man's potato farm for his pass crimes.

4 Following that brutal encounter I had with them, the Peri-Urban police became a tormenting presence in my life. Whereas in the past I had been more or less conscious of their presence in black life—as they stopped people in the streets and demanded passes, as they chased after *tsotsis* and other hoodlums, as they raided shebeens in search of illicit liquor, and as they launched an occasional pass raid into the neighbourhood—they now moved permanently into my consciousness. Scarcely a week passed without the neighbourhood being invaded by waves of black and white policemen.

They always came unannounced, at any time of day or night, and gradually I came to accept, and to dread, their presence as a way of life. They haunted me in real life and in my dreams, to the extent that I would often wake up screaming in the middle of the night, claiming that the police were after me with dogs and flashlights, trying to shoot me down. Word had it that our neighbourhood, because of the increasing presence of people whose papers were not in order, had been designated a "hot spot," which meant that it had to be raided constantly. So, barely six years old, I was called upon to deal with constant terror. The year was 1966.

By witnessing raid after raid, week in and week out, month after month, I began learning from my parents ways of recognizing and interpreting specific cues about the movement of police once they had invaded the neighbourhood, so I could react swiftly and warn my parents, or fabricate ingenious lies to prevent them from searching the house. Other children—three, four, five and six years old—were being taught the same lessons by their parents. Whenever we were out at play we were expected to act as sentries. Whenever the police came other children would scamper homeward shouting, "Mama, Papa, the police are coming! The police are coming!"

But I failed to do the same. That brutal encounter with the police had left indelible scars. The mere sight of police vans now had the power of blanking my mind, making me forget all I had learned, making me rely on my instincts, which invariably told me to flee, to cower, lest I end up face-to-face with a policeman and get flogged. I became a useless sentry. But it did not matter, for the raids now launched incessantly into our neighbourhood had an uncanny element of surprise. That the police would come was as certain a fact as the sun rising in the morning; what black people didn't know, and would have given everything in the world to know, was when and with how strong a force.

Each time the police launched a raid into the neighbourhood my mother by some miracle would manage to escape in the nick of time. She seemed to always have premonitions of their coming and would forewarn my father.

"You know," my mother would say, "I have a feeling Peri-Urban will visit us this week."

"There you go again," my father would retort. "Would you stop being paranoiac, woman? They were here just last week; how can they come again this week? Need I remind you that we're not the only people living in Alexandra?"

"Suit yourself," my mother would say. "Don't say I didn't warn you. You said the same last time, and didn't they nearly pick you up? If you hadn't left for work before they came, they would have. Anyways, I'm not the only one who has these dreams of their coming. Many other women do, and they tell their husbands."

My father would then say, "Have you women stopped and told yourselves that maybe the police keep on coming because you women think about them so often?"

My mother would then reply, "What else is there to think about?"

My father's response was more or less typical of that of other men in the yard. So when my mother and other women in the yard sought ways of escaping from the police—at times hiding in ditches, at times in outhouses, at times in trees, at times on rooftops, at times in secret underground hollows and at times waking in the middle of the night and leaving home to drift along some faraway street until the police were gone—he and other men would frown, and, with affectations of bravery, continue with business as usual. For a long time I did not understand why my father and other men acted this way, until one day I heard talk among the womenfolk that the real reason why their husbands refused to run away was that they considered it cowardly and unmanly to run away from other men.

The police, whenever my mother forebode, would indeed come, and many of the men of the yard would be caught napping, surrendering themselves with lamblike submission. Some of the men, my father occasionally among them, would pay hefty bribes to the policemen and would be let go. (Sometimes my father would escape arrest because, since his last arrest, he now left for work at three o'clock in the morning, and would not return until eight or nine at night, when most of the raids had already taken place.)

But other men were not so lucky. They had no money, having paid it all out in bribes over the course of many arrests. They would be carted in vans and trucks to Number Four, a notorious prison for black people in Johannesburg. Repeat offenders and those whose passbook crimes were considered more serious would be processed to a maximum-security penitentiary called Modderbee, on the outskirts of Kempton Park. I would often hear the womenfolk say that Modderbee was a "hell which changed black men into brutes, no matter how tough and stubborn they may be." Almost every night, before we went to bed, whenever my mother happened to have one of her premonitions, she would pray in earnest to our ancestral spirits that the day never come when my father would be sent to Modderbee.

"Will prayers stop the police from coming, Mama?" I asked one evening. Somehow I had the vague feeling that all my mother's prayers were useless, that no amount of prayer could stop the police from violating our lives at will.

"No," my mother replied.

"Then why do you pray?"

"I don't know."

Despite the terror of Peri-Urban, the lives of my family, neighbours and community continued to ebb and flow along a predictable, monotonous course.

On Mondays the blacks of Alexandra (my parents included) continued having *babalazi*—blue Monday hangover—after a weekend of feasting on Bantu beer and Western liquor in the shebeens. Much of this sottish drinking was meant to drown sorrows, and forget the troubles and hardships of black life.

On Tuesdays itinerant butchers continued coming by with their donkey- or pushcarts, peddling heavy bones with scraps of meat on them, *muhodu* (cattle's lungs), pig's knuckles, giblets and chitlings. And black women in tribal garb continued erecting their stalls by the dusty street corners, selling cooked or roasted maize cobs, cooked yams and spinach and chicken feet, mostly to migrant labourers from the tribal reserves, who had no wives to cook for them.

On Wednesday the Chinaman continued coming, in his flashy American-made car, to the runners' homes to pick up bets and announce winners in the numbers game of fah-fee.

On Thursdays kitchen girls and garden boys, dressed in their Sunday best, continued coming to the townships to spend their day off with their families and friends.

On Fridays black people continued to be paid for their toil in the white world, and *tsotsis* and other muggers continued robbing them of their hard-earned pittance, often hacking and stabbing them to death.

And on weekends black people continued to feast and drink heavily in an effort to unwind and prepare for another week of hard labour in the white world.

5 One night our dingy shack, which had been leaning precipitously on the edge of a *donga*, collapsed. Luckily no one was hurt, but we were forced to move to another one, similarly built. This new shack, like the old one, had two rooms and measured something like fifteen by fifteen feet, and overlooked the same unlit, unpaved, potholed street. It had an interior flaked with old whitewash, a leaky ceiling of rusted zinc propped up by a thin wall of crumbling adobe bricks, two tiny windows made of cardboard and pieces of glass, a creaky, termite-eaten door too low for a person of average height to pass through without bending double, and a floor made of patches of cement and earth. It was similar to the dozen or so shacks strewn irregularly, like lumps on a leper, upon the cracked greenless piece of ground named yard number thirty-five.

In this new shack my brother, George, was weaned. It was amusing to witness my mother do it. The first day she began the process she secretly smeared her breasts with red pepper and then invited my brother to suckle. Unsuspecting, George energetically attacked my mother's breast only to let go of it instantly and start hollering because of the hot pepper. This continued throughout the day whenever he wanted to suckle. Finally, after a few days, he began to dread the sight of my mother's breast, and each time she teased him with it he would turn his face. He was now weaned. My father bought a small white chicken, my mother brewed beer, a few relatives were invited, and a small celebration was held to mark George's passage from infancy to childhood. He was almost two years old. He now had to sleep with Florah and me in the kitchen.

Soon after George was weaned my father began teaching him, as he had been teaching me, tribal ways of life. My father belonged to a loosely knit group of black families in the neighbourhood to whom tribal traditions were a way of life, and who sought to bring up their offspring according to its laws. He believed that feeding us a steady diet of tribal beliefs, values and rituals was one way of ensuring our normal growth, so that in the event of our returning to the tribal reserve, something he insistently believed would happen soon, we would blend in perfectly. This diet he administered religiously, seemingly bent on moulding George and me in his image. At first I had tried to resist the diet, but my father's severe looks frightened me.

A short, gaunt figure, with a smooth, tight, black-as-coal skin, large prominent jaws, thin, uneven lips whose sole function seemed to be the production of sneers, a broad nose with slightly flaring nostrils, small, bloodshot eyes which never cried, small, close-set ears, and a wide, prominent forehead—such were my father's fearsome features.

Born and bred in a tribal reserve and nearly twice my mother's age, my father existed under the illusion, formed as much by a strange innate pride as by a blindness to everything but his own will, that someday all white people would disappear from South Africa, and black people would revert to their old ways of living. To prepare for this eventuality, he ruled the house strictly according to tribal law, tolerating no deviance, particularly from his children. At the same time that he was force-feeding us tribalism we were learning other ways of life, modern ways, from mingling with children whose parents had shed their tribal cloth and embraced Western culture.

My father's tribal rule had as its fulcrum the constant performing of rituals spanning the range of day-to-day living. There were rituals to protect the house from evildoers, to ward off starvation, to prevent us from becoming sick, to safeguard his job, to keep the police away, to bring us good luck, to make him earn more money and many others which my young mind could not understand. Somehow they did not make sense to me; they simply awed, confused and embarrassed me, and the only reason I participated in them night after night was because my father made certain that I did, by using, among other things, the whip, and the threat of the retributive powers of my ancestral spirits, whose favour the rituals were designed to curry. Along with the rituals, there were also tribal laws governing manners.

One day I intentionally broke one of these laws: I talked while eating.

"That's never done in my house," my father screamed at me as he rose from the table where he had been sitting alone, presiding over our meal. I was eating *pap 'n vleis* out of the same bowl with George and Florah. We were sitting on the floor, about the brazier, and my mother was in the bedroom doing something.

"You don't have two mouths to afford you such luxury!" he fumed, advancing threateningly toward me, a cold sneer on his thin-lipped, cankerous mouth. He seemed ten feet tall.

Terrified, I deserted the *pap 'n vleis* and fled to Mother.

"Bring him back here, woman!" my father called through the door as he unbuckled his rawhide belt. "He needs to be taught how to eat properly."

I began bawling, sensing I was about to be whipped.

My mother led me into the kitchen and pleaded for me. "He won't do it again. He's only a child, and you know how forgetful children are." At this point George and Florah stopped eating and watched with petrified eyes. "Don't give me that," snarled my father. "He's old enough to remember how to eat properly." He tore me away from my mother and lashed me. She tried to intervene, but my father shoved her aside and promised her the same. I never finished my meal; sobbing, I slunk off to bed, my limbs afire with pain where the rawhide had raised welts. The next day, as I nursed my wounds, while my father was at work, I told my mother that I hated him and promised her I would kill him when I grew up.

"Don't say that!" my mother reprimanded me.

"I will," I said stoutly, "if he won't leave me alone."

"He's your father, you know."

"He's not my father."

"Shut that bad mouth of yours!" My mother threatened to smack me.

"Why does he beat me, then?" I protested. "Other fathers don't beat their children." My friends always boasted that their fathers never laid a hand on them.

"He's trying to discipline you. He wants you to grow up to be like him."

"What! Me! Never!" I shook with indignation. "I'm never going to be like him! Why should I?"

"Well, in the tribes sons grow up to be like their fathers."

"But we're not living in the tribes."

"But we're still of the tribes."

"I'm not," I said. Trying to focus the conversation on rituals, my nemesis, I said, after a thoughtful pause, "Is that why Papa insists that we do rituals?"

"Yes."

"But other people don't."

"Everybody does rituals, Mr. Mathabane," my mother said. "You just don't notice it because they do theirs differently. Even white people do rituals."

"Why do people do rituals, Mama?"

"People do rituals because they were born in the tribes. And in the tribes rituals are done every day. They are a way of life."

"But we don't live in the tribes," I countered. "Papa should stop doing rituals."

My mother laughed. "Well, it's not as simple as that. Your father grew up in the tribes, as you know. He didn't come to the city until he was quite old. It's hard to stop doing things when you're old. I, too, do rituals because I was raised in the tribes. Their meaning, child, will become clear as you grow up. Have patience."

But I had no patience with rituals, and I continued hating them.

Participation in my father's rituals sometimes led to the most appalling scenes, which invariably made me the laughingstock of my friends, who thought that my father, in his ritual garb, was the most hilarious thing they had ever seen since natives in Tarzan movies. Whenever they laughed at me I would feel embarrassed and would cry. I began seeking ways of distancing myself from my father's rituals. I found one: I decided I would no longer, in the presence of my friends, speak Venda, my father's tribal language. I began speaking Zulu, Sotho and Tsonga, the languages of my friends. It worked. I was no longer an object of mockery. My masquerade continued until my father got wind of it.

"My boy," he began. "Who is ruler of this house?"

"You are, Papa," I said with a trembling voice.

"Whose son are you?"

"Yours and Mama's."

"Whose?"

"Yours."

"That's better. Now tell me, which language do I speak?"

"Venda."

"Which does your mama speak?"

"Venda."

"Which should you speak?"

"Venda."

"Then why do I hear you're speaking other tongues; are you a prophet?" Before I could reply he grabbed me and lashed me thoroughly. Afterward he threatened to cut out my tongue if he ever again heard I wasn't speaking Venda. As further punishment, he increased the number of rituals I had to participate in. I hated him more for it.

6 Toward the end of 1966 my father was temporarily laid off his job as a menial labourer for a white firm in Germiston, a white city an hour's bus ride southeast of Johannesburg. He had been told by his *baas* (boss) that he would be recalled as soon as the reorganization of the firm was complete: it was coming under new ownership. The first few weeks my father stayed at home awaiting the recall. It never came. As weeks slid past, he began making plans to seek another job, thinking that he had been permanently laid off. But first he had to go to BAD (Bantu Affairs Department)* to obtain a permit to do so.

I was out in the streets playing soccer one weekday afternoon when Florah came running up to me, crying. She told me that something terrible had happened at home and I was wanted immediately. When I reached home I found my mother pacing mechanically about the shack, murmuring helplessly, desperately, uncontrollably, clasping and unclasping her hands.

"It cannot be! No it cannot be! Not my husband! Not my husband!" She was saying to herself.

"What happened to Papa, Mama?" I said with fright as I flung myself at her. I thought that maybe he had been killed. For a while my mother did not answer; but finally she controlled her emotions and between sobs told me what had happened. My father had been arrested that morning at the bus stop—for being unemployed. A man who had been with him as they waited for the bus to Johannesburg to apply for permits had brought my mother the grim news. The man's story was as follows: as he and my father waited for the bus several police vans suddenly swooped upon the bus stop. People fled in all directions. My father was nabbed as he tried to leap a fence. His pass was scanned and found to contain an out-of-work stamp; he was taken in. His crime, unemployment, was one of the worst a black man could commit.

My mother sent me to fetch my father's relatives, with the hope that they might find some way to secure his release. The relatives came but couldn't help; neither could our neighbours. "What would happen to him now?" I asked my mother. She told me not to worry, that my father would come back home after serving the customary four weeks' sentence for being unemployed. Four weeks went by and still he had not come back. We began to worry. My mother wept every night. We children cried along with her. No word of his whereabouts came for yet another week. Suspecting the worst—that my father had been sent to Modderbee—my mother lost faith in herself and began to despair of our future.

"Things will be very different without your father, children."

We did not understand, and we simply cried and grew frightened.

Pangs of hunger melted my resentment of my father away, and

---

* Now renamed Department of Cooperation and Development.

now that he was gone I longed night and day for his return. I didn't even mind his coming back and shouting restrictions at me and making me perform rituals. I simply wanted him back. And as days slid by without him, as I saw other children in the company of their fathers, I would cry. His absence showed me how much I loved him. I never stopped asking questions about when he would be coming back.

One afternoon after it had been two months since I last saw my father, and we were now on rations, I asked my mother, "When will Papa be back?"

"I don't know," my mother said sadly. "He may be gone for a long, long time."

"Why does he get arrested so much?"

"Because his pass is not in order."

"Why doesn't he get it fixed?"

"He can't."

"Why?"

"You're too young to know."

"What's a pass, Mama?" I knew vaguely what a pass was, but not its reality.

"It's an important book that we black people must have in order always, and carry with us at all times." She took out hers and showed it to me. I remembered seeing the book; in fact, I remembered seeing it many times; and yet, each time I saw it, it appeared dreadfully new. There was something about it which made me fearful, helpless. But I could not figure out what about it made me feel that way. It seemed a mere book. Yet it was, I was to later find out, the black man's passport to existence.

Naively I told my mother that I did not have a pass, suggesting that the police would not take me away.

"You'll have to get one when you turn sixteen."

"Will they take me away too, Mama? Like they do Papa?"

"Hush. You're asking too many questions for your own good."

My father's latest arrest, true to my mother's predictions, changed our life-style drastically. Lunch was now out of the question, so was breakfast; and having *pap 'n vleis* became a sporadic, chancy luxury. My mother, who for some reason could not get a permit to work in Johannesburg, could not even afford to buy tea and brown bread. There came many days when we ate nothing at all, spending the long evening hours simply staring at one another, at the empty pots, and at the sun going down. George, Florah and I resorted to eating our own mucus.

Each day we spent without food drove us closer and closer to starvation. Then terror struck. I began having fainting spells. I would be out playing when suddenly my head would feel light, my knees would wobble, my vision would dim and blur and down I would come like a log. My playmate would then run away in shock (I would be told when I woke up), screaming that I was dead. My mother would then come and revive me, usually by pouring cold water over me, or slapping me on the cheeks, or both.

But there was sometimes a good part to my blackouts. Whenever I fainted near a store, I would get a piece of candy or fruit from the storekeeper upon reviving. Naturally, I loved fainting near stores. But my storefront fainting spells became so frequent that storekeepers —for fear of going broke, I suppose—no longer gave me anything.

One day I asked my mother if we had any savings, and she replied that we did not have a cent, that we were a hand-to-mouth household, that when my father had been around he had spent all his money on food, on paying rent, on busfare and on police bribes. I suggested that she borrow money from other people. Who? she asked. Our neighbours, I answered. She broke into a laugh, like that of a person being driven mad by hunger, and said, "Show me a black man with a penny to spare, and I'll bring your father back."

My father's long imprisonment began to wreak daily nightmares on everybody in the house. Without income we could no longer afford the rent for our dingy shack. One afternoon the landlord, a fat, grey-haired, no-nonsense *Mosotho* man came and told us that we would have to pack and leave at the end of the week, unless we came up with his money. He said that he had the longest list of people waiting to grab the shack at any price. And he wasn't lying: since word got around that we could not afford to pay rent, there had been a steady stream of shack-seekers at the custodian's door. My mother begged him to give us at least a month's extension, pointing out that eviction would automatically result in the family being endorsed out of Alexandra back to a tribal reserve.

"We have nowhere to go back there," my mother implored. "This is our only home. Please let us stay. We'll get you the money somehow."

The landlord relented and gave us until the end of the month to come up with the three months' rent we owed him. One weekday afternoon while my mother was out hunting for food and money to pay rent, and Florah, George and I were left alone in the house, two tall, powerful, belligerent Zulu men, armed with spears and *pangas* (machetes), burst into the house and demanded to see my father.

"He isn't home," I said with bated breath. George and Florah burst out crying.

"Your Mother?"

"She too."

They looked about the kitchen for a couple moments, and then stepped into the bedroom. They came back to the kitchen, wielding the *pangas* and spears. George, Florah and me clung to each other in terror.

"When they get back, tell them we've been here!"

I nodded vigorously. Without saying another word, they proceeded to strip the house of furniture, seizing the wardrobe, chairs and table, saying that the goods were payment for a mysterious debt of honor my father owed them. My mother came back, and I told her what had happened. There was nothing she could do to retrieve the furniture, she said. She could not even report the matter to the police, she added, for it would mean producing her passbook, which was not in order. As she sat figuring what to do, tears streaming down her cheeks, she said: "This is just the beginning."

A few weeks later George and Florah came down with a mysterious illness, which left them emaciated and lethargic, their stomachs so distended that I thought they would burst. Their bodies were covered with sores, which punctured and oozed pus, and their hair turned to a strange orange colour. There were times when, while fanning off blowflies with a piece of cardboard from their filmy, half-closed eyes, mucus-covered noses and bruised mouths, while they lay writhing with pain on the damp cement floor, I thought I could see their tiny, empty intestines. Seeing them like that made me cry. Occasionally, they excreted live worms with their bloody stools. Their tearing coughs kept everyone awake at night. Each time my mother gave them a morsel of food, whenever she could get it, they vomited. Their suffering made the days and nights unbearably long and gloomy.

My mother did not have the one hundred cents to take them to the clinic, and no witch doctor, our last resort, was willing to treat them on credit. But with determination, courage and love, she tried her best to nurse them back to health using some herbs Granny gave her. My brother and sister fought with the tenacity typical of African children to stay alive, but I wondered for how long. The strangest thing was that, except for a minor cough, I felt fine.

My father's arrest had come in September, and when Christmas was but two days away, my mother dropped a bombshell.

"There won't be any Christmas celebration this year," she said.

"What!" I cried, reacting as if I were a convict and my mother a judge condemning me to death for a crime I didn't commit.

Each Christmas, black families would celebrate by taking children of all ages to the Indian place on First Avenue to be outfitted with cheap garments, and some, the extremely lucky ones, with sneakers or shoes. The clothes were worn on Christmas and New Year's when families paraded their children on the streets in a pageantry designed to imply nonexistent wealth. Chickens, goats, sheep, pigs or cattle would be slaughtered by the various households, depending on each's level of affluence and religious beliefs, and, commensurately, big or small feasts would be held, to which relatives from near and far came to partake in the festivities. Scones would be baked and gallons of Kool-Aid or cider made to give to children on New Year's, while the adults went about each other's homesteads, drinking free liquor. And, for the families who could afford it, their houses would be elaborately decorated with trinketry, and the very affluent would have Christmas trees in their homes and exchange small gifts.

"How come we won't be celebrating Christmas, Mama?"

"Your father isn't here," my mother said.

"But Christmas is here," I said.

"Yes, I know," my mother said sadly. "But we don't have the money to celebrate it with."

"But we've always celebrated Christmas," I said.

"That's because your father had been around and working," my mother said.

"When will he be back?" I said, tears filling my eyes.

"I don't know," my mother said.

When Christmas came my mother locked my ailing brother and sister and me inside the house, while she went about the township begging for cookies, Kool-Aid and other foods to keep us alive. We children sat staring vacantly and longingly through the window at the bright streets teeming with children dressed in gaudy new outfits, sucking candy bars, munching cookies, laughing, playing and romping around, all the time singing Christmas carols. Florah couldn't bear the agony of seeing her friends all dressed up, playing and eating, and she burst into tears. As I closed the curtains to ease her agony, while trying hard to mask my own sadness, I consoled her, "Don't worry, Sis, Christmas is but for one day. It'll be over before you know it, and next year you'll be out there too, just like everybody else." Little was I aware that that first bleak Christmas was a portent for many similar ones to come.

January, February and March of the new year went by, still without any sign of, nor word from, my father. We could not visit him, for we had no money, and even if we had had the money, we did not know to which prison he had been taken. My mother told me that the relatives of black prisoners were seldom notified about the whereabouts of their loved ones. Gradually, my father's absence began to change my mother's personality.

She grew irritable and short-tempered, and any slight provocation made her explode in anger. She spent many an afternoon staring blankly through the window while singing songs of sorrow to herself, as though she were going mad or something.

She began to drink heavily. And whenever she was drunk, her hot temper got her involved in nasty fights with several women in the yards over such things as whose child had been shitting all over the place, or who had the right to draw water first from the communal tap in the middle of the yard. We had one tap for about one hundred people. Inside the house, much of her anger was, fortunately, verbal rather than physical, but its presence nonetheless created a tense atmosphere, making me always self-conscious of what I said, how I said it and when I said it. Her changed personality gradually began changing mine too.

I became cranky. Many days I could not sit still in the house; violent impulses would seize me whenever I was at play so that I would, for no reason at all, pick fights with other children. I abused my brother and sister. To quiet my hunger, I embarked upon a career of stealing beer and soda bottles from shebeens, and frequently ended up in trouble. Fat shebeen queens would engage in shouting matches with my mother, calling her all sorts of filthy names, and me, a bastard, promising to work the voodoo on me. In an attempt to keep me off the streets and out of trouble, my mother said one day: "No more streets for you until you behave." She then told me that from now on I had to help her with household chores. She did much of the work, and I was required to lug water from the communal tap, run errands and baby-sit my brother and sister.

One morning as I was baby-sitting, and watching my mother go about cleaning the house, my suspicions about something that was happening to her reached a peak. For some months I had been keeping a close eye on her stomach, and it kept on getting bigger and bigger by the day; while George, Florah and I were getting thinner and thinner. I took her oversized stomach to mean she was getting fat, perhaps from stuffing herself secretly with all sorts of food in the middle of the night when we children were asleep. I had heard of mothers who did that.

I began watching her like a hawk, expecting to catch her eating things alone. I followed her everywhere at all times of the day, including to the lavatory, where I would stand outside the door until she reemerged. Because my father was gone, George, Florah and I now slept in the bedroom, on the floor next to the bed. I would stay awake at night, even after the candle was snuffed, listening for any strange sounds that might suggest eating.

Though I followed my mother around all day, kept a nightlong vigil on her, there was nothing suspicious about her behavior. The crumbs of food she begged from people she shared with us. Yet her stomach kept on getting bigger and bigger, and we children were like scarecrows. How could that be? Finally, in desperation, I decided to confront her. It was early evening, and we were sitting about the smouldering embers of a brazier fire. My mother was busy patching our rags.

"Mama," I said hesitantly, hiding my face behind my hands to conceal embarrassment over what I was about to say, for I was still unconvinced that my mother, my own mother, the mother I loved, would dare eat food, without sharing it with us.

"Yes?" my mother said, lifting her eyes from her work to look at me.

I coughed once or twice, then asked, in a trembling voice, "Why are you getting fat?"

"Am I fat, child?" she laughed. Immediately I took that as an attempt to hide her guilt.

"Yes, Mama," I said nervously.

"I don't think I'm fat," she said. "Come over here. Take a look at my arm." She rolled up the sleeve of her gingham dress, all the way to the shoulder joint, revealing a bony arm with stringy muscles. "Is this fat?" she asked.

I shook my head embarrassedly. Her arm was a matchstick.

"Then what makes you think I'm fat?"

I eyed her carefully, suspiciously. Should I tell her? What would she think of me? I thought back to the many days I spent staring at empty pots and plates; how each such day shoved me closer and closer to the brink of starvation.

"It's your stomach, Mama," the words spilled out of my mouth before I could stop them, "why does it keep on getting bigger and bigger?"

She roared with laughter. My suspicions grew, I don't know why.

"Oh! this!" she exclaimed, pointing at the massive bulge. "That's not fat, silly."

"What is it then?" I asked, confused.

She paused pensively for a few moments, then said, softly, "It's a bloated stomach."

I looked at her, uncomprehending; finally, I said, bravely, "You haven't been eating too much, have you, Mama?"

She fixed a searching stare at me, and the smile vanished from her face. My question had shocked her. For a long while she said nothing, simply staring at me with silent amazement. I became tense. Had I said something wrong? What was she thinking? Was I right in confronting her so bluntly? I took the solemn expression on her face to mean that she understood my need to know why her stomach was so big. She hemmed several times, as if mulling over how to tell me whatever it was she was about to tell me.

A few minutes passed in deep silence, during which I averted my eyes from her gaze. With a calmness of manner which somewhat but not quite concealed her astonishment of a moment ago, she finally spoke. Her "bloated stomach," she explained, was of a different, strange, but harmless nature. It was not the result of eating too much food, she said emphatically. She asked me if I had not seen her with a "bloated stomach" before. I said no. She told me that she had had three of them already, one when I was born (which, she said, I could not have seen because I was still at the clinic awaiting delivery), the second when my sister was born, and the third when my brother was born. The current one, she said, would disappear as soon as she had received another baby from the clinic. I did not ask her what was in her stomach, content with puzzling over why she would want another mouth to feed when there was not enough food to feed the mouths already here. Later when I was older, my mother was to tell me all about the birds and the bees, and I reminded her of the "bloated stomach" episode, and we both laughed.

7 To prevent us from starving and to maintain a roof over our heads, my mother began running around the township soliciting money with which to pay the rent and to buy food, but very little came of it. A few people tried to help; but in the main, black people were burdened with their own survival.

When it seemed that no help was forthcoming, we resigned ourselves to the inevitable: eviction and starvation. Luck of some sort came when my maternal grandmother—who had been away in the Shangaan Bantustan attending a ceremony to exorcise evil spirits from a raving mad relative—came back unexpectedly. My mother told her of our plight. Granny had some money to spare.

She paid the rent a week before we were to be evicted; bought us bread, sugar and mealie meal*; and gave my mother one hundred cents to take George and Florah to the clinic, where their sickness was diagnosed as advanced malnutrition and chicken pox. More money was required to continue their treatment, and Granny gave my mother three hundred cents. Thinking her rich, I proposed to my mother that we move in with her until my father's return from prison. My mother told me that that could not be, that Granny was already overburdened with looking after herself and her other children and could not afford to take us in. Moreover, my mother said, my father's relatives would never sanction such a move.

"Why?" I asked. "We're starving as it is, and they aren't helping us in any way." I had close to a dozen relatives on my father's side scattered all over Johannesburg; yet since my father's arrest none had come forward to help us.

My mother explained that my father's relatives would not allow us to move in with any of her relatives because according to tribal marriage customs we were my father's property—her, myself, my brother and my sister; therefore, for as long as my father was alive, regardless of his being in prison, we had to stay put in his *kaya* (house), awaiting his eventual return.

The money Granny gave us soon ran out. Granny could no longer help us because what she had given us had been her "last money." My father was still not back. Where would we get rent money? Food money?

There was a small grocery store nearby where my father, before his arrest, had maintained a simple charge account. It worked in the

---

* South African term for corn meal.

following way: during the week he would buy things like candles, tea, sugar, paraffin, bread, matches, mealie meal and floor polish, on credit; and on Friday, payday for him, he would settle the account. But since his arrest, the account had not been used. One afternoon my mother and I went to the store to see if we could reopen it. The storekeeper, a lean Mosotho man with greying hair, told us we could not reopen the account, for there was no man in our house to settle it on Fridays. As my mother and I turned to leave, the storekeeper called us back. There was a way he could try and help us. If my mother would work at cleaning his house and washing his family's clothing, he could arrange to pay our rent. My mother agreed. She would be required to work on weekends. So our rent problem was taken care of. Now what about food? Word came that a new garbage dump, the Mlothi, had just opened, and many of Alexandra's poor were going there in search of scraps of food. We decided to go there too.

"I never thought the day would come when we would have to do this," my mother said.

The Mlothi was on the veld fringing Alexandra to the east, about half a mile from where we lived. Every weekday huge, grey trucks arrived to dump garbage from white people's homes. Each morning my mother would take Florah, George and me, and the four of us would join the throng of black men, women and children flocking down there. We always left home between six and seven in the morning so we could be among the front wave of people rushing the trucks as they came in, usually around ten.

The Mlothi provided us with many items we could not afford— clothes, knives, furniture, spoons, cribs, mugs, forks, plates and scraps of food. All at no cost. We simply had to be there very early in the morning, wait for the trucks to arrive and dump and then carefully dig our way through the heap of ash and refuse, collecting item after item as we worked the huge mound till sundown.

We would use sticks and iron rods to dig, but often we had to use our hands, especially on Mondays and Tuesdays when the garbage contained perishables like half-eaten sandwiches and cold cuts. One morning I was digging alongside my sister when my stick struck something soft buried deep in the debris.

"Mama!" I cried, "I think I've found something nice."

My mother, digging a couple yards away from me, asked what it was I had found.

"I don't know yet," I said. "But it felt soft. It must be food. And it's big."

Upon hearing the word *food*, all the ashen-faced men, women and children digging about me started inching toward where I was digging, their faces lit with expectation. "Mama!" I yelled, remembering previous fights which had erupted when families fought over rights to dig up white people's leftovers.

"Don't dig in my child's territory!" my mother screamed a warning and hurried over to protect my discovery by staking out the area I was digging in. "Where's your find, child?" she asked, sliding over to me.

"In there," I pointed excitedly at the huge mound where I was digging. "Among the broken bottles and papers."

My mother began digging delicately around the area, first with her stick, to clear the broken bottles, then with her gnarled hands to reach the object. My sister and I joined her in the digging. My brother was strapped to my mother's back.

"Careful about using your hands," she warned. "There's too much broken glass."

My sister and I stopped digging, and we waited expectantly alongside, our mouths drooling. One of the women digging nearby said to my mother, enviously:

"*Musadi* [woman], your children are lucky. They are the best diggers around. They seem to always know where the good things are. Just look at those sacks and boxes you have there with you; they're already full, and it isn't noon yet. I wish my children were like that, instead of the lazy fools my husband gave me." At that, she turned and pinched the ear of one of her children, a boy my age, and said, "Come on, dig! Why aren't you like Johannes! He finds his mother things, and you don't find me anything! You just eat, eat, eat!"

The woman, who lived in our neighbourhood, was envying boxes brimming with dented pots, knives, spoons, forks, broken mirrors and articles of furniture; things which, after being thoroughly cleaned, we would use as housewares. Since we began coming to Mlothi, our collection of housewares had increased enormously. We now even had a couple of blankets, a leaky washtub and a baby's crib. I was puzzled by what I thought to be wastefulness on the part of white people: they threw away, still in excellent condition, things that many black people could not even afford to buy secondhand. We had even managed to replace some of the furniture the two Zulu men had seized.

"They've learned well," my mother said proudly. She stopped digging momentarily and took a pinch of snuff and sneezed noisily. She resumed digging, and presently she excavated the package— square, wrapped in thick brown paper and tied with a strong cord.

Upon seeing the size of the package, an old woman nearby quipped, "Madam must have had one of her sumptuous banquets." Several women affirmed her claim.

Continuing, the old woman, in a hoary voice, said, "I worked for a madam a long time ago, when my papers were still in order, who had three refrigerators all stacked with food. And no children. And she would always throw away packages of meat because they were a day old. When I asked her to give them to me, she would reply: 'I buy you meat, girlie, is that not enough?' And the meat she was talking about was dog's meat."

"They eat well, them white people," said an old man nearby. "Yes sir, they eat well."

"They have everything," a jet-black woman said in a shrill voice, "and we have nothing."

"Maybe it's an entire elephant," jested a beady-eyed, one-armed man in tattered pants and without a shirt, referring to our package. "How I wish to find me a whole elephant, trunk an' all. All my meat problems would be taken care of."

My mother carried the brown package to a clearing where several men, women and children sat underneath a blazing sun; some rested, tired from digging; others munched hungrily at dug-up sandwiches and other viands.

"Mama," I whined hungrily, envious of all those people eating, "may I have something to eat too?"

"Me too, please, Mama," cried my sister.

"Take out one sandwich from the sack and share it with your sister," my mother said.

Grudgingly, because since hunger became a constant companion I had developed the habit of not wanting to share food with anyone, not even my sister, I took out one of the butter-and-jam sandwiches and broke it into two uneven pieces, giving my sister the smaller one.

"Mama," she whimpered. "Look at what he gave me."

I quickly gobbled up my lion's share.

"Give her some more, Johannes," my mother said, unaware that I had already eaten up my entire share. "She's your sister, you know," she added, wiping her brow.

"She's small," I mumbled with my mouth full.

"She may be small," my mother said, still unaware that I had nothing left, "but that don't mean her hunger is. You must learn to take care of your sister. She's the only one you have."

"I don' have any more," I said, throwing open my hands in triumph.

"He's eaten it all, Mama," my sister cried.

"Take out another sandwich," my mother said to me; and she added, sternly, "and this time give her a bigger piece than yours or you won't have any more."

I took out another butter and jam sandwich, broke it into four unequal pieces.

"Here." I gave my sister two of the smallest pieces. "You have two and I have two."

The equal number of pieces seemed to appease her, and she ate them in silence.

Suddenly, I heard my mother scream. "Yowee! Yowee!"

I turned and saw her leap away from the package she was opening. Everyone around the place started.

"What's the matter?" asked everyone.

"Get away from me, Satan!" shouted my mother, continuing to back away from the package as if fleeing a ghost. She trembled from head to toe.

"What's the matter, *musadi?*" asked several women as they rushed to my mother's side.

Zombielike, my mother pointed at the package, unable to utter a word, her face a mask of indescribable horror. My sister and I stood equally thunderstruck a couple of feet away from her, clinging to one another in fear, wondering what was happening to our mother. Several men and women left their places and hurried over to where the brown package lay half-opened.

"What the hell!" exclaimed one old man as he peered into the package. "There's a baby in here!"

"What!" several people gasped.

"There's a baby in here!" repeated the old man, backing away from the package in fear.

"Is it alive?" a woman asked.

"Are you mad," retorted the old man. "After being buried under such a rubble, who would still be alive?"

"What child is it?" asked one woman.

"Black child," the old man said angrily, and added, "what did you expect?"

"Boy or girl?"

"Still wrapped . . . can't tell."

"Go on, unwrap the rest," said the woman to the old man.

"Are you mad," cried the old man. "I'm touching no voodoo child."

Everyone stood back, terrified. In the meantime, my sister and I had joined my mother, who was still shaking. We did not say anything to her; we simply clung to the hem of her ashen dress. Baby? Black? What was a black baby doing in a package? I wondered.

"Whose baby is it, Mama?" I asked, fearful yet unable to contain my curiosity.

"Hush!" my mother scolded me.

While everybody stood about the package, petrified, an old woman with a decided limp in one leg hobbled from the back of the crowd to where the package lay.

"You're all pretending it's the first time you've seen a dead baby," she said as she struggled to kneel beside the package. "These things happen every day. They kill them and throw them away every day." Tears filled her wrinkled eyes as she proceeded to unwrap the rest of the package. "It's a girl," she said, "and she's beginning to rot."

Some of the women began weeping. The group of men and women started arguing what to do with the corpse, with the men insisting that for fear of getting entangled in a controversy that would certainly involve the police, the baby should be secretly buried in an unmarked grave. The women, however, unanimously refused to have the dead baby subjected to what they called "an inhuman burial," and insisted that for the sake of the baby girl's soul, she be handed over to the authorities for a decent burial. The woman prevailed, but another heated debate soon developed over who should do the actual handing over. While it raged without sign of settlement, my mother, still shocked, gathered everything we had dug up for the day, and we headed home. At home, as we washed the ash off our faces, legs and arms, and off the items we had gathered for the day, I asked her for more details about how a dead black baby ended up in a garbage dump. She told me that some maids and nannies who worked for white people, because of fears of losing their jobs in the event of an accidental pregnancy, would often smother the baby and dump the corpse in garbage bins so they could continue working.

"Wouldn't the police arrest such people for murder?" I asked in shock.

"Police don't arrest black people for killing black people," my mother said.

After the incident of the dead baby we stopped going to Mlothi. Instead, we began going to another site at the other end of the veld, where a chicken factory, Sunnyside, dumped loads of dead, diseased chickens, and rejected eggs. There we would search for eggs which were uncracked. We found many of them, as many as three dozen in a day, but on being cooked, many turned out to contain dead embryos in various stages of development. We stopped going to the egg-dumping site when, of all the eggs we dug up, something like 99 percent of them turned up dead embryos.

Long after I had ceased having thoughts of him; long after my mother had given him up for dead, following constant nightmares she had had of his being killed by a white farmer for insubordination, and buried secretly in an unmarked grave; long after my sister Maria was born, under difficult circumstances, at home, because my mother could not afford maternity care; long after we had adjusted to a life without him, my father walked in one afternoon, like a spook out of one of my mother's tales. After almost a year in prison, he was so changed that I hardly knew him. He had grown thinner, his body more bent, his skin blacker and coarse, his cheeks more hollow, his eyes so outward it seemed they were attempting to force their way out of the sockets: they seemed those of a man who had been through hell. And he was an embittered man. His attitude seemed that of a black man being changed into a brute.

He spent days telling my mother about the horrid life he had led in prison, about the thousands of black men locked inside simply because they, like he, had committed the unpardonable crime of being unemployed; thousands more because their papers were not in order; and still thousands more for entering the white world without permission. In particular he spoke of the backbreaking work he had to do on various white farms, and on chain gangs digging trenches and roads in the white people's world. A vindictive hatred for white people, which was soon to become the passion of his life, had crept into his speech, and as he spoke haltingly, his words ringing with anger and hatred, he punctuated each reference to white people with a four-letter word. He never stopped accusing various neighbours of being witches responsible for his arrest.

I was glad to see my father back, for his absence had meant biting hunger, and I thought his presence would mean food. But in the latter I was soon proved mistaken. Apparently—he told the story—the day he was arrested, he threw his pass away, so that when he appeared in court, he could plead guilty to a lost pass, rather than unemployment, which was a worse crime. But he now needed a pass before he could begin canvassing for a job in the white world. He began leaving home at four in the morning for the superintendent's office to apply for one. For some unknown reason, the authorities kept on giving him the runaround, telling him to bring this and that document, this and that certificate. Unable to read, and too proud to seek help from those who could, he kept on taking the wrong papers each time. Finally, through a process of elimination, and some luck, he was given the pass. But for yet another stretch of months no white man was willing to hire him because of his arrest record—stamped on his pass—and as a result hunger remained in the house, growing each day; and in its attempt to grow, it would gnaw at my guts, disorient me and make me hallucinate.

One evening while I was sitting by a brazier staring at its flaring coals and at a black empty pot on it and envying my three-month-old sister Maria suck lustily from my mother's breast, I began feeling dizzy. Watching my sister suckle filled me with hatred, and my hot head thought of forcibly wrenching her away from my mother's lap and sucking the succulent gourd of milk myself. Yet something made me refrain; something which was fanning the fire inside my head; something which was making my head spin crazily round and round.

Suddenly, I cried out. "Mama! The house is spinning. Make it stop! I wanna get off!"

I faintly heard my mother say, "Nothing is spinning."

But to me things spun, as if caught in a whirlwind. In desperation I clutched my head and attempted to rise, but I only managed to lurch about dizzily in the direction of the brazier. Instantly my mother reached out and grabbed me. I tussled with her as she tried to calm me down, to move me away from the brazier, lest in my frenzy I should tip it over. As she fought to subdue me, her hands clamped around my neck, I sunk my teeth into the nipple of her drooping breast. She shrieked in pain and I broke loose. I lurched forward and nearly fell onto the brazier. As I staggered dizzily about the kitchen, screaming, not knowing where to go or what to do to stop my spinning head, my mother, now recovered from the bite, came after me.

Suddenly, the gyrating objects developed huge mouths and began laughing at me, a roaring, crazy laughter, which split my head in two. As the maddening laughter continued, each whirling object suddenly contorted, enlarged, ballooned, stretched, shrank, into all sorts of grotesque, shifting monsters, all of them attempting to swallow me up. Each fiend had big, red, unblinking eyes and a wide red mouth without lips, from which protruded massive, shiny, razor-sharp teeth.

Suddenly all the monsters burst into flames.

"Mama!" I screamed as I staggered about the room, my mother chasing after me. "The house is on fire!"

"There's no fire!" my mother said.

"The house is on fire, Mama!" I repeated.

"There's no fire!" My mother's hands clamped around my neck.

She brought me down and continued yelling that there was no fire. But, to me, there was a fire—a huge fire, and I continued twisting to duck red hot planks hurtling from the ceiling toward me. My mother smacked me several times on the cheeks.

"Calm down!"

The next I knew I was soaking wet. My mother had somehow poured water all over me. My body cooled down. I stopped screaming. I felt spent. I breathed heavily and my mouth drooled. My mother stood me near the open window and rested my head on her lap. A cool breeze was blowing.

"There's no fire," she said, sighing lightly, "you're imagining things. Calm down. You'll be all right."

After a while my head stopped spinning, but I still felt light-headed and rickety. The fire inside my limbs cooled down. I felt so exhausted my limbs ached. My mother half-carried and half-dragged me to the cardboard mat and laid me down, swaddling me in a black blanket. She began singing folksongs and telling a story. I found it all soothing and my mind felt at ease. I went to sleep on her lap, no longer feeling hungry even though I had not eaten any food.

The next morning I awoke and found myself under the table, George and Florah asleep beside me. Pencil-like rays of spring sunshine streamed through the window and the slightly open door. I put on my ragged clothes and stepped outside to stretch and yawn while soaking in the sunshine and warmth. A cool, gentle breeze blew boiling small clouds of dust as my mother, Maria slung loosely about her back, swept the stoop with a grass broom.

"Mama," I said as I yawned and stretched. "I had a strange dream last night."

"Let's hear it."

I had dreamed of being marooned on a strange island, and as I wandered about the land, I came across a group of white men clad in loinskins who, upon seeing me, fell on their knees and worshipped me, as if I were a god. They then led me to a huge hut filled with mangoes, papayas, curried rice and fish, oranges, chocolate candy, milk, bread smeared with peanut butter and jam, bananas and guavas, where they clad me in a rainbow-coloured toga like a chieftain, set me upon a high boulder in the midst of all the food, and beseeched me to eat everything, saying that there were many other huts similarly filled with food, which was all mine to eat. I began gobbling all the food until my stomach burst open, revealing my cloyed intestines, which burst open too. However, I didn't die.

My mother, in divining my dream, told me that the events in it meant that some day I would find myself in a faraway place, among strangers, who would take me in, clothe me and provide me with all the things I wanted.

By some stroke of luck my father got his old job back. Now armed with a steady job, he set out to rebuild our former life. We now ate full meals, and dressed in clothes slightly better than rags. But things were never quite the same; there was now a definite change in our life. We could not regain the past; it seemed gone forever. A definite sense of insecurity and helplessness had entered our life, to stay for years to come. My father was now a completely changed man; so changed that he now began drinking and gambling excessively, and from time to time quarrelling with my mother over money matters and over what he called my mother's streak of insubordination not befitting "the woman he bought." But he still tried, in his own way, to be a father and a husband.

One evening he came staggering home, drunk as a sot. It was a Friday. He called Florah, George and me to the table, saying he had a big surprise for us. We kneeled in front of him, as we were not allowed to sit at the table, and watched him unpack a brown paper bag. There was *muhodu* and *mala* (chicken feet, intestines and heads), a delicacy the equivalent of a steak; a packet of candles; a small bag of mealie meal; packets of salt and sugar; and then the surprise—a packet of fish and chips wrapped in newspaper. We children were overjoyed; it had been ages since we last had fish and chips; we danced and sang with delight. George and Florah ran up to my father and embraced him. He blushed; I could see he was happy. My mother smiled. That was one of the few times I was to see our entire family happy.

8 Since staying at home meant hunger and chores, I began attaching myself to gangs of five-, six- and seven-year-old neighbourhood boys who daily roamed the filthy streets of Alexandra in search of food and adventure. These boys were like adults in their knowledge of the ways of the world. Together with them, I would spend time at the marketplace on First Avenue, watching shrewd Indian traders shout, "Come in, Mama; Come in, sir; *lo makulu* [big] bargain inside; *lo makulu chipile* [very cheap]," as they tried to lure unsuspecting black men and women into shops to buy cheap garments on layaway schemes; at the PUTCO bus terminal watching gold and green buses being washed by a fantastic machine; at the beer halls watching black women, with infants strapped to their backs, lining up outside barbed-wired fences, carrying drums and tins, waiting to buy Bantu beer, while inside the fences, black men sat in clusters, drinking and talking loudly, as gun-toting black guards patrolled the entrance gate.

At times we would watch, awestruck and envious, as *tsotsis*, dressed in new zoot suits and shiny shoes, played dice, smoked *dagga* (marijuana) and drank brandy and whisky, in the dark recesses of abandoned buildings. *Tsotsis* were Alexandra's legendary gangsters. And at times we would spend entire mornings scouring the streets for empty beer bottles and used bus tickets, to sell to shebeen queens and bus drivers. We used the proceeds to pay admission to the King's cinema, on First Avenue, where our appetite for bloody murder movies would be satisfied by a Western or gladiator or secret agent movie. King's Bioscope went out of its way to cater to our voracious appetite, it seemed, for almost always the movies shown were violent ones.

It was through watching such movies that I first began to form ideas about the nature of white people. Aside from the police, I rarely saw a white face in the township. And because black people were forbidden to enter the white world without a permit, I naturally saw the movies as one way to get a glimpse of that world: how it was structured, what kinds of people lived there; and how they functioned from day to day. To me the illusions and fantasy of the movies were the stark reality of a world I was forbidden to enter. From my experiences with white policemen, I had come to develop a deep-seated fear of white people; and seeing the bloody murders and savage beatings and indiscriminate shootings in the movies, that fear was fueled to phobic proportions. I vowed that never would I enter such a world, and I thanked the law for making sure I could not do so without a permit. Maybe, I repeatedly told myself, white people have placed these restrictions on the movement of black people in the white world because they did not want them to unwittingly wander into an Indian village or into a gladiator arena or into a cowboy shootout, and end up getting killed.

I had sense enough to know that there were white residential areas, where black maids and garden boys worked, and firms like the one where my father worked; but, in the main, I was fully convinced that somewhere in the white world, the events depicted in the movies were everyday occurrences. Otherwise, how were those movies made?

I remember well my first time at the movies. I was about three or four. My friends had dragged me there. As we sat in utter darkness, before huge, red curtains covering the silver screen, I was terrified.

"Why is it so dark in here?" I said. "I want to go home."

"Don't worry. The movie will begin soon, and you'll have the best time of your life."

"Why is that big man slapping all those boys sitting on the benches?" I pointed at the usher.

"He keeps order in the Bioscope. If you don't shut up, he'll give you the hot five."

Music rumbled. I turned my head to see where the door was, in case. . . . While my head was turned I heard the sound of a truck travelling at top speed. I whirled and saw a huge grey truck coming right at me! I screamed and leaped off of the bench to get out of its way.

"Sit down, you fool!" My friend pulled me back.

"The truck! The truck!" I screamed, pointing at the screen, my head turned to the door.

"What truck?"

I turned and looked at the screen. The truck had vanished. Instead a herd of elephants stampeded toward me.

"Mama, help me!"

The usher lammed me on the head with his flashlight. He ordered me to sit down or get out. I sat, shaken. My friends later explained how everything on the silver screen only took place in the white world.

9 One afternoon I was returning home from the King's cinema when, a few blocks away from home, I came across a group of strange-looking black men pitching a weather-beaten tent in an empty yard where the neighbourhood kids and I often played soccer. I stopped and watched, awed and fascinated. Suddenly two mud-covered jeeps swerved out of a corner three or so blocks from where I stood. Shielding my eyes from the sun with my hand, I could make out eight black men in fleece-white frocks sitting in the jeeps. Four of the men were shouting something through megaphones. As they went past me, toward the tent, I gathered what that something was: they were issuing invitations, in various tribal languages, to everyone in the neighbourhood to come to the tent where they would hear "good news" so glorious, so warming to the heart, so uplifting and comforting to a suffering soul, that their lives, their hearts, the situations in their homes, would be changed forever for the better.

I was still absorbed in the speech when out of the corner of my eyes I saw two tall white men coming out of the tent. White men in our neighbourhood! I gasped in terror, thinking it was the police. I bolted home, and along the way I heard several people whisper, "The evangelists have come."

Panting and out of breath I shouted as I came through the door, "Mama! Mama! the white man is here, the white man is here!" Immediately George and Florah bawled and ran into the bedroom to hide.

"Where?" my mother asked in a tense voice.

"There, there, see, see!" I babbled, taking her by the hand and leading her to the window, where I pointed at the huge tent in the distance.

"Oh, those there," my mother heaved a sigh of relief. "Don't worry, they won't harm you. They're evangelists."

"What are evangelists?" I asked.

"They are people who preach the teachings of the Christian God." Our household was not Christian; my father insisted that we worship only the tribal gods of his ancestors. Though we celebrated Christmas, we did so not because of the religious part of it, but because everyone, Christian or non-Christian, celebrated Christmas, for it was one of the few times when relatives could get together. Even witch doctors celebrated Christmas. Besides, the various white people my father had worked for since coming to Johannesburg allowed him time off from work only on Christmas.

Eager to go meet the representatives of the Christian God, I said to my mother, "Can you take me to the tent without Papa finding out?"

To my surprise, my mother said, "Yes. As a matter of fact, I was planning to ask your father to take us there."

"Really!" I exclaimed joyously at the prospects of going to the tent, but I quickly checked my enthusiasm when I thought of my father's vehement opposition to other religions, especially Christianity. His opposition had even led him to declare that there would be no churchgoing in his house in his lifetime; and that even after his death, if we broke his declaration, he would come back from the dead to haunt us.

"But will he take us, Mama? You know him."

"Don't worry," my mother said with assurance. "He'll take us there this time. Now go out and play; I've got work to do."

I left the house to witness the activities at the tent. I watched the evangelists bring in equipment in mud-covered jeeps, while pondering on what could have possibly made my mother say so positively that my father would take us to the tent to listen to what he called "white man's nonsense and lies." Had he not repeatedly refused my mother permission to attend any of the several churches in our neighbourhood?

Then suddenly I remembered snatches of long dreary conversations between my mother and father, in which my mother told my father that because of the hard times we had been experiencing continuously over the years, despite repeated sacrifices to tribal gods, it was high time we looked for new ways of dealing with our poverty and suffering, and that maybe Christianity might be one such way.

That evening I listened as my mother weaved a ploy to get my father to take us to the tent: she played on his obsession to acquire wealth and status by telling him that the prosperity of some of his neighbours, nominal Christians, was probably due to their conversion to the Christian faith.

My father listened, and afterward reflected deeply, seemingly trying to find a way to rebuff my mother's claims. But there seemed no way he could disprove them, for our Christian neighbours were indeed faring better than we and other adherents to tribal religions: they had better furniture, better clothing, more food on the table, radios and stoves, better shacks, more beds, and some of them even had used cars.

"And this afternoon," I put in, "I heard them say that those who came to the tent will hear 'good news' so glorious. . . ." I went on to restate the evangelists' invitation.

"Okay," my father said finally, uttering a statement I had never, even in my wildest dreams, thought I would ever hear him say, "I'll take you there, even though I don't believe in the bloody nonsense."

I was so glad I dreamt heavenly dreams that night.

The next evening, a Saturday, we went to the tent; it was opening night. We barely managed to squeeze in, for by the time we arrived, the tent was jam-packed, and the evangelists told scores of people to stand outside and listen to two huge loudspeakers. Inside the average-size tent, children sat up front on the yellowed grass, and grown-ups crammed together on the few long rickety benches. The place was stiflingly hot and noisy and buzzing with flies.

Soon the evangelists emerged from a flap on the side of the tent. There were twelve of them—eight men and four women—each wore a spectacular fleece-white robe, the back of which had a number between one and twelve embroidered in gold and green. The robes were further decorated with small silver buttons with silver wings. Each of the evangelists carried a wooden staff with a pair of tiny, shiny silver wings on top. Two of the men had cowhide drums suspended by leather straps from their necks, and two of the women had pairs of tambourines. One had cymbals. Two of the evangelists, a man and a woman, held hands and seesawed from side to side like babies being rocked to sleep, singing and humming excerpts from some cryptic hymns.

The two white men were not there. I was disappointed, yet relieved.

"Where are the two white people, Mama?" I asked. They had been around during the day.

"They went to their world," my mother said. "They are not allowed to remain in our world at night."

The leading evangelist, a short, fat, cross-eyed, baldheaded man with thick, woolen strings about his chest and neck and hands in the manner of chains, stepped forward and demanded silence. "We are the selfless messengers of Christ—the only true God," he proclaimed pompously, as he walked, with theatrical steps, between the tight rows of people, megaphone in hand. It was evident that the majority of the audience knew little about Christianity.

"We are here as a part of the covenant we made with Him," he continued, spreading his mouth wide in a smile, bending to touch a child, then waving his left hand this way and that at the audience, "to spread His word to all corners of Alexandra and save you from the tentacles of paganism."

At that a Zulu woman in tribal garb stood up and shouted: "We don't need Christianity. We have our religions of a thousand years. We don't need to worship a white man's god when we have our own."

The cross-eyed evangelist turned a full circle and faced the woman. He lifted his megaphone and directed it to the woman's head, took a deep breath and blared: "O, woman of little faith. The Bible is full of people like you, whose sins made them doubt that Christ is the only true living God. Unclean woman, did you know that our ancestors never knew Christ until the white missionaries came?"

"We had no need for Christ," the woman retorted.

"See how the devil speaks through you," the cross-eyed evangelist gloated. "Everybody needs Christ. Our forefathers, who for centuries had lived in utter darkness in the jungles of Africa, worshipping false gods involving human sacrifices, needed Christ bad. That's why God from his sacred seat in heaven one day looked at Africa and said to Himself, 'I cannot in all fairness let those black children of mine continue to follow the evil path. They've already suffered enough for the transgressions of their cursed father, Ham. I've got to save them somehow.' 'But how can I save them,' the mighty God wondered, 'for there's none among them who knows how to read or write, therefore I cannot send them my Ten Commandments.' God worried over the problem for days and nights, until one day he stumbled across the solution: He would send to Africa his other children in Europe, who already knew the Word. Indeed the white missionaries—valiant men like Dr. Livingstone—heard the call and braved treacherous seas and jungles and disease to bring our ancestors Christianity.

"After years of fervent preaching by the missionaries, many of our stubborn ancestors finally opened their dark hearts and grass huts to God's light. Some became full Christians, and discarded tribal ways of worship. Others, however, while they did take up Christianity, continued to worship tribal religions, under the delusion that they could have it both ways. Still others refused completely to see the light, and they passed that refusal to their descendants, down to this day."

Almost out of breath, the cross-eyed evangelist paused dramatically, gulped air into his lungs, and then continued: "That's why we're here today, brothers and sisters in Christ, to prepare you all so you can, when the Day of Judgment comes, be among those lucky few who will board that glory train to heaven."

At that, one young man stood up and challenged: "How do you know this heaven exists?" To which the evangelist replied: "By faith, young man, by faith alone." Bewildered, the young man pursued: "What has faith done for the black man?" And the evangelist said, "Young man, God isn't somebody to mess around with. Sit down, or else He'll have to take care of your insolence on Judgment Day." Reluctantly, the young man sat down, still shaking his head.

Having taken care of the young man, the evangelist returned to his sermon by thrusting his left fist, clenched, into the air for emphasis, and shouting with much animation, "Those among you, therefore, who, after tonight, will not, once and for all, terminate that hideous legacy by renouncing tribal beliefs and taking up Christianity, will not board—I repeat—will not board God's glory train. Your souls will roast at the hands of that horned black man with the fork and the pit of fire. So come on now, brothers and sisters," he beckoned with his fat hand, "come now to God, for He isn't gonna wait much longer. He's waited enough."

The evangelist's words cast an abrupt silence over the crowd. Most people appeared shocked, bewildered, some even angered by the evangelist's ominous message. Equally shocked, I turned and looked at my father. He stiffened, his mouth twitched, and his eyes blazed. The evangelist, by denouncing tribal religions, had entered the forbidden zone upon which my father stood guard. No one dared do that with impunity. And my father had support. A group of tribal men nearby heaved their massive chests in anger and clenched their fists.

"I wish the evangelist would stop saying that," my mother told a woman nearby, alarmed by the confrontational tone of the sermon. The woman nodded her assent. As for me, my excitement mounted: maybe my father and the tribal men would fight the evangelists!

Seemingly unaware of the mounting opposition to his sermon, the cross-eyed evangelist said, in an even louder voice, "Belief in ancestral spirits is sheer nonsense and hogwash. Those dead people you revere and worship are impotent and wouldn't harm a fly. I repeat: Christ is the only true God. So let all those with pagan hearts accept Him tonight and be saved."

At that, my father and several of the men from the tribal reserve leaped up and shook threatening fists at the evangelists, screaming, "Saved from what, you liars! You black traitors! You're the ones who need to be saved from the white man's lies! Who are you to tell us to renounce our gods for a white god! Heh, who are you! You can take your Christianity and shove it!" One of the tribal men lunged at the cross-eyed evangelist and had to be restrained and taken out of the tent. Fuming and uttering curses, my father grabbed my mother's hand, and we left the tent; many people followed suit.

When we reached home, my mother said to my father, who was still enraged, "You should have given the evangelists a chance to clarify their position. I'm certain there's more to Christianity than what they said."

"What more!" my father retorted. "Dammit, woman! Are you aware of what you're saying! You heard those white man's lies those black fools puked! I've heard those lies before; the white missionaries used them to take land away from my father. Those black fools won't fool me. I know who they're working for—the government." Slamming his fist on the table, he added, "From now on, I want no one to go near that damn tent." My mother did not argue; she knew my father well enough not to.

The next day, however, while my father was at work, my mother took us children to the tent. She was determined to know more about Christianity, it seemed. When we came back—long before my father came back from work—she and I began discussing Christianity while she cooked. I began telling her about my previous encounters with Christianity in the homes of some of my playmates. In particular, I told her about the portraits I had seen in several of the homes.

These portraits, made by a white company and sold through a local black grocery store, depicted various biblical events, figures and catastrophes, from the creation of the world all the way to Jesus' ascension to heaven. Two portraits in particular always had me thinking: one depicting heaven and God; the other, hell and the Devil. The former portrayed God as an old blue-eyed white man with a long white beard, sitting between white, fluffy clouds, flanked by two bearded white men. And all around heaven were groups of angels—all of them white people. The latter portrayed a naked black man, his features distorted to resemble the Devil with a tail, twisted horns like a kudu's, writhing vipers around the horns, big wild red eyes, and a wide mouth spewing flames and smoke. He carried a long fork, which he used to stab, one by one, the black men and women and children on their knees about him, begging that he not roast them in the pit of fire.

Though the Christian children and their parents simply laughed when I had asked them about the pictures, and considered them a practical joke by whomever made them, I, on the other hand, influenced in part by my father's denunciations of Christianity, and in part by my own skepticism, considered this blatant depiction of black as evil part of the teachings of Christianity, and had vowed never to let myself be fooled into believing otherwise.

My mother, in replying to my question about the portraits, said: "Christianity is essentially the religion of white people, therefore it makes sense that the Christian God should be thought of as a white person. Just like we, in our religions, have our black God."

"But why should the Devil and all the sinners be black?" I asked.

My mother began telling me stories about white missionaries; about how Africa was once considered, by Europeans, a dark continent overrun with black savages practising pagan religions; about how many white people in South Africa believed that the Devil was black, that all black people were descendants of the cursed Ham, condemned by God to be forever servants of the white man. I found the reality of what she was saying beyond my understanding; yet, emotionally, I believed her wholly. And as she talked, an idea that had been growing in my mind, flashed across my consciousness, and I said: "But Mama, aren't the Bible stories merely stories about white people? Black people tell stories about their own gods, and white people do the same." I wanted to relegate Christianity to the level of folklore, so I could deal with its fantastic claims about the nature of man and sin.

"Yes," my mother said, "Bible stories are like our stories. But they seem to have meanings which many of us black people can't understand."

Though the reality and meaning of the Bible stories seemed vast and alien, I still found the stories enthralling, so I said: "The Bible stories are nice."

My mother agreed.

"But yours are better," I said.

She smiled.

My father, who had been at work, happened to walk through the door, and upon hearing our discussion, he screamed at my mother: "I told you that I don't want any of that nonsense discussed in my house, you hear! If I ever hear you teach my son that nonsense, I'll cut out your tongue!" He then turned to me and shouted, "As for you, if I ever see you playing with those Christian children, I'll skin the hide off you!"

Such threats drove me further away from the few churches in the neighbourhood, and served to reinforce my own skepticism about Christianity. Daily I would hear my father denounce Christianity in various ways, and gradually, I began to believe his denunciations. I told myself that, like him, I would accept Christianity at no other level than that of being a collection of white people's "nonsense and lies," and I began regarding as fools all black men and women who daily came to our door demanding that we convert to Christianity or else suffer eternal damnation at the hands of a wrathful God.

10 At the beginning of 1967 our rent was hiked; my father's busfare was hiked; prices at the store were hiked; my father's wage remained the same. We now had very little money to spend on food, so we had to find other food sources. And we did.

First there were the locusts. My mother would often take us children to the veld on the outskirts of the township, and there, from sunup to sunset, we would scour for locusts, which were so hard to spot because of the camouflage provided them by the veld's yellowed grass and stubble. We would return home weary and sunburnt, carrying small jars half-filled with grasshoppers.

My mother would order me to nip their prickly wings while she cooked *pap*. She fried the locusts to a deep brown colour, salted them heavily and then served them with the *pap*. At first I adamantly refused to eat the locusts, calling them filth. My mother simply left me alone, and wouldn't force me to eat. Soon hunger would convince me that one can acquire a taste for something one doesn't like and I would munch, in the middle of the night, while everyone slept, the *pap* and the locusts she had left in a bowl.

Then there were the black, prickly worms called *sonjas*. These worms closely resembled leeches. My mother purchased them for sixpence a cup, from a fat black woman who erected a stall by the street corner every afternoon, peddling them with other exotic creatures. Her customers were mostly migrant workers returning in truckloads from the white world. The worms, my mother told me, flourished abundantly in the swamps of some of the tribal reserves.

The worms sometimes came live, and my mother would order me to squeeze their greenish entrails out and rinse them in warm water, so as to make them taste less sour. Whenever I ate these worms, whose skins were like those of miniature porcupines, my stomach would tighten in severe cramps, and I would have no bowel movement for days. Then there were the weeds called *murogo*. These greenish wild plants grew copiously near lavatories.

"Mama," I would say whenever she brought home *murogo*. "How can we eat such things? They grow near lavatories."

"What's wrong with that?"

"They feed on urine and *makaka* [shit]."

"You eat potatoes, don't you?"

"Yes."

"Did you know that potatoes are fed night soil so they can grow big?"

I did not believe the potato story and I continued to insist that *murogo* was filth. But, again, hunger educated my mind and prepared my stomach to receive.

And then there was the blood from "Mr. Green," the local abattoir on First Avenue. Each morning my mother and us children would wake up very early, tramp all the way up to Mr. Green, a distance of about one mile, so we could be first on line when the abattoir opened at nine-thirty. We carried various containers with us—my mother a small drum; Florah, George and I, small plastic containers.

At Mr. Green they killed cattle quickly and savagely. Many of Alexandra's poor flocked to Mr. Green to buy various parts of cattle —heads, entrails, hooves and heavy bones with scraps of meat on them. The good meat went to white people's butchers. Some of the black people who bought what was left resold it to others in the township, at a profit. We had no money, so we settled for the blood, which was free.

We would give our containers to the cattle killers—muscular tribal men who wore heavy boots and plastic aprons—and they would fill them to capacity. We would lug the dripping containers back home, where my mother would cook the blood in a large saucepan, let it simmer into a thick, pasty, brownish slush. We would then drink the boiled blood as soup. From all the containers we would get a week's supply. From watching Dracula movies, I hated drinking the stuff, fearing that I might turn into a vampire; but there was nothing I could do about it—short of starving to death. Relief from blood came when we stopped going to Mr. Green—the cattle killers began demanding payment even for blood.

Early one morning I found myself sitting on a rock in front of our shack; dreamily watching a pack of scrawny, nondescript dogs sniff hungrily about the rotting carcass of a cat; seemingly pondering how to get at what remained of the cat, without eating any of the thick white worms squirming about. I wanted to shoo the dogs away, to tell them that what they were debating of eating was horrible filth and would make them sick, or, possibly, die. But feeling hungry myself, I reasoned that it would be pointless to waste whatever little energy I had left in scatting them away, for they would soon return. One distinguishing feature of hunger I already knew was persistence: I, too, whenever I felt hungry, always returned to the source of food whenever I was scatted.

George, Florah and Maria, whom I was baby-sitting that day because my mother had left at dawn to go hunt for jobs and food, were playing in a small mud puddle. They seemed to be enjoying themselves with the toys I had given them: empty cans and bottles, and three plastic bags full of pebbles. They were half-naked, but the sun was up and flaring, so they didn't shiver, even though it was the middle of a bitter winter. I had brought them outside because they were shivering on the cold cement floor.

I was restless and bored. The streets were deserted, except for an occasional old man or woman doddering about. There were no children around. Some had left for school; others had left with their parents for some destination. I yearned for someone to come play with me—soccer, marbles, hopscotch, anything—but no one was in sight.

I picked up a couple rocks and started throwing them at the dogs, which were now nibbling at the reeking cat. I missed hopelessly.

I exhausted my rock supply. I gathered more rocks. Finally one landed with a thud on the mid-section of one of the lean dogs and sent it *auw-auw*ing behind the shacks. I gloated. The dog came back. I accepted the challenge. A new game had come to mind, and I collected more and more rocks. I began firing them rapidly at the dogs, laughing loudly when I made a strike, and sulking when I missed.

Presently a garbage truck came speeding down the road. Black garbage collectors, without shirts on, dangled from the sides. I jeered at them, shouting how silly they looked all ashened up, and running around picking other people's filth. One of them hurled a missile at me. I ducked; it missed me, but whammed Maria on the head and sent her plunging headlong into the mud. She bawled. I screamed obscenities at the disappearing truck. I fished Maria out of the mud and gave her a bottle of peanut butter to lick—the bottle was empty; it had been empty since a month ago.

As midday approached the sun grew very warm and soothing. Its penetrating warmth made me forget my hunger and loneliness. I dozed off by the rock and daydreamed of faraway places and things and food.

Shortly into my nap, I dreamily heard Florah's voice saying, "Look!" I opened my eyes, and saw Maria scooping, with her little fingers, her own feces and smearing herself all over. Two dogs were hungrily licking her. I went over and savagely kicked one of the dogs, and both scampered away. I ordered Florah and George to drag Maria and follow me to the communal tap.

A woman in tribal garb and multiple anklets had placed a drum underneath the gushing tap, so I waited. As soon as she left, balancing the dripping drum on her head without holding it with her hands, I shoved Maria underneath the tap and turned it on full blast. The cold water made her bawl; her teeth chattered; she sought to run away, but I told Florah to pin her down. I removed a few pieces of old newspapers that the wind had impaled against the fence and gave them to Florah to dry my sister with, while George held her down, and I stood by, watching and ordering her to wipe here and there.

Just before we left, a toothless old man, suffering from tuberculosis, came by to have a drink. We exchanged greetings. He hugged the tap with his thick, sore-covered lips and opened it halfway. After the drink, as he wiped his mouth with his soiled shirt-sleeve, I heard him say, amid a rasping cough, as I was walking away: "This water sure smells funny. But it's crisp and refreshing."

Later on that evening my mother came back with a loaf of brown bread and the bad news that she was unable to find a job.

Another evening Florah asked, "Why are you looking for work, Mama?"

"So that you children can eat," my mother replied. "Your father can't manage things alone."

"Why can't he?" I interjected. "He used to, didn't he?"

"The family is growing, and so are our needs."

"We should eat every day," I said. "Like my friends at their homes."

"We will someday."

"My friends say their fathers buy them food all the time," I said. "Why won't Papa do the same? We are his children, aren't we?"

"Yes."

"As his children he should buy us food all the time."

"He doesn't make enough money, I told you."

"Then he should borrow some."

"He can't afford to."

"Why not?"

"He's already up to his neck in debt."

"But we have to eat, Mama," I protested. I thought that regardless of the size of my father's debt, he should still borrow more. I don't know why I thought that. Maybe hunger made me. "We are his children, aren't we?" I repeated, implying that it was a father's duty to provide for his children no matter what.

"Why do you keep on saying, 'We are his children, aren't we?' " my mother said angrily. "Who told you you're not his children?"

"I heard him say that," I said, alluding to statements my father had often made when quarrelling with my mother. (Whenever the two went head to head, my mother would threaten to leave my father and take us children with her; and my father would retort: "Take those bastards with you, I don't care! I sometimes wonder if they're my children the way they disobey my laws!")

Before I knew it, my mother had given me a stinging smack across the mouth with the back of her hand, causing me to nearly choke on the marble I had been sucking in my mouth. I coughed violently, and nearly fell into the red-hot brazier in front of me. She caught me, steadied me, pulled my ears, beat my chest, and I puked the marble.

Shocked by my mother's actions, I began to whimper, gazing at her with questioning eyes. She told me that she was sorry that she had hit me; but that I had made her angry and lose her temper by what I said about my father. She began crying. She told me that going without a job was nerve-wracking, that she was tired of being turned away from jobs at the Indian place because she could not read or write, because she did not have a permit, because she had a suckling infant and because she was pregnant. She then told me that it was imperative that she find some kind of job soon for she would be needing diapers and baby food along with maternity care from the clinic.

Hearing all this made me forgive my mother for hitting me. I began feeling sorry for her. I cried even more. "Now, now, Johannes," she comforted me, wiping my tears with her dress. "Don't you worry about me. God will provide. God will provide." She gathered George, Florah, Maria and me around her and embraced us.

"Why don't you stop having babies, Mama?" I said.

My mother laughed. "I will stop one of these days, Doctor."

"Why not stop now?"

"Your father won't allow it."

"Why not? You have to carry the baby, don't you?"

"You're too young to know."

"You know what I think, Mama?"

"What?"

"You and Papa shouldn't have had me. I'm not happy in this world."

"Why do you say so?"

"Because life is so hard. No food. No clothes. The police. What's the use of living without food? And Papa is always beating me up and making me perform rituals."

My mother eyed me thoughtfully and said, "Things will get better."

But things didn't get better. If they did, I didn't notice it. Gradually, I came to accept hunger as a constant companion. But this new hunger was different. It filled me with hatred, confusion, helplessness, hopelessness, anxiety, loneliness, selfishness and a cynical attitude toward people. It seemed to lurk everywhere about and inside me: in the things I touched, in the people I talked to, in the empty pots, in the black children I played with, in the nightmares I dreamt. It even pervaded the air I breathed. At times it was the silent destroyer, creeping in unseen, unrecognized, except when, like a powerful time bomb, it would explode inside my guts. At other times it took the form of a dark, fanged beast, and hovered constantly over my dizzy head, as if about to pounce on me and gouge my guts out with its monstrous talons.

It made me seek solace, sympathy and companionship in the wildness of the streets. Playing pickup soccer all day long seemed to postpone my pangs of hunger somehow. But at the end of the day hunger would return, with even greater intensity, and, weary and lightheaded, I would stagger home, and, depending on whether there was anything to eat in the house, hunger would spend the night with me until the next day when I would again wander the streets in a frantic search for soccer games, which I would play with a passion rivalling my feelings of hunger. Thus I came to develop a passion for sports, and every day I would amble from street to street, neighbourhood to neighbourhood, searching for games to play.

In our neighbourhood there was a large compound that housed migrant workers from the tribal reserves. One evening while dragging myself home after a day of excruciating hunger, I stumbled across a group of boys my age who were pacing briskly and excitedly in front of the compound. A friend among them beckoned.

"Wanna make some money and get a lot of food also?" he said animatedly.

"All the food you can eat," echoed the others.

"Yes," I said eagerly. "Where?"

"In there." They pointed at the fenced barracks.

As we were talking, a tall, lean, hairless boy of about thirteen, nicknamed Mpandhlani (Baldhead) joined us. He had just left the company of a tall, muscular man with buckteeth. The man wore a gaudy blanket, one of the blanketed people who lived inside the compound.

"The man says not today," sulked Mpandhlani. A wave of dejection swept the group of five-, six- and seven-year-old boys. I didn't have the faintest idea what they were sulking over, and was about to ask, when my mother happened to be walking past. She saw me and yelled: "Let's go home, you night prowler. Can't you see it's dark already?"

Reluctantly, I left the group, without finding out how I could make some money and get all the food I wanted. But I was determined to find out, so I made it a point to seek those boys out as soon as I could escape my mother's watchful eye.

The opportunity to do so came when one Thursday morning, my mother left to go job hunting at the Indian place. She left me with orders to baby-sit Florah and George, clean the house and make a fire; but as soon as she was out through the door, I left for the streets. I left George and Florah alone in the house, for I thought that at three and five years old respectively, they were old enough to take care of themselves. As for cleaning the house and making a fire, well, I would do that later: the day was long, and my mother's job hunts often took her away from home for the whole day.

All day long I played soccer in various neighbourhoods, and toward afternoon, as hunger began gnashing at my guts, I left for home. I was rambling dizzily about one street when I saw a group of boys pacing briskly and excitedly about the entrance to a men's compound similar to the one in our neighbourhood. I recognized them as those of that night when my mother had ordered me home before I had had a chance to inquire how one got "money and all the food one could eat."

I joined them. They remembered me.

"Do you still want that food and money?" they asked.

"Yes," I said eagerly.

"Then wait here with us."

Presently, a tall, burly man with hideous vertical scars on his face —tribal beauty marks—and a left shoulder decidedly lower than the right, came by. He called Mpandhlani to his side. The two whispered to each other for a few minutes. Mpandhlani kept nodding eagerly. The man left and returned to the compound; on his way in, he whispered something to a black guard with apelike teeth sitting idly on an empty oil drum by the entrance gate leading into the barbed-wire enclosure. The guard wore a serape and a rusted miner's helmet, and smoked a long-stemmed pipe. A few minutes later, the guard called Mpandhlani to his side, and the two exchanged whispers. Afterward, Mpandhlani shouted that we should come in. The guard let us through the iron gate, smiling stiffly and squinting one eye.

We walked past the rows of brick structures with corrugated iron roofs to a big grey building in the back of the compound. Mpandhlani led the way, strutting about like a peacock and conversing with some of the men in a manner suggesting that he knew the place rather well.

About the compound yard were strewn empty beer cartons and bottles, papers, rotting porridge, rags, overturned trash cans, overturned nightsoil buckets, ash from burnt peat and coal. Huge flies buzzed about strands of rank meat suspended from wires placed in the sun so that it could turn into *biltong* (jerked meat).

For some unknown reason, I was fearful of the place and wanted to turn back, but the sight, nearby, of shirtless, muscular *impis* * engaged in mock fights using spears and knobkerries made me stay. Some of the men in the *impis* winked and grinned at us as we passed. Finally, we reached the building in the back and found the man with the scarified face waiting by the door.

Grinning, he led us in. The inside of the building was one long, dim, seemingly endless hall, partitioned into small, semiprivate cubicles by huge slabs of halfway-up concrete walls. The grimy walls were festooned with cobwebs and clippings of various tribal chiefs. Long, thick, concrete tables and benches streaked tediously, in two rows, from one end of the hall to the other. The ceiling of the building was high up and baring its rafters. Immediately below it were row upon row of threadbare clothes dangling from sagging ropes suspended across the ceiling like a gigantic spiderweb.

The place was stuffy and had a very bad smell, as of rotten eggs. From the small shut windows was suspended row upon row of fly-swathed *biltong*. The cement floor was a jungle of boxes, ragged pants, overalls, jackets, bicycles, unwashed pots and pans, opened cans of fish, empty beer bottles and cartons, old newspapers, greasy underwear and frayed suitcases.

The many unmade bunks with torn, faded blankets hanging limply from the sides suggested that a great number of men lived there. The man with the scarified face led us to the end of the hall where we found, sprawled leisurely on several bunk beds, muscular men without shirts on. The men told us to make ourselves comfortable while they prepared food for us. There were eight of them, including the one with the scarified face, and there were ten of us boys.

Two of the men began pumping up two Primus stoves, one with a black pot of corn mush upon it, and the other, with a large, black, greasy saucepan containing chunks of liver. The boys in the group flung themselves onto the bunk beds, giggling with the men, and went

* A group of Zulu warriors.

about wolfing bread, bananas and candy sticks the men had left out in the open—like bait for fish.

Not understanding what was going on, or who the men were, I was hesitant to touch or eat anything. I leaned against the wall, filled with anxiety. I watched the boys go about eating and laughing and talking with the men. One of the men saw me and said to Mpandhlani: "Why isn't he eating?"

"He's new," Mpandhlani said, giggling.

"Is he," the man ejaculated; and turning to me, he said with a fake smile, "Eat boy, eat all you want, the food is free."

I shook my head.

"What's wrong?" he asked. "Don't you like the food?"

I did not answer; I wanted to leave.

"Doesn't he like the food?" he asked Mpandhlani. "Tell him he can eat anything he wants. It's all right. Take this and give it to him." He handed Mpandhlani, who was busy munching an orange—the juice dribbled down the side of his mouth—a piece of liver.

Mpandhlani took a bite first, and then thrust the piece of liver in my face.

"Take!"

"I don't want it," I said and turned my head away.

"Aren't you hungry?" he asked.

I did not answer.

"Come on," insisted Mpandhlani, "don't be a fool, take and eat. You said you wanted free food, didn't you? Now eat; it's free."

Though I was hungry and my stomach growled because of it, I refused the piece of liver for the second time, and I moved a few paces away from the group.

From the corners of my eyes I saw Mpandhlani give the piece of liver to a five-year-old boy. I did not mind. The scarified man looked at me suspiciously, yet said nothing. My limbs tightened in apprehension. To escape his gaze I turned my eyes in the direction of the rest of the people in the hall. Two of the men still squatted near the Primus stoves, serving corn mush and liver. The rest of the men were busy clearing the area in front of three of the concrete bunk beds and putting layers of blankets on the floor of each bed. I wondered what they were up to but was afraid to ask.

Soon, everyone else had eaten his fill, except me, and two of the men began giving out palmfuls of gleaming coins to each of the boys

—Mpandhlani got a couple rands—and when they came to me, they stopped and said: "You'll get yours the next time."

I was ready to admonish myself for having behaved like a fool in refusing to eat, and in suspecting that the men might be up to something in giving out all that money, when one of the men said: "Are you ready now?"

Mpandhlani nodded to the boys, and they began to undress. My eyes widened. I heard the sound of running water and thought that the men were going to let the boys bathe or something.

"Take off your clothes!" Mpandhlani yelled at me.

"I don't want to take a bath," I said.

Mpandhlani was about to say something when one of the men interrupted him and breathed: "Maybe he wants to go last."

Go last? Where? What's going on here? As my mind was getting more confused, the men began taking their clothes off! Before I fully realised what was happening, the boys, now completely naked, had begun lining up along the three bunks. They then bent over and touched their toes, their black anuses high up in the air. One of the naked men brought out a large bottle of Vaseline and began smearing, lavishly, the boys' anuses, and then his long, swollen penis. My eyes darted to the other men; they too had begun smearing their penises with vaseline. I had never seen anything the like of this before, and when I looked at the boys' faces, expecting, somehow, to have them explain what was going on, I was met instead by looks of apprehension; the merry expressions of a moment ago had vanished. Meanwhile, Mpandhlani kept on whistling as he ate what was left of the food; he still had his clothes on.

I looked at the men, and one of them said to me, as he continued rubbing his long, veined penis with Vaseline: "This is a game we and the boys play all the time." He grinned; I tensed.

"What type of a game is that?" I asked, my suspicions and fear mounting by the second.

"Shut up!" Mpandhlani yelled. "Take your clothes off and keep your mouth shut!"

"I am not taking my clothes off!" I said.

"Don't be afraid, boy," said one of the men softly, breathily, dreamily. "It's only a game we play, and nobody gets hurt."

"It's a lovely game," added another man softly, breathily, dreamily. "You'll find out when your turn comes."

My turn!

"No!" I shrieked, backing away from where the boys and the men were.

"Don't be foolish now, boy," one of the men ejaculated. "Come back here."

"No!" I shrieked, continuing to back away toward the door.

One of the men rose to come after me. He stopped after only a few steps.

"Come back here, boy!" he said. "Come back here or you'll be sorry!"

I continued backing away, with quickening steps, sensing that the man was afraid to follow me because he was naked. I swept my head backward every second to see where the door was, I saw one of the men, farthest from me and nearest to the wall, position himself behind a boy who had his anus in the air. I turned and bolted for the door.

"Don't do that, boy!" I heard voices say but paid no heed.

"Mpandhlani, bring that boy back here!" the order was given. I stumbled on some object on the floor and fell. I quickly recovered, only to fall again as I missed a footing on the steps of the door leading out of the building. My mind swam in a fog of terror, my eyes were bathed in tears, and I saw only blurs as I tore through the yard toward what I hoped was the direction of the gate.

"Look at that boy go!"; "Boy, can he run!"; "Where did he come from!"; "Catch him!"; "He stole something!" I heard rough voices shout as I raced maddeningly toward the gate.

I thought only of reaching the gate, praying it was open, I saw it loom up ahead. It was open! I accelerated. The guard looked up and saw me coming. He rose.

"What the hell!" he yelled as I shot past him before he could reach the gate to close it. He tried to trip me but missed.

I never looked back as I tore down the street, dodging cars, leaping over *dongas* and fences and puddles; entering yards I did not know, only to leap fences again. Somehow, I managed to reach home, panting and breathless.

I never told anybody what had happened, not even my mother, afraid that I might be asked questions I could not answer, or worse, that there might erupt a big scandal if I so much as breathed a word about what actually took place inside the rows of barracks when groups of hungry black boys met with muscular blanketed men. I kept my mouth shut, knowing that if any of the blanketed people living inside the compound were to be in any way implicated in a scandal that could, I thought, have them deported back to the tribal reserve, the neighbourhood could become a bloody battleground. I had often seen the *impis* who lived in the compound go on a rampage with knobkerries and spears.

Little did I know then that what I had vowed to keep a secret until I died was actually an everyday occurrence known to every adult in Alexandra, including the police, and that nothing had ever been done, or was being done, to curb the prostitution behavior casually referred to as *Matanyula*.

Occasionally, I would run into Mpandhlani, the thirteen-year-old pimp, and his clique, and on seeing me, they would tease me and say, "You're a fool," while eating fish and chips no doubt bought with money earned from their prostitution escapades.

I was a fool all right, but I was a fool of my own free will. I was not prepared to prostitute myself for food or money. I would rather have died than do that. Mpandhlani and his clique, though while the compound was in operation never went hungry, fell on hard times when it was suddenly closed down, and the clique broke up. Each member of the group went his separate way; some became pimps at other compounds, others turned into *tsotsis* and ended up in penitentiaries, and in the grave.

Throughout all the years that I lived in South Africa, people were to call me a fool for refusing to live life the way they did and by doing the things they did. Little did they realise that in our world, the black world, one could only survive if one played the fool, and bided his time.

11 Though my parents differed on many things, including the usefulness of Christianity to black people, they agreed on one thing: the power of witchcraft. Both believed that many, if not all, of our household problems were somehow the result of bad voodoo inflicted upon us by evil-minded and jealous neighbours, and that a powerful witch doctor was needed to remedy things. There was no room for bad luck or chance in their lives. My mother thought that her inability to find jobs in the white world was not only due to her papers not being in order, but also because some neighbour out there simply did not want her to better her lot. We children were led to believe that the world was steeped in voodoo, witchcraft and sorcery.

One sunny Wednesday afternoon my mother, George, Florah, Maria and I were returning from visiting my grandmother when, turning a corner, we walked right into a police trap. Their van stood in the middle of the street, and they were stopping passersby and demanding passes. My mother tried to run away, but a black policeman spotted her.

"Where do you think you're going?" he yelled. "Let's see your pass."

My mother timidly untied ten-month-old Maria from her back, handed her to me, opened up her blouse, and from her bosom, removed her pass. She handed it to the policeman, who then quickly flipped through it.

"It's not in order," he said.

"I know, *murena* [lord]," my mother said. "I can't get it fixed."

"So why are you still living in Alexandra?" the policeman said. "You know that all those whose passes are not in order are supposed to be back in the tribal reserves."

"My husband is here, *murena*," my mother said. "We've been living here for over fifteen years."

"Then he's breaking the law by having you here. Do you have any money?"

"No, *murena*. I'm expecting soon, so I spent it all on the clinic people."

"Then I have to take you in."

"But I'm—"

"That's none of my business. You broke the law."

As my mother was being loaded into the van, she told me to take care of my brother and two sisters until my father returned from work. My father came back late that evening, and I told him what had happened. He went out to borrow some money from the landlord. He came back and sent me next door to fetch Mrs. Munyama, our neighbour's wife.

My father asked Mrs. Munyama if she could go to the police station the next day and get my mother released, because he dared not miss a day of work—he would get fired if he did. Mrs. Munyama agreed; her pass was in order. The next day my mother was back.

"They say next time they pick me up," she told my father,

"they'll deport me back to the homeland. And you, too, for having a wife without a permit."

"What can we do?" my father asked.

"If only I could get a permit," my mother lamented. My parents now lived the lives of perpetual fugitives, fleeing by day and fleeing by night, making sure that they were never caught together under the same roof as husband and wife. My brother, sisters and I, unable to fully understand why our parents had to constantly be on the run, would always ask our mother to explain. And she would reply with the following litany:

"Living like animals is not the way your father and I chose to raise you, children. In order for the family to remain together, we have to live that way. There's no other way. Illegal shacks are the only places we can call home. Your father could stay in a hostel if he wanted. But if he does, we would have to break up, and you and I would have to go back to the homeland while he remains and works. But we have no place back in the homeland. Your father and I met in the city. All you children were born in Alexandra. We have no other home but Alexandra. All we can hope and pray for is that God help us stay together until all you children are grown up." And each time she told us that, she would break down and cry, and we would cry with her.

Desperate to find a job, her only way to qualify for residential status in Alexandra, my mother, at my father's suggestion, began visiting several witch doctors, who prescribed various remedies, but to no avail. She continued without work.

But my mother was open-minded. Having apparently failed with witch doctors, she began exploring other options. One option came when, one day, a group calling themselves the Full Gospel Apostles of God came and told her about the miraculous ways through which the Christian God worked, hoping that she would renounce her tribal religion and convert to Christianity. My mother listened; questioned them here and there about aspects of the Old and New Testaments; and at the end of the two-hour revival sermon, she made them the following proposition: if the God they believed in could help her find a job, something tribal gods had thus far been unable to do for her, then she would gladly renounce her tribal religion and start believing in Christianity. Upon hearing that, the Full Gospel Apostles enthusiastically assured her that the moment she began going to church, got us children and herself baptized, God would in no time grant her her request. My mother told them she would think about it. But my father, when he came back from work, somehow heard of the Full Gospel Apostles' visit, and he confronted my mother.

"I hear you've been talking to those mad men and women again," he said as we sat down for dinner.

Laughing, my mother replied. "Yes. And I intend to become mad like them by joining their church."

"What!"

My mother repeated what she had said. A change had come over my mother over the last two years: she seemed no longer prepared to be ruled by my father, to play the role of a tribal wife who never dared assert her individuality.

"The minute you do that, woman," my father raged, "out you go from this here house and never come back. I'll get another woman to raise my children. There's no room for two men in this house. You either do as I say, or out you go."

"But I need a job," my mother insisted, "and haven't you noticed that all the Christians have jobs? Besides, going to church won't mean that I will stop worshipping your religion." She put an emphasis on the word *your*.

"You can't have it both ways, dammit," my father said angrily.

As I sat listening to my mother and father argue, I tacitly agreed with my father: there was no way the two religions could exist side by side in the house. We either converted to Christianity or remained tribal. Knowing my father, I knew that we were going to remain tribal for as long as he lived; and that for us to change, my mother would have to do something drastic—defy my father. As for myself, I cared less what happened, as long as I was left out of it. I was opposed to both.

A month or so later my mother defied my father and secretly took us to the local Full Gospel Church, where we were baptized. Though baptized, I still continued being skeptical about Christianity. As for my mother, despite openly and proudly calling herself a Christian, her tribal beliefs continued as strong as ever, latently when things seemed to be going right, and actively when things were going wrong. Hers was a Christianity of expediency.

12 A few weeks after we had become nominal Christians my mother collected our rent receipts, hers and my father's marriage license and passbooks, and once again began the ritual of going to the superintendent's office to seek a permit to go search for a job in the white world. At the end of each day she would come back home—after having been denied the permit because she lacked this and that document—tired and downcast, and tackle the chores of cooking, cleaning the house, washing and patching our rags and nursing back to health Florah and George who from time to time came down with malnutrition-related illnesses. Despite all that, she still found time to tell us stories, teach us tribal songs and pose riddles for us to grapple with, as we all gathered around the smouldering embers of the brazier. When I was younger some of the stories did not seem to have much meaning beyond being entertaining, but now, at six years old, they took on a new life, and I began to see them in a different light, and to understand their various shades of meaning. They made me feel and see and think in a way I had never before done.

My mother said that her stories had been handed down to her from past generations; and that, therefore, she was narrating them not only to entertain us children and to teach us morals, but also that we, in turn, would come to tell our children, and they, their children, and so on through posterity. She was such a mesmerizing storyteller that once she began telling a tale, we children would remain so quiet and so transfixed, like mannequins, our eager and receptive minds under her hypnotic voice, that we would often hear ourselves breathing. Whenever she ended a particular story, saying that it was past our bedtime, we would implore her to tell another one—a request she always heartily granted—until either my father screamed from the bedroom that the candle be snuffed, or we children simply dozed off into faraway worlds, our minds pregnant with fantastic yarns we wished never to forget.

My mother's vast knowledge of folklore, her vivid remembrance of traditions of various tribes of long ago and her uncanny ability to turn mere words into unforgettable pictures, fused night after night to concoct riveting stories.

On some nights, she would tell of chiefs, witch doctors, sages, warriors, sorcerers, magicians and wild, monstrous beasts. These stories were set in mythical African kingdoms ruled by black people, where no white man had ever set foot. She would recount prodigious deeds of famous African gods, endowed with unlimited magical powers; among them the powers of immortality, invincibility and invisibility, powers which they used to fight, relentlessly and valiantly, for justice, peace and harmony among all black tribes of the Valley of a Thousand Hills.

On some nights, she would quaintly and proudly tell legends about great and noble chiefs of her tribe, the Tsongas; chiefs who, along with powerful chivalrous warriors, undertook many daring and perilous missions into the unknown interiors of Africa, and there fought many a brilliant battle against ferocious enemy tribes. When the battles were won, however, instead of subjugating the conquered people as other tribes did, the Tsonga *impis* always allowed the vanquished to continue following their old beliefs, customs and tradition, and to worship their own gods, as long as they pledged to live in peace with, and to pay homage to, their conquerors.

On some nights, she would tell stories about animals. These animals, to whom she gave the complete gamut of human traits—strength, cowardice, love, hate, honesty, wisdom, magnanimity, cunning, treachery, fear and so on—behaved very much like humans, and she would highlight their interactions with human beings. The animals in her stories were always smarter than humans, and capable of making complex moral decisions.

And on some nights she would teach us tribal songs, proverbs and riddles, all of which she encouraged us to commit to memory, saying, "Memory to us black people is like a book that one can read over and over again for an entire lifetime."

There were dance songs, mimic songs and many others, which, she said, black people of long ago sang during harvest seasons, initiation ceremonies, burial ceremonies, witch hunts, auguries, ceremonies welcoming victorious warriors and other festivities and celebrations that formed the daily life of black people. The proverbs intrigued us children, and the riddles baffled us by their seeming unsolvable despite an abundance of clues. Each time my mother divulged the "easy" solutions, and uncamouflaged the pitfalls inherent in such exercises of common sense, I would marvel at her intelligence.

As we had no nursery rhymes nor storybooks, and, besides, as no one in the house knew how to read, my mother's stories served as a kind of library, a golden fountain of knowledge where we children learned about right and wrong, about good and evil.

I learned that virtues are things to be always striven after, embraced and cultivated, for they are amply rewarded; and that vices were bad things, to be avoided at all cost, for they bring one nothing but trouble and punishment.

I learned that sagacity and quick wits are necessary in avoiding dangerous situations; and that fatuity and shortsightedness make one go around in circles, seemingly unaware of the many opportunities for escape.

I learned that good deeds advance one positively in life, and lead to a greater and fuller development of self; and that bad deeds accomplish the contrary.

I learned that good always invariably triumphs over evil; that having brains is often better than having brawn; and that underdogs in all situations of life need to have unlimited patience, resiliency, stubbornness and unshakable hope in order to triumph in the end.

I learned to prefer peace to war, cleverness to stupidity, love to hate, sensitivity to stoicism, humility to pomposity, reconciliation to hostility, harmony to strife, patience to rashness, gregariousness to misanthropy, creation to annihilation.

13 Winter came, and turned out to be a very bad one. Our shack—like most shacks throughout Alexandra—had no heat, electricity or plumbing, and we had no stove, so my mother had to keep the brazier indoors, as she had done all previous winters. This particular winter, however, because of the severe cold, she would keep it inside the house until we children were asleep, which was usually round midnight, then she would take it out. The freezing cement floor made us children huddle together near the brazier each night, and my mother would cover us with old newspapers, cardboard and our two thin blankets.

One night in the middle of winter a fierce storm came along and shook the shack as if it were made of matchsticks, and shrieked at the ceiling like a poltergeist. Before we went to bed, my mother told us a story about how, one night in the long ago, a witch went flying during one such storm, blazing torch in hand, and at the clap of thunder, descended upon village huts and set them afire, as a way of settling grievances against the villagers who had burnt her child at the stake, claiming that mother and daughter were responsible for bringing drought through voodoo. I wondered why my mother would tell such a story on such a night, for it had George, Florah and me scared stiff. In fact, George and Florah became so terrified they could not sleep, and my mother had to reassure them by saying that our ancestral spirits would protect us against any evil.

We went to sleep. Toward the middle of the night, I was awakened by something choking me, as if two steel claws had locked themselves around my throat. I tried screaming, but no sound came out. My head felt unnaturally light, as if it were ballooning; I began thrashing in agony, feeling my limbs deaden. One of my wild kicks found Florah and sent her rolling. She hit something and let out ear-piercing screams: "Mama! Mama! I'm on fire!" Apparently my mother had forgotten to take the brazier out, and my sister had bumped into it as she was rolling. My mother came storming out of the bedroom.

"What's the matter?" she asked. Her voice sounded faint and distant, as if she were speaking from atop a high mountain.

I tried gurgling out a response, but still nothing intelligible came out of my throat. I began to sweat and gasp for breath.

"What's going on?" my mother repeated.

Through the thick fog which hung before me, my glassy eyes at last saw her, a hazy shadow as she grabbed a container filled with urine and poured it over my sister's burns (because we could not afford salves, urine was regularly used in the house to treat burns).

Somehow, I managed to gasp. "Mama! M-my t-throat!"

"What's wrong with it?"

"Mama! M-my t-throat! I-I ca-can't b-breathe!" I continued gasping, clasping my throat with both hands.

I saw her look at the brazier, then at me: she gasped, and without uttering another word, rushed over and grabbed and dragged me outside where a heavy downpour was falling from a blackened sky. Within seconds I was soaking wet; air gushed down my windpipe. I screamed, as if a big rock had suddenly been removed from my throat. My mother began beating my chest vigorously while applying pressure to the area below it. I began to vomit. After vomiting for some time, I felt the grip around my throat loosen, as if whatever had been strangling me had been somewhere in the vomit.

My mother rushed back inside the house, leaving me standing naked in the rain.

"Jackson! Jackson!" I heard her scream, calling for my father. "Come help me get the children outside! Yowee! Yowee!"

I heard footsteps thunder, and soon saw my brother and sisters staggering through the door, gasping for air and puking all over the place.

"Why the damn is the brazier still indoors!" my father screamed at my mother as we all stood outside.

"Because of the storm I forgot to take it out," my mother said.

My father shook his head and mumbled something to himself. He then stormed back into the house and flung all windows open.

"Are you all right children?" my mother asked.

My brother and sisters uttered timid "Yes, Mamas," but I merely nodded, too shocked to talk. I tried to figure out what it was that had been choking me, and where it had suddenly and mysteriously gone. Was it a witch? Presently my father brought the brazier outside and overturned it near the fence. Lightning flashed across the black sky, and I cowered in fear. A deathly silence hung in the air.

Finally, my mother said, in a whisper, "That's what nearly killed you, children," pointing at the coals from the spilled brazier, from which puffs of smoke coiled upward as raindrops fell on them.

"What was in there, Mama?" I asked, thinking that maybe witches had been in the coal.

"Poison gas," my mother said ominously.

"What's that?" I asked.

"It a deadly gas which comes from burnt coals."

My father called everybody back into the house. I went back to bed, but hardly slept a wink. At daybreak I stepped outside to look at the brazier; nothing was left but ashes, now grey and powdery. I scattered them with a stick and timidly touched them with my fingers: they were cold. Later on in the day my mother told me that I was lucky to be alive, thanks to my sister's screams, because poison gas and accidental fires were the number one killers of black people during winter months because many of the shacks they lived in had to be heated by braziers, and people often unwittingly left them indoors at night, as she had done.

14 A little thereafter Maria fell ill. Her mysterious disease was rampant in the neighbourhood and had already claimed an infant's life. A week went by, with my mother trying every traditional treatment on her to no avail. Her illness got worse. Alarmed, my mother decided to take her to the clinic, even though she did not have enough money to pay for her treatment. "There's nothing else I can do," she said one morning when she left me with orders to mind the house. "If they won't treat her because I have no money, then I'll just stay there at the clinic until she dies," she declared. She took George and Florah with her.

For much of the day I did chores: cleaned the house, gathered firewood, made fire and lugged water. Toward evening I found myself with nothing else to do. I paced aimlessly and listlessly about the house, brooding, searching for things to do or food to eat—there was neither. I longed for the day when I would have toys to play with and enough food to stuff my belly.

As I wandered about the kitchen I suddenly smelled feces and urine. The stench came from outside. I closed the door but the insufferable stench persisted. It was night soil collection night, the once-in-two-weeks night on which the shit-men—belligerent immigrant workers who, because of the work they did, were looked down upon by many black people—went about the communal lavatories picking up buckets of excrement.

Unable to take the stench any longer, I left the house for the streetcorner, where I knew a group of boys would be assembled—as they always did on such a night—to sing ditties denigrating the shit-men. I found about ten boys pacing excitedly about the dimly lit corner.

We waited, rehearsing our mean ditties. A while later the shit-men came down the road, trotting powerfully behind the night soil truck, dirty handerchiefs over their mouths and noses like cowboys during a stickup, dirty, thick plastic aprons about their thighs and savage-looking, gleaming metal hooks in their hands. They had no shirts or gloves on. The truck slowed down to a cruise to allow the shit-men time to go into the yards and come out with dripping buckets atop their powerful, bare shoulders. As the truck neared, we ran up to a ridge a few yards from the street and started throwing stones at the shit-men while gesturing obscenely, and singing tauntingly:

> *The shit-men feast on our feces*
> *They love to do so, just look at their faces*
> *Eat shit-men eat good my feces*
> *For they'll make good your kisses.*

The shit-men were in no mood for our mean ditties. The truck suddenly screeched to a halt abreast the ridge, and the driver signalled the shit-men to go after us. Caught unaware, we scattered in all directions, the shit-men hot on our heels, screaming like cannibals chasing a white man lost in a jungle. *"Mbambe! Mbambe! Mbambe, loyo mfana!* (Grab! Grab! Grab that brat!)" I stumbled over an unseen pothole, and two of the shit-men nabbed me. I bawled with terror, trying to tear myself away, as they dragged me back toward the truck. But the shit-men's hands were like a vise.

"Where's your home, boy!" the truck driver hissed as the two shit-men brought me before him.

I was paralyzed with fear and couldn't answer.

"I said, where's your home, boy!" the driver repeated.

"TALK, BOY!" one of the two shit-men said fiercely as he savagely twisted the metal hook in my face, a hook he used to haul buckets from beneath the privies.

"I didn't mean any harm," I begged, making piteous gestures. "Please le' me go."

"I said where's home, boy!" the driver said irately. His eyes grew fierce with anger.

"Over there," I pointed with a trembling hand.

The fuming driver ordered the two shit-men to take me home and confront my parents. They dragged me to the door.

"Who's in there!" the shorter of the shit-men bellowed. The door was slightly open.

"No one," I whimpered.

"You lying, boy. Who's in there?"

"No one. I swear."

The door being slightly open, the shorter shit-man peeped inside.

"There's no one," he told his comrade.

They looked at each other, like cannibals ogling a plump victim. To my utter horror, they ordered me to take my clothes off. I hesitated, remembering the Mpandhlani episode. But one of the shit-men made my mind up for me: he brandished the metal hook in my face. As I began undressing, the taller shit-man left for the gate. Still horrified I stood there naked and perspiring, wishing that the other shit-man would go away too. Suddenly, the taller shit-man came strutting back with a bucket brimming with excrement upon his right shoulder. He set it before me.

"Get in there, boy!" he bellowed, pointing to the bucket with his metal hook.

I was speechless. His voice came floating like an echo from a distant mountain so that I thought I was having a nightmare.

"Get in there, boy!" the order was repeated, louder than before, and I jolted back to reality. However, I did not move; I could not do so.

The taller shit-man advanced toward me, twisting his metal hook menacingly. "Jump in there before we make you!" he snapped.

Thinking that he probably was going to disembowel me if I didn't obey, I slowly lifted my legs and gingerly dipped them into the bucket. My body shuddered as the feces, urine and paper squished under my feet. The shit-men, watching me teeter as I attempted to secure my balance, broke into peals of maniacal laughter. Several people walking up and down the street stopped momentarily to witness the spectacle, but no one came to my rescue, for they knew the savage reputation of the shit-men. Meantime, I was knee-deep in the bucket. The shorter shit-man ordered me to march in place inside the bucket. I obeyed, and the gooey, reeking mess splattered all over my naked body. Some drops even fell on my face and lips. As I grimaced, the shit-men convulsed with laughter.

After a while, the taller shit-man rasped, "Let's make him eat some, maybe that'll teach him a lesson."

"I think he's learned his lesson," replied the comrade; and, turning to me, he bellowed, "Haven't you, boy!"

I nodded my head so vigorously in affirmation that I lurched forward, nearly pitching over. They ordered me out of the bucket. I got out. They spilled the contents right at our door and left, guffawing like madmen. Smelling like a cesspool, I staggered into the house and took pieces of rags, doused them in water and wiped myself, but the stench remained. My mother came back later, and I tearfully explained to her what had happened.

"Don't you ever make fun of those people again, you hear?" she rebuked me. She then went to Mrs. Munyama and borrowed a washtub and a thistle-brush and a dose of laundry detergent. As she scrubbed me, she lectured me: "These men do unpleasant jobs, and many of our people hate them for that. They themselves don't like their jobs; but they have no choice. Taunting them is bad. You're lucky they didn't make you eat the stuff."

Following that harrowing incident, I was sure of one thing: never again would I jeer at the shit-men, nor at anyone, for that matter.

15 My father was again laid off from his job, temporarily. Apparently shaken by the layoff, he decided to take a trip back to the tribal reserve to see a witch doctor, who would give him a talisman to guarantee him perpetual employment, and to replenish his supply of voodoo-combating medicines. One Friday evening a week later he told my mother that we would be on rations so he could save enough money to finance the trip. Two months of near-starvation went by, and finally my father had the money. Because minors didn't have to pay, he announced that he would take me with him.

Having never been outside Alexandra before, the prospects of the trip excited me for days. I was thinking that, finally, I would get a peek at the white world. Friday night a week later we crammed into an old truck with ten other people and an assortment of secondhand goods—cupboards, wardrobes, gramophones, pots, pans, tables, mirrors, cement bags, bricks, chairs and glass windows. The goods—belonging to migrant workers living alone in the city—were being sent to wives back in the tribal reserve. The truck belonged to a PUTCO bus driver who augmented his income by operating illegal monthly shuttles between Johannesburg and the Venda tribal reserve—taking goods there and smuggling back black men seeking work but unqualified to go through Influx Control.

To avoid detection by the white policemen staking highways leading in and out of Johannesburg, on the lookout for vehicles carrying blacks trying to enter the white cities illegally, we passengers were stashed deep in the back of the truck, amid the jangling pots and rattling crates and heavy furniture. A huge tarpaulin was tied over us. We left at midnight, and throughout the twenty-four-hour journey—to my greatest disappointment, for I had hoped to have a glimpse at the white world—we never saw daylight. When we were finally released we had come upon a strange black world.

The place was mountainous, rugged and bone-dry, like a wasteland. Straggling, unpaved roads, which became treacherous quagmires with each infrequent rainfall, were the only means of getting from one village to another. The soil was a baked reddish brown, like terra-cotta, with patches of dried-up stubble here and there. Intermittently, huge clouds of dust swelled upward, lingered a few moments in the air, and then settled down to make everything and everybody reddish brown.

The place was unbearably hot. The black people who lived there appeared secretive and docile and spoke Venda. Most were a pathetic lot. The houses they lived in were scattered about the wasteland, and were mostly little thatch-roofed huts with floors and porches decked smooth with cowdung. Others were made of crumpling adobe, and these stood among clumps of thorns. Still others were made of tin and cardboard and sacks. Only a few were like city houses.

As I wandered in confusion among so quirky a people—a people whom my father told me were kin—I was awed by the narrowness of their lives, which were even more circumscribed than those of blacks in the cities, with whom they seemed to share nothing in common, except poverty and suffering.

Following a visit with my father to the local village chief's kraal, where he paid overdue tribal taxes, I learned that the Venda tribal reserve, of which the village was a part, was soon to be granted "independence" from white South Africa. Yet, my father told me, despite independence, there would continue to be a white man behind every tribal chief, who would have the final say in all matters concerning the reserve.

Another thing that awed me was their almost total lack of information outside their milieu. They never stopped asking us about goings-on in the city and about the world of white people. Even though I had never been beyond the confines of Alexandra to know what Johannesburg was really like, I told them secondhand stories about it. They believed me completely, and thought me vastly knowledgeable; I felt superior to the lot of them. The way they went about their daily life reminded me of my mother's stories about primitive tribes, and I felt a slight revulsion at being connected, through my father, to what everyone in the city called a "backward" way of life. My father, on the other hand, seemed very much at home; I wondered why.

Everywhere I went nothing grew except near lavatories. Occasionally I sighted a handful of scrawny cattle, goats and pigs grazing on stubbles of dry brush. The scrawny animals, it turned out, were seldom slaughtered for food because they were being held as the people's wealth. Malnutrition was rampant, especially among the children. One time I saw an old jet-black woman, bent like an ostrich with its head in the sand, trying to cultivate the bone-dry soil with a broken hoe.

"This is a place where someday soon, all of our people will have to come to live," my father said to me one afternoon as we ambled about the tribal chief's kraal.

"Live here?" I asked.

"Yes," my father said emphatically. "Whether we like it or not."

"Why?"

"Because the white man tells us so," my father said, and added, with a touch of sarcasm, "I think it'll do you good to come live here. That way you can be raised like a true Venda boy should be raised." The statement made me leap backward in shock, as if I had been hit with a fist. I suddenly remembered the rituals my father had forced me to learn, and the many times he had said that he wanted me to grow up the way he did.

I began thinking all sorts of dreadful things: that the reason he had brought me along was to leave me behind; that he was being nice to me, which was not his nature, so as not to arouse my suspicions about his ulterior motives; and that the queer people in whose huts we were staying were always inviting me to go places with them with the intention of having me come back and find my father gone. I cursed myself for being a fool in agreeing to come with my father and began watching carefully his every move.

Toward the end of the first week of our stay my father received word that the witch doctor would now receive him. I insisted on going along with him, though I felt a vague terror at having to meet a witch doctor face-to-face. When we arrived at the witch doctor's kraal, a village of about six or seven huts in a circle below a craggy mountain, we were immediately taken, by one of the witch doctor's several wives, an old crone with drooping, wrinkled breasts, along a narrow path to a cave on the mountaintop.

As we entered the cave, a strange terror seized me. The interior was spookily dark, except for a dim corner where several sticks of incense burned, casting their dim flickering light upon an eerie shadow of a man sitting, back turned, cross-legged, head half-bowed and arms outstretched, on a reed mat on the ground. I followed closely behind my father as the old woman led us through—the way she looked and walked reminded me of Gagool in the movie *King Solomon's Mines*. On the rugged walls of the cave hung bones and skins of various wild animals; bark, roots and leaves of various plants; bottles containing grey, cloudy brews, from which pungent vapors came; dead frogs, snakes and other reptiles. And in one far corner, alongside a font bubbling an eerie mist, was perched a human skull!

I froze with terror, thinking that I had entered a cannibal cave; I wanted to turn back. My father calmed me somewhat by saying that the skull was part of the witch doctor's medicines.

"*Nda, Nganga ya Dinganga* [Greetings, O witch doctor of witch doctors]," my father said, and bowed several times in traditional greetings to a figure on the mat, who had an array of small bones and shells in front of him; I speedily did the same. The witch doctor did not answer back but continued to wave a *choya* (a short stick made from the mane of a lion) over the bones and shells, and murmur incantations. The old woman beckoned that we sit, cross-legged, opposite the witch doctor. She lit two candles and placed them in front of us. The increased light led to my first face-to-face meeting with a witch doctor. His looks nearly made me faint. He looked like a figure out of a Tarzan movie; he was dressed in animal bones, shells, bladders and skins, and his fat body and deadpan face were caked with red clay.

The ceremony began. My father listed his real problems and unrealistic needs. He needed medicines to safeguard his job, to "blind" the police so they could not see our shack during a raid, to cause the magistrate to impose a lenient sentence on him in the event of his being arrested, to make him earn more money so he could support his family, meet rental payments and retire his debts, to cure us children when we became sick, to make him win at dice.

The witch doctor searched my father's face with his bleary eyes; he picked up the bones and shells, slowly shook them in his gnarled, jet-black hands and threw them on the mat.

"*Vumani bo!* [Do you agree?]" he said in a deep, bloodcurdling voice.

"*Siyavuma* [We agree]," my father replied.

"*Vumani bo!*" the witch doctor repeated the chant.

"*Siyavuma.*"

The witch doctor then proceeded to divine the bones. My father's problems had one source, he said ominously: my father had totally lost contact with his ancestral spirits, and they were mad. The witch doctor offered the diagnosis: appeasement of the spirits through sacrificing a white chicken twice a year. The witch doctor then signalled the old woman to bring his medicine bag. From it he removed and handed to my father several small pouches filled with roots, ointments and bottles containing drops of the grey, misty brew—medicines for all his problems. My father was then led to the back of the cave where an ablution ceremony was held. The witch doctor made him drink spurting blood from a goat whose jugular had been ritualistically severed.

When we left the witch doctor's kraal three hours later, my father seemed a new man. He was happy, relaxed, self-assured, pleased as punch, like someone who had been terminally ill and, when all seemed lost, had been cured by some wonder drug and was now ready to conquer the world. The fact that he willingly, without question or protest, submitted to the witch doctor's rituals made him a stranger to me. The business of the witch doctor had somehow seemed unwholesome.

A day before we were to leave for Alexandra my father terrified me by saying: "What would you do if I were to leave you here and let that witch doctor raise you?"

My mind reeled. "I would run all the way back home," I gasped.

"You're mad," he retorted. "You'll never find your way back to Johannesburg. You'd get lost in the jungle and the lions would eat you. Don't you know the Kruger Game Reserve is just over that hill?"

"I'd rather die than live here," I declared.

"You're mad," my father repeated.

"Just try leaving me here and you'll see."

My father must have realised the depth of my resolve not to stay in the tribal reserve, for he simply laughed; he never brought the issue up again during our stay.

On the day of departure I asked a question that had been bothering me all along. I was talking to a thirteen-year-old, brown-teethed, scaly-skinned boy, who was wearing nothing but a greasy loinskin and who had been a constant companion and guide since my arrival.

"What happened to the men of this place?" Since coming, everywhere I had been in the tribal reserve I had come across very few able-bodied men.

"They've gone to the cities," the boy said. "And in a few years I'll be going there too."

Puzzled, I asked, "Why?"

"All men have to go to the cities to work in the mines so that people back here can survive."

Though I had seen no sign of industry I asked, "Can't they find work here?"

"Are you crazy? What kind of work can one do in a desert?"

"Do the men ever come back?"

"Some do during Christmas, but many don't. My father hasn't been back in seven years."

"What?"

"But he sends us money and goods every six months."

"Do you go visit him?"

"No, we children can't. Only my mother does. Once a year," the boy said. And leaning in close and dropping his voice to an important half-whisper, like someone about to divulge a big secret, he said, "And when she gets back, in no time she has a baby. So I think she can only go to him to make babies."

16 On the day that my father and I returned from the tribal reserve my mother gave birth to a baby girl, my third sister. In keeping with tribal tradition, she and the baby remained in seclusion for about two weeks, and for that period my father, George and I had to be housed by neighbours, for the presence of males was forbidden during seclusion. The day the baby was born, I spied, in the dead of night, midwives, under a cloak of great secrecy, digging small holes near the house. When I asked what the holes were for, I was told that "sacred things from my mother and the new child" were being buried to prevent witches from taking possession of the stuff and using it to affect the well-being of both.

At the end of the month a celebration was held to bless the coming out of the child. She was named Merriam. My father's measly wage of ten rands a week was stretched even tighter as a result of the new addition to the family. With the money he had to pay rent, buy food, pay bus fare and retire portions of his ever-increasing gambling debts. My mother could not afford diapers, so she used pieces of rags to diaper the baby. New clothes for any member of the family were out of the question. My mother patched and repatched the old rags. That year Christmas was not celebrated.

Six months after Merriam was born a new crisis hit the family. The authorities announced that Alexandra was soon to be demolished, for it had long been declared a "black spot." From stories I heard daily about the plight of blacks in other townships that had been declared "black spots," I knew well what the phrase meant. It meant that all family units were to be dismantled to make way for barracks housing only single men and women working in the white world. Those households with residential permits qualifying them to be in Johannesburg were to be relocated in Soweto and parts of Tembisa, a black township under construction outside Johannesburg. Those without were to be deported back to the tribal reserves.

Our family had no such permit. Where would we go? We had no home back in the tribal reserves. To compound our problem, my parents came from different tribal reserves, and in the event of the family breaking up, I did not know whether my mother would be allowed into my father's tribal reserve. If not, what would happen to my brother, sisters and me? How would we be split up? If we could somehow get a permit to transfer to another township, then there was hope of the family remaining together. But there was no hope of us ever getting such a permit; our papers were not in order. Where would we go? What could we do? The family was plunged into utter despair. We had little sleep each night, not knowing when the bulldozers would come to raze our home.

A month later, by some miracle, we were still in our shack. But I wondered for how long, for daily I heard stories of people refusing to move; of bulldozers moving in and levelling their houses, churches, playgrounds, schools; and of children sleeping in the streets and in the gutter while their parents were being chased by the police. Would the same happen to us? For the first time in my life I knew real terror —a terror which was mirrored in the helplessness of my parents, and in the suffering of the families around us that were being broken up.

One day word came that the authorities had decided not to demolish all of Alexandra at one go, but in stages. No explanation was given. My parents could not believe the news. It meant respite; we could look for another shack in parts of Alexandra that had been spared. My parents devoted all their energies to working around the clock to find another shack. Weeks went by. No vacant shack. One day word came that there was a vacant shack on Thirteenth Avenue, and finally, after months of anxiety, we packed our meager belongings and left for our new home.

The place on Thirteenth Avenue was another dingy two-roomed shack. The two ramshackle rooms, built from zinc and porous bricks, like the ones on Fifteenth Avenue, overlooked the street, and were part of a row of similarly constructed tenements partitioned by narrow, dark, rat-infested alleyways. Most nongovernment yards throughout Alexandra were similarly built. Collectively, the tenements, along with the one outside lavatory servicing them all, constituted yard number forty-seven, and our address, therefore, was Forty-seven Thirteenth Avenue. Rent was due the first day of each month, without exception. For our tenement we paid six rands, half my father's wage.

It was on Thirteenth Avenue that I first became aware of the fact that white people were the authors of apartheid.

I was walking along a street one afternoon when I saw a piece of magazine impaled against a fence of cacti. I freed it and found that it contained pictures of big beautiful houses, white people's houses. I took the magazine home and there told my mother that someday I would amass hordes of money and build her a house similar to the ones in the magazine.

"What makes you think you can build a house like that?" my mother asked me gently but in a tone touched with sarcasm.

"I'll have lots of money, so it will be easy," I said naively.

"Even if you had all the money in the world, my child," she said, "you wouldn't build that house."

"Why not? Money can buy everything, can't it?"

"Because it's against the law for black people to own houses," my mother said matter-of-factly.

"What law is that?" I asked. "White people build nice houses, don't they? So why can't we?" Though I had never been to places where white people lived, I knew from movies and magazine pictures and hearsay from black domestic servants that white people lived in big, beautiful houses.

"It's a law for black people only," my mother said, and added that such a law had long stripped black people of the right to buy land and own homes.

"Who makes such unfair laws?" I asked. The fact that white people made all the laws, ran the country alone, had not yet entered my mind. My encounters with whites in the movies had revealed none of the politics of the country.

"White people," my mother said.

"Why?"

"That's a stupid question to ask," my mother said. "White people make laws because they've been making all the laws since they took over our country."

"Can't we black people make our own laws? Alexandra is our world, isn't it? And white people have their own world." My conception of the world, of life, was wholly in racial terms; and that conception was not mine alone. It was echoed by all black people I had come across. There were two worlds as far as we were concerned, separated absolutely in every sense. But somehow, in my knowing about these two worlds, it had never occurred to me that though the two were as different as night and day, as separate as east and west, they had everything to do with each other; that one could not be without the other, and that their dependency was that of master and slave.

"Shut up!" my mother said in frustration. "You're still too young to be talking about such things."

I dropped the subject, for I knew that once my mother had said: "You're still too young . . ." I would get nowhere no matter how insistent I became. But I knew that I would bring the issue up another time, that I would attempt again to break down the wall of unanswered questions my mother had erected to deny me access to things I wanted to know.

Perhaps it was stubbornness which made me persist asking questions I knew would not be answered, phrasing them differently each time; perhaps it was some inborn insatiable curiosity to know that made me keep a mental tally of all unanswered questions, and made me construe my mother's reluctance to answer them as proof of their significance and relevance to life as it really was, as opposed to how she, my father and all the black people about me saw it, and wanted me and other children to see it.

Being new to Thirteenth Avenue, I began spending time getting to know the yard and the neighbourhood. I was slow in making friends but quick in knowing my way around, and soon I knew the yard and the neighbourhood like the back of my hand. When we arrived the former had alleyways partitioning its many shacks, but within a few months very few were left because the landlord had begun building shacks at breakneck speed to accommodate the seemingly endless demand for housing by people whose homes had been bulldozed. The demolition of uptown Alexandra had resumed, and it seemed the landlord wanted to make as much money as he could before his yard, too, was razed.

Despite the many shacks, a few narrow, dark, rat-infested alleyways still remained. Each household was required to help in the cleaning of the yard, but people were in such a constant state of flight from the police that no one was stationary long enough to even think of cleaning, let alone thoroughly.

One afternoon I overheard the black health inspector scream at the bald-headed custodian of the yard. "This place is in such a shocking state of disrepair and neglect that it's a menace to health. Even a sewer is better. Clean it up or you'll all die."

"We'll clean it up, *nkosi*," the hairless custodian said.

"You better. We can't afford to have a plague in Alexandra."

The health inspector left; the yard went uncleaned.

Sanitary or unsanitary, plague or no plague, to black boys and girls my age the yard was a paradise playground. Daily we dug for "hidden treasure" about the mounds of rotting dirt. We played "witch doctor" with the many odd-looking bones extracted from the rotting carcasses of dogs, cats and rats. We crushed the many empty liquor bottles littering the yard into "diamonds." We mischievously overturned the buckets of excrement reeking by the entrance gate awaiting pickup by the night soil men, who seldom came. We played "lorry" inside the many stolen, scrapped cars strewn about the yard. We lurched about holding beer cartons in our hands, mimicking the many drunken men and women we saw stagger out of shebeens. We powdered ourselves with ash to imitate ghosts.

The one lavatory was surrounded by a moat of urine, and we would race, as ships, bottle tops on its roily and reeking waters, rowing with our fingers.

We were forbidden to enter the lavatory, let alone use it, unless accompanied by an adult. One summer night while we were playing hide and seek, Dikeledi (tears), a small girl of five, hid in the lavatory. While in there, it turned out, she decided to relieve herself. She ended up tipping over and plunging, headfirst, into an overflowing bucket. Luckily, the bucket tipped and spilled and she crawled out through the bucket hole, smelling horribly. After that, we children began squatting in the narrow, dark alleyways separating the shacks to relieve ourselves. Our mothers and fathers would see us, but would simply turn a blind eye; some parents actively encouraged it, presumably finding it tedious to walk their children all the way up to the latrine only to tag onto the long line of people waiting to use it. Consequently, the alleyways became a stinking cesspool, swarming with flies the size of rats, and rats the size of cats. At home we dared not open the back window adjoining an alleyway, for fear of being overcome by the stench, or worse, being invaded by the giant flies and rats.

The ceiling of our shack began to crumble, and the door and wooden window frames began to rot, and in the winter icy winds would whip through. We were reliving the nightmare of Fifteenth Avenue. The slushed walls gradually peeled, inviting bats, rats and other nightly creatures to come live with us.

One day I asked my mother, "Why don't Papa fix the house?"

"It's not his house."

"Whose house is it?" I asked. "We live in it don't we?" Though I knew that we did not own the house, I thought that the least my father could do was to fix it; after all, we lived in it.

"Living in it doesn't make it our house."

"Whose house is it then?"

"It's the landlord's house."

"Why don't he fix it?"

"He doesn't want to."

"We pay him rent, don't we? He should fix it. If it falls, he won't be able to get rent no more."

"Yes, but he won't fix it."

"Why not?"

"HE WON'T FIX IT! NOW HUSH, DAMN YOU!"

I hushed, and the house continued decaying. Often, during the night, particularly after it had rained and the floor was soggy wet, my brother, sisters and I, after being gnawed by vicious red ants and scorpions burrowing through the porous cement floor, would wake up screaming from the floor where we slept. Rats never stopped eating our palms and feet, and we often were unable to walk or handle anything for days because both areas were like open wounds. Bedbugs and lice sucked us dry during the night. And just about every day my mother had to get new cardboard to make pallets because the rats were eating those too.

But all of this I passively accepted as a way of life, for I knew no other. The house, the yard, the neighbourhood and Alexandra were at the hub of my existence. They constituted the only world I knew, the only reality.

17 We had been living on Thirteenth Avenue but a few months when I became aware that the yard we were living in was nothing but a haven for refugees. They came from just about every tribe in South Africa, all of them on the run from the law because something was wrong with their passbooks or permits.

For days I pondered the many tribal affiliations, hardly aware that for all the years I was to live there I was never to know all our neighbours because of their sheer number and the constant and mysterious coming and going. It was because of this continuous stream of undocumented human souls that, a few months after our arrival, my mother warned me about the perils of a favourite habit of mine: begging for food.

My father had been arrested again. Hunger in the house was again acute. I was faced with two choices: starve or beg. Naturally, I chose the latter, and began waiting outside doors of various neighbours, diving for crumbs to still my hunger. My mother walked up to me one day and shook a finger in my face. "Stop begging for food, you hear! This isn't Fifteenth Avenue!"

"Why?" I asked.

"Because I don't want you going on begging for food, that's why."

I ignored her warnings and went on begging for food.

One late summer afternoon, as I was hovering expectedly about a door from which issued a mouth-watering smell of fried giblets, my mother sneaked up on me and grabbed me by the neck and dragged me home. I fought to break loose, and she fumed: "You'll know me well today!"

She dragged me inside the house, slammed the door shut and backhanded me across the face. I screamed, sensing deep trouble.

"Listen here, you pig!" she thundered as she latched the door and grabbed a switch from behind it.

"What's the matter?" I cried. "What did I do?"

"Shut up!" She took a swing at me. I ducked; the switch tore past my ears. I dove under the table.

"Come back here, you black swine!" my mother screamed. "Where do you think you're going? Come back here!" She towered alongside the table.

Warily I crawled out and stood myself at the opposite end of the table. Sensing that I had probably committed a deadly mistake for which I was about to be severely punished, I began thinking up excuses and hoping that for God's sake someone would walk in and save me. George, Florah and Maria were spending the day with Granny.

"How many times should I tell you not to beg for food?" my mother demanded.

"I wasn't begging for food."

"Don't lie to me, you hear! What were you doing outside Pule's house? Weren't you panting like a dog so you could get food?"

My mother had me cornered, so I decided to tell the truth, hoping that the truth might stop her from hitting me again.

"I'm not getting enough to eat here," I said.

"Even if you don't get enough to eat," my mother railed, "that's not license for you to go about eating poison!"

"What poison?" I asked incredulously.

"You fool, you'll die without knowing it."

"Who'll kill me?"

I listened with horror and utter disbelief as my mother told her voodoo story. She said everything with such forthrightness and conviction, with such calculated slowness, her face a mask of grimness, that everything she said sank in, and I believed her wholly, accepted all she said as undisputed fact.

She said that several of our neighbours—in particular, those who often gave me food—were witches who, at the dead of night, stripped themselves naked and rode on baboons and *thikoloshes** on various voodoo missions. These witches, she continued—I was now gasping for dear life—had a fetish of constantly poisoning food, which they gave to unsuspecting victims, particularly children, with the intent of validating the potency of their voodoo drugs. Among the people she implicated as witches were two old women who lived several doors from us, from whom I had often received morsels of food.

Regaining my breath, I screamed, "NO!" as I shook with the terror at the possibility that I might have eaten voodooed food: I had eaten something from the two old women just the day before.

"Yes!" my mother retorted. "They're witches!"

"NO!"

"Yes! And you'll die if you eat any food from them! Did you?"

"Yes, Mama."

"When?"

"Yesterday, Mama," I said, jumping up and down like a lunatic, clutching my stomach, which all of a sudden ached. Suddenly I burst out: "They should be killed, Mama! They should be killed! They should be killed!" thinking that if indeed I had been poisoned, then the culprits had to die. I had heard tales of children being fed *sejeso*

---

* Small, hairy beasts with faces squashed up like baboons and penises so long they had to be carried over the shoulders.

(voodooed food), which, upon entering the stomach, turned into miniature crocodiles, or lions, and began gnawing persistently at the victim's innards until that victim died.

"It can't be done that way," my mother said, lowering her voice and calming me down.

"Please get me a witch doctor to cure me, Mama," the words spilled out of my mouth unpremeditatedly. In my frenzy, I somehow believed, I don't know why I believed it, that only a witch doctor could help me.

"He's away in the tribal reserve," my mother said.

"Please help me, Mama."

"There's nothing I can do. We'll just have to wait and see."

Torturous days went by, whose hours I thought were my last on earth. I avoided the two old women as if they were afflicted with the plague and their house a haunted graveyard.

I now refused food from strangers, fearful that it might be voodooed. I even avoided standing anywhere near unfamiliar people, afraid that they might suddenly grab me and forcibly feed me voodooed food.

"Mama, why didn't I die from the poisoned food?" I asked about a month after the incident.

"You were lucky," my mother said. "They must have used weak poison."

"Is everyone in this place a *muloi* [witch]?"

"Not everyone."

"Then can I eat at the houses of those people who aren't witches?"

"You can eat at the homes of some of your friends," she said. "But," she cautioned, "eat only when they eat. Never eat alone. And if any stranger gives you food, hurry and bring it home without eating it, and I will tell you whether to eat it or not. Also, be on the lookout as to what your brother and sisters eat."

One evening a stranger from one of the houses gave me a piece of meat pie, and I brought it home without eating it. My mother placed a portion of it in a small bowl and left it overnight in a corner where there was a rathole. The next morning, we found, near the bowl, a stiff, hairy rat with a distended belly. The piece of meat pie was gone. I was horrified by the ghastly discovery. We did not have any mousetraps or rat poison in the house, and my mother had not been up to anything suspicious during the night. How the rat died forever remained a mystery.

18 My father came back, and our lives became somewhat normal again. But my instincts told me that that normalcy could be shattered at any moment—by another arrest. At this point in my life I realised that, willy-nilly, black people had to map out their lives, their future, with the terror of the police in mind. And that that terror led to the hunger, the loneliness, the violence, the helplessness, the hopelessness, the apathy and the suffering with which I was surrounded.

My father's repeated arrests gave me insight into the likely nature of my own future. As a black boy, the odds were heavily stacked against my establishing a normal, stable family when I came of age, for the minute I left boyhood and became a man, I, too, would be required to possess the odious pass, which had to be in order at all times. And the chances of it being in order at all times were nil, for I knew that, as with my father, the authorities would always find something wrong with my pass.

Knowing that, my heart sank, and I began to wonder whether life—black life—was really worth living. But what other life was there to live?

While I lamented the state of life in Alexandra, waves of men, because of rampant poverty in the tribal reserves, continued coming illegally to the ghetto. Some brought their families with them, and hid them in the shacks in illegal yards; others made their homes in abandoned cars and buildings. The threat of persecution and deportation if found, and the fact that Alexandra was being demolished, did not stop this stream of forced migration. Many of those who came settled in our neighbourhood and, as a result, before long my playmates included boys from various tribal reserves. These boys brought with them voodoo superstitions, more mysterious than the ones I already held. My sensibilities became sharpened to the point where I began paying singular attention to little oddities that previously I had dismissed without thought, now thinking that they were manifestations of witchcraft. For instance, I would be sitting outside at night, and a shiny object would suddenly streak across the sky and vanish mysteriously. I would bolt into the house and tell whichever adult was around that I had seen a witch. To my surprise some of the people around me would openly and publicly support my claims of witchcraft sightings, so that soon I began walking around with the paranoiac attitude that every strange thing that no adult could explain was the "deeds of witches," that strangers were not to be trusted, that every crone was a potential witch and out to get me.

I never climbed into strange vehicles because the occupants might be the Mai-Mai, notorious cannibals who regularly kidnapped people, carved them into pieces and sold these chunks of human flesh to witches and sorcerers back in the tribal reserves for use in voodoo ceremonies and in concocting magic potions.

If a foot wound did not heal, but swelled and continued to ooze pus, despite being treated with leaves and ointments from a witch doctor, then I must have stepped on a spot where a witch had recently urinated.

The many strange noises I often heard in the middle of the night, coming from the rooftop, were those of the *baloyi* (very wicked witches) riding their reluctant baboons and *thikoloshes* en route to a witches' human flesh-eating, blood-drinking and sex orgy.

Illnesses, bad luck and unemployment were caused by witchcraft, and only the timely intervention by my ancestral spirits—through a powerful witch doctor as an intermediary—could relieve anyone of such suffering.

The chicken blood my father used to cordon the house with twice a year was a sacrifice to my ancestral spirits, without whose absolute support, advice and guidance our household would experience unprecedented hardships whose enormity would cause everyone to die a macabre death. There was no room for chance in this world; all occurrences were preordained, and were caused either by the ancestral or evil spirits.

Because my navel was an "innie" and not an "outie," and because I was left-handed and not right-handed, I was destined to become the sage in the family, and someday would do something great.

Whenever I slept I "died a little," and during the "little death" my spirit would leave my body temporarily to wander mysteriously on its own, encountering and conversing and trying to reason with my ancestral spirits, who would then manifest their unconditional wishes through either pleasant dreams or chilling nightmares. For some people, however, the spirit would leave the body forever, and they would die in their sleep. There were supposed to be also instances when the spirits returned to the wrong bodies and the person suffered from amnesia. I therefore had to report each dream I remembered so that it could be interpreted by my mother or father.

If I ate more liver my patience would grow; if I ate more spleen my hatred of white people would grow.

It was taboo for my sisters to eat eggs until they were of a certain age because it would interfere with the development of their child-bearing organs.

I was told by my father I had no free will, no control whatsoever over my destiny, that each minute detail about my life, my existence —before, now and to come—were all contained in a big scroll made of brilliant sheepskin and as long as the days of my life, over which my ancestors pondered day and night as they alternately tossed random situations into my life.

Prior to age five I had blindly believed all this, but as I grew older, as the black life around me showed no signs of miraculous happenings and catastrophes, and as I came more and more under the influence of our Westernized neighbours, I began to doubt. I began asking my mother and father to offer concrete and lucid explanations concerning voodoo, the influence my ancestral spirits supposedly had on me, the mysteries of the world around me, and why calamities would befall me should I remain heedless of the dire warnings and signs my ancestors had placed along the course of my life to forewarn me of impending tragedy.

My father told me to believe and not ask questions, for to question what he believed was a sign of insubordination and disrespect. My mother tried to explain, yet each time she did I found her explanations vague, cryptic, obscure, ambiguous, enigmatic and too fantastic to be believable. Maybe had I grown up in a tribal reserve like my parents, maybe had all our neighbours been believers in voodoo and superstition, everything would have made sense to me. But fate had decreed otherwise.

In a vague way I began to feel that though my parents in general knew more about the ways of the world, about life and its mysteries, than I as a child did, it did not follow that what they knew and accepted as truth for themselves, I, too, had to accept as truth—especially against my own will. Knowing that, I felt that I could not just sit back and let them order my mind and shape my life as they saw fit, without my asking questions; that somehow I had to seek my own answers to the complex life around me. If it turned out that those answers I unearthed were no different from theirs—which I very much doubted—well, then I would believe everything they said with a clear conscience. But somehow I knew that, from the life around me, there would most likely come answers different from my parents'; if so, I knew that at some point I would have to go against their will

—particularly my father's, for in him the tribal values were most entrenched. Would I do it?

At seven years old I had sense enough to know that though I was beginning to oppose tribal values and superstitions, to declare my opposition openly without the evidence to defend myself would no doubt cast me, in the eyes of my father, as a tribal infidel. And I knew my father would not hesitate to drive me out of the house, and if my mother came to my defense, which I knew she would do, she too would be driven out. Therefore I told myself to feign belief, and to wait for the time when I would go out into the world, learn other ways of life and gather the evidence to confront my parents. If, then, they still refused to accept my new way of life, I would rebel, and face the consequences. After all, my life was my own to do with as I pleased.

19 With almost three years of constant police terror behind me, I had now become, at seven years old, so conditioned to expecting predawn police raids that each time my mother awakened me in the middle of the night, I would spring up and ask, "Are they here? I didn't hear any noises," thinking that the police had invaded the neighbourhood. And on many occasions it turned out they had.

One day my mother woke me at four o'clock in the morning and I jumped up from the pallet of cardboard on the floor where George and I were sleeping, stood up, heavy-eyed, and asked:

"Are they here? I didn't hear any noises."

My mother, now in the far corner of the room by another pallet where my sisters, Florah and Maria, were sleeping—my sisters no longer slept with me and my brother because we were of the age when tribal tradition forbade that boys and girls sleep together, lest they develop incestuous tendencies—turned around, looked at me hard and said: "No, silly. You've got to get the police out of your mind, you hear! Each time I wake you up doesn't mean they're here."

"Why do I have to get up, then?" I protested and started heading back to my bed of cardboard.

"Don't you dare go back to sleep!" my mother shouted as she continued rousing the rest of the brood.

"But I still want to sleep," I insisted.

"Don't we all," my mother said. "We have someplace to go today, so stop whining and put on your pants."

"Where are we going?"

"You'll find out. Now shut up and get dressed. Do you want you sisters to see you naked?"

I grunted disapproval and reached under the rag pillow for my tattered khaki pants and shorts. I dared not sleep with my clothes on because George had become a perennial bedwetter. While he and I dressed, my mother proceeded to dress my sisters, and to wipe their faces with the family's *waslap*. She then wiped her face too with the same *waslap*, then George's and then handed it to me.

"Where are we going?" I asked again as I wiped my face, curiously watching my mother wrap what remained of last night's porridge with old newspapers and put it inside a brown gunnysack. She also took containers of salt and sugar.

"You'll soon find out," she said brusquely.

We left without eating breakfast, for the porridge, sugar and salt were supposed to carry us through the day. It was still dark, and the air still misty and cold, when we trotted our way through the rock-strewn, potholed streets to the other end of Alexandra where Granny lived. Merriam, my youngest sister, was strapped to my mother's back; and my mother held Maria and George by the hand. Florah followed closely behind my mother, and I behind Florah, carrying on my head the gunnysack. Every now and then I would signal my mother to stop so I could rub some warmth into my hands and feet, which kept on getting frozen every short while. My mother would massage those of my brother and sisters.

"Some day I'll get you all some warm clothing and shoes," my mother said.

I smiled and wished that that "some day" would come soon. Along the streets we passed an assortment of people: old, ragged men and women drifting aimlessly about the fog like restless ghosts; sullen-faced men and women hungrily warming their limbs around small trash fires; grim- and blank-faced men and women hurrying to catch PUTCO buses to their workplaces in the white world. From inside some of the shacks alongside the road issued loud, mournful cries of hungry or neglected children (no longer a stranger to hunger, I recognized its cry everywhere). Along one street we saw a naked man and woman scaling a barbed-wire fence. The woman kept on falling.

Finally, she succeeded in going over the high fence, and disappeared behind a cluster of shacks.

"The police probably barged into their home before they had had time to dress," my mother said, replying to my brother's question why the man and woman had no clothes on.

Granny's home was a tiny, neat shack, measuring twelve by fifteen feet. It was perched unpretentiously on the edge of a *donga*, one of many similar shacks on Eighth Avenue. Its exterior was conspicuously flaked with old whitewash. Granny lived with her two children, Uncle Piet, thirteen, and Aunt Bush, fifteen. Her first-born, Uncle Cheeks, was somewhere in a black penitentiary serving a long sentence for burglarizing a white man's home. To help make ends meet, Granny rented out part of her lodgings to immigrant workers whose permits to live in Alexandra had expired and who were facing deportation orders.

Granny, an indomitable matriarch, had single-handedly raised all of her children after her husband had deserted her for another woman.

She had a statuesque figure—tall, lithe and ebony-coloured—like a Masai woman, complete with tribal garbs and multiple anklets, beads, earrings and bracelets. In that dazzling outfit, she could have easily been a chief's daughter. Her genial, brown eyes had the radiance of pristine pearls. She was, I think, the most beautiful black woman I had ever seen. Though somewhat grey-haired and wrinkled by the time I came to know her well, from the stories I heard of her youth she could have captured the heart of any man she wanted.

Despite the fact that she was now quite old, Granny still worked six days a week, from seven to five, manicuring lawns, raking leaves, clipping hedges, watering plants, sweeping driveways, cleaning yards and pruning trees for white people. She told me there were no social security or pension schemes for black people in her particular occupation, so she had resigned herself to working until all her children were of the age when they could take care of her, or as she often put it, until her last breath.

The sun was just rising behind the smoky, distant shacks when we reached her place.

"Thank God you came," she cried as we found her waiting anxiously by the gate. She appeared flustered, and as she spoke, her normally firm and authoritative voice trembled.

"What's the matter?" my mother asked.

"They've taken him away," Granny said, her eyes watery as if about burst into tears. "They've taken my Piet away."

"What! Who? Piet?" my mother cried in astonishment. "They couldn't have—"

Aunt Bushy, clad in a school uniform and standing alongside Granny, suddenly burst into tears at the mention of Uncle Piet's name.

"Piet! Piet!" she wailed. "They've taken him away; the police have taken him away!"

"Don't cry like that," my grandmother reproached her. "It's a bad omen."

"They couldn't have taken him away," my mother said disbelievingly. "How could they have? He's hardly old enough to carry a pass. How did it happen?"

As we filed sullenly into the shack, Granny leading the way, she began explaining how Uncle Piet, unusually tall for a thirteen-year-old, had been arrested by Peri-Urban that morning.

"It happened early this morning," she began, struggling to control her emotions. "It was about six or seven, I don't know. I had sent him, as I usually do when I have some money, to the corner store to buy a loaf of brown bread for them to eat before going to school. Whenever he went to the store, he never took long. But this morning, after a long time, he still hadn't returned." Granny could no longer control herself, and she broke down and cried, "Oh, Lord, what will they do to my son!"

"Nothing, Mama," my mother consoled my grandmother. "Nothing. Tell me the rest, and we'll see what can be done."

"When he didn't return, I got worried," Granny continued, pausing to take a little snuff from a small tin can and wipe tears off her cheeks, "and I was about to go out looking for him when in rushed one of our neighbours, Mama Vilakazi, shouting that she'd just witnessed something dreadful to do with Piet and the police. I went into a frenzy, suspecting the worst. She calmed me down and told me what had happened. She said she'd been hiding in a ditch when she saw my poor Piet being stopped by two policemen as he was coming out of the store. They started frisking him, Mama Vilakazi said."

"How did she know it was Piet?" my mother asked.

"She said she recognized the colours of his school uniform," Granny said. "And apparently he still had the loaf of bread in his hand. Mama Vilakazi said that it seemed as if Piet was protesting and trying to tell the police something, and he was repeatedly pointing in the direction of the house, but the police apparently wouldn't listen, for they marched him toward the police truck."

"Did you go outside to see if you could do anything?" my mother asked.

"Yes, as soon as Mama Vilakazi finished her talk, I ran outside, and sure enough, there was the police truck still standing by the corner; they already had my Piet in the truck. But I dared not go any nearer because the police were still stopping people and asking for passes. You know that mine is not in order."

"It's not? I didn't know that. I thought they had finally given you permission to continue living in Alexandra since Father had abandoned you."

"No, they didn't. They told me that I didn't qualify, that unless I married a second time I would have to leave Alexandra."

"You! Get married a second time! You must be pulling my leg; how could they have said that to you, Mama. Didn't they see who they were talking to?"

"You know that Peri-Urban never sees who we are but the numbers we are, and the laws they have to enforce. The superintendent himself told me that I would be breaking the law if I didn't get married again, and there's nothing he could do about it."

"So what do you propose we do about Piet? Do you have any money to get him out?"

Granny started weeping. She blew her nose in the palm of her hands and wrung them till they gleamed with mucus. "No," she said finally, "the last money I had I used to pay rent and school fees for the children. I don't even have a cent on me. I don't know who'll lend us money. I don't know what to do. I was hoping to work all this week."

"I don't have any money either," my mother said, "and we can't leave Piet in jail."

"Not on my life," vowed Granny, her limbs tightening in anger. Her big brown eyes blazed with fury as she spoke. "They'll have to kill me to keep him there. I won't let those beasts take my Piet to a potato farm."

Conditions on the potato farms in the Bethal area, where black prisoners were often taken to relieve the overcrowded jails in Johannesburg and provide cheap labour for white farmers, were described as inhuman. Prisoners were often kept in barbed-wire compounds, flogged, tortured, starved and hung from trees, and those who died buried secretly in unmarked graves.

My mother had to postpone her itinerary as she and my grandmother spent the entire day combing the township for relatives and friends who could spare some money or donate some of their meager belongings to be sold so that Uncle Piet could be released. Aunt Bushy was told not to go to school but to take care of the house. Toward late evening, Granny and my mother returned, dead weary, all for nothing: they had not gotten enough money to secure Uncle Piet's release.

The following day they pawned some of Granny's meager belongings. Then they left to get Uncle Piet. Two hours later, they were back—without Uncle Piet. It turned out that there was a law that stated that no black person could be released or tried on weekends, for the Bantu courts were open only on weekdays. So Uncle Piet remained in jail for the weekend.

On Monday Granny and my mother again went to get Uncle Piet. This time they came back with him. He had been released—without being charged—and given a warning that he better get himself a pass soon, for he was getting too tall and was beginning to wear long pants, factors which alone made him adult enough to carry a pass. The next day Granny took him to school and explained the matter to the principal, who then wrote Uncle Piet a note, which he had to carry with him at all times. The note was stamped with the school's official seal, attesting that he was a full-time student and only thirteen years old. Whenever an overzealous policeman arrested him despite the note, the principal had to personally call the police station and vouch that he was indeed a student.

20 A few weeks after Uncle Piet's release my mother again woke me at four in the morning and told me that the trip she had had to postpone had now to be taken. I again asked her where we were going. She told me that we were going to the superintendent's office. We again trotted all the way to the other end of the township, where we left George and my sisters under Granny's care—she was not working that day. At five my mother and I reached the superintendent's office on First Avenue and found a throng of black men, women and children waiting on line. The line was so long that it wound all around the big, grassy courtyard, all around the tall barbed-wire fence and snaked all the way down the wide, tarred road. Many of the women standing on line had infants strapped to their backs; others clutched fearful, scantily dressed, barefooted six- and seven-year-old boys and girls.

"What are we doing here, Mama?" I asked apprehensively.

"We've come to apply for papers."

"What papers?"

"Important papers."

"What do I need important papers for?"

"You need them."

"Why?"

"You need them. Now hush."

We stood on line and waited. A scrawny black woman nearby, a bawling infant strapped to her back by a piece of worn goatskin, asked a fat black man guarding the superintendent's office what time it was. The guard, wearing a heavy blanket, and smoking a pipe gave a terse reply, "Six." The scrawny woman then asked, "When does the office open?" The guard gave another terse reply, "Ten." An icy wind howled, whipping its way through my scantily dressed limbs, and the thought of waiting another four hours numbed me. I looked about and saw flames licking the air not too far away from where I stood.

"Can I go warm myself at that fire over there," I asked, pointing to a small trash fire around which a group of sullen-faced black men, looking as pathetic as a bunch of workless men out of the depression, squatted on their hams, some with chins buried in their hands, others with elbows resting on their thighs while supporting their bony cheeks.

My mother palpated my face.

"My feet are frozen too," I said.

"You can go," she said. "Ask the men nicely, now."

As I approached the fire, one of the men squatting hungrily about it saw me coming, and he yelled, "Don't come near this fire, you vagabond!" I stopped dead in my tracks and scuttled back to my mother and told her what happened. She took me by the hand and led me back to the fire.

"Could you good men please allow my son to warm his little feet?" she begged. "We've been out here since five." The group of men stared at my mother, then at me—my teeth were chattering.

"*Eke nwana waho, musadi?* [Is he your child, woman?]" the man who had chased me away said apologetically in Sotho. My mother nodded. The man went on, "We didn't know that. We thought he was one of the regular runaways and pickpockets who sleep in the gutter waiting for fires like this one to go up. You can't tell these days, you know?"

"Yes, I know," my mother said humbly.

I probably fit the description of a vagabond—my clothes were ragged, my body was scarred with sores and bruises, mucus dribbled from my nose into my mouth, and my tightly curled mop of wooly black hair was unkempt and teemed with lice. And I smelled.

The man then called me to him and asked me which part of my body was the coldest. I told him all parts but that my feet were frozen. He invited me to sit on his lap, and he began vigorously massaging my feet. As he did, they seemed to thaw, and feeling once again surged through them. I sat and enjoyed the fire, listening to the men talking and cursing about their difficulties in obtaining passes, in obtaining permits to go look for work in the white world, in obtaining permission for their families to come live with them; talking and cursing about the brutality of the Peri-Urban police, the lack of justice in the Bantu courts, the insensitivity of white people in refusing to hire black people with prison records; talking and cursing about the lack of decent-paying jobs and the abundance of pain and misery in their lives. Suddenly a convoy of trucks, packed with grim-faced black men wearing gaudy blankets, went by.

"Who are those men?" I asked a middle-aged man squatting nearby, his buttocks, sticking from a huge hole in what was left of his ragged trousers, almost touching the ground.

The man turned his head, looked at me, twitched his mouth to reveal several rotten buckteeth, spat a huge blob of mucus into the fire, and then broke into a long, scornful laughter.

"Those, my boy," he guffawed. "Those, my boy, are not men. Those are leeches from the tribal reserves. They're coming here to work in the mines."

At his saying that, everyone around the fire broke out laughing— a sort of sardonic laughter intended to convey deep-rooted rancor and hatred. Thinking that I had probably asked a dumb, or worse, a wrong question, I coyly dropped my eyes and stared at the smouldering flames. I did not pursue my question; I simply sat in silence and listened to the men's talk. Half an hour later, another convoy of trucks carrying more grim-faced black men in gaudy blankets went by.

"There goes that vermin, again," a man with a hideous scar on his left cheek remarked, making an obscene gesture at the passing trucks.

"Why are there so many of those men?" I blurted out.

"Those aren't men, boy, that's vermin," the scarfaced man retorted. There was fire in his big bloodshot eyes as he spoke. "That vermin is being brought here to get gold for the white man, boy," he went on, "to make the white bastards fat and rich and powerful and deadly." He paused and took three deep draws from tobacco wrapped in brown paper. "If all these years that vermin hadn't been licking the white man's ass, boy," he went on, making another obscene gesture with several stub fingers in his left hand, at another passing truck, "we would have long had political rights in this country. And I wouldn't be standing here freezing my ass off waiting for the bloody offices to open so that I could have my pass stamped so that I could hunt for a job so that I could feed myself, my wife and my brood so they wouldn't die." His run-on sentences throbbed with anger and hatred. It seemed as if somehow my questions, naive and unpremeditated though they were, had, nonetheless, provided him with some long-awaited opportunity to vent his pent-up frustrations and bitterness. The way he denounced the blanketed people, and the way the rest of the men around the fire supported what he was saying, made it seem that, somehow, their inability to find work, to earn a living, to have self-respect and dignity, to be real men in the eyes of their wives; in short, the disintegration of their lives, was blamable on the convoys coming into the township. Somehow, in their anger and hatred, I could see traces of my father's anger and hatred. What created men like these? I did not know.

Seven hours after we had waited on line, been told to go to this office and that, been told to produce this paper and that paper, we were finally ushered into a small, empty room by a black policeman with a gun about his waist. Terrified at the sight of the policeman, I clung to my mother, hiding behind her dress.

"Wait here for the *baas*," the policeman said, pointing to the side of the door. There were two chairs nearby, but we were not allowed to sit on them. The policeman took our papers and stepped outside. Presently, he came back.

"The *baas* will be with you shortly," he said. "He's still having lunch."

"We will wait, *murena* [sir]," my mother said humbly.

The black policeman again left. Feeling exhausted and lightheaded from standing up all morning, I asked my mother if we could sit down, forgetting that the policeman had told us not to.

"Are you mad?" she retorted. "Here you don't sit down unless you're told to!"

We waited for about an hour; no one came. Well into the second hour, the black policeman came back.

"The *baas* says he can't see you today," he said, removing a fancy overcoat from a nail behind the door. "He's got to rush home."

"Can't you help us, *murena*," my mother entreated. "We've been here since five in the morning. All I need are papers for my son. Please tell him I desperately need the papers for my son. Please, *murena*, please."

"You've heard what I said, *musadi*," the black policeman said with annoyance, showing us the door. "The *baas* has an important dinner date, and there's nothing I can do about it."

"I understand, *murena*," my mother begged. "But can't you tell him I only need a simple paper. Please, *murena*, I pray you."

"You're wasting your time with me, *musadi*," the policeman said with mounting irritation. "I told you before that the *baas* wants to go home, and there's nothing I can do about it. He is the *baas*, you know. I don't tell him what to do. He tells me what to do. If he wants to go home an hour early, he does; and that's fine with me. If he feels like going home two hours early, he does; and that's fine with me too. I don't care nothing. I only work for my children."

"When can we come back?" my mother asked despairingly, as she took the papers from the outstretched hand of the policeman.

"In a month," the policeman said.

"But—"

"*Musadi*, I've had enough of your complaints," the policeman cut my mother short. "You're not the only one here, you know. There are hundreds other people waiting to be attended to."

We left.

A month or so later, on a Friday (the mysterious papers my mother was seeking were only issued on Fridays), we were up at three in the morning; by four we had arrived at Granny's, where we left George and my sisters, and by five we were again waiting on line at the superintendent's office. It was still dark. From the voice of the scores of people already on line I could make out that many of the men and women who were with us the last time were back. I also recognized the voices of some of the children in the clutches of some of the women. This time the fire was not there. At seven the truckloads of blanketed men did go past again, this time in the opposite direction. The blanketed men sang boisterously.

"Why are the trucks going the other way today, Mama?" I asked. "And why are the blanketed people singing?"

"They're going to work," my mother said. "White people live that way. And they are singing because they're happy."

"They were not happy the last time I saw them."

"They're happy today because it's Friday. They get paid on Friday."

"Doesn't Papa get paid on Friday too?"

"Yes."

"Why is he never happy?"

My father's metamorphosis was now complete. In his new personage he was always cold, sullen, distant, contemplative; always wrinkling his brow and scratching his balding head and wringing his hands and muttering curses and complaints, especially on Fridays. Our emotional lives and his now moved on vastly different planes. My sisters could no longer run up to him, as he came through the door from work, and welcome him with a hug or a kiss as other children did their fathers on Fridays. They tried it once, but he simply shoved them aside and warned them never to do it again. He never even said goodnight to any of us at bedtime. I dearly and desperately wanted to love him as I loved my mother. I tried, persistently but in vain, to reach out for his love and understanding, and each time he reciprocated by becoming more distant and inscrutable, more morose and frightening to me. Gradually I came to fear him, to fear even the sound of his voice, even the sight of his shadow. I came to spend days and nights wishing he were dead; wishing he were blotted out of my life; wishing that a better father had taken his place.

"Your father is never happy because his job gives him too many worries," my mother said.

"But you too have worries, Mama, don't you?"

"Yes," she said, "but mine aren't as many as your father's. Also, I try my best not to let them make me unhappy."

"Worries are terrible things," I said philosophically.

It was again late afternoon when we were ushered into the same office of a month ago by the same black policeman with the gun. As my mother and I nervously entered the small room I looked up and had the most terrifying experience of my seven-year-old life. Seated on a reclining easy chair by a small open window and wearing a khaki safari suit, a holstered gun slung loosely about his fat waist; stockinged feet clad in shiny brown boots and placed leisurely and obliquely on a long mahogany table; his big, red, soft and hairy hands twirling a golden pen; his red neck hairy and thick; his spectacles resting lazily upon the ridge of a bulbous freckled nose with flaring, hairy nostrils; his face broad and red and freckled and topped by a bang of carroty hair; and his thick red lips curled around a thick brown and burning cigar, was the white man.

I gasped with terror when I saw him. He resembled the same white man who had led a raid into the neighbourhood some time ago. I ran behind my mother and cowered behind her long dress. I started screaming.

"What's the matter with you?" my mother shouted as she turned around and faced me.

The white man leaped from his chair, flabbergasted by the storm of screams in his office.

"It's him, Mama! It's him!" I bawled in terror as I pointed a trembling finger at the white man. "Get me out of here!"

The white man shouted something to the black man, who then scuttled over to the door where my mother was desperately but vainly trying to calm me down.

"Take him outside, *musadi!*" the black policeman bellowed. "Take him outside!"

My mother dragged me outside toward the rear of the building, out of sight of the white man. And as we went, she whacked me across the face several times, screaming, "What's gotten into you, you black fool! Are you mad! What's gotten into you!"

"It's t-the white m-man, Mama," I kept on whimpering. "H-he's the o-one who l-led the r-aid the other day. It's him, M-m—"

"Shut your filthy mouth! I know it's him!" my mother said, wrenching my arm. "But don't say that here, you hear! Not here!"

"But it's him, Mama."

"Shut your mouth!" she screamed. "Don't you have enough brains in that big head of yours to realise that you can't talk like that here! Not in front of him! You know what he'll do when he hears you talk like that about him? He'll shoot you dead, that's what he'll do! Now calm down and keep your mouth shut, when we get in there!

He won't hurt you so long as I'm with you. Keep your mouth shut, you hear?—or you're dead."

I nodded, yet fear of the white man still tormented me.

"That's a wild pickanninny you've got there," the white man, smiling wryly, said to my mother as we reentered. "What's the matter with him?"

"Yes, *mei makulu baas* [my big lord], he's *makulu* [very] wild," my mother said, smiling nervously. "He's not used to seeing white people."

"Tell him we don't bite," the white man said, breaking into a laugh.

The black policeman laughed too, in nervous spurts.

"You heard what the *baas* said?" my mother said to me.

I nodded.

"John here tells me that you want papers for pickaninny," the white man addressed my mother. He was now back in his easy chair, in his former attitude before I had alarmed him.

"Yes, yes, *mei makulu baas*," my mother said.

"Was the pickaninny born in Alexandra?" the white man asked.

"Yes, yes, *mei makulu baas*."

"Are you sure?"

"*Makulu* sure, *mei makulu baas*."

The white man turned to the black policeman standing at the opposite end of the table. "John," he called as if he were calling a child, "bring me this woman's dossier from the filing cabinet. Hurry, boy."

John scuttled like a rabbit to the filing cabinet in the corner.

"Which one, *baas*?" he asked servilely as he leaned over the cabinet.

"The one on Influx Control," the white man said.

"Okay, *baas*," John said, pulling a stack of papers out of the filing cabinet. He then ran them back to the table, where he set them before the white man. The white man perused them.

After a few minutes the white man slowly lifted his eyes from behind his spectacles, gazed at my mother and said, in a cold tone, "Your son's name is not here, woman. We don't have any indication that he was born in Alexandra. Are you sure he was?"

"Yes, *mei makulu baas. Mina* [I] *makulu* sure."

"Then why don't we have his name in the files?" the white man said, continuing to flip through the papers.

"He's Alexandra's child, *mei baas*," my mother said, "I swear he was born here."

"Do you have the papers from the health clinic to prove it? Is he registered?"

An expression of shock swept my mother's face. She groped for words. She began sweating and her eyes widened. For a few seconds she could not speak. Finally, she manage to stammer: "*M-mei, b-baas, L-lo* p-pickaninny don't h-have the c-clinic papers."

"How come? Is he a bastard? Are you sure you're his real mother? Does he have a father?" the white man fired at my mother. "I know you Kaffir women breed like rabbits."

"He is my child, *mei makulu baas*," my mother said, tears streaming down her cheeks. "The reason he doesn't have the clinic papers is that he was home-delivered."

"Never mind home delivery," the white man retorted, "most Kaffir bastards are born that way anyway. He should have the clinic papers. After you had coughed him out you should have gone to the clinic and had him registered. Those papers are important, you know? —more important than him."

"But I went to the clinic, *mei makulu baas*," my mother said, "and they refused to give me the papers until I bring them papers from here first."

"But we need the clinic papers first, woman."

My mother was flabbergasted. Perspiration poured down her brows. "But I did go to the clinic, *mei baas*," she pleaded in a trembling voice. "But the clinic people sent me over here. They say they can't give me the papers without authorization from this office."

"John," the white man called the black policeman to his side, "come here." John ran to the white man's side. "Explain to this woman here that we can't give her any papers until she brings us proof that the pickaninny was born here. And she has to get that from the clinic."

"*Musadi*," John addressed my mother in an important tone. "You have things the wrong way. The big *baas* here won't give you the papers until you bring him the pickaninny's birth certificate from the clinic. He needs the birth certificate in order to register him. Otherwise, how is he to know your pickaninny was born here? You *have* to get the certificate first. Without it there's nothing he can do. That's the law, and there's absolutely nothing he can do about it. Go back to the clinic and tell them we want the birth certificate."

"But I've already been to the clinic four times," my mother said despairingly. "And they keep on telling me that they can't issue my child a birth certificate because the clinic didn't deliver him."

"Go back again and tell them we need the certificate," the black policeman insisted. "Tell them the big white *baas* needs it."

"What if they turn me back again?" my mother said. "Can I have a note from the big *baas* to show them that I've been here?"

The white man scribbled a short note and handed it to my mother.

"What does it say?" my mother asked.

"It tells them what I just explained to you," John said in another important tone.

We left the superintendent's office. The Alexandra Health Center and University Clinic was located at the other end of the township, and because darkness had begun creeping in, and it was a Friday, the most dangerous day in the ghetto, my mother decided against going right away.

"We'll go there first thing Monday morning," she said as we headed home.

Monday morning, we arrived at the Clinic at five o'clock—that was a mistake, we should have gone there earlier—only to find that though the place wasn't scheduled to open till nine-thirty, it was already packed with black people awaiting treatment and seeking papers of various kinds. The sight about the clinic was sickening— bleeding heads and chests, burn victims, skinny pregnant women, malnourished infants with oversized heads and stomachs, TB sufferers, tramps, deformed children, people with gouged eyes and severed fingers and so on. The clinic was filled with pain, lack, suffering and neglect. We tagged onto the long line leading to the office where incoming patients registered. It turned out to be the wrong office for our purpose, and it wasn't until an hour or so later when it was our turn at the window that we found out. The proper line, the one leading to the office responsible for issuing birth certificates and other documents, turned out to be longer than the other one, so we waited another hour.

While we stood in line, my mother, in an attempt to allay her doubts about the contents of the note, asked a man in front of us to read it to her. The man told us that the note, contrary to what John had said, merely stated that my mother had a problem; it didn't explain the nature of the problem, or state the fact that we had twice been to the superintendent's office. All in all, the note was worthless.

And its immateriality became obvious when we reached the window and the black man in attendance told us that he could not give us a birth certificate until we had brought him the papers from the superintendent's office. My mother, bewildered, tried to explain that we had already been there, but the black man did not believe her. My mother vowed not to go anywhere until she had the birth certificate. The black man called a black guard, and my mother was forcibly removed from blocking the line.

We stationed ourselves on the porch in front of the office, for something like two hours of anguish and hunger, waiting for a change of heart. The office closed for lunch and later reopened, and we were still sitting there. I spent the hours gazing at the types of victims, all black, crawling in by the scores. I could not believe the extent of some of the injuries I saw. One man came limping in, unassisted, on a gangrened leg teeming with worms. A handful of young student doctors from a white university ran around all day trying to treat the endless number of black patients. Their task seemed so impossible that, figuratively speaking, they were like people attempting to put out a huge fire with their saliva.

As we sat outside the door, my mother plaintively intoning a Tsonga song about her misfortunes, a white woman, wearing a white dress and a black wimple came by, apparently to pick up something from the office.

"Sister," my mother accosted her and begged, "please help me—please help my child."

The white woman stopped, turned around, her hand on the doorknob, and faced my mother. She smiled and asked my mother what the problem was. My mother told her of our plight. The white woman listened, spellbound, her hand still clasping the doorknob as if paralyzed. She gasped several times and shook her head in disbelief as my mother told her about our trials and tribulations in attempting to obtain my birth certificate.

When my mother ended her story, the white woman, almost in tears, stormed into the office, fuming. We stood ourselves by the door and heard a brief altercation take place inside the office. In a matter of minutes, my mother was called to the window, where an irate young black man, who earlier had ordered that my mother be towed away, shoved a piece of paper in her face. We finally had the birth certificate. My mother fortressed it in her bosom, as if it were a golden nugget. I had never seen a happier mother than the one who, as we trotted home, kept on singing songs of praise about the white "sister." She even proudly said: "You see, child, not all white people are bad; remember that."

I simply grumbled, little realising that my entire future had actually depended on that one piece of paper she had fought so long and so doggedly to secure. I had, though I hardly knew it then, cleared the first, and most difficult, hurdle toward eventually enrolling at school. Without a birth certificate I would have never been allowed to enroll at any of the tribal schools in Alexandra.

PART TWO

PASSPORT TO KNOWLEDGE

21

"Education will open doors where none seem to exist."

When my mother began dropping hints that I would soon be going to school, I vowed never to go because school was a waste of time. She laughed and said, "We'll see. You don't know what you're talking about." My philosophy on school was that of a gang of ten-, eleven- and twelve-year-olds whom I so revered that their every word seemed that of an oracle.

These boys had long left their homes and were now living in various neighbourhood junkyards, making it on their own. They slept in abandoned cars, smoked glue and benzene, ate pilchards and brown bread, sneaked into the white world to caddy and, if unsuccessful, came back to the township to steal beer and soda bottles from shebeens, or goods from the Indian traders on First Avenue. Their life-style was exciting, adventurous and full of surprises; and I was attracted to it. My mother told me that they were no-gooders, that they would amount to nothing, that I should not associate with them, but I paid no heed. What does she know? I used to tell myself. One thing she did not know was that the gang's way of life had captivated me wholly, particularly their philosophy on school: they hated it and considered an education a waste of time.

They, like myself, had grown up in an environment where the value of an education was never emphasized, where the first thing a child learned was not how to read and write and spell, but how to fight and steal and rebel; where the money to send children to school was grossly lacking, for survival was first priority. I kept my membership in the gang, knowing that for as long as I was under its influence, I would never go to school.

One day my mother woke me up at four in the morning.

"Are they here? I didn't hear any noises," I asked in the usual way.

"No," my mother said. "I want you to get into that washtub over there."

"What!" I balked, upon hearing the word *washtub*. I feared taking

123

baths like one feared the plague. Throughout seven years of hectic living the number of baths I had taken could be counted on one hand with several fingers missing. I simply had no natural inclination for water; cleanliness was a trait I still had to acquire. Besides, we had only one bathtub in the house, and it constantly sprung a leak.

"I said get into that tub!" My mother shook a finger in my face.

Reluctantly, I obeyed, yet wondered why all of a sudden I had to take a bath. My mother, armed with a scropbrush and a piece of Lifebuoy soap, purged me of years and years of grime till I ached and bled. As I howled, feeling pain shoot through my limbs as the thistles of the brush encountered stubborn callouses, there was a loud knock at the door.

Instantly my mother leaped away from the tub and headed, on tiptoe, toward the bedroom. Fear seized me as I, too, thought of the police. I sat frozen in the bathtub, not knowing what to do.

"Open up, Mujaji [my mother's maiden name]," Granny's voice came shrilling through the door. "It's me."

My mother heaved a sigh of relief; her tense limbs relaxed. She turned and headed to the kitchen door, unlatched it and in came Granny and Aunt Bushy.

"You scared me half to death," my mother said to Granny. "I had forgotten all about your coming."

"Are you ready?" Granny asked my mother.

"Yes—just about," my mother said, beckoning me to get out of the washtub.

She handed me a piece of cloth to dry myself. As I dried myself, questions raced through my mind: What's going on? What's Granny doing at our house this ungodly hour of the morning? And why did she ask my mother, "Are you ready?" While I stood debating, my mother went into the bedroom and came out with a stained white shirt and a pair of faded black shorts.

"Here," she said, handing me the togs, "put these on."

"Why?" I asked.

"Put them on I said!"

I put the shirt on; it was grossly loose-fitting. It reached all the way down to my ankles. Then I saw the reason why: it was my father's shirt!

"But this is Papa's shirt," I complained. "It don't fit me."

"Put it on," my mother insisted. "I'll make it fit."

"The pants don't fit me either," I said. "Whose are they anyway?"

"Put them on," my mother said. "I'll make them fit."

Moments later I had the garments on; I looked ridiculous. My mother started working on the pants and shirt to make them fit. She folded the shirt in so many intricate ways and stashed it inside the pants, they too having been folded several times at the waist. She then choked the pants at the waist with a piece of sisal rope to hold them up. She then lavishly smeared my face, arms and legs with a mixture of pig's fat and vaseline. "This will insulate you from the cold," she said. My skin gleamed like the morning star and I felt as hot as the centre of the sun and I smelled God knows like what. After embalming me, she headed to the bedroom.

"Where are we going, Gran'ma?" I said, hoping that she would tell me what my mother refused to tell me. I still had no idea I was about to be taken to school.

"Didn't your mother tell you?" Granny said with a smile. "You're going to start school."

"What!" I gasped, leaping from the chair where I was sitting as if it were made of hot lead. "I am not going to school!" I blurted out and raced toward the kitchen door.

My mother had just reappeared from the bedroom and guessing what I was up to, she yelled, "Someone get the door!"

Aunt Bushy immediately barred the door. I turned and headed for the window. As I leaped for the windowsill, my mother lunged at me and brought me down. I tussled, "Let go of me! I don't want to go to school! Let me go!" but my mother held fast onto me.

"It's no use now," she said, grinning triumphantly as she pinned me down. Turning her head in Granny's direction, she shouted, "Granny! Get a rope quickly!"

Granny grabbed a piece of rope nearby and came to my mother's aid. I bit and clawed every hand that grabbed me, and howled protestations against going to school; however, I was no match for the two determined matriarchs. In a jiffy they had me bound, hands and feet.

"What's the matter with him?" Granny, bewildered, asked my mother. "Why did he suddenly turn into an imp when I told him you're taking him to school?"

"You shouldn't have told him that he's being taken to school," my mother said. "He doesn't want to go there. That's why I requested you come today, to help me take him there. Those boys in the streets have been a bad influence on him."

As the two matriarchs hauled me through the door, they told Aunt

Bushy not to go to school but stay behind and mind the house and the children.

The sun was beginning to rise from beyond the veld when Granny and my mother dragged me to school. The streets were beginning to fill with their everyday traffic: old men and women, wizened, bent and ragged, were beginning their rambling; workless men and women were beginning to assemble in their usual coteries and head for shebeens in the backyards where they discussed how they escaped the morning pass raids and contemplated the conditions of life amidst intense beer drinking and vacant, uneasy laughter; young boys and girls, some as young as myself, were beginning their aimless wanderings along the narrow, dusty streets in search of food, carrying bawling infants piggyback.

As we went along some of the streets, boys and girls who shared the same fears about school as I were making their feelings known in a variety of ways. They were howling their protests and trying to escape. A few managed to break loose and make a mad dash for freedom, only to be recaptured in no time, admonished or whipped, or both, and ordered to march again.

As we made a turn into Sixteenth Avenue, the street leading to the tribal school I was being taken to, a short, chubby black woman came along from the opposite direction. She had a scuttle overflowing with coal on her *doek*-covered (cloth-covered) head. An infant, bawling deafeningly, was loosely swathed with a piece of sheepskin onto her back. Following closely behind the woman, and picking up pieces of coal as they fell from the scuttle and placing them in a small plastic bag, was a half-naked, potbellied and thumb-sucking boy of about four. The woman stopped abreast. For some reason we stopped too.

"I wish I had done the same to my oldest son," the strange woman said in a regretful voice, gazing at me. I was confounded by her stopping and offering her unsolicited opinion.

"I wish I had done that to my oldest son," she repeated, and suddenly burst into tears; amidst sobs, she continued, "before . . . the street claimed him . . . and . . . turned him into a *tsotsi.*"

Granny and my mother offered consolatory remarks to the strange woman.

"But it's too late now," the strange woman continued, tears now streaming freely down her puffy cheeks. She made no attempt to dry them. "It's too late now," she said for the second time, "he's beyond any help. I can't help him even if I wanted to. *Uswile* [He is dead]."

"How did he die?" my mother asked in a sympathetic voice.

"He shunned school and, instead, grew up to live by the knife. And the same knife he lived by ended his life. That's why whenever I see a boy-child refuse to go to school, I stop and tell the story of my dear little *mbitsini* [heartbreak]."

Having said that, the strange woman left as mysteriously as she had arrived.

"Did you hear what that woman said!" my mother screamed into my ears. "Do you want the same to happen to you?"

I dropped my eyes. I was confused.

"Poor woman," Granny said ruefully. "She must have truly loved her son."

Finally, we reached the school and I was ushered into the principal's office, a tiny cubicle facing a row of privies and a patch of yellowed grass.

"So this is the rascal we'd been talking about," the principal, a tall, wiry man, foppishly dressed in a black pin-striped suit, said to my mother as we entered. His austere, shiny face, inscrutable and imposing, reminded me of my father. He was sitting behind a brown table upon which stood piles of dust and cobweb-covered books and papers. In one upper pocket of his jacket was arrayed a variety of pens and pencils; in the other nestled a lily-white handkerchief whose presence was more decorative than utilitarian. Alongside him stood a disproportionately portly black woman, fashionably dressed in a black skirt and a white blouse. She had but one pen, and this she held in her hand. The room was hot and stuffy and buzzing with flies.

"Yes, Principal," my mother answered, "this is he."

"I see he's living up to his notoriety," remarked the principal, noticing that I had been bound. "Did he give you too much trouble?"

"Trouble, Principal," my mother sighed. "He was like an imp."

"He's just like the rest of them, Principal," Granny sighed. "Once they get out into the streets, they become wild. They take to the many vices of the streets like an infant takes to its mother's milk. They begin to think that there's no other life but the one shown them by the *tsotsis*. They come to hate school and forget about the future."

"Well," the principal said. "We'll soon remedy all that. Untie him."

"He'll run away," my mother cried.

"I don't think he's that foolish to attempt that with all of us here."

"He *is* that foolish, Principal," my mother said as she and Granny began untying me. "He's tried it before. Getting him here was an ordeal in itself."

The principal rose from his seat, took two steps to the door and closed it. As the door swung closed, I spotted a row of canes of different lengths and thicknesses hanging behind it. The principal, seeing me staring at the canes, grinned and said, in a manner suggesting that he had wanted me to see them, "As long as you behave, I won't have to use any of those on you."

Use those canes on me? I gasped. I stared at my mother—she smiled; at Granny—she smiled too. That made me abandon any inkling of escaping.

"So they finally gave you the birth certificate and the papers," the principal addressed my mother as he returned to his chair.

"Yes, Principal," my mother said, "they finally did. But what a battle it was. It took me nearly a year to get all them papers together." She took out of her handbag a neatly wrapped package and handed it to the principal. "They've been running us around for so long that there were times when I thought he would never attend school, Principal," she said.

"That's pretty much standard procedure, Mrs. Mathabane," the principal said, unwrapping the package. "But you now have the papers and that's what's important.

"As long as we have the papers," he continued, minutely perusing the contents of the package, "we won't be breaking the law in admitting your son to this school, for we'll be in full compliance with the requirements set by the authorities in Pretoria."

"Sometimes I don't understand the laws from Pitori," Granny said. "They did the same to me with my Piet and Bushy. Why, Principal, should our children not be allowed to learn because of some piece of paper?"

"The piece of paper you're referring to, Mrs. Mabaso [Granny's maiden name]," the principal said to Granny, "is as important to our children as a pass is to us adults. We all hate passes; therefore, it's only natural we should hate the regulations our children are subjected to. But as we have to live with passes, so our children have to live with the regulations, Mrs. Mabaso. I hope you understand, that is the law of the country. We would have admitted your grandson a long time ago, as you well know, had it not been for the papers. I hope you understand."

"I understand, Principal," Granny said, "but I don't understand," she added paradoxically.

One of the papers caught the principal's eye and he turned to my mother and asked, "Is your husband a Shangaan, Mrs. Mathabane?"

"No, he's not Principal," my mother said. "Is there anything wrong? He's Venda and I'm Shangaan."

The principal reflected for a moment or so and then said, concernedly, "No, there's nothing seriously wrong. Nothing that we can't take care of. You see, Mrs. Mathabane, technically, the fact that your child's father is a Venda makes him ineligible to attend this tribal school because it is only for children whose parents are of the Shangaan tribe. May I ask what language the children speak at home?"

"Both languages," my mother said worriedly, "Venda and Shangaan. Is there anything wrong?"

The principal coughed, clearing his throat, then said, "I mean which language do they speak more?"

"It depends, Principal," my mother said, swallowing hard. "When their father is around, he wants them to speak only Venda. And when he's not, they speak Shangaan. And when they are out at play, they speak Zulu and Sisotho."

"Well," the principal said, heaving a sigh of relief. "In that case, I think an exception can be made. The reason for such an exception is that there's currently no school for Vendas in Alexandra. And should the authorities come asking why we took in your son, we can tell them that. Anyway, your child is half-half."

Everyone broke into a nervous laugh, except me. I was bewildered by the whole thing. I looked at my mother, and she seemed greatly relieved as she watched the principal register me; a broad smile broke across her face. It was as if some enormously heavy burden had finally been lifted from her shoulders and her conscience.

"Bring him back two weeks from today," the principal said as he saw us to the door. "There're so many children registering today that classes won't begin until two weeks hence. Also, the school needs repair and cleaning up after the holidays. If he refuses to come, simply notify us, and we'll send a couple of big boys to come fetch him, and he'll be very sorry if it ever comes to that."

As we left the principal's office and headed home, my mind was still against going to school. I was thinking of running away from home and joining my friends in the junkyard.

I didn't want to go to school for three reasons: I was reluctant to surrender my freedom and independence over to what I heard every school-going child call "tyrannous discipline." I had heard many bad things about life in tribal school—from daily beatings by teachers and mistresses who worked you like a mule to long school hours—and the sight of those canes in the principal's office gave ample credence to rumors that school was nothing but a torture chamber. And there was my allegiance to the gang.

But the thought of the strange woman's lamentations over her dead son presented a somewhat strong case for going to school: I didn't want to end up dead in the streets. A more compelling argument for going to school, however, was the vivid recollection of all that humiliation and pain my mother had gone through to get me the papers and the birth certificate so I could enroll in school. What should I do? I was torn between two worlds.

But later that evening something happened to force me to go to school.

I was returning home from playing soccer when a neighbour accosted me by the gate and told me that there had been a bloody fight at my home.

"Your mother and father have been at it again," the neighbour, a woman, said.

"And your mother left."

I was stunned.

"Was she hurt badly?"

"A little bit," the woman said. "But she'll be all right. We took her to your grandma's place."

I became hot with anger.

"Is anyone in the house?" I stammered, trying to control my rage.

"Yes, your father is. But I don't think you should go near the house. He's raving mad. He's armed with a meat cleaver. He's chased out your brother and sisters, also. And some of the neighbours who tried to intervene he's threatened to carve them to pieces. I have never seen him this mad before."

I brushed aside the woman's warnings and went. Shattered windows convinced me that there had indeed been a skirmish of some sort. Several pieces of broken bricks, evidently broken after being thrown at the door, were lying about the door. I tried opening the door; it was locked from the inside. I knocked. No one answered. I knocked again. Still no one answered, until, as I turned to leave:

"Who's out there?" my father's voice came growling from inside.

"It's me, Johannes," I said.

"Go away, you bastard!" he bellowed. "I don't want you or that whore mother of yours setting foot in this house. Go away before I come out there and kill you!"

"Let me in!" I cried. "Dammit, let me in! I want my things!"

"What things? Go away, you black swine!"

I went to the broken window and screamed obscenities at my father, daring him to come out, hoping that if he as much as ever stuck his black face out, I would pelt him with the half-a-loaf brick in my hand. He didn't come out. He continued launching a tirade of obscenities at my mother and her mother, calling them whores and bitches and so on. He was drunk, but I wondered where he had gotten the money to buy beer because it was still the middle of the week and he was dead broke. He had lost his entire wage for the past week in dice and had had to borrow bus fare.

"I'll kill you someday for all you're doing to my mother," I threatened him, overwhelmed with rage. Several nosey neighbours were beginning to congregate by open windows and doors. Not wanting to make a spectacle of myself, which was something many of our neighbours seemed to always expect from our family, I backtracked away from the door and vanished into the dark street. I ran, without stopping, all the way to the other end of the township where Granny lived. There I found my mother, her face swollen and bruised and her eyes puffed up to the point where she could scarcely see.

"What happened, Mama?" I asked, fighting to hold back the tears at the sight of her disfigured face.

"Nothing, child, nothing," she mumbled, almost apologetically, between swollen lips. "Your papa simply lost his temper, that's all."

"But why did he beat you up like this, Mama?" Tears came down my face. "He's never beaten you like this before."

My mother appeared reluctant to answer me. She looked searchingly at Granny, who was pounding millet with pestle and mortar and mixing it with sorghum and nuts for an African delicacy. Granny said, "Tell him, child, tell him. He's got a right to know. Anyway, he's the cause of it all."

"Your father and I fought because I took you to school this morning," my mother began. "He had told me not to, and when I told him that I had, he became very upset. He was drunk. We started arguing, and one thing led to another."

"Why doesn't he want me to go to school?"

"He says he doesn't have money to waste paying for you to get what he calls a useless white man's education," my mother replied. "But I told him that if he won't pay for your schooling, I would try and look for a job and pay, but he didn't want to hear that, also. 'There are better things for you to work for,' he said. 'Besides, I don't want you to work. How would I look to other men if you, a woman I owned, were to start working?' When I asked him why shouldn't I take you to school, seeing that you were now of age, he replied that he doesn't believe in schools. I told him that school would keep you off the streets and out of trouble, but still he was belligerent."

"Is that why he beat you up?"

"Yes, he said I disobeyed his orders."

"He's right, child," Granny interjected. "He paid *lobola* [bride price] for you. And your father ate it all up before he left me."

To which my mother replied, "But I desperately want to leave this beast of a man. But with his *lobola* gone I can't do it. That worthless thing you call your husband shouldn't have sold Jackson's scrawny cattle and left you penniless."

"Don't talk like that about your father, child," Granny said. "Despite all, he's still your father, you know. Anyway, he asked for *lobola* only because he had to get back what he spent raising you. And you know it would have been taboo for him to let you or any of your sisters go without asking for *lobola*."

"You and Papa seemed to forget that my sisters and I have minds of our own," my mother said. "We didn't need you to tell us whom to marry, and why, and how. If it hadn't been for your interference, I could have married that schoolteacher."

Granny did not reply; she knew well not to. When it came to the act of "selling" women as marriage partners, my mother was vehemently opposed to it. Not only was she opposed to this one aspect of tribal culture, but to others as well, particularly those involving relations between men and women and the upbringing of children. But my mother's sharply differing opinion was an exception rather than the rule among tribal women. Most times, many tribal women questioned her sanity in daring to question well-established mores. But my mother did not seem to care; she would always scoff at her opponents and call them fools in letting their husbands enslave them completely.

Though I disliked school, largely because I knew nothing about what actually went on there, and the little I knew had painted a dreadful picture, the fact that a father would not want his son to go to school, especially a father who didn't go to school, seemed hard to understand.

"Why do you want me to go to school, Mama?" I asked, hoping that she might, somehow, clear up some of the confusion that was building in my mind.

"I want you to have a future, child," my mother said. "And, contrary to what your father says, school is the only means to a future. I don't want you growing up to be like your father."

The latter statement hit me like a bolt of lightning. It just about shattered every defense mechanism and every pretext I had against going to school.

"Your father didn't go to school," she continued, dabbing her puffed eyes to reduce the swelling with a piece of cloth dipped in warm water, "that's why he's doing some of the bad things he's doing. Things like drinking, gambling and neglecting his family. He didn't learn how to read and write; therefore, he can't find a decent job. Lack of any education has narrowly focused his life. He sees nothing beyond himself. He still thinks in the old, tribal way, and still believes that things should be as they were back in the old days when he was growing up as a tribal boy in Louis Trichardt. Though he's my husband, and your father, he doesn't see any of that."

"Why didn't he go to school, Mama?"

"He refused to go to school because his father led him to believe that an education was a tool through which white people were going to take things away from him, like they did black people in the old days. And that a white man's education was worthless insofar as black people were concerned because it prepared them for jobs they can't have. But I know it isn't totally so, child, because times have changed somewhat. Though our lot isn't any better today, an education will get you a decent job. If you can read or write you'll be better off than those of us who can't. Take my situation: I can't find a job because I don't have papers, and I can't get papers because white people mainly want to register people who can read and write. But I want things to be different for you, child. For you and your brother and sisters. I want you to go to school, because I believe that an education is the key you need to open up a new world and a new life for yourself, a world and life different from that of either your father's or mine. It is the only key that can do that, and only those who seek it earnestly and perseveringly will get anywhere in the white man's world. Education will open doors where none seem to exist. It'll make people talk to you, listen to you and help you; people who otherwise wouldn't bother. It will make you soar, like a bird lifting up into the endless blue sky, and leave poverty, hunger and suffering behind. It'll teach you to learn to embrace what's good and shun what's bad and evil. Above all, it'll make you a somebody in this world. It'll make you grow up to be a good and proud person. That's why I want you to go to school, child, so that education can do all that, and more, for you."

A long, awkward silence followed, during which I reflected upon the significance of my mother's lengthy speech. I looked at my mother; she looked at me.

Finally, I asked, "How come you know so much about school, Mama? You didn't go to school, did you?"

"No, child," my mother replied. "Just like your father, I never went to school." For the second time that evening, a mere statement of fact had a thunderous impact on me. All the confusion I had about school seemed to leave my mind, like darkness giving way to light. And what had previously been a dark, yawning void in my mind was suddenly transformed into a beacon of light that began to grow larger and larger, until it had swallowed up, blotted out, all the blackness. That beacon of light seemed to reveal things and facts, which, though they must have always existed in me, I hadn't been aware of up until now.

"But unlike your father," my mother went on, "I've always wanted to go to school, but couldn't because my father, under the sway of tribal traditions, thought it unnecessary to educate females. That's why I so much want you to go, child, for if you do, I know that someday I too would come to go, old as I would be then. Promise me, therefore, that no matter what, you'll go back to school. And I, in turn, promise that I'll do everything in my power to keep you there."

With tears streaming down my cheeks and falling upon my mother's bosom, I promised her that I would go to school "forever." That night, at seven and a half years of my life, the battlelines in the family were drawn. My mother on the one side, illiterate but determined to have me drink, for better or for worse, from the well of knowledge. On the other side, my father, he too illiterate, yet determined to have me drink from the well of ignorance. Scarcely aware of the magnitude of the decision I was making or, rather, the decision which was being emotionally thrust upon me, I chose to fight on my mother's side, and thus my destiny was forever altered.

22 Two weeks later, on a Monday in early February, I had my first full day at school. It turned out to be such a nightmare that had I not made the solemn pledge to my mother that I would go to school till kingdom come, I would not have returned for another day.

The day began at 6:00 A.M. as my mother and Granny left me at the school's entrance gate. (Since the fight between my parents, my mother and the children had been staying at Granny's, until, according to tribal custom, penance had been done on my mother's behalf, by Granny and a group of elders, so that my father could "accept her back.") Granny went off to her gardening job in the white suburbs, and my mother took off to hunt for a job at the Indian marketplace so she could finance my schooling in light of my father's refusal to assume the responsibility.

"Be good now," they both said before departing. "Don't be afraid. Even if anything bad happens, don't be alarmed. Remember, it's only your first day. You'll get used to school in no time. And remember to learn as much as you can for the day."

I carried a heavy slate (tied to my neck to avoid losing it), a pencil, two thin slices of brown bread sprinkled with brown sugar and a mind full of confusion and anxiety. After Granny and my mother left, I reclined on top of a huge boulder nearby and gazed eastward at the flickering stars slowly vanishing from a bleak eastern sky. Bluish-white smoke from early-morning braziers billowed upward in stream-lined wisps. The school was, except for myself, deserted. The sun came up, gradually, and I marvelled at how, as it emerged mysteriously from behind the distant shacks and veld, everything suddenly sparkled and filled with warmth and sprang to life. I dozed. I was abruptly awakened by the loud ringing of a churchbell, signalling the start of the school day. The nightmare began. Apparently while I had been napping the schoolyard had been steadily filling with apprehensive children on their first day of school, many of whom were crying. All of a sudden a group of neatly dressed men and women began corraling the bawling children, using the canes I had seen in the principal's office. The teachers herded us into a narrow, sandy courtyard where, I heard a veteran schoolgoer say, morning assemblies were held.

"Welcome everyone, new and old," announced the principal in a loud, excited voice. His words were immediately drowned by the din from the throng of about two thousand schoolchildren, many of whom

—those on their first day at school—screamed and cried and begged for their parents to come and take them home. The principal was without the help of a voice amplifier.

As he stood there, in his pin-striped suit, upon a makeshift podium (a row of steps leading to one of the classrooms) overlooking the courtyard, he kept on brandishing his cane to demand silence. Immediately behind him, at the bottom of the steps, teachers stood in rows.

We were so tightly packed into that narrow courtyard that some children fainted from excessive heat and stuffiness. There were no nurses, so the few teachers who patrolled the columns attempting to maintain order, along with several older schoolgirls, attended to the fainted victims. I stood in the front row with children so young that had there been enough kindergartens in Alexandra (and black people been able to afford them), I would have been one of the few remaining in the row. Many of the toddlers screamed that they were hungry, dizzy and wanted their mothers to come and take them home.

"The name of our school is Bovet Community School," shouted the principal, trying his best to raise his voice above the storm of noise. "I and the people you see behind me," he pointed at the teachers with his cane, "are here to see to it that you get a little Bantu Education inside those waterlogged skulls of yours. Most of you are obviously too young to understand what an education is. But I hope you'll be around long enough to find out. Listen carefully now to the rest of what I have to say, for attentive listening will, as from now on, mean the difference between this"—he waved his cane—"and that" —he pointed at a teacher with a fake smile.

As he rattled on for more than an hour, during which time about half a dozen children fainted and were revived, some only to faint again, he drew serious attention to the following:

—We should have respect for him and all teachers.

—All newcomers should memorize, as soon as possible, several special hymns, the Lord's prayer and several passages from the Bible, to be sung and recited during morning assembly and at dismissal in the afternoon.

—We should remind our mothers to be prompt in buying us books and a uniform and other school paraphernalia. Most important, we should remind them to pay each quarter's school fees ahead of time.

—We shouldn't be alarmed to see him or one of his staff whip some of us, for such was the rule of the school—to punish those who broke school rules.

—Some of us children, due to a chronic shortage of buildings, desks, blackboards and benches, would have to be relocated in shacks down by the river.

—No lateness would be tolerated, whether in the morning, for assembly, or at lunch. Any latecomer would be subjected to whipping.

—Every child enrolled at the school should attempt to learn whatever he or she could, for in us—and our peers at other tribal schools—was embodied the hope for a meaningful future for black people.

—We should not be terrified when, occasionally, we saw white people about the school, for they would not eat us.

—The school's only medium of instruction was Tsonga; therefore anyone speaking any other language had better leave before it was too late.

—School, for many of us, would be a rough and a constantly uphill battle; but he hoped that some of us would remain in school long enough to learn to write our names.

After a few words—mainly a repetition of what the principal said —from several of the senior teachers, a hymn was sung and a prayer said. We were then ordered to dismiss. The veteran schoolboys were led by several male teachers to clear the jungle of weeds that had grown in front of and behind the buildings during the holidays, and the veteran schoolgirls were led by some of the female teachers to clean the classrooms. All the newcomers were herded into a big church hall. More than two hundred screaming, sobbing, trembling and confused children jammed the badly ventilated hall, and, for lack of enough benches, most of us stood up like bristles.

The place was like a madhouse. Outside, still more children were attempting to squeeze their way in. Having been in the first wave of schoolchildren flooding the hall, I found myself in front, near the blackboard. The bedlam continued for some time till a young girl, who couldn't have been more than sixteen, appeared at the door and attempted to jostle her way through the jungle of screaming black children, to the front of the hall. But the jungle was impenetrable. Somehow, after much effort, she finally managed to push, claw, elbow and kick her way through to the front. My impression of her as she made her way to the front of the hall was this: here is some young girl who has to take her little brother or sister away. Not only was I shocked when it turned out she was to be our teacher, but there and then I instinctively knew that whatever the principles of proper teaching were, she did not possess them.

"Good morning, children," she said in a soft, timid voice, mopping her sweaty brow with the sleeve of her faded blouse. Her words were immediately swallowed up by the pandemonium. She seemed so fatigued and so unprepared to handle what was going on that she became increasingly flustered and angry when no one paid attention to her.

"Sit down, please," she sighed despairingly. She should not have said that, for no sooner had she finished uttering the sentence that, everywhere, children began fighting each other for the right to sit on the handful of rickety benches about the hall. I punched a boy in the nose for having the audacity to contest a sitting spot with me.

"Stop fighting and sit down quietly, please," the young girl begged. We paid no heed; I punched another boy for trying to push me off the bench.

"STOP FIGHTING AND SIT DOWN!" she screamed. The fighting stopped. Many of the children who had lost the right to sit on the benches resigned themselves to sitting on the cold cement floor.

"I'm your teacher," the young girl groped for words, seemingly not knowing what to do or where to begin. "My name is Miss Mphephu, and I'll be your teacher for Sub-standard A. Please listen to me," she begged for attention, but no one gave it to her.

"LISTEN TO ME!" she screamed, expecting everyone to listen. Instead, all hell broke loose. Everywhere children screamed and cried. This made her scream even louder, but her screams proved useless, as she still was unable to gain the attention of a single child. As the disorderliness continued, becoming, it seemed, too much for her to handle, she broke down, and became downright hostile. She slapped children and screamed obscenities at them. Suddenly she grabbed a long, thick cane from behind the blackboard and began using it. I left the bench and stole into a corner, afraid that, considering how indiscriminately she was using it, she might turn on me. In those few moments that she went on a rampage, my dread for school increased a thousandfold, and I swore that, despite the pledge I had made to my mother, I would never come back. The vicious circle of screaming, beating, screaming, beating, continued until the principal, whose office adjoined the hall, came in.

"Stop that ruckus!" he railed, brandishing his own cane. "What's going on here? Why are there so many of them in here! How many shifts are here?" he asked the teacher.

"I don't know," replied the young girl. "Have they been divided into shifts yet, sir?"

"Yes, what did you think!"

The young girl turned and faced us. "All those supposed to be attending the eleven o'clock shift instead of the eight o'clock one, please step outside."

"Don't 'please' them!" cried the principal as he descended on us with the cane. "Out! Out! Out!" he screamed as he lammed children on the head. I wasn't in the eleven o'clock shift, but I was more than happy to leave. We were told to wait outside the schoolyard until the churchbell rang at eleven; then, and only then, should we reenter the classrooms. I was told to come back to the same hall, and I shook with dread. I longed to run away, never to set foot inside a classroom again.

When the churchbell rang at eleven, I went back to the torture chamber. I was hungry, wilted and disillusioned about the idea of school. I found it hard to concentrate. Whenever I talked, my voice came out sapless.

Our teacher was again the young girl.

"SAY 'AAAA; EEEE; IIII; OOOO; UUUU!' AFTER ME!" she ordered with her big mouth wide open, like a hippo's.

Everyone started yapping incoherently. We spent a third of the class time learning "aeiou's," a third learning how to count to twenty in Tsonga and a third how to sit and stand upon command. At two-thirty the churchbell rang for recess, and everyone fled the room. On the way home I overheard some children vow never to return; others vowed to relate to their parents the day's atrocities. At home, mother told me that I should keep on going to school, despite the beating.

"As long as you learn something," she said, "it's worth it."

23 My attitude toward school grew more ambivalent. On the one hand, I dreaded the whipping the teachers meted out, without exception, day in and day out, to all who violated the school's strict code of discipline. I was often a victim of such punishment, usually for such things as: lack of a school uniform, having long nails, uncombed hair, lack of primers, failing dictation, failure to pay school fees on time and a bully-boy image.

Also, I was often punished for carrying on cross-conversations when the teacher was busy writing things on the blackboard, or for having my name on the "noisemakers list"—a list compiled by the class prefect, the most hated fellow in class—whenever the teacher temporarily left the classroom. Further, there was punishment for being lackadaisical during choir rehearsals and morning drills (I would often be so hungry in the morning that I could not drill, and I would be so fatigued by the end of the day that I could not sing), for being late for school (I was consistently late because each morning my mother had to leave to go hunt for jobs, and I had to take my brother and sisters to Granny's).

Along with all that, I hated the mountains of homework—for which we were punished for not doing, or doing incorrectly.

On the other hand, four things happened to make me stay in school. First: The sixteen-year-old teacher was dismissed within a month after she suffered a severe nervous breakdown. An older, lovable woman, with children of her own in the class, replaced her. Even though she too whipped us, she didn't do so with the unchecked brutality of the young girl; besides, she punished her own children also, as severely as the rest of us, which led me to conclude that she was at least fair.

Second: I began making friends, some of whom came from "affluent" homes, and thus constantly had lunch money. One boy my age whom I had befriended on the first day of school had a father, a store owner who daily gave him one rand as an inducement to going to school and working hard.

Third: A nutrition program called *Hebelungu* was established near the school, by Catholic sisters from the Alexandra Health Clinic. This facility provided children from my school and other tribal schools in the area with a low-cost lunch—peanut-buttered brown bread, and a mug of skimmed milk. All for four cents. At lunchtime, therefore, those with four pennies—a kingly sum—would wait in line, always long; sometimes though, there wouldn't be enough bread or milk to go around. My mother tried her best to furnish me with four cents each day, and often I would bring my brother and sisters leftover pieces of peanut-buttered bread, and some skimmed milk. When my mother didn't have the four cents, I would cling to my "affluent" friends like a parasite—they didn't seem to mind.

Fourth and last: The opening up of a new and intriguing world of words, songs and numbers gradually established in me a desire to learn more. I was thrilled at being able to recite arithmetic tables, and the letters of the alphabet forward and backward. We were taught everything in Tsonga. When I finally learned how to count up to ten, and to spell my first and last names, in English, I was so overjoyed that I constantly begged my mother to listen to me "talk" English. The greatest benefit of my crude English was that, for the first time, I could understand a few stock phrases in the movies.

One hot December afternoon, toward the end of my first year at school, the principal interrupted classes and summoned everyone to the courtyard. The entire school was there, including those who took classes in the tin shacks by the river.

"Today is the last day of school," he announced as he stood upon a makeshift podium. (Our school began in January, and continued till December, with only a few weeks' break each quarter.) As soon as he said that, the columns of schoolchildren standing under the blazing sun erupted in excitement. "I know it's been a rough year for many of you," he continued, shielding his narrow eyes from the sun with a foolscap. "But I must say that I'm delighted to see that many of you are still with us, which is a slight improvement from last year's awful dropout rate. I hope you will all stay the course. School is very hard work, I agree, especially when there aren't enough books and desks and classrooms—not to mention enough teachers. But it's worth the toil, won't you all say?"

A mighty wave of nos mixed with giggles swept the crowd. Changing the subject, the principal went on: "As we've now come to the end of the year, I would like to wish each of you a safe and pleasant Christmas holiday. Those of you who'll be going to the tribal reserves to visit relatives, may God clear your paths and bring you back safely. Those who'll be remaining in Alexandra, stay out of trouble and don't eat too much."

He paused and then whispered something to one of the senior teachers standing behind him. The latter handed the principal a note. By this time all the children were beside themselves with joy at the prospect of the oncoming holidays. Turning to us the principal said: "Before we sing the customary 'Hip! hip! hurrah!' I will, as is the custom each year, call upon your hardworking, dedicated and grossly underpaid teachers to announce the year-end examination results and class standings."

Suddenly everybody became very quiet.

"We'll begin with the results for the Sub-standard A's," said the principal, and he vacated the podium. Along came four female teachers—no male teachers taught the Sub-standards—including mine, each carrying in her hand a class register containing the pupils' names, their ages, their grades, their attendance records throughout the year and whether or not they had paid school fees.

My teacher went first. Everything occurred so quickly after she had ascended the podium and uttered the words: "Out of 164 pupils enrolled in my class this year, and out of 400 Standard A pupils in the entire school, the top pupil, with a total of 794 marks, 50 marks ahead of his nearest rival, is Johannes Mathabane," that I did not grasp the significance of her remarks until I found myself being called to the podium, and once there, being congratulated by the various teachers.

"Wonderful achievement, boy."

"Keep it up."

"Well done."

"That's the way to work hard."

"That's the way to sock up the competition, boy."

"Your parents ought to be proud of you."

When I recovered my senses, the teacher handed me a white, sealed envelope, and told me not to open it, but to give it to my parents. She then went back to announcing the rest of the results. I returned back to my row. I was on cloud nine. My classmates looked at me with envious eyes. The teachers of the other classes read the names of the top students in their respective classes, and these students were called to the podium to be congratulated and to receive their envelopes. Afterward, the principal called upon the assembly to give all the top achievers a round of applause. Then, breviary in hand, one of the female teachers led us in singing hymns and reciting psalms. After that, the principal led us in prayer—a prayer which all tribal schoolchildren were expected to know by heart, regardless of the religious beliefs of their parents. The prayer went thus:

> *Our Father, who art in heaven*
> *Hallowed be Thy name, Thy kingdom come,*
> *Thy will be done on earth, as it is in heaven.*
> *Give us this day our daily bread. . . .*

The principal then shouted: "Hip! hip!" at the top of his voice, three times, and the assembly roared "Hurrah! hurrah! hurrah!" Thereafter, he again wished everyone happy holidays; then the following perennial closing hymn was sung:

> *God be with you till we meet again*
> *By His counsels guide uphold you*
> *His sleep securely fold you;*
> *God be with you till we meet again. . . .*

The assembly was ordered dismissed. Some of the students who had been around the school longer, and had caught the full spirit of the end-of-the-year festivities, hugged and kissed and shook hands with each other; some even cried. I felt a slight sadness at the thought of not seeing my friends for two months, the length of the Christmas holidays.

That night, my mother, upon hearing the news that I had come out number one in my class, hugged and kissed me so many times and made me so many promises. Before the night was over, the yard was buzzing with news of a teacher-to-be at the Mathabanes' household. Granny was told the good news, and she promised me many things. I felt happy and proud. I even began to like school. What was so remarkable about my first-year performance was that I had come out number one despite chronically lacking books, having had to resort to paying more attention during class lectures, borrowing other children's books to do homework and relying on a picture-book memory during exams.

My accomplishments at school must have touched my father's heart, for one Friday night, in my second year of school, he did something that made me cry.

"Johannes, come here," he called; I went. He had just arrived from work and was sitting by the table, waiting for dinner, which my mother was busy serving. Florah was singing lullabies to Merriam; Maria was playing placidly with her frayed rag doll; and George huddled near the brazier, sleeping.

"How much is a slate?" he asked.

"Twenty cents."

"School fees?"

"One rand twenty for the entire year."

"That much!" my father cried, astounded; the amount was a tenth of his wages. "Where in the hell do teachers think we black people can get that type of money! They must be mad. Black people aren't flushed with money like white people are!" Turning to my mother, he said, "I told you, woman, not to take him to the damn school. Now where do you think he will get money to buy slates and pay school fees? Not from me."

Humbly, my mother said, "Well, I bought him that one slate. He broke it and kept using the pieces for a year. And I've already paid his school fees for this year."

"Where did you get the money?" asked my father suspiciously.

"I didn't use your money, if that's what you're thinking," my mother said. "Granny gave me from the little she had."

"Now, who is going to pay for him next year, and the next, and the next?"

"Won't you have a change of heart, Jackson?" my mother asked. "He's your son, you know. The money you're wasting on liquor and gambling could pay for his school needs. He's already done well his first year, and who knows, if he keeps on doing well, someday he may get a good job and take care of you in your old age."

"I don't believe in schools, woman," my father said emphatically. "How often do I have to tell you that. Just look at all those so-called educated people. What has education done for them? They pick garbage, wash cars, work as garden boys and delivery boys. Is that what people pay all this money to go learn at school? I myself wouldn't go even if school were free."

"There are teachers, doctors and nurses," my mother said. "He can become a teacher."

"And how much will he be paid?" my father returned sarcastically. "There are teachers I know who are making half of what the garbageman makes."

All that this talk did was confuse me.

"How much did you say a slate was?" my father turned to me and asked.

"Twenty cents."

"And that other book, how much is it?"

"You mean a primer? Forty cents."

"Here's sixty cents," he said, reaching deep into his pocket.

My mouth dropped. I thought I was dreaming. My mother's face broke into a wide smile.

"Come on, what are you frozen for?" my father said to me. "Do you want the money or don't you?"

I timidly reached out and took the money. Tears stood in my eyes. I wanted to kiss him, fall on my knees and worship him, do anything to show him how thankful I was.

"Say thanks to your father," my mother said.

"Thanks, Papa," I said in a trembling voice.

"But don't you get any ideas, now," my father said. "This doesn't mean I am going to buy you everything for school. When you've learned how to read and write letters, I want you to stop going. That's all the education you will need to get by in this world."

Florah was now six years old. At my mother's insistence, she, too, began school; the burden of financing both our educations rested entirely on my mother, even though my father tried to help from time to time. She begged and borrowed to pay for Florah's school fees, which were demanded upon registration.

I was now in Standard One, having passed Sub-standard B at the top of my class. My school needs had increased. When I asked my mother how she thought she was ever going to keep us both in school, considering she was having enormous difficulties keeping me there, she calmly replied, "I'll tackle each problem as it comes, and God will help me." The problems kept on coming, but God's help didn't.

School turned into a nightmare.

I began coming home with bruises, unable to sit down or sleep for days because I had been whipped by teachers for failing to pay my school fees on time, and for lacking in books and a proper uniform.

I would occasionally attempt to lie my way out each time I was threatened with a beating, by telling teachers that I would be getting the required books and uniform, and would be paying my school fees, by the end of the month. However, months would go by, with no job in sight for my mother, and I would continue without school paraphernalia. My father tried to buy my sister and me a few exercise books, worth about ten cents or so each, and pay the three hundred cents a year each for school fees, but he soon gave up the idea because he was paid so little, our household needs were so many and school was a low-priority item in the house. Survival was first.

"How many months have to end before you pay your school fees and start wearing the proper uniform?" a teacher asked me one morning during uniform inspection. "And where are your primers?"

I dropped my eyes to the floor and lied. "My mother said I would be getting everything at the end of the month."

"The end of which month?" the teacher said with a touch of sarcasm. "This one, the next one or the one ten years down the road? You've been saying 'the end of the month' since the beginning of the year, and school is nearly over. And other teachers who've had you in their classes over the years have told me that you've been giving them the 'the end of the month' line too."

My eyes still on the floor, I mumbled. "The end of this month, sir."

"Look at me when I speak to you!" the teacher screamed at me.

I looked at him, or rather, beyond him and at the blackboard mounted on the red-bricked wall, as he stood akimbo next to the cupboard where he kept his array of canes. I was standing in an aisle between benches, on exhibit before the entire class. During uniform inspection, the entire class of boys and girls was required to stand, at ease between the aisles, and each pupil would be told by the teacher to sit down, provided he or she was properly dressed, had the required books and had passed the "neatness" test—trimmed nails, combed hair, polished shoes and so on.

"Do you know you're the only one who doesn't have the proper uniform and primers?" the teacher said. "And do you know that it's the law to have those things? And do you know that you may fail as a result? Do you know?"

I nodded feebly, my head cast down like a victim awaiting sentencing.

"Why aren't you like any normal child, heh?" the teacher said, fixing a stern look on me. Shaking his head, he went on, "It's still a mystery to me how you manage to come out number one in the class. What's the problem?"

I kept my head down and didn't answer him; he knew what my problem was. I was growing angry over the public interrogation, yet there was nothing I could do but endure the ordeal.

After verbally humiliating me, the teacher called me up to the front of the class, grabbed a thick cane out of the cupboard, told me to straddle the table and whipped me a dozen lashes. Tears welled in my eyes, I clenched my teeth and in my mind called him all sorts of obscene names as he lashed me mercilessly.

Week after week the pattern repeated itself. Some teachers, particularly the women, were sympathetic and did not whip me. Others, however, simply said, "You're no different from other schoolchildren. They too have parents who have trouble getting jobs; yet they have uniforms and books." I began hating all teachers. I became disenchanted with school. I began asking myself: Why was it a crime to be without books and a proper uniform? I desperately wanted to learn how to read and write, but if learning meant being whipped constantly for things I had no control over and probably never could have, I was prepared to seriously reconsider my desire to learn.

One day I decided to have it out with my mother.

"Mama, I don't want to go to school anymore," I said.

"What's the matter?" my mother asked.

"I can't take the punishment any longer."

"Can't you bear it just a little longer—until I get a job?" she said. "Then I'll be able to buy you school things."

I told her that I would go back only when I had a uniform and books.

"But you'll lose much while you're away," she said, "and you may never be able to catch up. Who knows how long it'll take for me to find a job."

"Then I'll leave school altogether," I declared. I was only nine years old.

"If you leave school, what will you do? What job will you get?"

I was tongue-tied. Yes, if I left school at that age, what would I do? How would I earn a living? What kind of job could a nine-year-old who could barely write a complete sentence of English do? Though I had friends who had left school and their homes at seven and eight years old, and were now living in junkyards and dilapidated buildings, supporting themselves through stealing and handouts, I had no confidence in myself that I could do likewise. But what other choice did I have, as a Kaffir boy?

"What should I do, then, Mama?" I said in despair. "I'm tired of being punished all the time for books and a uniform I may never have."

"Stay in school, child," my mother said. "Stay in school," she repeated, in a tone full of hope, "and as soon as I find a job, the first thing I'll do with my first wages, will be to buy you and your sister books and uniforms. I may not be able to buy you everything all at once. But I'll do my best. And before you know it, both you and your sister will have everything and be just like other schoolchildren."

Soon after that conversation, a miracle occurred. My mother at last found a housekeeping job at the Indian place on First Avenue (she was able to take it because she didn't need a permit to work in Alexandra). The backbreaking job required her to work six days a week, scrubbing floors, washing clothes, cleaning windows, cooking and tending babies and washing diapers for an Indian trader named Shortie, who had a very large family. Though six months' pregnant with her fifth child, my mother took the job; in fact, she was ecstatic over it.

"For you, children," she said the day she found the job. "I'll sacrifice even my life." Tears came to my eyes when I heard that. She began talking about what she was going to do with her wages—twenty rands a month—buy diapers, books, uniforms and pay school fees, and pay for maternity care at the clinic so that nurses could attend to her when the time came. (My arithmetic told me that twenty rands couldn't accomplish all that.) And so, each morning she would get up at six, and walk all the way from Thirteenth Avenue to First Avenue —a distance of about two miles to and fro. Sometimes she would get lifts from kind bus drivers. When she got home late in the evening, she brought with her curried leftovers, mangoes and other Indian food.

My father stopped giving my mother grocery money. "You're working, now," he said one Friday night. "So you too can help pay for things around the house." My mother didn't argue. At no other time did I hate my father more than when he did this. I swore in my heart that someday I would make him pay, dearly, for it. As far as I was concerned, I had no father. He used the extra money to gamble and buy alcohol.

"Mama, when will I get the books?" I asked her a month after she had been working.

"You will get them soon, child. I bought groceries with what I would have used for your books, because your father didn't give me grocery money this week. Have patience."

One evening my mother returned home from work carrying on her head a big box. "I have books for you, Johannes," she said with a smile. "And a new slate for you, Florah." I was overjoyed. The box contained curried leftovers, bruised mangoes and a dozen or so books, which my mother said she had bought at a flea market near where she worked. As my brother and sisters clawed each other over the food, she and I went over the books.

"Can you use this one?" she asked eagerly, showing me a book written—I didn't know till later—in Chinese.

I took it and flipped through the pages, pondering the alien script. Unable to decipher the abstruse writing, I shook my head. "No."

"What about this one?" she said, showing me a book written in French.

I again shook my head. "No."

"And this one?" A book written in Arabic.

"No."

"This one?" A book written in Hindu.

"No."

"This one?" A book written in German.

"No."

"And this one?" A book written in Afrikaans.

"No."

"Are you sure they don't use any of them at your school?" my mother asked.

"I'm sure, Mama," I said emphatically.

"Why—they're books, aren't they?"

"Just because they're books, Mama," I said, "doesn't mean we use them at school. They're written in languages we don't use at school. Our school uses only the Tsonga language."

"What languages are they written in?"

"I don't know."

"How, then, can you tell?"

"I can't read them, Mama, that's how. If they were written in Tsonga, I could at least read them."

My mother doubted me, for she said, "Let's take the books to Mr. Brown." Mr. Brown was one of the few persons in the yard with the equivalent of a high-school education. He was a bus driver for PUTCO, but he also operated a sort of moving service, transporting people and goods between Alexandra and the tribal reserve of the Vendas. "Maybe he can tell us what languages they're written in, and whether you can use them in later classes."

"I don't think I'll ever be required to use them, Mama."

"How do you know?"

We went to Mr. Brown's shack.

"You say you bought these books for your son, heh?" Mr. Brown asked my mother as he skimmed through the books, his brow knitted, giving him a look of someone very learned.

"Yes," my mother said humbly.

"Where again did you say you bought them?" Mr. Brown asked, "and how much, may I ask?"

My mother told him.

"No wonder you got them so cheap," Mr. Brown said, laughing. "They're worthless to your son. Tribal schools don't use these books, for they are written in French, German, Arabic, Hindu and Chinese, languages which I, too, can't read."

"But the people at the flea market told me these were school-books," my mother said.

"They're schoolbooks all right," Mr. Brown sighed deeply. "But only white people and Indians use them." A look of dejection crossed my mother's face, and her bony shoulders drooped in resignation. As she began putting the books in the box, like someone collecting the pieces of a shattered dream, Mr. Brown suggested, "Listen, Mrs. Mathabane. I'll buy your child a few primers if you agree to give me these books."

"What use will they be to you?" my mother asked. "You just said you can't read them."

"They'll look beautiful on my shelves." Mr. Brown smiled.

My mother gave him the books, and a week later, I had two primers.

24 Despite the fact that, with my mother working, I could now afford a few books and a uniform, I continued wondering what I was being educated for. Over the years, since I began school, I had from time to time heard people around me say that whites had built blacks schools only to teach us how to be their slaves.

Hearing this type of talk confused me even more about the objectives of all I was learning. Yes, I was coming out at the top of my class —yes, I could read and write things in Tsonga—yes, I could recite arithmetic tables—yes, I knew how to draw the map of Alexandra— yes, I could sing hymns and recite Scriptures—but what did it all mean?

And my father's constant preaching about how schools were, like

Christianity, simply another white man's tool of keeping the black man down didn't help much either. One of his strong points whenever he argued with my mother about the pros and cons of schooling, was that blacks, before the coming of the white man to Africa, had always taught their offspring ways of being useful and productive in the villages while they were still in the cradle, and that by the time boys and girls were five, six, seven and eight years old, they were already making meaningful contributions to tribal society. On the other hand, he pointed out critically, the white man's education did not and could not do that.

"A man who knows nothing about books," my father said to me one day, "but can feed himself and his family, is a million times better than a man who has read a million books but cannot feed himself and his family."

Another day he said, "What a man does is more important than what he knows."

Still another day he said, "I don't know why your mother is breaking her neck to pay for your schooling, for the white man will not look at you any better even if you were the most educated black man in this world. There are people with degrees at my job, and I'm their boss, boy, how about that?"

I couldn't understand.

But it came as no surprise when, hardly three years after I had begun school, the novelty of learning began to fade. Despite my continued successes at school, I failed to find real meaning in what I was being taught; more important, I failed to find, among the black people I lived with, and with whose accomplishments in life I was familiar, those particular individuals whom I could identify as having benefited from an education, and whose accomplishments in life could act as landmarks to orient me and help me set goals in life. Where were the lighthouses to guide my newly built ship of knowledge just setting sail on a perilous journey upon a vast, turbulent and unknown ocean of life?

One afternoon after school I was sitting on a tin chair near the window doing homework when I heard a medley of voices shouting out in the streets. Instantly I abandoned my books and rushed outside to investigate.

Coming down the street in a cloud of dust, twelve to fifteen variously shaped black men in overalls, waving copies of newspapers over their heads, were chanting, "ALI! ALI! ALI! ALI! ALI! ALI!" as they leaped in the air, stomped their feet, and embraced each other in ecstasy.

"What's going on?" I asked of an older boy leaning with me against the fence and watching the group of men. People all over the yards leaned over fences, witnessing the spectacle.

"Haven't you heard?" He bulged his eyes at me.

"Heard what?"

"Where have you been since this morning?"

"At school. Why?"

"Didn't you hear people talk about it there?"

"Talk about what?" I asked, growing impatient at the suspense.

"Talk about the boxing fight, you fool," the boy said importantly. "The big boxing fight that took place in America yesterday."

America? What strange name is that?

"Who fought who?" I asked eagerly. I understood what boxing meant, but I hadn't the faintest idea where America was.

"Ali," the boy said, jabbing his fists high in the air as a sign of victory. "Ali," he repeated reverently, "a black man. As black as all the people you see around here. The greatest fighter that ever lived in this world. He beat to death a white man."

"Hunh!" I gasped in disbelief. "A black man beat a white man to death? Where, in this country?"

"No, fool. Not here, in America."

"Where's that?"

"Overseas."

"Where's overseas?"

"I don't know."

The shouting men came abreast of where we were standing. The boy leaped over the railing and followed them as they went down the street, chanting and stomping their feet in fits of joy. I had to look after the house, so I didn't follow. The chanting of Ali's name, however, continued throughout the rest of the afternoon, well into the night. Throughout the week, on street corners, in stores, at shebeens all over the neighbourhood, the talk was about the fight, and black people everywhere were enraptured by Ali's feats. Boys everywhere called themselves Ali, and emulated his "float like a butterfly and sting like a bee" routines. I, too, rejoiced along with everybody— simply because a black man had finally "beaten to death" a white man. (It turned out that the boy was exaggerating; by "beat to death" he meant a knockout.) Secretly, I dreamed of some day becoming as good a fighter as Ali, and "beating to death" all the white men I could lay my hands on, beginning with the superintendent and all the white men on the police force. (I considered the black policemen's crimes against their own people so heinous that, once I became a fighter, "beating them to death" wouldn't be enough punishment—I would squash them like vermin under the wheels of a bulldozer I would have bought with my boxing revenues.)

That dream of becoming a boxer, however, was shattered when one evening I accompanied a group of neighbourhood boys to the local boxing club: a stuffy, dimly lit, bare-walled cubicle with a cement floor so damp and slippery that it seemed a miracle how the throng of furiously sweating, shirtless men and boys managed to work out without falling and breaking a limb. The place was used as a classroom during the day.

"We want to learn how to box," the leader of our group said eagerly to the gym owner, an old man with a receding hairline.

"Want to box, heh—how old are you?"

We gave him our inflated ages.

"Okay," he said, "stand over there," motioning us to a semidark corner, where a group of older boys was already assembled.

The gym teemed with shirtless men and boys doing different things. Some skipped rope, some punched an old, patchy bag hanging from the ceiling and some did sit-ups and push-ups.

"What are those men doing hitting at thin air?" I said to one of the boys, giggling.

"They're shadowboxing."

"What's that?"

"They're hitting at their own shadows."

"What for?"

"They become good boxers that way."

I began bombarding the boy with questions concerning pugilism: it seemed so different from the way we fought in the street—it was cleaner. Soon, the gym owner came over, carrying two sets of worn oversized gloves, and bellowed: "Who among you wants to go first?"

One of my friends pointed at me, laughing. I thought it some kind of a joke, and I laughed too. The old man called me over; I went. He told me to take my shirt off. He turned his head toward a cluster of mean-looking boys in the far corner.

"Who among you wants to fight this boy?" he asked.

I gasped. Who? Me? I looked about. Yes, he meant me.

"I don't know how to box, sir," I whimpered. "I've never boxed before."

"Don't be a sissy, now," the old man said. "There's nothing to it. Haven't you used your fists before? Or are you afraid of him because he looks big?" A boy with thick thighs and muscled arms and a shaved head full of sores had volunteered to fight me. My pride was on the line. I told the gym owner that I wasn't afraid of anybody. "That's the spirit, boy," the old man said, patting me on the shoulder. "Ali was much smaller than the white man, yet he knocked him out cold."

Hearing this gave me some courage.

"You boys fight every day in the streets," the old man went on, as he gloved me. "Here you'll learn the art of boxing."

My opponent's eyes were big, red and shining, as if he were high on benzene. He looked so mean and deadly that, as his large, scaly, muscled hands were being gloved, I had second thoughts about wanting to mess with him. A circle formed around us. The old man announced that he would referee the fight, which was slated for three rounds. A wave of excitement surged through the tight crowd, and people started making predictions and bets. I was assigned a corner consisting of two boys in their teens.

"You'll be Ali," the old man said to me, as he brought my opponent and me together in the middle of the "ring." Turning to the hairless boy, he said, "And you'll be Schmeling."

"But I want to be Ali," the hairless boy complained.

"You'll do as I tell you," the old man retorted. Turning to the crowd of spectators, he said, lifting my hand high up, "This here is Muhammad Ali, alias Cassius Clay." Lifting the hairless boy's, "And this is Max Schmeling."

"YEA! YEA! YEA! COME ON ALI," someone said.

"ALI! ALI! ALI! ALI!" the crowd erupted into a chant.

"Come on, 'Smelling,' " said a lone voice.

I bubbled with fear and excitement. The gloves I had on were so heavy I could hardly lift up my arms.

"Shake hands," the old man said.

Instinctively, I swung at the hairless boy, catching him on the jaw with a wicked, unexpected left. He staggered, grimacing, but didn't fall. He came back, with fire in his eyes. He was about to fling himself at me when the old man interposed himself between the two of us, and said to me, angrily: "You don't hit when I say 'shake hands.' " I was about to tell him that I didn't know any of the rules, when he cried, "Box on!" Before I knew what was happening, a vicious right landed on my nose. It sent me crashing into the human wall. The wall pushed me back. Fuming, I went at my opponent like a maddened bull seeing red, punching the best I could given the immense weight of the gloves. I kept on swinging and missing and spinning.

"KILL HIM! KILL HIM! KILL HIM!" the cry went out.

I didn't know whether they were telling me to kill the hairless boy, which I didn't want to do; or him to kill me! While pondering the matter, a lightning uppercut to my jaw spun me 180 degrees. I spit blood. I had bit my lips and tongue. While still dizzy from the blow, another came, then another, then another, to the nose, to the stomach, to the head, to my crotch. I had become a punching bag.

"Stop! Stop! Stop, please," I bawled, trying in vain to parry the blows, staggering about in a fog. "I can't see."

"Pretend you didn't hear him say that," I heard the old man tell my opponent. I tried to cover my face with the heavy gloves, but I couldn't. The blows kept coming. I felt my knees wobble.

"Fight back, boy! Fight! Don't be a wimp, fight!"

"I can't," I whimpered. "I can't see."

The blows kept coming. Suddenly everything became blurred, then dark. My feet gave way under me. I slumped to the floor— knocked out. Reviving, I found myself in a corner; the old man was busy dabbing my forehead with a wet, dirty sponge. My friends who had led me to the slaughter came over and offered words of consolation. I shrugged them aside. I hated them. The old man said, "Not a bad fight, boy, not a bad fight at all. You'll learn. Are you all right?" he asked, as he saw me rubbing my puffed eyes.

"Yes," I nodded, though my head felt like a lump of lead, "I'm fine." I told him I wanted to go home.

"Will you come back tomorrow?" he asked hopefully. "You didn't box that badly, you know. The mistakes you made can be easily corrected. Anyway, the other boy is one of my seasoned fighters. With a couple more fights, who knows, you could be on your way to becoming another Ali. You've got potential."

"To hell with Ali," I told myself as I left the gym. From that day, I hated boxing.

25 On a cold grey morning in 1968 I woke up and found the world deep in mourning. Throughout the long and confused day, wherever I went, I met black people with grief and rage in their eyes. At school I heard teachers whisper to one another in uneasy, subdued tones.

"The white bastards finally killed him."

"Yes, they assassinate them over there; and they jail them and throw away the key over here."

"The white bastards are the same the world over; they differ only in their tactics to keep the black man down."

"His death will be avenged; just you wait and see."

Wondering who it was that had been killed, and why his death had aroused so much anger and grief, I began asking questions of some of the older boys at school.

"It's a black man that's been murdered."

"He lived in America."

"I don't know his name."

As I went about the township throughout that long, grief-stricken afternoon, rumours began filtering into my always inquisitive ears that the black man being mourned was a preacher and a leader of august stature in America, and that he had been assassinated by a white man.

I wondered why there was so much fuss over his death, considering that he was a black man. I had heard many stories in my history classes about black men who had been butchered, gunned and hanged in cold blood by whites, but none of those deaths, to the best of my knowledge, had ever had such widespread reverberations, and enraged so many black people. What seemed more absurd was that this dead black preacher and leader was not even from Alexandra. Throughout the township, in every street I went, I saw grown-ups assembled in clusters to read the papers and to whisper about its dark and dastardly contents. Because a newspaper was never bought at home, I went to the newsstand on Twelfth Avenue, in the hope of catching a glimpse of the newspaper photo of the man, if there was any, who was causing so much furor. However, so many people were crowding the newspaper boy that day that I couldn't get near enough to have a look at the papers. As I stood debating what to do, my eyes wandered about, and fell upon several placards, in red ink, impaled upon a nearby fence.

The placards read:

EXTRA! EXTRA!
KING
IS
DEAD.

I ran back home, pondering who this "king" was. At home I found my mother breast-feeding the new baby, Dinah.

"Who's that man that got killed, Mama?"

"I don't know who he is," my mother said in a tone expressing a reluctance to talk about the subject. "I've never heard of him until today."

"His name is 'King.' Was he some kind of a chief?"

"I don't know. He didn't live in this country."

"He lived in 'America,' Mama," I said naturally, as if I knew where America was. Somehow the name *America* had stuck in my mind since the day Ali won the boxing match.

"Who told you that?" my mother asked.

"I heard," I said.

"Yes, they say he lived in 'America.' But I don't know where that is. All I know is this country. This 'King' you're asking about, I hear many people—those that went to school and can read newspapers— say that he was a God-fearing man who died fighting to set his people free. To get them equal rights."

"What are equal rights, Mama?"

She thought pensively for a moment or two, then said, "Equal rights are laws which give black people the same opportunities as white people."

"Do black people in this country have equal rights?"

"No."

"Why not?"

"Because white people have taken away all our rights."

White people again. Why were they seemingly behind every major issue I wanted to know about? Why were they always the architects of every woe the black man had? Why were they always taking things away from black people? Were they never satisfied with what they've got? Why weren't black people fighting them? Was it because white people had, as I had seen in movies, guns, swords, bombs and tanks?

"Has anybody fought to get them back?" I thought that if black people were somehow able to get hold of bombs, tanks, guns, swords and machetes, then white people would be in for it. And oh, how I yearned for the day when armies of black peasants would invade the white world, and butcher, guillotine, hang, machine-gun, bury alive and drown in hot lead every bad white man alive.

Again my mother paused for a moment to reflect. "You're very curious, child," she said. "I doubt if the story will mean anything to you."

"I want to know, Mama," I said.

"Once, I remember," she began. "Black people did attempt to fight for their rights. It was the year in which you were born. A group of learned black people organized a march of protest to show white people that they didn't want to carry passes no more."

"Did they get those rights?"

"No."

"How come?"

"Many of those people who marched were shot and killed by the police."

"How many?"

"Sixty-nine."

"That many?" I gasped. "Where was this?"

"It was in Sharpeville, near a police station."

"Why didn't the black people fight back? Didn't they carry guns too? Didn't they shoot back?" I said blindly.

"No," my mother said, "black people can't carry guns. It's against the law."

"Has anyone since fought for any rights?"

"No."

"Why?"

"Because everyone is afraid."

"Afraid of what?"

"Afraid of dying, silly. Now stop asking questions and go do your homework."

"When I grow up, Mama," I said stoutly, as I took my books to go do homework with a friend who lived in the neighbourhood, "I'll fight for my rights."

My mother stared at me, but said nothing.

26 One day, following a series of months during which I had been repeatedly punished by teachers for being without certain reading books, I decided to quit school permanently. Now, there was a rule in my school which gave teachers authority to expel a pupil who was absent from school for over a month without a solid reason.

Aware of the existence of such a rule, I stayed away from school for something like three weeks. I would leave home saying I was going to school when in truth I was headed for the junkyard on Fourteenth Avenue, where I rendezvoused with a group of boys from other tribal schools who also played hooky. The average age of the group was eight. We would spend the day scouring the ghetto for warehouses where shebeen queens stored their illicit hooch. We would bust in using crowbars and steal beer and whisky bottles, which we sold and used the proceeds to go to King's Bioscope. We would attend the afternoon show, usually featuring films about the Wild West and gladiators. Upon leaving King's we would go to the open veld, where we would imitate the various fighting methods—using sharpened sticks and iron rods—we had seen in the pictures. We thought we were imitating the reality of white people

At sunset, I would leave for home.

"Why are you home so late?" my mother would ask.

I would lie to her that I was late because I had to stay behind for choir rehearsals. Because my mother couldn't read, there seemed no way for her to find out the truth. What I didn't know, however, was that each time I came back and lied that I had been to school, she would wait for me to leave the house, then take my exercise books to a next-door neighbour to find out whether the material appearing on the last pages of each book was indeed the latest work. Finding out that it wasn't, that in fact the last entries were dated, she kept count of the number of days I was absenting myself from school. She meticulously kept the record for three weeks, and in the fourth, she went to my school and had a talk with the principal. She did all this without arousing even the slightest of my suspicions.

One Monday morning, toward the end of what would have been my fourth week away from school, she followed me secretly to find out where I was actually going. She gave the information of the whereabouts of the junkyard to the principal.

Two days later, on a Wednesday, I left home on the pretense that I was headed for school. Instead, I headed for the junkyard. I found the gang lounging lazily atop the hood of a scrapped '65 Chevy, basking in the flaring morning sun waiting for me.

"We must get to the Bioscope early today," announced the gang leader, a twelve-year-old boy named Mnyamani (The Black One); "there's a great double feature," he added, and continued to pass around small bottles of glue and benzene for the others to smoke. I didn't smoke because each time I tried to, I ended up feeling nauseated and dizzy, and would vomit.

"By the way, what's playing?" I asked.

"*Spartacus* and *For a Few Dollars More*."

"I thought that was next week," I said as I stashed my books underneath the dashboard. "I thought *Street with No Name* and *Cemetery without Crosses* were playing."

"They moved those to next week because of the Easter holidays."

While we waited for Mnyamani to map out our bottle-stealing itinerary for the day, out of the corner of one eye I saw a group of schoolboys coming down the street, heading in our direction. I paid no particular attention to them until they had surrounded the junkyard.

"Johannes!" a voice boomed from somewhere behind me, taking me unawares, "We've come to take you back to school!"

I whirled in the direction of the voice, and instantly I froze with fear as I came face-to-face with the towering figure of Mandleve (Big Ears), Bovet's notorious truant-hunter, barely three yards away from me.

"You're not taking me back!" I yelled, leaping upon the hood and preparing to defend myself.

"Don't be foolish," said Mandleve, advancing toward me. "There are too many of us. Besides, if you come peacefully, nobody will get hurt."

"We have done nothing," my friends whimpered as they deserted me.

"I am not going back!" I said, starting to panic.

"Then we'll have to take you back by force!" Mandleve said. The group closed in. Realising that they were about to rush me, I reached under the hood of the dashboard and grabbed a crowbar that the gang used in opening bottle stockades.

"Don't come any closer or I'll kill you!" I yelled, brandishing the crowbar.

"We are too many for you," Mandleve pointed out. "Give yourself up peacefully, and I'll tell the principal and the teachers that you didn't give us any trouble, and they'll take it easy on you."

"No!" I shook my head. I knew he was lying. Once they had me back at school, it was the end. No teacher would ever entertain the thought of mitigating, in any way, the punishment of a truant. I had seen other truants being lashed mercilessly.

"Go back to school," I said. "Go back and I promise to be at school tomorrow, on my own accord." I was lying. I was thinking of running away from home, forever, and living in a junkyard somewhere.

"Come on," said Mandleve. "What's the difference? Come with us now and get it over with."

"I don't have any books with me," I lied.

"You don't need any books today," said Mandleve. "There's no regular school but choir rehearsals in preparation for the competition next week."

"I'm in no choir," I said. "So I won't be needed."

Mandleve apparently decided that he had bargained with me enough, for he suddenly lunged at me. Instinctively, I let go of the crowbar. He ducked, and the heavy bar crashed harmlessly into the hood of the Chevy. The swing was so powerful that it dented the metal. Mandleve grabbed my legs, and I came crashing down to the ground. Bleeding from the mouth and nose, I tried to fight, yelling, "Turn me loose, turn me loose!" but the boys were simply too many and too powerful. Within minutes they had me bound—hands and feet—with a thick rope.

At school I found the principal and all the male teachers waiting for me, their faces cold and menacing, as they tested their canes between their hands. My mother was also inside the principal's office.

"Whip him good," she impassively gave the order—which was not necessary—and there and then I knew it was the end. She left the office and stood outside. The teachers descended upon me like starved vultures out of the sky. They commenced the savage beating, taking turns whenever one teacher's hand got tired. I fainted. They revived me, only to whip me some more. I spent an entire week bedridden, unable to sit up or sleep. For the rest of my primary school years I seldom, if ever, cut school for any reason. Even when I was gravely ill, I would crawl to school, and the teachers would send me back home.

27 My tenth birthday came and went away, like all the other nine, uncelebrated. Having never had a normal childhood, I didn't miss birthdays; to me they were simply like other days: to be survived. Strangely, however, on each birthday I somehow got the feeling that I had aged more than a year. Suffering seemed to age me more than birthdays. Though I was only ten, black life seemed to have, all along, been teaching me the same lessons of survival, and making the same demands upon me for that survival, as it was doing to grown-ups. Thus, emotionally, I had aged far beyond my ten years.

Alexandra continued being the decaying shantytown it was before I was born. The police continued with their raids; children continued dying of malnutrition; the gutters continued to overflow with filth, and hovels continued mushrooming all over the place; families continued being deported to the tribal reserves; I continued going to school and to the movies and playing soccer; waves of immigrant workers continued arriving in Alexandra—this time, however, they were being housed in newly built hostels (constructed where houses had been demolished) instead of compounds, and there was talk that eventually, the whole of Alexandra would be nothing but hostels; our neighbours continued accusing one another of witchcraft; my father continued drinking and gambling, and quarrelling with my mother, often beating her up. In short, the suffering of black people continued on the increase, and I continued getting the feeling that we, blacks of Alexandra, were like animals, quarantined inside a cage—by the white man—fomenting ignorance and death—and that there was nothing we could do about it but await, each, our violent end.

One late Friday evening when I was nearing the end of my tenth year an event occurred that precipitated the greatest crisis of my childhood: I was an eyewitness to a murder. Upon that night—as on every Friday night—the dark and dusty streets of Alexandra swarmed with black workers returning home from work, and about to begin celebrating the start of a weekend, a time when many of them would be drowning their pain, sorrow and suffering with all-night orgies and feasting in shebeens throughout the township.

I was returning home after a long afternoon of playing soccer at the stadium on Twelfth Avenue. As it was payday, all along the streets I met black men hurrying, hurrying, hurrying, the pittances of an eight days' week in sweatshops jingling in their deep pockets. Some hurried home, there to feed the many hungry mouths awaiting their arrival; others headed for the crazy comfort of shebeens where, in one fleeting moment of glory, they could be masters of their destinies.

As I turned the corner into Thirteenth Avenue, I saw, coming down the street, a group of about six *tsotsis* chasing two men. Remembering my mother's warning about what to do when encountering *tsotsis*—"When you see *tsotsis*, child, run for the nearest cover until they're gone"—I fled into a nearby yard. I dove into the patch of tall dried grass in front of the gate.

I lay flat in the tall grass and watched the scene in the street. The *tsotsis* were rapidly gaining on the two men, who were being slowed by the heavy paper bags they were unwilling to let go. The chase reached alongside the spot where I was hiding. I held my breath and kept still. Suddenly, one of the men being chased swung into the yard where I was hiding, apparently thinking that he might get help from the inhabitants of several of the shacks in it. He was mistaken, for no sooner had he entered the yard than shutters were closed and doors barricaded. The *tsotsis* followed him in, letting the other man go.

"Please don't kill me! Please don't kill me!" the man begged as the *tsotsis* caught up with him. "Take everything I have, but please don't kill me!"

"Shut up!" came the acrimonious reply as the *tsotsis*, like a pack of scavengers, surrounded him. The moon was full, and it seemed daylight.

I craned my neck to see what was going on. What I saw made me gasp with horror. Having drawn gleaming, sharp knives, meat cleavers and tomahawks, the *tsotsis* began carving the man as he howled for mercy. "Don't kill me, please don't kill me. I have ten children, please don't kill me. Take everything I have, but please don't kill me."

The *tsotsis* paid no heed to his pleas; in fact, they grinned at his cries.

Through some superhuman effort, it seemed, the man, now bleeding heavily from gaping wounds, managed to break through the cordon of butchers and make a mad dash for the street. The *tsotsis* didn't chase after him immediately, tarrying a while to rummage through the packages he had dropped. The wounded man staggered left and right, clutching his slashed throat, which spewed blood. I was now bathed in perspiration. My breath was coming out in spurts. As the wounded man staggered past me, I detected tubelike things unwinding like a spool of thread through his slashed overalls. His guts were spilling from his belly! Nausea overcame me. I wanted desperately to faint and be away from it all. I thought I would panic any minute. The fatally wounded man turned his bleeding head in the direction of the fortified shacks, as if pleading for them to open and let him in. There was a dreadful glint in his eyes, the glint of death creeping in. I can never forget the look on his face for as long as I live.

The *tsotsis* caught up with him before he even reached the street. Their gleaming weapons of death remorselessly went about their unfinished, infernal mission.

The wounded man uttered hideous guttural sounds through his slashed throat. Gradually the sounds grew fewer and fainter. Suddenly his body lurched forward with outstretched arms, and his limbs twitched violently; he pitched forward, uttering one last, ghastly, gurgling sound, as if some beast were lodged within him and were struggling furiously to be set free. He slumped to the bone-dry ground, like a bundle of old newspapers. Before the corpse even hit the ground, the *tsotsis* were already upon it, stripping and searching it, like a bunch of ravenous hyenas wrenching pieces of flesh from a carcass. The *tsotsis* turned the dead body supine, and removed its shoes, its not-worth-anything coat and frisked the back pockets. In a matter of minutes the six shadowy figures had accomplished their dastardly act and were heading for the shadows of the eerie moonlit night, the spoils of their foray ensconced between their murdering paws, their bloodshot eyes gleaming and their teeth grinning like those of cannibals after a kill.

An icy chill of death froze the world around me. For a long time I remained stock-still in the tall grass, in the limpid night, scarcely breathing, watching the naked, mutilated, lifeless body contorted on the ground, in a pool of blood. Each gaze made it seem to come alive, to stir, to slowly rise, like an entombed Egyptian mummy coming back to life. I panicked, and shot out of the grass as though I had been shot out of a cannon, howling like a maniac, as if tenscore devils were after me. Blinded by terror, I was mindless of my safety as I ran all the way home without stopping, dodging cars, bumping into obstacles and people, and leaping over *dongas*. Upon entering the house I fainted. My mother revived me by pouring water over me.

"What happened?" she said, as I lay upon the damp floor, shaking like a leaf in the wind.

With bated breath, I tried to gasp out what I had seen, but only managed to utter unintelligible, guttural sounds. Sweat poured in streams from my brow.

"What happened?" my mother repeated.

My mouth twitched as I strained to utter something, but still no words came out. Again I fainted.

What I remember on waking up was that it was early Saturday morning, and I was lying under the table. My mother was in the far corner of the kitchen preparing breakfast. As she saw me rise, she came over and asked, "How are you feeling?"

"A bit drowsy," I said as I stretched and yawned. "My head feels heavy, and I'm aching all over."

"Did you have any bad dreams?" she said guardedly.

"No," I said, "why?"

"Oh, nothing," my mother said.

Then it all came back, the witnessing of the grisly murder. I luridly recapitulated everything I had seen. My mother's face grew pale, and lines of deep concern furrowed her brow.

"I saw the corpse this morning as I was going to the store," she said. "It was covered with newspapers."

"Do you know who it was?" I asked.

"No," my mother said, adding, "but I heard this morning that several people in the neighbourhood were killed last night."

There was a moment of strained silence, during which time my mother eyed me thoughtfully.

Sighing, she said, "What were you doing out so late anyway?"

"I was out playing soccer," I said. "The team always practises till six on Fridays."

"With all this soccer, when do you ever get the time to do your homework?" my mother said concernedly.

"I always do my homework before I go to soccer practise," I said.

"When do you ever read? I've never seen you with a reading book."

"You know I don't have any books to read, Mama."

"Then borrow some from your friends."

"They don't have any either."

My mother muttered something to herself and left to continue preparing breakfast. That afternoon I went past the spot where the man had been killed. The corpse had been removed, but there were still traces of dried blood on the ground. I shrank. That evening the first of the nightmares about the incident began. For weeks they continued, festering like an open wound, and I, without an effective way of nursing them, simply withdrew into myself, and shut myself from the rest of the world. I wallowed in a mire of helplessness and despair. Gradually I developed a fatalistic resignation from life.

My parents, thinking I was bewitched, took me to a witch doctor, who made me drink a strange brew and bled me with a razor blade, all to no avail: I continued withdrawing into myself. What made this death different from the many others I had seen previously I do not really know.

One thing I do know was that I could not understand the morbid cruelty and satanic impulses that drove people to kill others. For what? I asked myself. What is to be gained from killing a fellow-sufferer? Why, instead of reaching out and helping each other, were some black people bent on hurting one another? Why, in the place of love and compassion, were there implacable hate and anger and jealousy? I could not see myself living the rest of my life under such conditions—to me life meant love, understanding, compassion. Yet, I asked myself, "What other world was there to run to?"

The question drew a blank. I began pitying myself for living in those times. I became a loner; I could not eat; I could not sleep; my schoolwork suffered; and I seldom went out to play as I used to. I would instead spend days brooding over my helplessness and the senselessness of the unbroken cycle of pain and suffering searing my mind and sapping my strength day after day. Why was life so hard, so without hope and promise?

I could not answer. Would life ever change for me? My sensitivity to the world around me made me soak all its suffering like a sponge soaking brackish water. Soon my mind was saturated, my being enervated, yet my soul continued to live and hope for better days. At ten years old I thought myself young; that maybe things would get better as I got older and was able to take responsibility for my own life. I filled myself with such hope and continued to cling to a silver lining, which seemed to disappear as rapidly as my desperation to cling to it increased. I had never felt more alone and helpless in the world.

28 A few months after I witnessed the grisly murder a strange feeling that I should end my own life suddenly came over me. I don't know why I felt that way, though the feeling seemed connected with the witnessing of the murder. All the memories of my childhood suffering came back and multiplied to a lifetime of continuous suffering, and I felt I could take no more.

I was weary of being hungry all the time, weary of being beaten all the time: at school, at home and in the streets. I felt that somehow the whole world was against me. I felt that the courage, the resiliency and the unswerving, fanatical will to survive, to dream of a bright future, to accomplish, to conquer, of early years had deserted me.

Since I was four years old I had held dear my mother's protracted and impassioned urges to keep on fighting, to keep on trying regardless, to never succumb to poverty, fear, pain and suffering, to study hard and to keep on knocking at the doors of opportunity and patiently wait for them to open eventually. "Stay in school, study hard and keep on trying, child," my mother had always told me. "And things will get better."

But that lone winter afternoon my fighting spirit had ebbed to an all-time low. Suffering seemed unconquerable. I had become frustrated, embittered and disillusioned about knocking at doors of opportunity, which seemed to shut more the harder and more persistently I knocked.

I felt unloved, unwanted, abandoned and betrayed by a world that seemingly denied me an opportunity to find my niche. A world that seemed to hold out nothing to me but hunger, pain, violence and death. I didn't feel that the world or anybody owed me anything, but I felt that the world and everybody had to at least give me an opportunity to prove my worth, to make something of myself, whatever that something might be.

That lone winter afternoon, however, I felt that I had lived long enough. I felt that life could never, would never, change from how it was for me. Suffering had finally succeeded in penetrating to my very soul and established within my consciousness a certain fear of living. Thus, as I stood dreamily by the stoop, twirling a switchblade knife between my trembling hands, oblivious to the world around me, I thought of killing myself. How was I going to do it?

My mind went back to the many afternoons I had spent watching movies about powerful and fearless white gladiators with sharp swords and glistening daggers. One of the stock phrases I had learned from watching these movies was "to die with honour." I recalled how a humiliated or troubled or helpless or vanquished gladiator would elect "to die with honour," by secretly removing himself from all eyes of restraint, from all human presence, to a spot known only to himself, and there end his miserable life—usually by plunging a long, sharp and gleaming sword or dagger into his heart or guts.

That afternoon I was predisposed to exacting the same justice on myself. I felt that if I had to die—and that afternoon I wanted to die —then I would die like a gladiator. There was unanimity among the boys I played swordfights with that the best way was to die like a gladiator.

As I stood there on the stoep, however, my mind was in utter confusion. Doubts, fears, restraints cluttered my thoughts. Should I go ahead and do it? If so, when? Should I leave a note for my mother? Where should I leave it? How did it feel when someone died? Where should I plunge the knife: in the stomach or in the heart? Would I die a quick death or a lingering one? What would everybody say when they found my corpse? Would anyone cry? Would anyone care? Did I have the courage to do it?

While standing there, lost in a world of confusion and fear, my mother unexpectedly joined me. I tried hiding the knife behind my back, but she had already seen it. She remained still alongside me, alternately looking at me, then at the knife. Overwhelmed with guilt, I dropped my eyes. A few moments passed in tense silence. Still she didn't say anything, seemingly waiting for me to say something, to explain the reason for the knife, and why I was trembling.

After a long while, I said, in a soft, trembling voice, "Mama, what would happen if I were to die? Would anybody miss me? Would anybody care? Will it matter to anyone?"

As I said that, an expression of deep concern swept my mother's face, and she tried to hide it. She didn't say anything for a long time. She seemed deep in thought. It made me feel even guiltier. Her hand reached out and touched me. Her eyes strained and became watery. I wondered what she was going to do or say.

Finally, in a surprisingly calm voice she said: "Look at your sisters over there." She pointed at Merriam and Dinah playing in the mud. Though they had been there since I came out to the stoep, I hadn't been conscious of their presence till now. I looked at them, twirling little sticks inside tins filled with mud, pretending to be cooking, porridge maybe. Blowflies droned about them, from time to time settling on the mucus dribbling from their noses into their mouths. They seemed lost in their own little world of mud, pebbles and tins, and oblivious to my suicide attempt.

"They'll miss you very much," my mother sighed deeply. The tone of her voice had changed, suddenly, to one full of sorrow. "They'll have no big brother to help them and to protect them. They'll have no big brother to look up to. They'll have no big brother to help them go to school when they grow up. They'll miss you very much."

I was very much touched by what she said. I remembered the many times my sisters had turned to me for help whenever anyone harassed them. I remembered the many times I had told my mother that when I was done with school, I would go out and work so that I could help my sisters go to school and become nurses and teachers. Remembering all that made me start crying. My mother wrapped her arms around me.

"Don't cry now," she said, "you're a big boy."

I felt stupid.

"Will you miss me too, Mama?" I sobbed.

She held me tighter and said: "I would miss you more than anyone else. I too would want to die if you were to die. You're the only hope I have. I love you very much."

I continued weeping. The tears seemed to want to come out. I felt deeply ashamed and guilty of some unknown wrong.

"Now give me that knife," I heard my mother say. I couldn't see her because my eyes were now swimming in tears. I extended my hand and opened my palm, and she took the knife.

"Promise me you'll never again think of doing what you were thinking of doing with the knife," she said.

I nodded penitently, and broke into a weak smile. Following that incident my mother kept a close watch on my temperament, and whenever I seemed unusually moody, sullen, angry or depressed, she would call me aside and we would talk about whatever was bothering me. I always felt better after talking to her, and gradually, my life became normal.

For years afterward, I was to think of that suicide attempt in the following terms: whenever the troubles of the world seem too much, it helps to have someone loving and understanding to share those troubles with; and life takes its true meaning in proportion to one's daily battles against suffering.

29 Granny unexpectedly lost one of her two gardening jobs. For some time she was fearful that with only eight rands a month from her one job, she would not be able to pay rent, buy food and keep Uncle Piet and Aunt Bushy in school. But she was lucky. Through a friend she found another gardening job in Rosebank, one of Johannesburg's posh whites-only suburbs. Her new employers were an English-speaking family, the Smiths.

Not long after she starting working for the Smiths, she began bringing home stacks of comic books: *Batman and Robin, Richie Rich, Dennis the Menace, The Justice League of America, Tarzan of the Apes, Sherlock Holmes Mysteries, Superman, The Incredible Hulk, Thor—God of Thunder, The Fantastic Four* and *Spiderman.*

Having never owned a comic book in my life, I tirelessly read them over and over again, the parts I could understand. Such voracious reading was like an anesthesia, numbing me to the harsh life around me. Soon comic books became the joy of my life, and everywhere I went I took one with me: to the river, to a soccer game, to the lavatory, to sleep, to the store and to school, where I would hide it under the desk, reading it furtively when the teacher was busy at the blackboard, and getting caned each time I was found out.

Because I had comic books, every kid in the neighbourhood wanted to be my friend. I started a small business of charging a penny to lend one out. I was very happy, living in this world of fantasy and escapism.

A year went by. The Smiths continued giving Granny comic books. Wondering why white people would bother giving a black person anything, I said to her one afternoon: "Granny, why are your white people giving you all these comics?"

"Well," she said with a smile, "Mrs. Smith once asked me if I had any little boys. I told her all about you and your good work at school, and she started giving me the comics. She has a son about your age."

I couldn't quite understand why white people would suddenly give a black child things. Out of the goodness of their hearts? No, white people had no hearts—that I had been learning every day of my life. They were to be feared and hated.

"What kinds of white people do you work for, Granny?" I asked.

"What do you mean?"

"You've been working for white people all your life," I said, "and they have never given you as much as a rag. You yourself always said that."

"The Smiths are nice white people," she said, "but there aren't many like them around."

Midway into my eleventh year, Granny started bringing home strange-looking books and toys. The books, which she said were Mrs. Smith's son's schoolbooks, bore no resemblance whatsoever to the ones we used at my school. Their names were as strange to me as their contents: *Pinocchio, Aesop's Fables* and the fairy tales of the brothers Grimm. At this point, because of reading comic books, my English had improved to a level where I could read simple sentences. I found the books enthralling.

The chest of toys contained nursery-rhyme booklets, Monopoly and word-association games, building blocks, Snakes-'n'-ladders, jigsaw puzzles and many other kinds of games no black child ever dreamed of having. My mother called in the Coloured woman next door, who had once worked as a nanny for white people, to come and explain the games to me. I learned the rules rapidly and was soon teaching George and my sisters.

These books and toys revealed to me a new reality. They moulded my thoughts and feelings and made me dream. My interest in learning increased. I no longer spent all my time playing soccer or fighting in gangs or hunting for money to go to the Bioscope. Instead I now stayed indoors, engrossed in attempting to master the Monopoly game, form English words with Boggle and figure out how the various toys worked, by meticulously taking them apart and reassembling them again.

Sometimes I would have a few friends over to play with me. At night, instead of my mother telling stories, I would tell stories of Hansel and Gretel, Pinocchio, Cinderella and the fables of Aesop. I was struck by the similarities between black and white people's stories.

Because of my habit of walking around telling my favourite stories to anyone who cared to listen, word soon got around the class that I knew nursery rhymes and stories teachers didn't know. My teacher got wind of it and called me before the class one morning to recite something.

I told the story of Hansel and Gretel.

"Where did you learn that?" the teacher gasped.

"From books, sir," I said with guarded pride.

"You—books—where did you suddenly get books from?" he demanded, mindful of my reputation of lacking in schoolbooks.

"From my grandmother, sir."

"If your grandmother has the kind of money to buy you expensive white people's books," the teacher said, "why can't she buy you cheap black books to use in school?"

"She doesn't buy the books, sir."

"Oh, yeah, where does she get them?"

"From the white people she works for, sir."

"How does she get them—steal them?" the teacher demanded.

"No," I cried defensively. "My grandmother doesn't steal. White people give them to her."

The teacher chuckled. He clasped the lapels of his faded, tight-fitting jacket and said, "Did I just hear you say that they give them to her? White people, my boy? Are you mad? What kind of white people would give books to a black man?"

"Nice white people, sir."

As if I had just uttered the joke of the century, the teacher burst into peals of maniacal laughter. The class joined in the guffaw. I boiled with anger and resentment.

"Listen here, my boy," the teacher said authoritatively, "I've been in this damn world long enough to know white people inside out, so don't lie to me. There's no such thing as a nice white man. Now, how does she get the books? Remember, 'honesty is the best policy,' and God can't stand black liars. So tell the truth—how does she get the books?"

"I swear, sir, white people give them to her," I said, almost in tears.

"What work does she do for them to give her books?"

I could not answer. I was embarrassed to reveal that Granny raked leaves and weeded gardens, afraid of being laughed at. Many of my classmates had parents who held jobs in factories, which made them look down on students whose parents did gardening. The teacher stared at me for an answer; I debated whether to lie.

Pride won out, and I decided to tell the truth and let them laugh if they wanted to. After all, I told myself, she was my grandmother, and was proud of me and loved me.

"She works in the garden, sir," I said, the words barely audible, and the word *garden* hardly coming out at all.

"What did you say?" demanded the teacher, obviously not having heard me.

"She works in the garden," I repeated softly; perspiration stood on my brow.

"Speak louder!"

"She works in the garden!" I shouted, and started crying. I hung my head in shame, expecting a salvo of laughter. There was none. A few students snickered; these the teacher went to with a grim face, cane in hand, and said in a deadly tone, "Get up and touch your toes!" The three students did as told, and the teacher lashed their buttocks. "Don't do that again!"

Turning to me, he said, "What's shameful about working in white people's gardens? My grandmother too worked there when I was going to school. That's how I was able to go through school. That's nothing to be ashamed of. Those are the kinds of jobs white people have in abundance for us. You should be thankful she's working there, otherwise you wouldn't be getting all those books."

From that day onward, I never again felt ashamed to tell people, when they asked me, that Granny was a gardener, or that she, my mother and my father never went to school. In a way, that incident helped me overcome the type of shame that leads many people to deny their heritage, to forget where they come from, for the sake of acceptance.

Shebeens gave life and soul to township drinking. In our neighbourhood there were about a dozen of them. Almost every household was a drinking parlor of some sort; those that weren't had neighbours that were.

Shebeens were considered illegal by authorities, for they took business away from government-run beer halls. The Peri-Urban Police therefore regularly raided them, arrested the owners and confiscated all kinds of hooch. But still shebeens thrived, for they were an irresistible and indispensable way of making ends meet, providing much-needed income to augment slave wages received from working for white people.

Many shebeens sold brandy, whisky and cartoons—a fermented sorghum brew made by the government, especially for black tastebuds. Cartoons were still fermenting when sold, and because of the pressure, sometimes exploded in the hands of some careless drinker. Along with selling cartoons, shebeen owners sold illegal concoctions brewed in the backyards, often under unsanitary conditions.

It was not uncommon for some desperate, enterprising shebeen queen to throw dirty shoes, tobacco leaves or dirty underwear into the brew to speed up fermentation, so as to sell it before the next raid. So intoxicating were these illegal drinks, that they had special names: *Mbamba* (Catch me), *Sibapala Mazenke* (Grab onto a fence after you drink me) and the perennial favourite, Kill Me Quick.

Bootlegging was a serious crime and those caught during raids were handed huge fines. Some were given long jail sentences or deported to the tribal reserves. Yet despite such hazards, the bootlegging club continued to grow; new members were added each day, more than making up for those arrested daily.

It came as no surprise, therefore, when one Friday evening my father said to my mother, as the family sat for dinner: "Now that we're both working, how about starting a little beer business. Other wives are doing it. Look at our neighbours, they've made such big profits they've even bought a new bathtub and a wardrobe."

Aware of the risks involved, my mother was quick to reply, "You know about raids on shebeens, don't you? Our pass and permit problems are enough to worry about."

"I'm not saying you should sell any of the illegal stuff," my father said, a thick lump of porridge in his hand. He dipped it into the *xixevo* (meat dish), stuffed the gravied porridge into his small mouth, chewed for one second, then swallowed with difficulty.

"What's not illegal about selling any kind of liquor without a license? You know Peri-Urban wants beer halls to be the only sellers of liquor in this township. So that the government can have money to spend on black programs, instead of spending that of white taxpayers."

Moulding another thick lump of porridge in his hand, my father said, "Then let us join stockvel. We don't need a license for that."

Stockvel was in vogue throughout the township. Carried out under the guise of a party, it worked in the following way: a group of households would get together and form a sort of club; under the terms of the club, each weekend a different member would host a party, which all other members are obligated by prior agreement to "support."

"Support" came in the payment by members of a fee, "stockvel money," to the host; and in return, they would be given free liquor and "stockvel plates"—dishes of chicken, rice and vegetables. The host raked in money from nonmembers as well, who paid cash for liquor and stockvel plates during the fete.

Stockvels had such a spirit of community to them that they were always well attended. It was not uncommon for a stockvel host to double, even triple, his investment.

But to become a stockvel member required large amounts of start-up money, the resourcefulness and shrewdness of an Indian trader and the elusiveness of a double agent, during police raids.

"Where do you think we'll get the kind of money needed to join a stockvel?" my mother asked.

"By combining our incomes," my father said. He asked for a second helping of porridge and giblets.

"My hard-earned money will be used for nothing but the children's schooling," my mother said.

"Don't give me that rubbish, woman," my father said hotly. He always raved when he could not get his way immediately. "You know I can't do it alone. Those damn bloody white bastards aren't paying me enough even to afford a pair of used underwear. I intend to quit the bloody fucking job as soon as the beer business is successful. I'm bloody tired of being told, '*Kom jong, kom jong; ons moet werk, ons moet werk; tyd is geld, tyd is geld!* [Come, boy, come, boy; we must work, we must work; time is money, time is money!]' by white boys the age of Johannes here, while they lounge about in easy chairs sipping whisky and brandy bought with money filched from my pay-check. It's high time I stopped being a slave and became my own boss."

A sarcastic smile playing on her face, my mother replied, "Maybe if you'd been saving all these years you've been working, instead of squandering money on liquor and dice, you'd have long become your own boss. Who knows, you might even be a millionaire. You have brains, Jackson, I will tell you that. But you choose not to use them. Whatever happened to that ambitious, hardworking, thrifty family man who swept me off my feet thirteen years ago? The man who once vowed to make it despite what white people told him?"

My mother's remarks wounded my father's pride. He leaped off his chair as though it were a brazier full of red-hot coals. "Don't lecture me, you hear, woman, don't lecture me!" he fumed. "I'm the man of this house. I wear the pants, not you! Watch your tongue or I'll cut it out, you hear! I'll cut it out!"—he shook a meatless chicken foot at my mother—"this bloody business of telling me, your husband and lord, how to run this house has to stop! Right at this moment, or you'll know why I'm called Mathabane!" He stamped a fist on the table; the table wobbled. Sinking back into his chair, he went on, blisteringly, "You seem to forget that I bought you! I own you. Your duty is to look after my children, cook for me and do what I say. And talking about cooking"—here he spat into his bowl of porridge—"this porridge tastes like shit. Whatever happened to your cooking skills!"

Not giving my mother an opportunity to answer, he went on, "Instead of putting your energies into cooking and raising children, as a good woman should, you put your energies into trying to be the man in this house. What kind of woman are you, heh?"

"I'm just what a woman should be," my mother said, with such coolness and poise that even I was shocked. "A woman who wants the best for her husband and children."

"If that's what you want," my father said complacently, "then let's work together. We both want the same things."

"Not until you mend your ways," my mother said. "Until you become a true husband and father, who cares about his family, and not waste money like one of those young men without responsibilities, I don't see how I can support you as a wife."

My father shook his balding head in disbelief. He said, "Do you know that what you're saying is grounds for my divorcing you? Were it not for *my* children, and the fact that your parents have long devoured my *lobola*, I would have long sent you packing. You're a good-for-nothing wife. Other wives uncomplainingly obey their husbands, who know best. But you—you—your words and behavior are like daggers driving into my back. What's possessing you, heh, woman? *Swikwembus* [demons]? How do you think we'll ever get ahead if everything I say you go against? Do you realise that stockvel may be the only way out of this pit of poverty?"

"That's where you're wrong, Jackson," my mother countered. "Educating our children is the only way out of this pit of poverty."

"Me? Wrong?" my father said, stupefied. "Are you calling me a liar, is that it? Am I a liar?"

"No one said you're a liar," my mother claimed. "I'm only telling you what I feel. Educating our children is the only way of securing our future. And for as long as I have an ounce of strength left in me, I'll work toward that goal."

Silence cloaked the room. My mother appeared uncompromising. My father scratched his head and knitted his brow, deep in thought. Suddenly his face lit up, like that of a man who, faced with utter and humiliating defeat, at the last minute strikes upon a brilliant, face-saving idea.

"You say I've not been a good husband and a father," my father said cagily. "Maybe you're right. But I'm prepared to turn a new leaf."

"What do you mean?" my mother asked dubiously.

"I'm prepared to make the following sacrifices if you'll agree to our joining stockvel. I'll quit gambling, and once we have our own beer business, I'll stop visiting shebeens. Isn't that what you've always wanted? My coming home every Friday night with the full paycheck?"

By now I had finished eating and was sitting in a corner pretending to be doing homework, although I was listening to all this incredible talk with keen interest. Had it not been for the tribal law which forbade children from intruding in adult conversations, I would have long said something, for I too had strong opinions about what was being discussed.

For instance, I had seen the kinds of miracles stockvel had wrought on families who took the risks. Their houses had been instantly transformed into what seemed liked palaces. They could afford new furniture, new beds, *tapeits* (linoleum flooring), cupboards stacked with food, kerosene lamps, gramophones and even used cars. The list was endless.

And more important to me, children from these families bought new schoolbooks and uniforms each year, went on all the school trips and spent lavishly during lunch breaks. Thinking about all this, I could not help but agree with my father, and wish my mother would too. Maybe this was the panacea we had been desperately searching for all these years.

To my surprise, my mother wasn't persuaded by my father's dramatic concessions. "Your quitting gambling and starting to bring home your full paycheck is no sacrifice, Jackson," she said, "not even a small one. As a man with a family to fend for, you should have been doing that all along. That's your responsibility as a father, and mine as a mother. So I'm glad you're assuming yours now. I'll continue with mine, which is to pay for the children's schooling. I admit we're struggling, we're poor—we may even get poorer the way things are going. And I'm not making much from working for that *Mgula* [Indian] Shortie. But the little I'm making has enabled Johannes to reach Standard Two. Florah Sub-B and soon, God willing, George will start Sub-A. So as far as I'm concerned, that's a lot to be thankful for."

"Do you think that with the peanuts you're making," my father sneered, "you'll be able to pay for their needs in years to come—till they reach university? Do words pay for books, school fees, uniforms, slates, shoes?"

"I may not be able to pay for all that," my mother said, "but I'll keep on trying. Besides, my mother says a friend of her employer wants a reliable washing girl, even if she doesn't have a permit. So maybe I'll finally have a better job. And I'll be able to pay for my children's schooling, seeing that they have no father to do it."

Confronted with my mother's resolve, my father appeared stymied. I wondered what he could possibly say to make my mother change her mind.

Breathing heavily, he said, "I don't know what's come over me to make me tolerate such blatant insubordination for so long. You must have bewitched me, or else I must be going mad."

Laughing, my mother said, "There's no witchcraft or madness about it. I don't think I'm being less of a wife by insisting on the best for our children. What future will they have without an education, tell me? Just look around you and you'll see what kind of jobs those who never went to school have. Garbage collectors, miners, maids, night soil collectors. Do you want our children to do the same? I don't. And when these children are through with school, and working and bringing in good money, and we're no longer living in this leaking shack, eating crumbs and leftovers, would you still be saying, 'I don't believe in schools?' Not if I know you well. And after thirteen years of being your slave, I know you, Jackson. You'll be boasting to the whole world that had it not been for you, the children wouldn't have become what they are."

How right my mother was. My father, in light of my continued successes at school, had begun claiming all the credit. For instance, each time we had visitors, my performance at school would come up for discussion, and my father would be quick to point out that I had "inherited his exceptional brain." Yet the next minute he would be

Granny with one of her great-grandchildren. (*Hajima Ota*)

My mother and father at home in Alexandra in 1985. (*Hajima Ota*)

Stan Smith and Bob Lutz on their way to the SAB (South African Breweries) Open Doubles Championship in 1977. (*Marjory Smith*)

Arthur Ashe during a tennis clinic in Soweto in 1973. (*Carole Dell*)

My brother, George, and sister Linah (*far right*) in front of our house in Alexandra. (*Hajima Ota*)

Full Gospel Church of God where my mother, brother and sisters and I were baptized. (*Hajima Ota*)

Aerial view of Johannesburg, also known to blacks as *Goli* (City of Gold). (*Hajima Ota*)

Children at communal tap, which often is the only source of water for over a dozen families. (*Hajima Ota*)

Whites-only restroom—an ever-present reminder of apartheid. (*Hajima Ota*)

Alexandra tennis courts where I first learned the game. (*Hajima Ota*)

Stan Smith posing with me at my graduation from Dowling College in 1983.

Bovet Community School—my primary school.

Children praying at assembly. (*Jeanne Moutoussamy-Ashe*)

A typical ghetto yard, an area containing shacks that house often a hundred people. (*Jeanne Moutoussamy-Ashe*)

Non-whites bridge. (*Jeanne Moutoussamy-Ashe*)

A bus for the so-called "Coloureds." (*Hajima Ota*)

warning my mother not to "waste money on school materials, because an education was a worthless thing to have as a black man." I could not understand the apparent contradiction.

My mother, who I thought had every right under the sun to bask in the glory of my success, was, on the contrary, willing to let my father upstage her. That also I could not understand; yet her humility made her dearer to me. I knew that deep in her heart, she was the proudest of all mothers because of my work at school. Of all the reasons that kept me plodding along the long and hard road of Bantu Education, the most important was that my mother and Granny were proud of me.

"Listen," my father said after a long pause. "If I pledge that part of the liquor profits be used to pay for the children's schooling, would you agree to back me up?" At this, he dug into the back pocket of his shabby overalls and pulled out a small brown envelope. "To show you I mean what I say," he went on, brandishing the envelope, "here's my wages for the week. Every penny." Turning to me, he said, "Johannes, count this money for your mother."

My mother stared at my father in astonishment. With trembling hands, I took the envelope and slowly counted the money. It was all there—ten rands and forty cents. This was the first time in years my father had brought his full wages home.

"So," my father said with deep satisfaction, "does this change your mind?"

Before my mother could answer, I said, "Please say yes, Mama. Please say yes."

"There's someone with good sense," my father said patronizingly. "So that education may not be that bad after all."

"Your father finally won you over, I see," my mother said, laughing.

"It's worth a try, Mama," I said. "Many children at school have parents who sell beer and run stockvels. And they have everything they need for school. Maybe Florah, George and I could be like them."

Our entrance into the beer-selling business didn't exactly work the miracles I had dreamed of. But my father did stop gambling. He now brought his full paycheck home every week. Also, he no longer stayed out late drinking; instead, he brought his drinking friends home.

With the beer-selling profits, my mother paid rent, took care of our school needs the best she could, sent any sick child to the clinic, bought luxuries like peanut butter, Milo, Pro-Nutro and Jungle Oats, and whatever was left of the money went into a small savings account —the family's first—which she had opened at Barclays Bank.

The liquor business flourished. Every Friday and Saturday night our two tiny rooms were packed with migrant workers, menial labourers and garbage collectors, buying drinks till well past midnight. There was no privacy for anyone. Each time we children wanted to sleep, we simply stole into a corner or under the table, shut out the noise and prayed that we were not stepped on or pissed on by drunks. Aside from an occasional ruckus, the atmosphere was one of conviviality.

With my knowledge of arithmetic, I became the household accountant. I got my mother to buy a notebook in which I wrote the names of all our customers, and the amounts they owed. Because many of our customers could not read, I at times felt tempted to cheat them by overcharging or making them pay for drinks they never had. I never yielded to the temptation; I made enough on tips.

I kept such meticulous records that soon I gained the trust of many of our customers. One group of illiterate migrant workers began asking me to read and write letters to and from the wives and children back in the tribal reserves.

They paid me, and I used the money to buy things for school. Many of the letters from the tribal reserves were about the day-to-day struggles of living there: children forced to leave school for lack of books and school fees; infants afflicted with polio, cholera, kwashiorkor, tuberculosis and various malnutrition-related diseases, many dying because there was no money to pay for medical treatment; plots of land confiscated by greedy tribal chiefs and their cohorts because of taxes in arrears; crop failure because of drought and pestilence; witchcraft accusations and persecutions—the list of miseries was endless.

I often cried when I read these letters, especially those detailing the suffering of children. One day I was reading one such letter to a migrant worker named Phineas, when I was overcome with feelings and started crying. Phineas patted me on the shoulder, consolingly, as we both sat on a makeshift bench of milk crates in his tiny shack.

"Now, now, my boy," he said. "I admit things are bad back

there, but not that bad. Look at it another way. If this one child is going to die, as the letter says, I'll still have six others left. I'm working seven days a week," he continued, "and one of these days I'll amass enough money to be able to take care of all their needs. Just you wait and see. Maybe I'll even afford to bribe one of those Peri-Urban bastards into giving me papers allowing my family to come live with me."

"But will they ever give you the permit?" I asked. Phineas had been working as a security guard in the city for ten years, and in that time, because of Influx Control laws, he had visited his wife and children only ten times. They had never been to see him.

"I'll keep on trying," he said, as a look of despair crossed his haggard face. A huge, black fly clung to the grimy cardboard wall in front of us. Phineas saw it. Grinning, he gathered in one sweep all the mucus in his flaring nostrils and let fly a blob as thick as a hailstone. The fly never knew what hit it.

Phineas was one of thousands of black migrant workers in Alexandra forced to live hundreds of miles from their families because of Influx Control laws, which discouraged black family life in what the government called "white South Africa." In the township, no other group lived as unnaturally as the migrant workers. Housed mostly in sterile single-sex barracks, they were prey to prostitution, *Matanyula*, alcoholism, robbery and senseless violence; they existed under such stress and absorbed so much emotional pain that tears, grief, fear, hope and sadness had become alien to most of them. They were the walking dead.

Stripped of their manhood, they hated the white man with every fibre of their being. Anger would leap into their eyes each time the words *white man* were uttered. Rage would heave their chest each time something or someone reminded them that it was the white man who kept their families away from them. Each time I saw that anger and hate, I knew that they felt a pain so deep it could not be expressed; that though they laughed and chaffed with one another, as they tried in vain to drown their sorrows in gourds of liquor, something inside them was slowly dying.

There is a death far worse than physical death, and that is the death of the mind and soul, when, despite toiling night and day, under sweltering heat, torrential rain, blistering winds, you still cannot make enough to clothe, shelter and feed your loved ones, suffering miles away, forcibly separated from you.

30 No longer able to afford rent for her shack, Granny moved from Fifteenth Avenue to a smaller shack on Eighth Avenue. As often as I could, I spent evenings at her place. Each time I was there she made it clear that I was her favourite grandchild. She would treat me to traditional cooking and tell me marvellous stories of her youth. Whenever I needed a particular book for school, and my mother didn't for some reason have the money to buy it, Granny would. She was very proud of my schoolwork.

Also, whenever I was at Granny's, I would read Uncle Piet's and Aunt Bushy's schoolbooks, even though both were several standards ahead of me. They were now in Standards Four and Six respectively. Granny had serious doubts about being able to see them go any further, for the cost of black education had risen dramatically, and her earnings from gardening had not. There was even talk that Aunt Bushy would have to leave school upon completing Standard Six, and look for a factory job, so she could help pay for Uncle Piet's schooling.

One late afternoon Granny returned from work very excited. I was sitting by the kitchen window memorizing a tribal poem for presentation at school when, as she came through the front door, she dropped the stack of old newspapers she was carrying on her *doek*-covered head, and hobbled toward my mother, who was busy cleaning around the kitchen.

"Mujaji, he's agreed! He's agreed! He's finally agreed!" Granny cried, throwing her long, bracelet-covered arms wide open to embrace my mother.

"Really," was all my mother uttered as she leaped from the floor and threw herself into Granny's arms. The two started dancing about the kitchen. Both then came to where I was sitting, puzzled. Granny hugged and kissed me, while my mother looked on, beaming with smiles.

"What's going on?" I said, pulling away from Granny in bewilderment. "Are you both mad?"

"Glory be to God in the highest," Granny said, almost out of breath. "A miracle happened today, child," she added enigmatically.

"What miracle?" I wrinkled my brow. In a flash, remembering that Granny had once said that it would be a miracle if she were ever to find some decent man to marry her, I said, with an understanding smile, "Congratulations, Granny, who's the lucky man?"

Granny stared at me with baffled eyes. My mother interjected, laughing, "No silly, your grandma didn't get married. The miracle concerns you."

I was about to ask for an explanation when Granny jumped in excitedly and said, "Remember the games and books I'm always bringing you?"

"Yes, what about them?"

"You know about Mrs. Smith, don't you?" Granny went on. I nodded. "Well, some time ago I asked her if I could bring you with me so she could see you. She agreed, but said that she had to get permission from her husband because it is uncommon for black children to be in white neighbourhoods. Today she's told me that he's also agreed. So next Tuesday I'll be taking you with me."

"I'm not going," I declared.

"What!" Granny cried.

"I said I'm not going," I repeated, casually going through the stack of newspapers and removing the comic sections.

"Of course you'll go, silly," my mother said.

Turning and facing her, I said, impetuously, "How can I go! How can I go! I can't afford to miss school on Tuesday. We have exams," I lied.

"Don't worry about school," my mother said. "I'll get permission from the principal. It's very important that you go with your grandma."

"I don't want to go," I insisted. "I don't want to have anything to do with white people."

Granny shook her head mournfully and muttered, "Lord, hear this foolish child." She stared at me as though she did not know me. I had wounded her feelings. I wished there was some way I could communicate to her the naked terror the sight of white people evoked in me, some way to convince her that the last thing I wanted to do in this world was to set foot in the white world.

"Why are you doing this to me, child," Granny said at length, in a quivering voice. Tears stood in her wrinkled eyes. "You don't know how long I begged Mrs. Smith to let me bring you. You don't know what this means, do you child? Don't you love me? Don't you love your grandma?" Her voice sounded so hurt that for a minute I thought of giving in.

"I love you very much, Granny," I said with feeling. "You're not the problem. I—" I felt so guilty I couldn't go on. I grabbed several comic strips and headed out-of-doors, away from it all. But my mother, who had been standing alongside the door, reached out and grabbed my arm as I turned the doorknob. "Wait just a minute, you ungrateful fool," she said in a deadly tone. "Before you leave this house, I want to hear you tell your grandma, 'I'll go with you next week,' Either that, or you leave this house for good."

She meant it. Searching for a way out, I said, "Why do Granny's white people all of a sudden want to see me? What's so special about me? Why not someone else? George or Uncle Piet, for instance."

Granny replied. "Because since I started working for them a year ago, I've been telling them what a smart grandson I have. That's why they've been giving you all those books, games and toys. Now they've finally agreed to see you in person."

"Why?"

"Stop asking why, you fool," my mother said, her face working up in anger. "Mrs. Smith's son is about your age. You know what that means? It means you'll get lots of *magabulela* [hand-me-downs] once they get to know you personally. This is a once-in-a-lifetime opportunity. You're always complaining about not having decent clothes to wear during Christmas, about not having books to read, yet here you are throwing away a chance to get all those things, and more. Remember what I once told you about knocking at the doors of opportunity? Well, this time those doors are wide open, and all you have to do is walk right in."

"Your mother is right, child," Granny said in support. "Mrs. Smith's son gets so many new things every day that he doesn't know what to do with the old ones, except throw them away. Don't throw away this opportunity, child, or you'll regret it the rest of your life."

"Over my dead body will he throw it away," my mother declared. I capitulated. But not before asking Granny to promise to be by my side at all times while we were in the white world; she agreed. She then lectured me on how to behave when among whites: "Talk only when talked to; wear a smile, preferably your widest one, at all times; say, 'Yes, madam,' to Mrs. Smith, and 'Yes, *baas*,' to Mr. Smith, and 'Yes, master,' to their son." That evening my father gave permission that I could go. He added, "Ask the *baas* if he's got any old clothes he wants to get rid of. I badly need underwear and socks."

On Monday, the eve of the biggest day in my life, my mother went to the principal and told him that I would be absent from school the next day. That evening I had the most thorough bath ever, more thorough than the one I had on my first day at school. Though by this time teachers at school had whipped the saying "Cleanliness is next to Godliness" into me—I now washed my face regularly, trimmed my fingernails every week with my father's razor, kept my hair short, combed and free of dandruff and lice, and brushed my teeth each morning using my left index finger as a toothbrush, and ash from the brazier as toothpaste (real toothbrush and toothpaste were luxuries we couldn't afford)—my mother insisted on scrubbing me herself.

"But I'm man enough to wash myself," I protested.

"You may be," she replied. "But I'm not taking any chances. You're going to spend an entire day among white people, the cleanest people on earth. The last thing they need is a filthy black boy contaminating their home. This bar of Lifebuoy soap will make you smell like fresh flowers," she added, smiling.

"I don't want to smell like flowers," I said, rubbing my eyes of suds, "I'm not a girl."

Now came the time to decide what to wear to look presentable in front of whites. The choice was easy; my sparse wardrobe took care of that. I had a shabby, tight-fitting khaki safari suit my parents had bought me two Christmases ago. My mother went next door and borrowed a pair of matching shoes, but the shoes were so big I had to stuff them with paper to be able to walk without leaving them behind. My father loaned me one of his three moth-eaten, gaudy ties, with a tongue so wide it spanned the width of my waist.

The seven o'clock bus for blacks to Johannesburg was jam-packed with men and women on their way to the white world to work. A huge sign above the driver's booth read:

AUTHORIZED TO CARRY ONLY 65 SEATED
PASSENGERS, AND 15 STANDING.

But there must have been close to a hundred perspiring people squeezed into the stuffy bus. People sat on top of one another, some were sandwiched in the narrow aisle between the rows of seats, and some crowded on the steps. I sat on Granny's lap, in the middle of the bus, by a large smudged window. As the bus droned past Alexandra's boundaries, I glued my eyes to the window, anticipating my first look at the white world. What I saw made me think I had just made a quantum leap into another galaxy. I couldn't stop asking questions.

"What are those?"

"Skyscrapers."

"Why do they reach all the way to the sky?"

"Because many white people live and work in them."

Seconds later. "Wow! look at all those nice houses, Granny! They're so big! Do many white people live and work there too?"

"No, those are mansions. Each is owned by one family."

"By one family!" I cried in disbelief. Each mansion occupied an area about three times that of the yard I lived in, yet the latter was home for over twenty families.

"Yes," Granny said matter-of-factly. "Your grandpa, when he first came to Johannesburg, worked for one such family. The family was so rich they owned an aeroplane."

"Why are there so many cars in the white people's homes?"

"Because they like to have many cars."

"Those people dressed in white, what game are they playing?"

"The men are playing cricket. Master Smith plays that too. The women are playing tennis. Mrs. Smith plays it too, on Tuesday and Thursday."

Suddenly the bus screeched to a halt, and people crashed into each other. I was thrown into the back of the wooden seat in front of me. Smarting, I asked, "Why did the bus suddenly stop? I didn't see any robots [street lights]."

"Look over there," Granny pointed. "White schoolchildren are crossing the road."

I gazed through the window and for the first time in my life saw white schoolchildren. I scrutinized them for any differences from black schoolchildren, aside from colour. They were like little mannequins. The boys were neatly dressed in snow-white shirts, blazers with badges, preppy caps with badges, ties matching the badges, shiny black and brown shoes, worsted knee-high socks. The girls wore pleated gymdresses with badges, snow-white shirts, caps with badges, blazers with badges, ties matching badges, shining black and brown shoes. A few of the girls had pigtails. On the back of each boy and girl was slung a schoolbag; and each frail, milky-white arm had a wristwatch on it. It suddenly struck me that we didn't even own a clock; we had to rely on cocks for time.

The white schoolchildren were filing out of a large, red-brick building with many large windows, in front of which were beds of multi-coloured flowers. A tall black man wearing a traffic uniform, a whistle between his thick lips, stood in the middle of the paved road, one hand raised to stop traffic, the other holding a sign that read in English and Afrikaans:

CHILDREN CROSSING
STOP
KINDERS STAP OOR

None of this orderly and safe crossing of the street ever took place at my school; we had to dash across.

The red-brick building stood on a vast tract of land with immaculate lawns, athletic fields, swings, merry-go-rounds, an Olympic-sized swimming pool, tennis courts and rows of brightly leafed trees. In the driveway leading to the entrance of the building, scores of yellow school buses were parked. Not even the best of tribal schools in Alexandra—in the whole of South Africa—came close to having such magnificent facilities. At our school we didn't even have a school bus. Oh, how I envied the white schoolchildren, how I longed to attend schools like theirs.

Minutes after all the white schoolchildren were safely across, traffic moved. At the next bus stop, we got off, and crossed the street when the robot flashed green. As we walked along the pavement, headed for Granny's workplace, I clutched her long dress, afraid of letting go, lest I be swallowed by the tremendous din of cars zooming up and down and honking in the busy streets. I began feeling dizzy as my eyes darted from one wonder to the next.

There were so many new and fantastic things around me that I walked as if in a dream. As we continued down the road, I became increasingly conscious of the curious looks white people gave us, as if we were a pair of escaped monkeys. Occasionally, Granny and I had to jump off the pavement to make way for *madams* and their poodles and English toy spaniels. By constantly throwing my eyes sideways, I accidentally bumped into a parking meter.

We went up a side street. "There is Mrs. Smith's house," Granny remarked as she led me up a long driveway of a beautiful villa-type house surrounded by a well-manicured lawn with several beds of colourful, sweet-smelling flowers and rosebushes. We went to a steel gate in the back of the yard, where Granny rang a bell.

"I'm here, madam," she shouted through the gate. Immediately a dog started barking from within; I trembled.

Granny calmed me. A door creaked open, and a high-pitched woman's voice called out, "I'm coming, Ellen. Quiet, Buster, you naughty dog, it's Ellen." The barking ceased. Presently the gate clicked open, and there appeared a short, slender white woman with silver hair and slightly drooping shoulders. She wore white slacks, a white sweater, white shoes and a white visor.

"I was just getting ready to leave for tennis," she said to Granny; she had not yet seen me.

"Madam, guess who I have with me today," Granny said with the widest smile.

I appeared like a Jack-in-the-box. "Oh, my, you finally brought him with you!" Mrs. Smith exclaimed.

Breaking into a wide smile, revealing gleaming teeth, several of which were made of gold, she continued, "My, what a big lad he is! What small ears!"—touching them playfully—"Is he really your grandson, Ellen?" The warmth in her voice somehow reduced my fears of her; her eyes shone with the same gentleness of the Catholic sisters at the clinic.

"Yes, madam," Granny said proudly; "this is the one I've been telling you about. This is the one who'll some day go to university, like Master Clyde, and take care of me."

"I believe you, Ellen," said Mrs. Smith. "He looks like a very smart pickaninny." Turning to me, she asked, "How old are you?"

"Eleven, madam, eleven," I said, with so wide a smile I thought my jaws would lock.

"He's a year younger than Master Clyde," Granny said, "though the master is much bigger."

"A little chubby, you mean," Mrs. Smith said with a smile. "If you knew how much the little master eats, Ellen; I'm afraid he'll soon turn into a piglet. Sometimes I regret not having had another child. With a sibling, Master Clyde might have turned out differently. As it is, he's so spoiled as an only child."

"Pickaninny has one brother and three sisters," Granny said of me, "and the fifth one is on the way."

"My God! What a large family! " Mrs. Smith exclaimed. "What's the pickaninny's name?"

Using pidgin English, I proceeded not only to give my name and surname, but also my grade in school, home address, tribal affiliation, name of school, principal and teacher—all in a feverish attempt to justify Granny's label of me as a "smart one."

Mrs. Smith was astounded. "What a clever, clever pickaninny!" She turned to a tall, lean black man with an expressionless face and slightly stooping shoulders, dressed in housekeeper's livery (khaki shirt and pants), who had just emerged from the house and who led a poodle on a leash, and said, "Did you hear that, Absalom? Bantu [black] children are smart. Soon they'll be running the country." Absalom simply tortured out a grin and took the poodle for a walk, after receiving instructions to bring brandy, whisky, wine and gin from the bottle store. Granny remarked that I was a "clever pickaninny" because of all the toys, games and comic books I had received from Master Clyde. Mrs. Smith seemed extremely pleased to hear that.

Before Mrs. Smith left for tennis, she said, "Ellen, your breakfast is near the washing machine in the garage. I'll be back sometime this afternoon. Please see to it that the flowers near the pool are watered, and that the rosebushes near the front of the gate are trimmed."

After a breakfast of coffee and peanut butter-and-jam sandwiches, Granny took out her gardening tools from the shed, and we started working. As the two of us went about the large yard, I raked leaves and watered the flowers; Granny weeded the lawn. Mrs. Smith's neighbour's children kept on casting curious glances over the fence. From the way they looked at me, it seemed they were seeing a black child for the first time in their lives.

At midday, despite a scorching sun, Granny, seemingly indefatigable, went about with impressive skill trimming the rosebushes as we talked about trees and flowers and how to best cultivate them.

"Someday I'll build a house as big and beautiful as Mrs. Smith's," I said to Granny. "And a garden just as big and beautiful."

"Then I'll be your gardener," Granny said with a smile.

Toward early afternoon Mrs. Smith returned. She called me to the car to remove several shopping bags from the backseat. She took her tennis rackets, closed the doors, then sighed, "Phew, what a tiring day. Don't ever play tennis," she said to me, "it's a killer."

"What's tennis, madam?" I asked.

"You don't know tennis?" she exclaimed. "What sports do you play?"

"Soccer, madam."

"Ugh, that dangerous sport. Soccer is too rough. You should try tennis someday. It's a gentlemen's sport. Wouldn't you like to be a gentleman?"

"I would like to be a gentleman, madam," I replied, even though I hadn't the faintest idea what constituted a gentleman.

"Do you have tennis courts in Alexandra?"

"Yes, madam." The stadium where I played soccer was adjacent to four ramshackle sand courts, used primarily by kitchen girls and kitchen boys on their day off.

"Then I'll see if I can find an old racket for you," she said.

As we were talking, a busload of white schoolchildren stopped in front of the house, and a young boy, with a mop of rebellious brown hair, alighted and ran up the driveway toward Mrs. Smith. After giving her a kiss, he turned and demanded, "Who is he, Mother?"

"That's Ellen's grandson. The one you've been giving all those comic books and toys to."

"What is he doing here?"

"He's visiting us."

"What for? I don't want him here."

"Why not, Clyde," Mrs. Smith said, "he's a nice pickaninny. Ellen is always nice to you, isn't she?"—the boy nodded with pursed lips—"now be nice to her grandson. Now run along inside and Absalom will show you the things I bought you today."

"Did you get my new bicycle and roller skates?"

"Yes, they'll be delivered Saturday. Now run in and change, and have something to eat. Then maybe you can play with pickaninny."

"I don't play with Kaffirs," the white boy declared. "At school they say we shouldn't."

"Watch your filthy mouth, Clyde," Mrs. Smith said, flushing crimson. "I thought I told you a million times to leave all that rubbish about Kaffirs in the classroom. Ellen's people are not Kaffirs, you hear! They're Bantus. Now go in and do as I told you." Turning to Granny, pruning a rosebush nearby, Mrs. Smith said, in a voice of someone fighting a losing battle, "You know, Ellen, I simply don't understand why those damn uncivilized Boers from Pretoria teach children such things. What future does this country have if this goes on?"

"I agree *makulu*, madam," Granny said, wiping her sweaty brow with her forearm. "All children, black and white, are God's children, madam. The preacher at my church tells us the Bible says so. 'Suffer little children to come unto me, and forbid them not; for of such is the kingdom of heaven,' the Bible says. Is that not so, madam? Do you believe in the words of the Bible, madam?"

"I'm afraid you're right, Ellen," Mrs. Smith said, somewhat touched. "Yes, I do believe in the Bible. That's why I cannot accept the laws of this country. We white people are hypocrites. We call ourselves Christians, yet our deeds make the Devil look like a saint. I sometimes wish I hadn't left England."

I was struck by the openness of the discussion between Granny and Mrs. Smith.

"You're not like most white people I've worked for, madam," Granny said. "Master and you are kind toward our people. You treat us like human beings."

Mrs. Smith didn't answer; she hurried back indoors. Shortly thereafter, Clyde emerged in a pair of denims and a T-shirt advertising a South African rock group. He called out to me. "Come here, pickaninny. My mother says I should show you around."

I went.

I followed him around as he showed me all the things his parents regularly bought him: toys, bicycles, go-carts, pinball machines, Ping-Pong tables, electric trains. I only half-listened: my mind was preoccupied with comparing my situation with his. I couldn't understand why he and his people had to have all the luxuries money can buy, while I and my people lived in abject poverty. Was it because they were whites and we were black? Were they better than we? I could not find the answers; yet I felt there was something wrong about white people having everything, and black people nothing.

We finally came to Clyde's playroom. The room was roughly the size of our house, and was elaborately decorated with posters, pennants of various white soccer and cricket teams, rock stars and photographs of Clyde in various stages of development. But what arrested my attention were the stacks of comic books on the floor, and the shelves and shelves of books. Never had I seen that many books in my life; even our school, with a student population of over two thousand, did not have half as many books. I was dazed.

Sensing that I was in awe of his magnificent library, Clyde said, "Do you have this many books in your playroom?"

"I don't have a playroom."

"You don't have a playroom," he said bug-eyed. "Can you read?" he smiled sinisterly. "Our boy Absalom can't. And he says black children aren't taught much English at school."

"I can read a little English," I said.

"I doubt if you can read any of my books. Here, read," he ordered, pulling one out of the shelves. The book was thick, looked formidable.

I nervously opened a page, toiled through a couple lines, encountering long words I could not pronounce, let alone understand their meaning. Shaking my head in embarrassment, I handed the book back, "I can't read this type of English."

"Then you must be retarded," Clyde laughed. Though he might have meant it in jest, my pride was deeply wounded. "This book is by William Shakespeare," he went on, waving it in my face, "the greatest English writer that ever lived. I could read it from cover to cover when I was half your age. But I don't blame you if you can't. My teachers tell us that Kaffirs can't read, speak or write English like white people because they have smaller brains, which are already full of tribal things. My teachers say you're not people like us, because you belong to a jungle civilization. That's why you can't live or go to school with us, but can only be our servants."

"Stop saying that rubbish, you naughty boy," Mrs. Smith said angrily as she entered the room just in time to catch the tail end of her son's knowledge of black people's intelligence, as postulated by the doctrine of apartheid. "How many times have I told you that what your teachers say about black people is not true?"

"What do you know, Mama?" Clyde retorted impudently, "you're not a teacher. Besides, there are textbooks where it's so written."

"Still it's not true," insisted Mrs. Smith. "Everything that's in your books is not necessarily true, especially your history books about this country." Changing the subject, she said, "Show him your easy books, and then get your things ready so I can drive you over to your friend's birthday party." Clyde quickly ran down his long list of "easy" books: *The Three Musketeers, Treasure Island, David Copperfield*, the Hardy Boys series, the Sherlock Holmes series, *Tom Sawyer, Robinson Crusoe, The Swiss Family Robinson, The Hunchback of Notre Dame, Black Beauty, A Tale of Two Cities*, and so on. Oh, how I envied Clyde's collection of books. I would have given my life to own just a handful of them.

The remark that black people had smaller brains and were thus incapable of reading, speaking or writing English like white people had so wounded my ego that I vowed that, whatever the cost, I would master English, that I would not rest till I could read, write and speak it just like any white man, if not better. Finally, I had something to aspire to.

Back with Granny, I told her to be on the lookout whenever Mrs. Smith junked any books. At the end of the day, as Granny and I prepared to leave, I was given a small box by Mrs. Smith.

"It's from Clyde," she said. "He's sorry that he treated you badly. He's promised not to do it again. I'll see to it he keeps his promise.

Come and help Ellen in the garden whenever you can; that way you'll earn some pocket money."

The box contained a couple shirts, pants and jerseys. Underneath the articles of clothing was a copy of *Treasure Island*.

31 To learn to express my thoughts and feelings effectively in English became my main goal in life. I saw command of the English language as the crucial key with which to unlock doors leading into that wonderful world of books revealed to me through the reading of Robert Louis Stevenson's gripping tale of buried treasure, mutiny on the high seas, one-legged seamen and the old sea song that I could recite even in my dreams:

> *Fifteen men on a dead man's chest*
> *Yo-ho-ho, and a bottle of rum.*

My heart ached to explore more such worlds, to live them in the imagination in much the same way as I lived the folktales of my mother and grandmother. I reasoned that if I somehow kept improving my English and ingratiated Mrs. Smith by the fact, then possibly she would give me more books like *Treasure Island* each time Granny took me along. Alas, such trips were few and far between. I could not afford to skip school regularly; and besides, each trip did not yield a book. But I clung to my dream.

A million times I wondered why the sparse library at my tribal school did not carry books like *Treasure Island*, why most of the books we read had tribal points of view. I would ask teachers and would be told that under the Bantu Education law black children were supposed to acquire a solid foundation in tribal life, which would prepare them for a productive future in their respective homelands. In this way the dream of Dr. Verwoerd, prime minister of South Africa and the architect of Bantu Education, would be realised, for he insisted that "the native child must be taught subjects which will enable him to work with and among his own people; therefore there is no use misleading him by showing him the green pastures of European society, in which he is not allowed to graze. Bantu Education should not be used to create imitation whites."

How I cursed Dr. Verwoerd and his law for prescribing how I should feel and think. I started looking toward the Smiths to provide me with the books about a different reality. Each day Granny came back from work around five in the afternoon, I would be the first to meet her at the gate, always with the same question, "Any books for me today?" Many times there weren't any. Unable to read new English books on a regular basis, I reread the ones I had over and over again, till the pages become dog-eared. With each reading each book took on new life, exposed new angles to the story, with the result that I was never bored.

My bleak vocabulary did not diminish my enthusiasm for reading. I constantly borrowed Mr. Brown's pocket-size dictionary to look up meanings of words, and would memorize them like arithmetic tables and write them in a small notebook. Sometimes I would read the dictionary. My pronunciation was appalling, but I had no way of finding out. I was amazed at the number of words in the English language, at the fact that a word could have different shades of meaning, or that certain words looked and sounded alike and yet differed greatly in meaning. Would I ever be able to learn all that?

At the same time I was discovering the richness of the English language I began imitating how white people talked, in the hope of learning proper pronunciation. My efforts were often hilarious, but my determination increased with failure. I set myself the goal of learning at least two new English words a day.

At this time Uncle Pietrus, on my father's side, had moved into our yard. A bachelor with some education, he read the *World* and the black edition of the *Star* every day. Each evening I would go to his shack to borrow the two papers. I often found him through with chores, and the two of us would sit and discuss the mainstay of black news: crime, sports (mainly boxing and soccer), murder stories (the staggering statistics and the gruesome ways through which blacks killed blacks) and the latest police raids and shebeen swoops.

On Mondays and Fridays we filled out Jackpots (crossword puzzles that paid cash prizes to winners). We never won anything, but my vocabulary benefited from the exercise. I began looking for opportunities to use my improved vocabulary in conversation. But such opportunities were rare: all talk, all teaching, all thinking for that matter, at my school was in Tsonga. The only time I encountered English was during the English period, one of the shortest in school, devoted mainly to honing servanthood English. For lack of practise I soon forgot many of the words and had to relearn them, only to forget them again, only to relearn them. I refused to quit.

My love for reading removed me from the streets and curtailed my involvement in gangs. This infuriated the leaders of my gang, the Thirteenth Avenue Tomahawks. Friends within warned me that there was a plot afoot to teach me a lesson for not showing up at the gang's fights. The Thirteenth Avenue Tomahawks fought just about every week, against this or that street's gang, for reasons ranging from territorial disputes to harassment of each other's girlfriends.

One weekday afternoon while I was splitting wood in front of our house the leader of the Thirteenth Avenue Tomahawks, a sixteen-year-old delinquent named Jarvas—whose claim to notoriety was that he once stabbed a rival to death over a girl he later made pregnant and dumped—and several of his henchmen approached me. The Tomahawks were in the middle of a protracted, two-pronged war against rival gangs, the Mongols from Sixteenth Avenue and the Dirty Dozen from Eleventh Avenue.

"Are you still one of us?" Jarvas demanded, in a tone suggesting that he normally let his knife do the talking, but was doing me a favour by giving me a chance to exonerate myself.

My heart was no longer into gangs, but I replied, "Yes."

"Then why haven't you been in any of our recent fights?"

"I've been too busy."

"So busy you neglect your gang duties?" he sneered.

"I've had too much schoolwork."

"Oh, too much schoolwork, heh," he said, doffing his worn-out beret in mock salute. "Excuse us for bothering you, Professor, we didn't know you were that busy." At this, his cohorts, who were smoking several bottles of glue, laughed.

I kept silent, sensing that Jarvas was provoking me into saying something that might give him an excuse to stab me. I bore the stream of filth he and his cohorts spewed at me, for I knew that it was better to act a coward and live than to act a hero and end up six feet under.

"What have you to say, wimp?" Jarvas sneered. "Will you fight, or will you hide behind your mama's apron like a little girl?"

"I'll fight in the next fight," I said.

"Better be there," Jarvas said, "if you know what's good for you."

The group left, and I sank into despair. Just when things were beginning to turn around in my life, this had to happen.

The next fight was on Saturday. It was a hot day. The Tomahawks were locked in fierce combat against the Mongols. Traffic was at a standstill as the two gangs went at each other with every type of weapon imaginable: tomahawks, machetes, bottles, rocks, daggers, slingshots, crowbars.

I was in the middle row of the Tomahawk formation, slingshot in hand. I had been grazed several times by rocks and bottles, but fought on. Mothers called their sons home, but we paid no heed. Amidst whistling, yelling and cursing, something whizzed past me, barely missing my head, but struck a barrel-chested thirteen-year-old boy to my left. He clutched his face and shrieked. "The bastards. They've hurt my eye." A couple of us rushed to his side. Someone said, "Let go of your face and let's see." He removed his bloodied hand from his face. His right eye had been completely gouged out by a stone from a slingshot.

Blood spurted out from the socket, down his cheeks like giant teardrops. There were no cars nearby, no phones, no means of getting him to the clinic. He might bleed to death, and he would be one-eyed for the rest of his life. Those thoughts numbed me. Then and there I decided to quit the gang, permanently.

On the way home, voices kept ringing in my head. Why do you fight when you don't want to? It could easily have been you with the gouged eye. Are you willing to pay such a price for conformity? Leave the gang, leave it now, while you still have both eyes, and your life; leave it now and be called a wimp for the rest of your life, if need be; but do not needlessly, recklessly and foolishly jeopardize your future.

I never again fought for any gang.

My leaving the gang, however, brought hostility and harassment. Jarvas warned me that my days were numbered, but I was resolved on quitting. Now an outcast and a marked man, I seldom travelled alone at night. During the day, I promptly came home after school and spent the rest of the day doing homework, reading and helping around the house. Occasionally, I would go out and play soccer with boys who did not belong to gangs.

My parents had known all along that I was involved with gangs and had said nothing, but when the harassment increased, I decided to tell them that I had quit gang life.

My mother, when she heard the full story behind my decision, heaved a deep sigh of relief and said, "You had two paths to choose from, just like every black boy in Alexandra: to become a *tsotsi*, or not to become a *tsotsi*. You chose the difficult way out. From now on, the going will be rough, for your *tsotsi* friends will try everything to make you change your mind. I hope you will remain firm in your decision. If you do, chances are you'll live to be old enough not to regret it."

My father in a typical remark said, "Watch out they don't kill you." He paused, then added, "Maybe it's about time I sent you to a school back in the homelands, where they'll make a warrior out of you."

32 After severing my ties with gangs, I had more time for my studies and books. I continued my above-average work, and was soon promoted to Standard Four, with the highest marks in the class. Teachers began forecasting great things for me: some said I would make a good teacher, others maintained that I had the brains to become a doctor. But all these predictions depended upon one thing—money. I was fast arriving at the point where many a black child, eager to continue learning, had to drop out because parents could not afford school fees, books and uniforms. I tried not to dwell on it. "Learn as much as you can, while the opportunity is still there," became my motto.

Though tribal indoctrination was still the focus of our curriculum in Standard Four, a few new and challenging subjects were introduced. In literature, we read a Tsonga translation of Booker T. Washington's autobiography, *Up from Slavery*. Teachers exhorted us to be like him, to lift ourselves from poverty by our bootstraps. We were required to memorize passages from the book, including "The Atlanta Exposition Address." For some reason, I never quite liked the book. It had an unsettlingly familiar ring to it.

But that was not the case with Tsonga translations of Greek and Roman mythology. I was drawn to the stories of Atalanta, Philemon and Bacchus, Odysseus and the Trojan War, Jason and the quest for the Golden Fleece. Admittedly they resembled much of African folk-lore, but they had a freshness that appealed to my imagination. I regularly chose to read them as prose during exams. My animated orations consistently scored high marks. I soon became one of the best prose and poetry readers in school, and would often get picked to represent the school whenever white inspectors came to assess our progress.

Another thing that caused a stir among teachers and students was my peculiar way of writing: I wrote upside down, literally. When I first learned how to write in Sub-standard A, I found it natural to write upside down, for it seemed that somehow my brain and left hand could only coordinate when I wrote upside down. To me, writing this way was the most normal thing; yet those who saw me do it shook their heads in disbelief and remarked that they had never seen anyone who wrote like me.

After a dozen or so trips to the white world, I began to feel somewhat comfortable amid the sea of white faces. There were still remnants of my childhood dread of white people somewhere in the recesses of my mind, but nothing major happened to rekindle it. On the contrary, the Smiths' kind treatment of me each time I visited them, though in most ways paternalistic, did much to alleviate that fear, and I began to naively assume that maybe white people weren't all that bad after all.

But one day something happened to cause me to think twice before declaring white terror more the fantasy of movies than the reality of day-to-day living.

It was a Saturday, and Granny took me along to her other gardening job in Pretoria, the capital of apartheid, because she needed help. Thinking that this was another way of getting books, I eagerly accompanied her. We spent the day doing the usual: raking leaves, pruning bushes, watering flowers and weeding the lawn. I washed cars, swept driveways and polished the *baas*'s shoes. At four, dead tired, we left for the bus stop about a mile away.

As we waited for the bus to Alexandra, Granny untied a rag from her waist, in which she kept money, and said, "Wait here, child, I'm going to the store across the street to get some change. These black drivers may leave us if we don't have the proper change. Be on the lookout for the bus. If it comes while I'm still away, kindly ask the driver to wait. Don't wander away from here or you'll end up in trouble."

I understood well what she meant by "trouble." It being a sunny Saturday afternoon, white people milled all over the place—walking in and out of boutiques, in and out of flowershops, in and out of hotels, in and out of department stores, in and out of Mercedes Benzes, Rolls-Royces and other expensive cars, in and out of tennis courts, in and out of houses and flats, and in but never out of my consciousness.

Granny hobbled across the street. Exhausted by the day's work, I sat on the bundle of newspapers, took out a comic book from my knapsack and buried my face in it. I had been reading for some time when I heard a bus screech to a halt not too far from where I sat. Dropping the comic book, I rushed to the door, so I could tell the driver to wait for Granny, who was waving vigorously at me from across the street, yelling something I couldn't quite make out. Lifting my head up as I came up the steps, I saw that I was in a "white" bus. I froze. My presence on the bus so startled several white old ladies who were about to disembark that they fled to the back.

"*Vootsek,** off this bus, Kaffir!" thundered the red-necked white driver. "Don't you see this is a white bus!"

Realising the tragic mistake I had committed, I tried to fly off the bus, but I could not. I thought I was in some kind of nightmare, and the fact that I had thought white people never rode buses because of all the cars they had made everything the more unreal.

But reality came in the venom the white bus driver was spitting as he reached for the side door to come after me. "I said get off the bloody bus, Kaffir!" I shut my eyes. I felt a pair of cold hands clutch my neck and yank me off the bus. I tumbled down the steps and landed on the concrete pavement. I must have prayed a million times.

Thinking that anytime I would be kicked in the face by the white bus driver, I started begging for mercy.

"Sorry, *mei baas,*" I whimpered, "Sorry, *mei baas.* Me make big mistake. Forgive me, *mei baas.* This Kaffir did not know bus for white people."

All this time my eyes were shut.

Suddenly I heard, "He's my pickaninny, *baas.* I'm at fault." It was Granny's voice. I opened my eyes to find her standing behind me, facing the white bus driver, who was in front of me. Apparently it was she who had jerked me off the bus.

"He's harmless, *mei baas,*" Granny went on in the most grovelling of voices. "He no cause *lo* trouble. Me to blame, me, *baas.* Me left him alone."

"Never mind who's to blame," the white driver said hotly, "why do you let him get into the wrong buses! You know I could have you both arrested for it!"

"He no know, *mei baas.* He no know. He only *kind* [child]."

---

* Invective commonly hurled at dogs.

"What do you mean he doesn't know," the white bus driver returned. "Don't you teach Kaffir children anything about the laws?"

"He can't learn, *mei baas*," Granny said dramatically, "*Lo* pickaninny *lo mal* [The pickaninny is deranged, my lord]," Granny gestured with her hands to indicate that mine was not a normal insanity. She then shoved me aside, and to my moral horror, began wiping with her dress the steps where I had trodden. This appeased the white bus driver, for after unleashing a tirade of how stupid and uncivilized black people were, he returned to the bus and drove off. Granny dragged me—I was in some sort of stupor—by the neck back to the black bus stop.

"What do you mean climbing into white people's buses, heh?" She shook with rage. "Do you want to get us killed?"

"I didn't know it was the white people's bus," I said contritely.

"You black liar," Granny exploded. "What do you mean you didn't know? Haven't you got eyes to see?"

"Granny, I swear I didn't know. I had never seen white people riding buses before, so when I heard this bus coming, I thought it was ours."

"Don't lie to me." She shook a finger in my face. "Can't you tell a black bus when you see one! Are you colour-blind? Or have you really gone mad! It must be all those books you're always reading!"

"I promise it won't happen again."

"If that's how you're going to behave each time you're among white people," Granny continued her verbal fusillade, "then this is the last trip you'll make with me. You know that had that white bus driver not been kind, we would now be in Number Four, you know that?"

"But Granny, I only stood on the steps," I said. "I would have understood had I sat on any seat."

"Shut up, you black imp," Granny screamed. "Shut up before I make you! You're always doing things you shouldn't be doing! That's your nature and you know it! You can get away with your bad behaviour in Alexandra, among black people, but not here! This is the white world!"

I remained silent, wondering whether I had underestimated the enormity of my crime of standing on the steps of a white bus. Were the poor white passengers going to die as a result?

After a long pause, during which she calmed down, Granny said, "Forgive me for the outburst, child, but what you did was no small thing in the eyes of white people and the law. There's something you ought to know about how things are in this country, something your Mama I see has not told you yet. Black and white people live apart—very much apart—that, you already know. What you may not know is that they've always been apart, and will always be apart—that's what apartheid means. White people want it that way, and they've created all sorts of laws and have the guns to keep it that way."

"We live in our world," she continued, after taking a pinch of snuff and loading it under her tongue, "and white people live in their world. We're their servants, they're our masters. Our people fought hard to change things, but each time the white man always won. He has all the guns. Maybe another generation of black people will come which will defeat the white man, despite his many guns. But for now, he says how things should be, and we have to obey. Do you see those two things over there?" Granny pointed across the street.

"Yes, Granny, they're phone boxes."

"That's right," she affirmed. "But they are not just phone boxes. One is a *black* phone box, the other a *white* phone box. Don't forget that. And for as long as I've been working for white people, and God knows I've been working for them for centuries, I've never seen a black person in his right mind go into the wrong one. It might be a matter of life and death, and still he wouldn't. Even blind people know which is which."

"Which one is for black people, Granny?" I asked, somewhat confused, for the two phone booths were exactly the same in all respects—colour, size and shape.

"I don't know which is which," Granny groped for words, "but there's always a sign on each door, to tell which race is allowed to use which phone."

As she said this, it struck me that she could not read, like millions of other blacks who worked for whites. How did they function normally in a world totally ruled by signs?

Thus my consciousness was awakened to the pervasiveness of "petty apartheid," and everywhere I went in the white world, I was met by visible and invisible guards of racial segregation. Overtly, the guards—larger-than-life signs that read, European Only, Non-European Only, Whites Only, Non-Whites Only, *Slegs Blankes, Slegs Nie-Blankes*—greeted me, and led me as a blind man would be led to the door I should enter through, the elevator I should ride in, the water fountain I should drink from, the park bench I should sit on, the bus I should ride in, the lavatory I should piss in.

The invisible guards, however, did not greet me as conspicuously to orient me about my place in life. Instead, remarks such as "You're in the wrong place, Kaffir," "We don't serve your colour here, Kaffir," "Who do you think you are, Kaffir?" "Are you mad, Kaffir?" told me it was still the guards of Jim Crow talking.

Because the guards of segregation were everywhere in the white world, and I saw black people who unwittingly disobeyed them cursed, beaten or thrown in jail, I became increasingly self-conscious with each step I took.

Through a school friend I landed a job selling newspapers after school plus Saturday and Sunday, from morning till noon. I liked the job partly because I made extra income to help finance my schooling, and partly because I got to read well-written papers like the *Star*, the *Rand Daily Mail*, the *Sunday Times* and the *Sunday Express*, on a regular basis.

I was now in Standard Six, my last year of primary school. Combining my modest income as a newspaperboy with what I made from reading and writing letters for migrant workers, I could now afford to go on some of the annual educational school trips to interesting places in the white world.

One such trip was to the Johannesburg Zoo. As with everything of worth the zoo was built primarily for whites, and groups of blacks had to apply for special permits to visit. After the principal received the permit Florah and I paid to go, along with half the school. One Tuesday morning four hundred excited schoolchildren were packed like sardines inside three buses. So happy were we that as the buses left Alexandra we began chanting and stomping our feet: it was not every day that sons and daughters of Africa got to see animals which their ancestors were keepers of. As we entered the white world, teachers attempted to keep the noise level down, but many of us, aware that we were among people who loved peace and quiet, shouted and stomped our feet the more. Some of us even stuck our heads out and hollered at stupefied white passersby. What an effect this had on people living on borrowed time. Bewildered white women scuttled indoors and bolted doors, simultaneously unleashing vicious dogs to patrol yards, seemingly misconstruing the busloads of black boys and girls as a prelude to a black invasion.

The zoo gatekeeper was a short white man with a fat face. Beaming, he told us that the zoo was all ours for the day because whites seldom came in great numbers on Tuesdays. There were a handful of whites entering through the "Whites Only" turnstile. We went through the "Non-Whites Only," but once inside, whites and blacks walked along the same paths to see the same animals.

"Why do they bother putting the bloody signs up if black and white people end up mingling once inside?" one boy snapped.

"Only God knows," a teacher said.

I chuckled; I had encountered so many such contradictions in the white world that I no longer spent sleepless nights trying to make sense of them. To me, and to many blacks, whites were a race peculiarly obsessed with creating contradictions that they, and they alone, could understand—if indeed they really could understand them in the strict sense of the word.

Most students obeyed the principal's rules and flocked like sheep when wolves are on the prowl. But a few maverick friends and I deliberately strayed from the herd. While wandering about the zoo, in awe of the caged animals, and at the same time feeling caged ourselves, we came upon a baboon cage in front of which stood a cluster of white schoolchildren in preppy green-and-white uniforms.

"Look," cried one of them in Afrikaans, as he saw us coming. From the startled look on his face, there was little doubt he was seeing black schoolboys for the first time in his life; the same could be said about the rest of his colleagues.

"Here come the small baboons," yelped another white boy.

"Let's turn back," someone in our group suggested.

"Yes, why don't we," a voice said in support. "We don't want to get into any trouble. Let's go see the lions over there instead."

"No," eighteen-year-old Phineas, leader of our group, said, in a defiant tone. "We paid too much money not to see everything in this fuckin' zoo."

"Yes." I gnashed my teeth. "Let's go. We have as much right as they to see the baboons. If they start anything, we'll respond in kind."

"Are you mad?" another boy said. "Do you want to get expelled?"

"Those who aren't cowards," Phineas said, "and will come with Johannes and me, over to this side."

The group divided into two roughly equal factions. Phineas boldly led us toward the white boys and the baboon cage while the others slunk away.

"Hey, *kyk* [look], the little baboons *are* coming to be with the big baboons," shrieked one white boy, and his mates roared with laughter.

There was no adult among them, except, some distance away, in front of a cage filled with playful spider monkeys, a tall wiry white man with silver-rimmed glasses stood bemused. He was wearing the same colours as the white boys. We disregarded his presence and jostled our way through the startled white boys to the front of the cage.

One of the white boys cursed, "Bloody Kaffir," as I deliberately kicked him in the shin.

"Kaffir is your mother," I said in Tsonga. My friends heard me and roared with laughter. The white boys didn't know what to do. They couldn't understand a single word of Tsonga, it seemed; yet we understood everything they were saying in Afrikaans.

Pretending to be talking about baboons, we proceeded to compare the mothers, fathers, grandmothers and grandfathers of the white boys to the various baboons in the cage. Sensing that we were talking about them, but not understanding what we were saying, the frustrated white boys strung one "bloody Kaffir" epithet after another.

Their headmaster came and took them to the lion's cage. We too soon left, laughing and singing, and rejoined our group. We had triumphed over them. After lunch we went over to the war museum across from the zoo. We saw among the relics of the many wars South Africa has been involved in relics from the Anglo-Boer War of 1899–1902, a colonial war so bitterly and closely fought that it left between the English and the Afrikaners wounds of mutual suspicion and hatred so deep that true reconcilement has never taken place to this day.

33 Constant police raids caused the family beer business to flounder a year after it was begun. Ultimately we went out of the business altogether. My father's old vices returned; first the gambling, then the heavy drinking to forget his losses. I found a job as a butcher boy for a Chinese family that owned a chain of stores and butcheries in Alexandra, and my mother worked as a washing girl in one of the neighbouring suburbs. She still did not have a permit, but her employers simply overlooked the fact, just like the thousands of other whites who did the same for their servants in similar straits.

With my father squandering his money on drink and gambling,

my mother became the breadwinner. I helped by using my wages to offset part of my siblings' school costs. Aunt Bushy had, as expected, left school after Standard Six and was now working at a garment factory on the outskirts of Alexandra. A little while after she started working she became pregnant: she was unmarried and eighteen. What was unexpected was Uncle Piet leaving school. He was only sixteen, but he could not stand seeing Granny work herself to death, and as the only man in the house (Uncle Cheeks was still in prison), he wanted to provide for her.

Uncle Piet and Aunt Bushy would have experienced the same difficulties and frustrations in getting work permits as Mother had not Granny bribed black policemen who specialized in getting people illegal documents. (These blacks were so many yet were never caught, because white officers either condoned or were part of the scheme.) Granny used her life savings for the bribes.

My mother became pregnant again. She had no money for maternity care and diapers, so she continued working until the baby was born. The little my father had given her over the course of her pregnancy had gone toward food, rent, bribes (whenever she was arrested during a police raid) and paying for Florah's and George's schooling. When the baby girl, named Linah, finally arrived, the family was dead broke, and my mother had to beg for money to buy diapers and baby food and medicine.

One Monday at four in the morning, my father woke me up and said, in an embarrassed tone: "Can you lend me thirty cents for bus fare so I can go to work?"

He had lost every penny of his wages at dice over the weekend; he had asked everyone in the yard to loan him some money—they had refused.

"I don't have any money," I said.

"But I saw you counting pennies and shillings last night," he retorted.

"So what?" I said. "It's my money, and I have plenty of uses for it." I said all this in an angry tone, for my father had gone on gambling, despite my mother begging him for some money to buy clothes for the infant.

"Don't talk to me like that," he bellowed. "I'm your father, you know."

"So what?" I said arrogantly; his tough talk no longer frightened me, and he knew it. At that moment I had more money in my pocket than his net worth, and I wasn't going to give him a penny of it, even if he were to fall on his knees and beg me.

"I need to go to work, son," he tried to smooth-talk me. "Just give me fifteen cents for one way. I'll ask for fifteen cents return fare from my friends at work. If they don't give me, I'll simply sleep in one of the factory buildings and come back Friday. I'll give you your fifteen cents back, with interest. I'll give you a rand: my boy, what do you say?"

"Just let me go back to sleep, will you?" I said. "I don't owe you any money."

"I said lend me some."

"I don't have any," I said, grabbing my pants from a chair nearby, in case he should have ideas. The money in my pockets jingled.

"Aha, what's that!" my father cried, and his eyes gleamed under the flickering candle. "I told you you had some money. Let me have some," he extended his gaunt hand anticipatingly, "or I'll miss the bus."

"I have use for this money," I said, folding my pants, and tucking them under the pillow.

"All of it?"

"All of it."

"On what?"

"On books and baby food."

"Damn the books and baby food. I want to go to work."

"I'm not stopping you."

"Give me the money, damn you!" he screamed.

I lost my temper. "It's my damn money and I have use for it!" I screamed back.

"Are you screaming at me," my father said, incredulous, "at me, your father. You-you-you my own flesh and blood," he stammered. "This school business has taught you to be cheeky, I see. Because you're working and making a few pennies, you think you're a man, heh. Well, let me tell you, my boy, let me tell you. I'm still man around here"—he beat his chest—"I call the shots. Either you give me the money or leave my house right at this minute."

Without a word, I stood up, dressed, gathered my books and left for Granny's place; it was five o'clock in the morning.

"I'll cut you down to size yet, my boy," my father shouted after me. "Wait until I send you to the mountain school back in the homelands, where they'll teach you respect. Just you wait and see."

I stayed at Granny's a week, and then returned home. My father said nothing, but I sensed that he was planning some sort of retaliation. I was ready for anything.

He couldn't *donder* (whip) me as he used to when I was a child, for I was growing stronger and more stubborn every day. We both knew that we were on a collision course. I was set in my ways, he in his. He disparaged education, I extolled it; he burned my books at every opportunity, I bought more; he abused my mother, I tried to help her; he believed all that the white man said about him, I did not; he lived for the moment, I for the future, uncertain as it was.

It soon became evident that the reason my father lived for the moment was because he was terrified of the future—terrified of facing the reality that I was on the way to becoming a somebody in a world that regarded him as a nobody, a world that had stripped him of his manhood, of his power to provide.

Years of watching him suffer under the double yoke of apartheid and tribalism convinced me that his was a hopeless case, so long as he persisted in clinging to tribal beliefs and letting the white man define his manhood.

His suffering convinced me that there was no way he could come to understand reality the way I did, let alone understand the extremes of emotions which had become so much a part of me and were altering my perspective toward life, that I no longer seemed his son, and he, to me, seemed no longer the father whose blood still ran in my veins.

By pining for the irretrievably gone days of drums, of warriors, of loinskins, of huts and of wife-buying, I knew that he could never travel, in thought and in feeling, the course my life was embarking upon, because everything he wholeheartedly embraced, I rejected with every fibre of my being.

The thick veil of tribalism which so covered his eyes and mind and heart was absolutely of no use to me, for I believed beyond a shadow of a doubt that black life would never revert to the past, that the clock would never turn back to a time centuries ago when black people had lived in peace and contentment before the coming of the white man.

Failure to tear away that veil had turned my father into an anachronism. Ignorance and tribalism claimed him so wholly—mind, body and soul—that he was baffled why the world, his wife, his children, were seemingly turned against him.

Even as he wasted away, trying desperately but in vain to establish order to the chaos of his life, he failed to realise, even in the slightest, that this chaos was partly of his own creation, of his continued clinging to values which had long outlived their usefulness; while at the same time attempting to function in a world the white man had long ago changed for his purposes, progress and whims.

Tribal ways and ignorance so ruled supreme over my father's life, and over many of those of his generation, that for as long as I was to know him, he was like some spectre wallowing in a bottomless hole of unreality, groping in it, trying, with great futility, to surface from it —to materialize into reality.

34 When Mrs. Smith gave me an old wood tennis racket one Saturday after I had done what she called "a splendid job" in cleaning her silver and brassware, and shining Mr. Smith's half a dozen pairs of shoes, I was already beginning to get bored with soccer.

"Practise hard," she said, "for one day I want to read about you in the papers, as our next Arthur Ashe."

"I don't know if I can be like him, madam," I said apologetically. "He's good." I had been reading about Arthur Ashe's exploit in the old tennis magazines Mrs. Smith regularly gave me. I couldn't even begin to imagine how a black man could become so good in a sport dominated by whites. Besides, what kind of a black man was he to be allowed to mix with whites, compete against them, even beat them? What kind of society did he live in which allowed a black man to become rich and famous at the expense of whites, instead of the other way round?

How could I begin teaching myself tennis? I was almost fourteen years old, had never handled a tennis racket in my life and knew absolutely nothing about the rules of the game. What I had read in the tennis magazines simply confounded rather than enlightened me.

I began pounding the tennis wall at the Alexandra Stadium. The one thing I liked about tennis was that it was not a team sport like soccer. My success and improvement depended upon my own efforts.

At Bovet there was no tennis. But I heard that the sport was played in some of the black colleges throughout the country. Would I ever get to college? Following the folding of the beer business, the economic situation in the house had worsened. My mother continued to work, but there was now another mouth to feed. I had left my job at the butchery, and was now doing piecework for Mrs. Smith and a few of her neighbours on weekends: washing cars, weeding gardens, shining shoes, cleaning silverware, cleaning pools and so on.

All my earnings went toward feeding the family and paying for my schooling. One evening while sitting by the table reading a torn copy of Alan Paton's *Cry, the Beloved Country,* I turned my eyes at my mother kneeling by the brazier, cooking porridge, Linah strapped to her back and bawling. My mother looked so worn out, I thought, the result of her working long hours for white people who she said "worked her like a mule, treated her like vermin, yet paid her nothing."

"Ma," I said, closing the book, "I'm going to leave school as soon as I finish Standard Six."

"Why?"

"Because you have six children and a useless husband to look after. I want to help."

"I can manage."

"No, Ma," I said. "You think you can, and you believe you should. But you can't do it alone. You need help."

"So you want to quit school just at the time when you're doing so well, is that it, child? What happened to your dreams of someday becoming a teacher or a doctor?"

"I can still do that through correspondence school."

"What job do you hope to get if you leave school now?"

"Anything a Standard Six graduate can do."

"Which is what? Picking up garbage for white people? Delivery boy? Is that what you've endured eight years in school for? Is that what I've sacrificed so much for?"

"I can work in a factory," I said, "just like Uncle Piet."

"Is that what your heart really wants to do? I know that's not what you want to do."

"How do you know my mind?"

"I'm your mother, remember," she said. "I carried you in my womb for nine months. You sucked from my breast; I saw you learn how to crawl and take your first walking steps. Child, I know you more than you know yourself."

She was right. I didn't want to drop out of school after Standard Six, if I could help it. I wanted to continue on to Form One, Two, Three, then do two years of matric (matriculation), then on to university to study engineering or medicine. I badly wanted to do that; no one in the family had done it; that was my dream.

But at the same time, I couldn't bear to watch my mother kill herself as she struggled against impossible odds to keep the family alive.

If I were to work, no matter at how menial a job, I could at least help her. I could make sure that my brother and sisters got all the education they wanted; I could compensate for my shattered dreams by helping them realise theirs.

"I want you to go on if you pass Standard Six," my mother said after a long pause.

"Where will the money come from?"

"From somewhere," she said. "I'll even break my back if that's what it takes to keep you going."

"Why, Ma?"

"Because I want you to become educated, that's all."

"But I'm educated," I countered.

"No, you aren't," she said emphatically. "I might not have gone to school, but I can tell an educated person when I see one."

My mother and I continued arguing until we reached a compromise: I would continue on to secondary school only on condition that I obtained a First Class pass. Otherwise, I would don overalls and begin working at one of the factories ringing Alexandra.

Had I been able to find part-time jobs to fill my spare time, I probably wouldn't have continued playing tennis. As it turned out, part-time jobs were as scarce as money to pay for school. The more I read about the world of tennis, and Arthur Ashe's role in it, the more I began to dream of its possibilities. What if I too were someday to attain the same fame and fortune as Arthur Ashe? Would whites respect me as they did him? Would I be as free as he? The dreams were tantalizing, but I knew they were only dreams. Nevertheless, I kept on dreaming; after all, what harm could that do me?

One weekday afternoon I was at the stadium practising against the wall when a big Coloured man, with a face full of freckles, approached the court. He leaned against its fence and watched me play.

"Hit that backhand! Hit that backhand!" he said insistently, "don't run around it."

I tried hitting one backhand; the stroke was horrible; I returned to only whacking my forehand, my best stroke.

"You fool," the Coloured man said, "practise that backhand, or you might just as well forget about tennis. Have you no common sense! Don't you know you never work on your strength but your weakness! And your backhand is atrocious."

The man's name was Scaramouche. He resented being called "Coloured," but according to apartheid, that was his official designation as one of over two million people of mixed race who were more than a blemish to the white man's theory of racial purity. According to the government Coloureds were neither black nor white, even though some of them were as black as the blackest black man, or as white as the whitest white man. Coloureds were allowed to live with blacks, though special areas had been set aside for them under the Group Areas Act.

The government generally treated Coloureds slightly better by giving them better jobs, better housing and better education than blacks. As a result most of the Coloureds were ashamed of their black blood, and often their prejudice against blacks was fiercer than the white man's. But a new generation of young Coloureds, which saw itself as more black than white, was emerging, and it embraced the entire range of black aspirations.

Scaramouche, a self-employed painter, was one of the best tennis players among people of colour in Johannesburg. An excellent coach, he was well connected in white and black tennis circles. He evaluated my game this way: I had potential to become a decent player provided I was prepared to work hard to unlearn the numerous bad habits I had taught myself. He agreed to be my coach.

PART THREE

PASSPORT TO FREEDOM

35 It was only a matter of time before tennis replaced soccer as my favourite sport. Scaramouche turned out to be not only a good coach but a confidant and a surrogate father. He was firm and demanding but not authoritative and stifling. Instead of teaching me his style of play, which would have been easy for him to do, he let me acquire my own. He was lavish with praise when deserved, but was a severe critic of sloppiness and laziness.

Whenever I visited his home on Second Avenue we often talked about the state of black tennis. Through Scaramouche I learned that the South African National Lawn Tennis Union (S.A.N.L.T.U.), an organization that ran black tennis, was so underfunded, so understaffed, its officers so embroiled in a power struggle, that it could manage to host only a handful of badly run tournaments a year.

This was in stark contrast to the white tennis body, S.A.L.T.U. (South African Lawn Tennis Union), which had the best facilities and administrators, almost limitless funding and hosted close to a thousand tournaments of mostly professional calibre each year. Scaramouche would often say, "You know, my boy, if we blacks had half the money and coaches as white people, we would have long produced several Arthur Ashes, Althea Gibsons and Evonne Goolagongs."

Scaramouche regularly gave me tennis instruction manuals and magazines. Soon I knew so much about the history of tennis that had the criteria for success in the game been knowledge of its history, I would certainly have been a superstar. I even knew the history of such players as Suzanne Lenglen and Bill Tilden.

My life began revolving around school, reading and tennis. On rainy days I would play shadow tennis: hitting at an imaginary tennis ball. I became so wrapped up in the game that my mother issued the following warning: "Tennis isn't everything, Johannes; don't forget school is more important."

"I won't, Ma," I said, and went ahead anyway thinking that man could live by tennis alone.

My father regarded tennis as a "sissy's sport." He would have

215

been thrilled had I shown an interest in tribal war games in which men and boys fought each other with spears and knobkerries.

"So," he said one evening as I was busy putting shoe polish on my sneakers, "not only are you trying to become a woman by crying and not bearing pain like a man, but I see you're also trying to become an imitation white man by playing this silly thing called tennis."

"Whites have no monopoly on tennis."

"I really doubt if you're my son, you know that?" he said. "There is no way I could have fathered a wimp."

"Leave me alone," I said angrily.

"By playing this thing tennis," he went on, "especially against women, one would indeed think you were a woman who only happened to have a penis."

"Just leave me alone!"

"Aha, you're mad because it's true, is that not so?" he said with a grin. "Well, all is not lost yet. There's still a way to cure you of all the books, all the tennis and all the white man's behaviour."

To avoid further confrontation I left the room.

36 That my mother's suffering at the hands of my father had led me to form an alliance with her to oppose his tyranny was true; that on most occasions I was more likely to listen to her advice than his I made no bones about; and finally, that my life was taking its shape and meaning largely due to her efforts and encouragement went without saying.

Yet there was one area in which she failed to exert any influence on me: religion. She had now become a devout member of the Full Gospel Church of God on Twelfth Avenue. Every Sunday she would take George and my sisters there to sing hymns of praise to the Lord and ask for renewal of strength to face and overcome the trials and tribulations strewn about our lives like grains of sand on the seashore.

I flatly refused to sit under some leaking roof listening to a demagogue out to make money by sending people on guilt trips and pretending to speak in tongues. That was the nature of some preachers in Alexandra, whose extremely obedient flocks were variously known as "The Donkey Church," "The Seven Wives Church," "The Hundred Rand Net Worth Church."

I frowned upon organized religion for the simple reason that about me I saw it being misused: by the government in claiming that God had given whites the divine right to rule over blacks, that our subservience was the most natural and heavenly condition to be in; by some black churches to strip ignorant black peasants of their last possessions in the name of payment for the salvation of their souls; and by the same churches to turn able-bodied men and women into flocks of sheep, making them relinquish responsibility for their lives in the hope that faith in Christ would miraculously make everything turn out right.

Worst of all, I found among members of some churches a readiness to accept their lot as God's will, a willingness to disparage their own blackness and heritage as inferior to the white man's Christianity, a readiness to give up fighting to make things just in this world, in the hope that God's justice would prevail in the hereafter, that the hungry and the oppressed and the enslaved of this world would feast on cornucopias while singing freedom songs and hosannas in a heaven without prejudice. In short, organized religion made blacks blind to, or avoid or seek to escape from, reality.

Maybe my mother did see reality in all its shades and colours, and was simply using organized religion to cultivate qualities like patience, resiliency, fortitude, hope and optimism. I do not know. All I know is that I wanted to carry the burden of my own life, to use whatever talent I had to carve a niche in a world where the odds were against my doing so. I instinctively knew that organized religion would hinder rather than help me; would torpedo my best-laid plans.

My mother tried to convince me that the preacher, herself and myself should work together as a trio to accomplish these goals I had set myself in life, but I wouldn't be convinced. What did the preacher know about tennis?

"Don't you think God has had some influence on the way your life is turning out?" she said one night after I had just finished reading her Scriptures. Because she could not read, my mother always requested that I read her several verses every night before she went to sleep. I gladly obliged; that was the least I could do at the moment to show appreciation for all she had done and was doing for me. Besides, I loved reading the Bible, mainly for the beauty and richness of its language, the earthy wisdom contained in many of its passages, and that sharpness which comes to the mind when one listens to the case of the existence of God being persuasively argued by men and women of different viewpoints who walked this earth in time immemorial.

"I have no way of telling, Ma," I said, "except that I do somehow believe there is something more powerful than man out there in the universe. Some call if a Force, some call it God, some call it luck."

"What do you call it?"

"I call it 'The Force,' " I said, laughing.

"Do you think 'The Force' may be working through our pastor, for instance?"

"I doubt that very much," I said, "but I have no way of telling."

"Putting it another way, do you think 'The Force' is in the church?"

"Maybe."

"They why don't you come?"

"I didn't say it's present only in churches. It could be right here in this house, for instance. As a matter of fact, I believe it is," I said, a smile on my face. "Otherwise, how does one account for the fact that Papa hasn't killed all of us yet, himself included in the bargain, as he's threatened so many times to do?"

"You know he doesn't mean it."

"I can't be *that* sure. Can I go to bed now?"

"Read me another verse, the last one, Corinthians thirteen."

One of the migrant workers for whom I read and wrote letters was a short, barrel-chested, pockmarked-faced man named Limela, who hated and distrusted Christianity so much that the mere mentioning of it, or the mere sight of evangelists who went about the township from house to house, expounding the doctrine, would send him into a fitful rage. He made it a personal crusade to visit shebeens regularly, and there, amid intense beer-drinking and boisterous talk, denounce Christianity as a "clever ploy through which whites sought to keep blacks forever slaves."

His repudiations of Christianity had as their launching pad the popular African expression "when the white people came, we had the land and they had the Bible; now we have the Bible, and they have our land"; an expression he always used to accuse priests, pastors, evangelists, and Jehovah's Witnesses of collaborating with what he called "descendants of treacherous white missionaries."

He was illiterate, and had a wife and six children back in a tribal reserve. His wife regularly wrote him lengthy, urgent and impassioned letters requesting money for food, clothing, rent, medicine, school fees, books, seeds and money to repair broken ploughs and leaking roofs.

One evening I was in his leaking shack reading him the bad news that his few lean cattle back in the tribal reserve had been confiscated by authorities there as partial payment for outstanding rent on the plot of land his wife and children lived on, and that they were facing eviction if the rest of the rent wasn't paid on time, when, after a faint knock, in walked a short, dumpy black man with tufts of crinkly greying hair, dressed in a green-and-white frock with sleeves up to the elbows. He had no shoes on. Following closely behind him was an equally short and plump black woman. She too was dressed in an outfit similar to the man's, except hers had a few cheap embroideries. The two clutched stacks of pamphlets in their hands.

"Not you again!" Limela exclaimed in fury as the two walked in. The man, already a foot or so inside the shack, cleared his throat while the woman stood silently by the doorway, and said, "Can we sit down?"

"No!" Limela said indignantly.

The evangelists sat down anyway, on a makeshift bench of bricks and planks.

"I told you never to set foot in my house again, *mfundisi* [preacher]," Limela raged. "I don't want to hear any more about your white God. Why, then, do you keep on coming? Do you think because you call yourself 'man of God' I won't kick your ass?"

"I'll gladly let you kick my ass for the glory of God," the *mfundisi* said humbly. "We are his shepherds and are expected to go after even the wildest sheep."

"God loves you, you know," shrieked the woman. "You may hate the white man, but do not hate God."

"Who's this God! Who's this God!" Limela fumed. "Isn't he a white man's God?"

"God is colour-blind," said the *mfundisi*. "White people, too, need to come to him so he can forgive them their sins."

Limela was beside himself with rage. "You're stark raving mad, *mfundisi*," he declared with flaming eyes. "You mean to tell me that white people aren't aware of what they're doing to us? You mean to tell me that they aren't aware that my family is starving because of their laws? Do you mean to tell me that God will forgive them all that? Any God who'll forgive white people's sins is as mad as you are, *mfundisi*."

Their brows shiny with perspiration, the evangelists sat speechless as Limela unleashed his blasphemous tirade, drawing parallel after parallel between Christianity and witchcraft. I enjoyed every minute of the confrontation. Perversely I wished Limela would throw the *mfundisi* out.

"They keep on returning, my boy," Limela said, shaking his head despairingly. "And each time they tell me, in different ways and each way more devious than the last, that this God of theirs forgives all sins, be they a black man's or white man's. Boy, would you, if you were God, forgive white people for what they're doing to us?"

"Never," I said.

"Don't lead the children astray, now, Limela," said the *mfundisi*. "Jesus said, 'Let the children—' "

I cut him short. "I'm not a bloody child, mister, and I'm going to no fucking Jesus." Warming up, I continued, "I know people of your kind. You're dirty stinking liars! You make people forget reality and dream about some stupid heaven no one really knows exists! If people like Limela don't confront reality in the face, who'll do it for them, heh, tell me, who? Who'll fight for their rights, their honour, their dignity?

"And let me tell you this, too. You and your kind are also cheats and thieves. How often do you, *mfundisi*, and your kind, strip people of everything they've got in the name of salvation? You would even rob them of their souls if you could get at them."

"My child," the *mfundisi* said with stupefied eyes. "Ignorant as you are, your soul right now is tumbling into hell! By blaspheming against God and His Holy Word, you're committing a sin so huge one hell won't be enough for your damned soul to roast in."

"Don't give me that rubbish, *mfundisi*," I sneered. "We all know that the existence of God is a matter of speculation. The Bible is nothing but a collection of stories by whites."

"You'll burn in hell," the *mfundisi* declared.

"I'm already going through hell under the white man's rule," I said, "so another ordeal in hell won't make much of a difference. I wonder where you'll end up, cheat and liar, betrayer of your own people."

The *mfundisi*'s jaws dropped and he stared at me stupidly. The woman emitted gasps of horror. I became self-conscious and turned my eyes away from the two.

"Is that so?" Limela grinned triumphantly. "So the Bible is nothing but a simple storybook. I thought so. The white man's storybook.

We black men don't need the white man's tales, do we, boy? We have our own, better ones, don't we?"

I nodded.

The *mfundisi* had apparently regained his composure, for he said, in an inspired voice, sweeping his arms toward heaven, "It's not too late for both you two to escape from the clutches of Diablos"—I marveled at his courage—"the kingdom of heaven is yours if you only allow me and my sister in Christ here to exorcise by prayer the evil spirits raging inside you; that way you'll be counted among those lucky ones who'll someday soon enjoy the overflowing bliss of the glorious life to come."

"Which life to come, liar," I said angrily. "Which life to come! There's only one life and this is it. And how are black people faring in it? Are we enjoying it like white people are? Are we getting Rolls-Royces, mansions and swimming pools from it—or are we getting hunger, disease, poverty and suffering? Why are you without shoes? Is it because walking on streets strewn with sharp rocks, thorns and broken bottles is a thrill? Tell me, *mfundisi*, why are white people having their paradise in this world, instead of suffering like us in anticipation of eternal bliss? You know why? They are smart. They know the game, for they invented it."

"Tell them, my boy," cheered Limela, clapping his hands, "tell them good."

"Child," the *mfundisi* said. "You must be born of the Devil."

Before I could insult the evangelists further, Limela said, "*Mfundisi*, I don't need your God. My gods are the spirits of my ancestors."

"Those things are impotent," said the *mfundisi*. "They can do nothing to save your soul from eternal damnation."

Limela sprung to this feet and cocked his fists, "Get out of my house, you bastard," he screamed at the *mfundisi*. "Get out before I fling you out!"

Silently the *mfundisi* and the woman rose and left; however, they intentionally left a couple pamphlets on the bench where they were sitting.

"What's that, boy?" Limela asked, as he saw me perusing the pamphlets.

"Oh, another pack of lies; so-called testimonials of black people who recount their 'meetings with God.' "

"Another of the white man's tricks, heh," Limela said. "I'm shivering, boy. What about us making a cozy little fire outside."

I understood what he meant; he wanted to use the pamphlets to make a fire. We stepped outside. The night was cold and the sky overcast. We gathered some wood and cardboard. The pamphlets made a roaring fire.

37 One winter evening while I was reading *Drum* magazine under candlelight my father burst through the front door, accompanied by two pitch-black men as huge and wild as grizzly bears. My mother was in the other room helping George and my sisters try on some secondhand clothes she had bought at a jumble sale.

"There he is," shouted my father the minute he saw me, as if he were a witch doctor accusing a villager of witchcraft. "Get him!"

The two men started toward me.

Instinctively I leaped from the chair, grabbed a long knife that had been on the table and stood against the wall. My mother heard the voices and came running to the kitchen.

"What's going on?" she asked.

"These men have come to take him to circumcision school," my father declared, a smile of deep satisfaction playing on his lips.

Under Venda tribal law, every boy, before being admitted into malehood, had to attend a "mountain school," usually situated in wooded, mountainous areas remote from the villages. During attendance at the school, the proselytes are put through various rituals by a group of circumcised men, including the main ceremony where the boys' penises are cut by razors without anesthesia.

My mother started. "What led you to decide this without telling me?" she asked.

"He's my child," my father said.

"And mine also," returned my mother.

"He's become too cheeky around my house," my father railed. "It's time he went to the mountain school to learn his proper role. He's not taking after me."

"Take after you!" I cried, "take after you! What have you done that I could emulate! Your drinking—your gambling—your ignorance—your irresponsibility! I'd rather be dead than be like you!" I spat.

"Hear how he talks to me, his father. He even spits at me."

"Okay, now, boy," growled one of the men. "Put that knife down and come quietly. You'll only be gone for three months."

"Three months," exclaimed my mother. "He can't afford to be gone that long! Exams are coming up soon."

"This is the most important exam of his life, *musadi*," said one of the men. "He's to be tested for his manhood."

"Maybe he can go next year."

"I'm not going anywhere, ever," I said. "If I need to be circumcised I'll go to the clinic. I'll kill anybody that dares lays a hand on me."

"He's only bluffing," my father said. "He won't use that knife."

"Try me," I gnashed my teeth.

The men hesitated.

"He's a *tsotsi*," my mother said.

The two strangers exchanged glances. "Talk to your son, Jackson," said one of them. "We'll come back tomorrow and pick him up."

They left, and my father left with them. I immediately packed my books and clothes and left for Granny's place, where I stayed for two weeks and then returned home. The issue of circumcision school never came up between me and my father, but there was no doubt that the incident had strained our relationship to a breaking point. He seldom talked to me, and I never as much as breathed a word to him. Living like this turned me into a nervous wreck. I began to experience problems with my health. Without money to go to a doctor I had no way of finding out what was ailing me. My imagination told me that my father was trying to poison me. I became paranoid. I thought I would go insane. I was only fourteen.

Despite being under considerable stress because of the bad blood between my father and me, I went ahead and sat for the Standard Six final exams. I had to do very well in these exams, for there was a possibility I could win a scholarship to help me on to secondary school. Under normal circumstances I would not have doubted my ability to do very well in an exam. In my eight years of school I had never placed below the top one percent in any class. But the falling out with my father had left me demoralized and without confidence. I felt I would be lucky to pass. I conferred with my mother about my plight, and as always she had an encouraging word. She was the eternal optimist.

"Have faith in yourself, child. You've done very well so far. There's no reason you can't do well now. Believe in yourself."

I sat for the exams with as much confidence as I could muster under the circumstances. When the results came out a few months later I found myself along with half a dozen other students the toast of the school. We were among the highest scorers in all of Alexandra's tribal schools. I had obtained a First Class pass, barely missing the highest honour, Distinction.

A day after the results appeared in the *World* the principal called me to his office, where I found several teachers full of smiles and congratulatory remarks. The principal motioned to my teacher to speak.

"You're without doubt one of the best students Bovet has ever had," he began. "We are all very proud of you. Though I may at times have caned you more than others, I knew deep in my heart that you were a bright student, that with the proper dose of punishment and encouragement you could achieve great things. I hope you'll retain the spirit of hard work, of curiosity, of doubting, of asking questions even if you know that answers are impossible. God bless you."

Everybody clapped. I was at a loss for words. The principal rescued me by saying, with effusive pride, "Johannes, I'm proud to inform you that you've been awarded, based on your academic record, a government scholarship to pay for your schooling for each of the three years of secondary school."

I could not believe my ears; I did not know whether to jump up and down or cry. How could it have happened? How could I have done it? Was it real?

The principal went on. "It's all true, my boy. It couldn't have happened to a more deserving student. It's a fitting crowning achievement to a remarkable career at this school. Your academic records will surely stand for years to come. Of course there's no need to tell you that the scholarship is contingent upon your continuing to do well academically. Do you think you will?"

I was too speechless to say anything.

That night my mother cried tears of joy. "God lives, child. He does live. He does listen to prayers," she sobbed. Granny, Uncle Piet and Aunt Bushy were informed and promised to help me become the family's first doctor. Even my father said, "Will the government give you a job when you're finished with school?"

Had I not hated the tribal reserves I would have gone with friends from the graduating class to boarding school in Giyani, the tribal reserve for the Tsongas. I chose instead the local secondary school, and as it turned out, that may have been the most important decision of my life: Alexandra Secondary School had a tennis team.

Alexandra Secondary School was the only mixed school in the ghetto. Students from various tribal primary schools studied together for the first time. Obviously the medium of instruction could not be any of the tribal languages. English, as the most common language in the country, was used in teaching mathematics, history, geography, physics, biology, religious instruction, woodworking and domestic science. Each student's curriculum was rounded off by the Afrikaans, English and vernacular languages.

The school had better facilities than the primary schools, but it lacked many things, and overcrowding was still a serious problem. The motto of the school was *Labor Omnia Vincit* (Labour Conquers All), and the dozen or so teachers, along with the principal, ran a tight ship: no drugs, proper uniform every day, corporal punishment to enforce discipline, compulsory cleaning of the school compound and a decree that English be spoken at all times instead of tribal languages. I could not have been happier with the rules, particularly the last one. Finally, here was a clear opportunity to strive toward mastering the language of John Bull.

Because many of the subjects were taught in English, and I had had a head start in the language through my connection with the Smiths, I quickly became one of the better students in school. I came out at the top of the Form One class in exams at the end of the first quarter. My performance was above average in all subjects, but I excelled in languages and the sciences. I was on the debating society my first year and was chosen to represent the school in Afrikaans, Tsonga and English prose and poetry reading during inspection. It was a lot of responsibility, but I still found time to practise tennis. Many of the boys and girls I had grown up with left school because they lacked money to continue. The dropout rate in primary school was 98 percent. The scholarship I had paid for books and school fees. I had to buy my own uniform and meet all other expenses; this I tried to do by working part-time for the Smiths.

The little I made was augmented by help from Aunt Bushy and Uncle Piet.

"One of these days I'll make you all proud for all the help," I told Uncle Piet after he had bought me a new white shirt and a pair of long grey flannels.

"Don't worry, Nephew," Uncle Piet replied. "Just keep up the good work. I doubt that had I been able to stay in school I would have accomplished half of what you have. Because of you I'm being recognized in the streets as 'that smart boy's uncle.' Remember that day your exam results appeared in the *World?* I took a copy with me to work, and you know, I was the envy of the whole factory. White people even greeted me. If you keep up the good work, kid brother, who knows, I may even be promoted."

Aunt Bushy, who regularly gave me lunch money and paid for my school trips, said about the same. Granny, always irrepressible, said, "As long as I have you, child, I don't need a husband. I couldn't find one as handsome, as brainy, as caring as you in the entire world. Wherever I go nowadays, grandmothers and mothers tell me they have granddaughters and daughters beautiful and smart enough for you to marry. But I say, 'He's already taken.' They ask. 'Who's the lucky girl?' And I say, 'You're looking right at her.' "

The fact that I could rely on getting help from the three whenever I needed it made it easy for me to devote more time to tennis. Improvement was slow. I came up with a regimen to help me play better. I started visiting bookstores in Johannesburg with a notebook in hand and would read scores of tennis and exercise books, jotting down pointers. To improve my concentration and flexibility I began practising yoga. To keep my energy level consistently high I vowed never to become sexually active until "I had made it." (I had read somewhere that sex drained one's energy and single-mindedness.)

Much to my surprise my game began improving. I started triumphing over players I had once been trampled by. For the first time since I began playing tennis I defeated Scaramouche. As if this was not enough to make me worship my secret formula of success, I became the number-one player at my school. The year was 1972. In final exams that year, held in December, I led the Form One classes.

Nineteen seventy-three proved a great tennis year. I was selected captain of the team, played number one in singles and doubles and led the school to several important victories against long-standing rivals. Scaramouche entered me in a couple of black tournaments held in Soweto, Pretoria, Tembisa, Daveyton and Kwa-Thema. I did not do well in them, but the experience was valuable. Scaramouche managed to get me a few old tennis rackets from his wealthy white tennis friends, and I was able to concentrate on my game without worrying about a broken racket or string.

In June I met Tom, a lanky Zulu tennis player who had just come out for the tennis team. He immediately stood out from the rest of us because his tennis clothes and rackets were worth at least twice the tennis team's annual budget. Tom was too harmless-looking to be a thief, so one day I asked him where he got the stuff. He started telling me about a tennis ranch in Halfway House (so-called because the place was roughly halfway between Johannesburg and Pretoria) where he worked but was about to quit to take up a better offer at another ranch. The tennis ranch in Halfway House was called Barretts, after the construction company that was one of the major builders of tennis courts in South Africa. A German immigrant named Wilfred Horn ran the place.

"How long has he been in South Africa?" I asked.

"Not long enough to have turned into an Afrikaner SOB," replied Tom. "He grew up during the Second World War and once told me that he thinks the mad ideas of Hitler and his Nazis are the same as the National party's [the ruling Afrikaner party, the creators of apartheid]."

"Interesting fellow."

"Wilfred respects black people," Tom said. "He and his South African–born wife, Norma, and their four-year-old son, like most whites, have an entourage of servants. But they treat them well."

"If they have a tribe of servants, what do you do?"

"I play tennis, brother," he boasted.

"I thought you said you worked there."

"Yes. I work at my tennis game."

"Who do you play with? Are there black players and black courts at this ranch?"

"No. It's as lily-white as the Broedersbond [a secret white male society that has produced all of South Africa's leaders]. I was the only black there. I played whites."

"You-played-against-whites!" I gasped. "Who are you?"

"I'm Tom, just plain, simple Tom."

Half my mind told me that Tom might be a police informer. Of all the categories of blacks, informers were the one group most likely to enjoy cordial relations with whites, the whites, of course, being the police. Maybe the ranch was nothing but a retreat for white secret agents and black informants.

"I'm not what you're thinking," Tom interrupted my thought. "I'm no Uncle Tom. The members of this ranch are mostly wealthy Germans and English liberals who don't mind—in fact they like—

mixing with blacks. The right blacks that is. Yes, there are a few Afrikaner bigots, but who cares? Anyway, these liberals love me because I'm neat, I'm in secondary school, I can speak English, Afrikaans and German fluently. What more could white liberals want? If all our people were like me, I strongly believe there would be no need for apartheid, not among white liberals anyway."

That was his opinion.

"And you say you're leaving this place?" I asked.

"Yes. At the end of the month. I've found a better paradise."

"Tom, I pray you," I said, "please take me to this paradise you're leaving. Introduce me to Wilfred, and for as long as I live, I'll worship the ground upon which you walk. My sister is beautiful, you know."

Wilfred turned out to be just as Tom had described him. We immediately liked each other. He was impressed by my English (which I spoke better than him) and my distinguished academic record. Details of my childhood and life in the ghetto shocked him. For some reason I gave my name as Mark.

"But how could people allow this to go on, Mark?" he asked in a heavy German accent. "In Germany we read about apartheid, but what you tell me we knew absolutely nothing about."

"I'm not surprised," I said. "Not even the whites in this country know the truth about ghetto life."

"I can never live in this country," he said in disgust. "But what a beautiful country." He paused and then said, "It'll be my pleasure to have you play at my ranch. Maybe you can educate us about the reality we whites don't know but should know."

38 In November of 1973 the government finally allowed Arthur Ashe to set foot on South African soil. For almost six years he had been persona non grata. The case against him was simple. He, a black man, had repeatedly impugned the government of South Africa and its policies of apartheid. But the straw which finally broke the camel's back was the remark Ashe supposedly made at a press conference in London, namely that he would "drop the H-bomb on Johannesburg" as a way of bringing the government to its senses.

"I don't think Arthur Ashe meant the remark to be taken seriously," I said to David one afternoon as we were reading the paper heralding Ashe's pending arrival. We had taken a break from tennis practise, and were headed for the local café to get some cold drinks. "He must have spoken it in anger."

David was the number-two singles player on the team, and he and I played number-one doubles. He was a soft-spoken, politically sensitive, brilliant Zulu student, whose love for the English language probably equalled my own. We frequently exchanged books, did English homework together, read prose and poetry together, trained together, and sat on the same seat during tennis trips. He was the first close friend I ever had. The one thing which differentiated us was that he was a womanizer and I was not (I still clung to my secret formula).

"This bloody government is so damn sensitive to what black people say," David said, "that it overreacts to everything they say."

"You know," I said in a whisper, "if Arthur Ashe had been living in South Africa, he would have been immediately arrested for making that statement."

"Shipped him off to Robben Island is what the bastards would have done with him," David returned angrily. "Or if they wanted, they would have allowed him to hang himself by his racket strings while under police custody."

We broke out laughing, a nervous laughter, our eyes darting about to see if we were being watched. In a country where the writing of political slogans on walls was considered a serious crime, talking about political matters was tantamount to treason, punishable by hanging, if you were black.

As David and I were talking, I remembered reading in newspapers about cases of black people mysteriously hanging themselves while under police custody. Black political activists were from time to time found dangling from belts, shirts, pants, blankets. At school, much of the furtive talk during lunch break was over such "suicides," as the police labelled them. We called them "cold-blooded murder."

David's political awareness had come about, he said, largely because some of his distant relatives had been involved with the ANC (African National Congress), before the movement was forced underground, and subsequently outlawed in the country.

Because it was illegal for black schools to teach black political history (except tribal political history, which the government had concocted to suit the apartheid ideology), my friendship with David enlightened me a great deal about the ANC liberation movement.

It was founded in 1912 by a group of black intellectuals, many of whom had studied in England and America. It began as a nonviolent movement, inspired by the work of Mahatma Gandhi, who lived in South Africa from 1894 to 1914, and it sought to peacefully bring about a South Africa free of racial prejudice.

Its leaders believed that white South Africans could be persuaded, on moral and humanitarian grounds, to end segregation. But the National party refused to end apartheid; instead, each year the system was fortified by the promulgation of laws to entrench white rule and privilege.

Black civil rights leaders continued to agitate, but the apartheid machinery ground on unheeding. Peaceful protesters were gunned down. Scores of civil rights leaders were arrested and sent to serve life sentences in the maximum-security penitentiary on Robben Island, in the cold Atlantic Ocean. Among the prisoners were Nelson Mandela, Gouan Mbeki, Walter Sisulu and Robert Sobukwe.

Those leaders who escaped went underground and continued their fight against injustice and racism. And because nonviolent measures had failed, they took up arms, and *"Umkhonto We Sizwe"* (Spear of the Nation) was formed. Yet they remained prepared to lay them down any minute to discuss the future of South Africa with whites, and their goal still was "to establish a free and democratic South Africa, where all people live in brotherhood and sisterhood, enjoying equal rights and opportunities."

Despite the escalating black rebellion, the government still refused to talk. So it was that my generation was born into a decade of heightened conflict. And as the realities of apartheid became evident to many of us, as anger, hatred and frustration became more and more a part of our daily lives, we began to look for ways of dealing with these destructive emotions.

Those of us who knew about black liberation history and the ANC's part in it opted to emulate the Mandelas, the Mbekis, the Sisulus and the Sobukwes, individuals who gave selflessly of themselves to the liberation struggle. Those of us who did not know black liberation history and the ANC's role in it still looked around for models to emulate. I was still looking when Arthur Ashe came to South Africa.

His coming meant so much to blacks, who literally worshipped American blacks who proved that they could triumph in a white man's world, a world that many of us believed was booby-trapped with all sorts of obstacles designed to sink blacks deeper into the mire of squalor and servitude, where white people wanted them to belong.

The day Arthur Ashe arrived I was on my way to the Barretts Tennis Ranch. I had begun practising there about three or four times a week. Wilfred too had heard the news of Ashe's arrival and seemed very excited about it.

"I've seen him play in Germany," he said. "He's awesome. One of the best serve-and-volleyers in the world. And he's such a gentleman. The game couldn't have had a better ambassador. If he had been in politics, he would have made an excellent politician."

"I would like to meet him," I said.

"As a matter of fact, I already have tickets for us to go see him play."

"I would like to meet him face-to-face," the words spilled out of my mouth. I was so emotional about wanting to meet Ashe that it did not occur to me that I was asking Wilfred the remotely possible.

"Even with my contacts," Wilfred said, "there are things I can't do."

The same week that Ashe arrived another historic landmark was being established in the annals of South African sports. For the first time ever a black man was to fight a white man in a boxing matchup hailed everywhere as the greatest breakthrough in sports apartheid since the government began allowing publication of photographs showing a black boxer pummeling a white boxer: in the past such photos were banned as fomenting racial tensions.

The boxing match pitted Bob Foster, a black American and the light heavyweight champion of the world, against a white challenger from South Africa. But I was no longer a boxing fan, since that incident years ago, so when Uncle Pietrus, a boxing fanatic, obtained two scalped tickets and invited me along, I refused.

The decision not to attend the fight was not based solely on my hatred of boxing. There was another, more compelling, reason why I refused to go. And that reason had nothing to do with the senselessness or brutality of the sport. It had to do with one of the fighters—Bob Foster.

I just didn't want to see the man. Why? I had begun to hate him. Since his arrival in the country, he had made various public statements that infuriated many black people. Statements like: he was in South Africa only to fight, and not to engage in politics; therefore the press should stop hounding him for comments on apartheid. That he felt South Africa was not such a bad place after all, and he was thinking of someday building a vacation home here.

What angered black people the most, however, was that he was trying his utmost to distance himself from us, as if we were subhuman blacks, wretches afflicted with some kind of racial leprosy that would rub off on him should he come into contact with any of us. By shutting himself in the white world and refusing to come to any of the ghettos, he was looked upon as a traitor, an Uncle Tom. As far as I was concerned, he might as well have been another white man, a Boer preferably, for he seemed so hopelessly out of touch with reality—my reality, his reality. I pitied him. And scoffed at all opportunities to see him fight.

Instead I concentrated all my efforts toward seeing Arthur Ashe. Though he, like Bob Foster, was a Negro and stayed, too, in the white world during his visit, his condemnations of apartheid made him one of us; he did not pretend he was a white man erroneously painted black.

We blacks in South Africa looked up to, and worshipped, people like Ashe.

We didn't feel, however, that each time black Americans came to our country—be they singers, athletes or actors—they had to ignore or compromise what they had come for (mostly to make money, some to prop up floundering careers) and, instead, undergo some kind of penance by, for instance, staying in a shack in Alexandra or Soweto, as a show of solidarity.

We could care less if they stayed at the five-star hotels into which they were allowed as honorary whites, and which, after all, they could afford and seemed to generally prefer. All we wanted them to do was to be true to the realities of their colour, to show concern for our plight, to not condone or appear to condone apartheid, to come out to the ghettos and meet us, because so few of us had the means to go see them perform.

Also, we felt that because they were black Americans, they were in a safer position to criticize apartheid, something which was prohibitively dangerous for us to do, as shown by the conspicuous absence among us of people like them.

I went to Ellis Park on a Tuesday, the first day of the tournament. Wilfred had a heavy load of tennis lessons and could not come with me; but he gave me money to cover expenses for the day. Arthur Ashe was scheduled to play his first-round match in the afternoon. As I got off the black bus on North Street, and was making my way toward the tournament site, I wondered what my first time attending a tournament full of world-class players would be like? The event was made even more significant by Arthur Ashe's presence—the first black man ever to play.

The stadium was jam-packed. The few black people at the tournament, much to my surprise, mingled freely with whites, as the two groups walked about the courts, eagerly seeking autographs from the tennis stars. Arthur Ashe was favoured to win his first-round match against Sherwood Stewart, a bearded, lanky American from Goose Creek, Texas.

The bleachers at centre court were supposed to be fully integrated, but most black people kept to themselves, sitting in a cluster in the northeast section of the stands, an area without a canopy and fully exposed to the torrid Transvaal sun. I tried, along with a couple friends from Soweto, to "integrate" with a group of whites who looked as though they were from Pretoria, but the atmosphere became so tense that we abandoned the effort. We went back to the black section.

Directly across from where we sat stood a large sign advertising a brand of Scotch whisky called Black & White. The sign read: (It's) Time to Serve Black and White. There were two dogs, one black and one white, and a grandfather clock, in the centre of the picture.

Arthur Ashe won his match in straight sets: 6–1, 7–6, 6–4. During the match, whenever he won a point, whether through hitting a winner or through an error by his opponent, the minority of black spectators rent the stadium with clapping and cheering. I chuckled at catching subtle expressions of disdain on several white faces as a black man trounced a white man. Many white spectators, however, did root for Arthur Ashe. I wondered what would have been the situation had he been playing against a white South African.

At the end of the day, as I was headed home in a packed black bus, the jubilation I had felt throughout the day waned. Stark reality once again overwhelmed me. Throughout the entire day at Ellis Park I had been exisiting in a different world, a sort of make-believe world. I had breathed fresh air, walked on paved roads, mingled freely with white people, rested upon green grass and eaten free hot dogs given to me by whites.

But as the packed bus rattled along Louis Botha Avenue, leaving behind the city of gold with its neon lights for a ghetto of darkness, smog, fear and violence—and all around me I saw sullen, worn, tired and sad faces of black workers—my spirits sunk. Sadly, I mulled over the day's events. Now that I had seen Arthur Ashe play, I found it hard to believe he was a black man. How could a black man play such excellent tennis, move about the court with such self-confidence, trash a white man and be cheered by white people?

"Am I being realistic?" I asked myself as I hurried home amid choking smog and a fear of *tsotsis*, "in thinking that I could ever be like him? Or am I simply dreaming?"

How did Arthur Ashe get to be so good in a white man's sport? What miracles did the environment in America provide that nurtured blacks into great athletes like Arthur Ashe? Were the blacks in America really like us? Or was there something mixed up in their blood, maybe in their brains too, which made them capable of accomplishing prodigious feats, which seemed beyond the capability of even the best among us?

I had read somewhere that there were, among blacks in America, singers, educators, politicians, mayors, inventors, scientists, actors, actresses, judges, army generals, pilots, writers and so on—people whose names weren't African, yet some of whom were as black as I was. W. E. B. Dubois, Frederick Douglass, Martin Luther King, Jr., Joe Louis, Muhammad Ali, Jesse Owens, Harry Belafonte, Marcus Garvey, Paul Robeson, Richard Wright, Sammy Davis, Jr., Nat "King" Cole, Lena Horne, Booker T. Washington, James Baldwin, Jesse Jackson, Sidney Poitier, Duke Ellington, George Washington Carver, Malcolm X, Marian Anderson, Ralph Bunche, Jackie Robinson, Thurgood Marshall, Ella Fitzgerald, Eldridge Cleaver, Langston Hughes, Louis Armstrong, and the list went on and on.

I came across these names in newspapers, magazines and books. On reading of their accomplishments, I found it beyond me to believe that they, whom history depicted as descendants of slaves, slaves taken from the *very* Africa in which I lived, could have achieved so much.

We in South Africa had never been called slaves, though, all along, day in and day out, we had been treated worse than slaves. None of our ancestors, as far as I could tell from our distorted history, had ever been shackled and considered chattel, bred and traded like cattle, as the ancestors of the American black had been.

Yet somehow, in a mysterious, diabolical way, our growth as a people, our aspirations as individuals, our capacity to dream and to create, our hopes for the future as a nation united, had been ruthlessly stunted by whites who possessed our lives from birth to death.

It seemed as if the haunting belief, held firmly by many a white South African, especially advocates of white supremacy, that we blacks were an inferior race, denied by nature and by God the ability to achieve anything great, was being affirmed as years went by without a single person attaining any measure of success that could be termed prodigious by worldwide standards of excellence.

Yes, we had a few writers, singers, educators, actors, actresses and so on, but few had attained the international stature of their American counterparts.

Could I ever be like Arthur Ashe?

Gradually I became aware that I could never be like him for as long as I remained in South Africa. For reasons still unclear, America, the land that had given birth to Ashe and nurtured him, loomed bright as the place to go to realise my fullest potential in tennis, in life. There, it seemed, blacks who had the talent, the will, the resiliency, the ambition, the drive to dream, were turning their dreams into reality.

I kept returning to Ellis Park to watch him play, to study his mannerisms, and to weigh his attacks on apartheid. I even skipped school expressly to see him.

He continued his winning streak; the results made headlines in all the black newspapers; blacks all over the country rejoiced, including those who knew nothing about tennis. Arthur Ashe's triumphs on the court were becoming triumphs for the black race. His name was everywhere: in stores, in schools, in churches, in shebeens, in the madam's kitchen and garden. Every day I asked my mother to request a special prayer at her church for Arthur Ashe to win the tournament. I do not know why I did that, considering I was skeptical about religion. I must have wanted Ashe to win so badly that I felt all powers known to man had to be on his side.

Presumably Arthur Ashe knew that the success of his mission to South Africa would be measured not by the amount of his criticism of apartheid, but by how well he did in the tournament. If he were to win it, which, considering the way he was playing, was conceivable, then he would have proven that blacks had the ability to succeed—if allowed the opportunity.

If, however, he were to lose, say, to some white South African, then the myth of black inferiority would remain entrenched in the minds of whites, and it would become doubly hard, if not impossible, for black athletes to break down racial barriers.

One afternoon I followed a throng of spectators to a tent on a patch of green next to centre court. Arthur Ashe was scheduled to make an appearance. I tried to get to the front of the tent so I could hear him speak, from close up, but a multitude of white people—schoolchildren, adults and newspeople—mobbing him, for autographs and comments, prevented me.

Though I was some distance away, I could still hear snippets of his speech. His English sounded strange, heavily accented. He was so eloquent that white women giggled in admiration. It was as if he were talking through his nostrils. After answering reporters' questions for a while, he left for a waiting car. I marveled at how proudly he walked. I had never seen a black man walk that proudly among whites. He appeared calm, cool and collected, even though he was surrounded by a sea of white faces.

One thing I found remarkable about Arthur Ashe was that he was not afraid to dismiss questions from white people if he considered them worth ignoring, and say what he considered important. I had never seen a black person do that, unless he or she was mad or something. You answered everything the white man asked, and more.

Toward the end of Arthur Ashe's first week in South Africa, a story appeared in the World that he would be conducting a tennis clinic in Soweto. Several white South African players, among them Ray Moore, had volunteered to help him. Ray Moore was an interesting fellow. An avowed critic of his government's policies of apartheid, especially in sports, he was typical of South African liberals, who from time to time found themselves torn between conscience and patriotism. He was unequivocally opposed to racial segregation, yet he led an all-white South African team to its first-ever Davis Cup victory (won by default when the other finalist, India, refused to play in protest of apartheid).

Young black tennis players from all over the southern Transvaal were invited to take part in the clinic, but I was overlooked, though I was unarguably the best junior player in Alexandra. The reason: petty township politics and jealousy. Apparently, selectors of participants in the clinic left me out because of my association with the Barretts Tennis Ranch. I was disappointed but decided to go to Soweto anyway, for I wanted to see Arthur Ashe once again: he had made such a big impression on me that I hoped this time to get near enough to ask him a few questions about America.

I did not have train fare. Wilfred gave me a couple rands. He had now become my unofficial tennis sponsor; from time to time he gave me money to enter tournaments and travel to them, gave me tennis clothes, rackets and balls; and once in a while he would buy me a schoolbook, or help my family through hard times. And he did it all out of the goodness of his heart, without any trace of condescension or paternalism. It was the knowledge that white people like him existed that reinforced my belief that though whites in South Africa were generally prejudiced toward blacks, and in many cases treated us as less than dogs, there were, among them, those handful who would bend over backward to help black people—not as servants, but as equals. Such white people are the only hope for South Africa; the more their numbers increase, the better the chances for peaceful change.

The train ride to Soweto was a living nightmare. People dangled from windows and from the top of the train because the coaches were packed. In the coach I was in, a sickly black baby girl of about six months, strapped loosely in a cloth slung to her mother's back, was being crushed by the masses of black bodies packed like sardines, leading its mother to cry: "Stop killing my baby!"

"Why did you bring the damn thing here!" someone retorted.

Meantime, on the opposite tracks, trains for white people passed by, almost empty except for an occasional passenger relaxing on one of the cushioned seats, feet hung on the opposite, unoccupied seat.

Two black youths were electrocuted while riding on top of the train when it reached Croesus Station.

"Two more have bit the dust," said an old man.

"But why do they do it?" asked a short, jet-black man, obviously a stranger to Soweto.

"Where will they ride?" replied the old man.

"They could wait for other trains. With this one so packed, surely there's bound to be a roomy, if not empty, one shortly."

"Are you mad, brother?" said the old man. "There's never a roomy or empty train to Soweto. You think this one is packed? Wait till you see it during morning and evening rush hour, and during weekends. Then people get zapped not only while they're on top, but as they dangle from windows too. Others get crushed underneath. Wait till then, brother, and you'll sing a different song."

The stranger to Soweto shook his head in disbelief.

I arrived at my destination without further incident. As I made my way toward the tennis courts, however, I saw a man being robbed and murdered, in broad daylight, by a gang of *tsotsis*. I backtracked, and took the long way to the courts. When I reached the two potholed courts with tattered nets and broken fences, I found assembled about them the largest crowd of black people I had ever seen about a tennis court. As I made my way through the thick crowd, a one-eyed drunkard blocked my way and hiccupped, "Sipho is here, brother."

"Who's Sipho, brother?" I asked.

"Don't you know him, brother?" the man mumbled. "He's one of us."

"Who's one of us?"

"The one from Amelika," said the drunkard, and he staggered away. "The one with the Afro," he said over the shoulder.

So Arthur Ashe was considered a gift (*sipho* is Zulu for "gift"), a saviour. He had become the black messiah sent from strange shores to come liberate us. By attacking apartheid in a way no other black American entertainer or athlete had done, Arthur Ashe did appear to be a sort of messiah.

To me it seemed he had come expressly to reveal some previously hidden truth about what we black people can accomplish; a truth on which to focus my life, hopes and dreams. The difference between him and me, I deduced from that truth, was that he had risen above his suffering, that he had conquered his fear of the white man, that he had learned to beat white people at their own game. I knew that if my desire was (and to the umpteenth time it was!) to reach where Arthur Ashe had been, then I too had to rise above my suffering; I too had to conquer my fear of the white man; I too had to learn to beat white people at their own game.

I had to believe in myself and not allow apartheid to define my humanity.

Somehow, deep inside, I felt that I was on the right track. That it was simply a matter of time before something happened to make my dreams come true. I don't know why I felt that way.

Again, I could not make it close to Arthur Ashe. I circled around the courts a couple times, desperately looking for an opening; there was none. I resigned myself to standing at the back of everyone. Near where I stood, a group of young black demonstrators began to gather. A few carried placards the wording of which I couldn't distinguish.

"Go home, Arthur Ashe, go home," one of the demonstrators cried. "We love you, brother, but go home. We admire all you've done, but go home. We don't need you here, for your presence legitimizes the system. Go home, brother, and leave us alone. You're doing more harm than good by coming to South Africa. Tell the same to the brothers and sisters in America."

Amid the heckling and the jarring noise of passing trains, I tried to listen to what Arthur Ashe was saying through a megaphone. I couldn't hear a thing. In a desperate attempt to convince myself that I had heard him say something—because I dared not face up to the possibility, which was slowly becoming a reality, of having to leave without getting near him—I imagined him as having said the following militant speech:

"Don't give up the struggle, brothers and sisters, don't give up. Stay united, fight hard on all fronts, and some day soon you shall all be free. Your brothers and sisters throughout Africa have become free, millions more are becoming free every day. The drums of *Uhuru* [Freedom] cannot be stopped. The die is cast.

"Some day soon, apartheid will be no more, and democracy will prevail. One man, one vote will be the rule. In the meantime, learn to use the white man in the same way as he uses you. Above all, unite, brothers and sisters, for in unity lies your strength. Don't allow the enemy to divide you. Unite and fight for what you and the rest of the world believe is right, just. Truth is on your side, the numbers too. It's only a matter of time before the struggle is won."

There was no doubt that what Ashe had really said had come nowhere close to the militant speech I attributed to him; but emotionally, I believed that he had said the militant speech, and that I was able to hear it through some sort of ESP. So, when I left for the train station, I was glad I had made the nightmarish trip to Soweto.

Arthur Ashe lost in the finals to Jimmy Connors. The match was a thriller. Arthur Ashe played like a man possessed; and had Connors not been at his best, Ashe would have been crowned the champion. Despite the loss, Ashe's trip to South Africa was not in vain. He won the doubles with Tom Okker, a Dutchman, thus becoming the first black man in the history of tennis in South Africa to have his name enshrined among those of whites, for future generations to mull over its significance, or lack of it.

During his final days in the country, Arthur Ashe met with high-ranking government officials, and urged them to abolish apartheid in sports, or else the rest of the world would continue boycotting South African teams. One paper quoted him as warning whites to start extending equal rights to blacks, in all spheres of life, because time was running out, black patience was becoming exhausted, and black moderates were turning into radicals and revolutionaries.

Arthur Ashe left an enduring monument in South Africa. He established the Black Tennis Foundation (BTF), along with Owen Williams, a white liberal who ran professional tennis in the country, and one of the persons instrumental in bringing Arthur Ashe to South Africa. The BTF was funded by some of the country's major corporations, and was administered by a multiracial body of officials. Its mission was to make the game of tennis accessible to every black child in South Africa, from the cities and from the tribal reserves, who wanted to play tennis but had no resources to do so.

I began working even harder at my game because a few youngsters in Alexandra saw me as someone worth emulating. How I wished to succeed in tennis so that they would really have something to emulate. For the first time I told Scaramouche my dream of gaining passage to America through tennis, and he urged me to write to Arthur Ashe.

"You think he'll answer back this time, Oom [Afrikaans for Uncle] Scary?" I asked. I had already, through the BTF, written one letter and got no reply. I jotted down an emotional ten-page letter detailing the reasons why I felt I was worthy of a tennis scholarship. I again sent it through the BTF. Again there was no reply. My hopes of ever going to America fizzled. I continued teaching six-, seven- and eight-year-olds the little I knew about tennis, with the hope that they might someday succeed where I had failed. But the obstacles facing them were many, almost insuperable: they had no rackets, no balls, no decent tennis courts, no shoes. All they had was the determination, courage and resiliency so typical of African children.

Because of all the tennis work I was doing in the township, some of the people who hated me for playing tennis at the ranch began acting friendly, even going to the extent of telling me to let sleeping dogs lie. But there were those whose hatred and jealousy were implacable. These continued to call me an Uncle Tom, and to threaten me with death. I therefore was careful never to travel alone, to always keep in the open, to curtail my trips to the ranch and to do everything not to give them reason to carry out their threats. I guess I could have appeased them by simply staying away from white tennis players, but that I was not prepared to do. I somehow felt that my only chance to make something of myself depended very much on my cultivation of genuine friends among whites, who, after all, had the means to help me in times of need. Also, I had come a long way from my days of fear, hatred, ignorance and stereotypes to turn back.

39 In 1974, two and a half years after I began tennis, I won my first championship, the Alexandra Open, defeating David in the final. The trophy became my most prized possession. I became the talk of the school, and teachers pointed to me as "a student who mixed sports and studies well." When I took the trophy to the ranch Wilfred was full of praise. "I wish I had been able to see you play," he said. He had been refused a permit to enter the ghetto.

My trophy was prominently displayed in the bar, and whites were so full of praise and encouragement to win more that I felt saddened that most black children did not have the opportunities to learn about different whites as I did.

"So Wilfred's lessons are paying off, heh?" said a short, German fellow with whom I played from time to time.

"Yes, Wolfgang," I said. "I hope you'll be able to keep up the next time we play." Many whites at the ranch had accepted me as an individual, an equal, that I called them by their first names, instead of *baas*, and could joke with them. That was unheard of in many parts of South Africa.

"Soon we'll have to start a fund for you to play in all the big tournaments overseas," said Wolfgang. "Think you'll win Wimbledon some day?"

"As long as I keep on practising with you," I said, laughing, "I don't stand a ghost of a chance." He laughed. I served him liquor; he bought me a large glass of Coca-Cola. We exchanged banter, sitting at the same table. Thinking that I could be jailed for such behaviour if the police were ever to get wind of it did not prevent me from being spontaneous. "You've already crossed the Rubicon," I told myself.

Of course, this cheery view of life ended each day at the threshold of the ranch. Beyond, I was subjected to the same dehumanizing laws as any black. I came to develop a dual personality, and in the beginning, I could switch from one to the other as the situation warranted.

Gradually, however, like Jekyll and Hyde, one personality began to predominate. I could no longer pretend, fawn or wear the mask of servility, without my true self violently rebelling.

I knew that I had to find a safe way to be myself without breaking the law, or else I would surely go mad.

One afternoon I returned home from school and was preparing to leave for tennis practise when my mother, who had been away all day, burst through the door crying, "I've been saved, child, I've truly met the church of God and His messengers."

My reaction was, "Oh, hell, here we go again," but I went ahead and listened.

My mother proceeded to tell me about her meeting that afternoon on the bus from work with members of the Twelve Apostle Church of God, who subsequently proselytized her to their religion. The church, she said, was like no other she had ever come across.

"These people prophesy," she said animatedly. "They have the gift of tongues, just like the apostles in Jesus' time."

"Ma," I said, "can't you ever learn not to be taken in by quacks? Can't you ever learn, heh? Every one will profess anything to make money. There's no such thing as speaking in tongues, and you know it. Probably all it is is some gibberish someone cooked up to fool people like you, and make money doing it. I thought you were smarter than that, Ma."

"This is no gibberish, child," my mother insisted. "I've heard gibberish before. These people are for real. God has inspired them. What's more, they demand no money from anyone. All they say is that you have to become convinced of the power of God in your own good time. And child, the power of God *is* with these people. I've never seen a happier group. I'm going to become part of them."

"Well, do what you want," I said, "it's your life."

A week after my mother switched churches, her employer in Randburg, a suburb of Johannesburg, had her registered and given a work permit. How this came about, after all the years her application had been denied, I will never know. As if this weren't miraculous enough, she also found two other washing jobs the same week. My mother was quick to point out that God had a hand in all this.

The Twelve Apostle Church of God had such influence on her that she not only attended Sunday morning and evening hour-long services, but went to choir practise on Tuesdays, hour-long services on Wednesdays, and Thursday afternoon, her day off, she and other members went about the township visiting the sick and bringing more sheep to the fold.

The house became a pulpit. Everyone who passed through our

house had to be told about my mother's God. Her new God turned her into a believer that every problem was solvable, every obstacle surmountable; she never got angry or wished anyone ill or hated her enemies, for she believed that her all-loving God would not approve of such emotions. Even her criticism of my father lessened; she tolerated every abuse he hurled at her; she even gave him money. She loved to share the little she had and would often bring home complete strangers off the streets—tramps, prostitutes, lunatics and even *tsotsis* —and would share with them whatever little food was there, and occasionally she would let them sleep over for a night or two.

"Are you going mad, Mama?" I said to her one day as she came in with a crazy, filthy woman whose rags teemed with lice. The inside of her legs were lined with dried urine, and she smelled of shit.

"Isn't she a human being like you and me?" my mother asked, and proceeded to prepare a meal for the crazy woman who, meantime, kept scratching herself till she bled. She was sitting so close to my bed that I asked her to move away for fear that the vermin that were eating her might invade it. She laughed childishly, and moved closer to the bed, almost touching it.

I was enraged. "Mama, tell this bloody woman to move away from my bed, or else . . . !"

My mother asked her politely, and she complied.

As they were eating, out of the same bowl, my mother told her about God and how He could work miracles for those who believed in Him with all their hearts and accepted Him as their personal saviour.

"Do you know that God can cure you if you believe in Him with all your heart?" my mother asked the crazy woman, who replied by laughing and saying something in babytalk. She seemed more concerned with devouring the food. Shrugging aside the fact that the sermon was falling on deaf ears, my mother continued preaching in earnest, as if the crazy woman were the most attentive of listeners and on the verge of being converted.

I felt utter disgust. I stood up and left, wondering if indeed my mother was mad. Was the burden of black life finally muddling her brain? I could not face the possibility of an insane mother, yet each day, the more she became closer to her God, the stranger her behaviour became—so strange that some neighbours publicly called her a lunatic.

Concern for my mother's mental health led me to decide to go to her church and find out exactly what was going on there. If there was anything fishy going on, I would denounce it. The church was a zinc structure with wooden pews. The congregation was diverse: Zulus, Sothos, Tsongas, Xhosas and Coloureds. As I chatted with several members before services began I was struck by how similar their demeanour was to my mother's: they were passionate about their God, optimistic about the future and patient to the point of disgusting me. Saints and angels could not have behaved any better.

They laughed and smiled a lot, as if the world had no sadness or tears. They greeted each other as "brother" and "sister." The church hierarchy consisted of a priest, whose duties included interpreting dreams. Below him were eleven male deacons who helped in the running of the church. During services they sat behind the priest.

After several hymns the priest fell into a long prayer. Suddenly my mother, sitting in the front pew, leaped and let out a half-scream, which died as suddenly as it began. I stared at her in amazement, wondering what she was about. The priest stopped right in the middle of the prayer and extended his right arm in the direction of my mother, who then started speaking in tongues. I could not make out what she was saying, except that the voice was simply not hers. It had the gurgling sound of someone being choked. As she spoke, her limbs shook like an epileptic's, her pupils dilated. She seemed locked in deadly combat with a sinister force.

She prophesied for five minutes or so and then stopped, sweating as though she had been running a marathon, her face drained of all expression. Two women nearby fanned her with their handkerchiefs and sat her down. My youngest sister, whom my mother had been suckling when "the force" hit her, was returned to her by Florah, who was sitting alongside. The priest proceeded to interpret my mother's prophesy, but I was too anxious about her well-being to pay any attention to what he was saying. Directly after he finished the interpretation, two other women began speaking in tongues too. What they said was as unintelligible as my mother's gibberish; they too experienced the same physical symptoms as she. Again the priest offered interpretations, which were as meaningless to me as if he too were speaking in tongues.

I left the church as confused as I had entered it. But one thing was certain: my mother wasn't insane. She could in some mysterious way communicate with her God. But I knew I could never have her kind of faith; I could never believe as deeply in a God who seemed oblivious to the pain of blacks and seemed to favour whites, for suffering had made me, at too young an age, too dependent upon my own free will.

40 In June of 1975 I was chosen to represent the southern Transvaal black junior tennis squad in the National Tournament in Pretoria. I was the first player chosen from Alexandra. The thought of competing against top black juniors from all over the country led me to overtrain and I ended up doing poorly in the individual competition; but I helped southern Transvaal win the team trophy.

The two weeks in Pretoria opened my eyes fully to the stark realities of black tennis. All the junior players I talked to, from as far away as Natal, the Orange Free State and Cape Province, echoed the same problems: poor facilities, lack of tennis equipment, sponsorship or qualified coaches. As long as apartheid remained the way of life, I saw no future for me in black tennis. This realisation made me even more thankful that I had access to the tennis ranch. Wilfred was by no means the best white coach in the land, but he was better than all the black coaches put together, and the ranch facilities were superior to anything black children ever dreamed of having access to. Under his tutelage I knew I could afford to have dreams about tennis, about life. Without him I would most likely have ended up along one of those dead-end roads many black youngsters found themselves on.

A week or so after I came back from the National Tournament, my eyes began to hurt. At first I paid little attention to the pain, attributing it to fatigue. I had had many ailments in my life from sore teeth to migraines to pneumonia—but because medical attention was sought only in life-and-death situations by many blacks, I had simply waited for nature to take its course. I did the same with my sore eyes.

They got worse. They swelled and ached to the point where I could hardly read or keep them open for long, especially in light. My mother became alarmed. Everyone suspected witchcraft.

"The swines," my mother said when I told her I feared going blind; I had even stopped going to school. "They couldn't get at you any other way, so they went for your eyes. They've bewitched you, child."

I was amazed. "But I thought you were a Christian," I said to my mother.

"Being a Christian doesn't make voodoo stop existing."

"I don't think I've been bewitched," I said. "There must be some rational explanation to the whole thing. As soon as I have enough money I'll go to the clinic and have doctors check me."

Three weeks later on a Friday my mother gave me part of her monthly wage, and I went to the clinic. I found the place overcrowded with black women, men and children seeking treatment for all kinds of diseases and injuries. I waited on the long line; it became afternoon; still I was not attended to. By the time I was through with the paperwork many doctors had gone, and those that remained were giving priority to emergency cases. Apparently the fact that I was going blind was not considered an emergency; there were dying people around me. I returned on Monday (there was no outpatient service on weekends) and the story was the same—even worse because it was following a weekend.

"Ma," I said when I returned without receiving treatment. "Maybe I ought to go and see a specialist." A few white doctors were allowed to practise in the ghetto, but only the wealthy could afford to go to them.

"That would mean going a month without food," she said. "Why don't you go to Tembisa Hospital or Baragwanath; I can at least give you bus fare."

I went to Tembisa Hospital, which was two hours away by bus; Baragwanath was four hours away. What I found at Tembisa Hospital was even worse than at Alexandra Clinic. There was a long waiting list of emergency cases. I was told to come back in about a week's time, as my case was not a matter of life and death. At this point my eyesight was as good as a blind man's.

"Child," my mother said. "Let me take you to the witch doctor before it's too late."

I agreed. The following day we took a three-hour bus trip to Hammanskraal, a rural ghetto outside Pretoria, there to see what my mother described as the greatest diviner in the country. She was a short, fat woman with long strands of hair braided with red clay; a blown goat's bladder was tied to the end of one strand of hair; beads and bones circled her neck, and copper and silver bangles her arms; her face was caked with yellow mud; she was draped in goatskin.

After introduction ceremonies, my mother, the diviner and I went to a hut, where we sat on mats on the floor, opposite the diviner, as she arranged her divining bones and shells. My mother asked the diviner to tell us why we were there; this was supposed to be a test of the diviner's powers. The diviner took the array of bones and shells in her fat hands, shook them, muttering incantations, then threw them on the mat in front of her. She carefully watched the bones and shells roll and come to a stop. She stared at them as in a trance.

I simply could not believe what happened next. She began telling me my life's story, with such accuracy, from childhood all the way to the present, that all I could do was gasp. Things that I had done but forgot came to life as she unravelled my past; some of these things nobody but myself knew.

Am I dreaming? my mind reeled. I sought rational explanation for what seemed the supernatural. Had my mother told her about me? No, she couldn't have: I had been with her all the time. Besides, there were many events that the diviner mentioned that even my mother knew nothing about.

The diviner gave the diagnosis of my ailment. Several individuals, she said, some of them distant relatives, were implacably jealous of my successes in school. Because these people dared not kill me, for my ancestors were jealously protecting me, they had resorted to do the next best thing to murder—blind me.

Naturally, with my Western education, I found such an explanation preposterous; I decided to "test" the diviner.

"How are they bewitching me?" I asked.

"Even though that question is to test me," the diviner said, making me start, "to set your mind at ease, I'll answer it. But remember this: I can read all your thoughts." After a minute's silence, she said, "Set aside the white man's bifocals for a moment. See the world according to eyes native to you. Don't attempt to explain what I say or do the white man's way, for you will not understand. Be a son of Africa, and you'll understand." She again paused.

Then, after staring at me for such a long time that I thought I was naked, she said, in a voice of someone in a trance: "They've been doing it all along. And they are doing it now, these children of hell. And they'll continue to do it until they achieve their aim, if they're not stopped."

She paused.

"You write letters for people, don't you?" she resumed.

"Yes," I said in a quivering voice.

"Why?"

I told her.

"And you read letters for people, don't you?"

"Yes."

"Beware, then!" she said ominously, her voice suddenly booming. "That's how they're getting at you. That's the cause of your blind- ness. And if you don't stop, beware!"

I didn't know what to say or do. Those people I wrote and read letters for seemed as innocent as Jesus Christ and his mother, Mary.

"If I cure you, will you stop doing that?" the diviner asked.

"Yes."

The treatment began. She made me eat two bowls of soft porridge treated with a bitter, grey powdery substance cooked in a blackened earthenware pot. She gave me a pouch of the powder with instructions to take a couple teaspoonfuls with my meals. We went to a shallow stream nearby where she abluted me. She brought me back to the hut, where with an herbally treated razor blade she nicked two vertical cuts below each of my eyes and then smeared some strange ointment along the cuts.

"This should do it," she said mysteriously. "The evildoers can no longer harm you. But stop reading and writing letters for strangers, you hear?" she warned me as we were about to leave.

"Even my teachers?" I asked incredulously.

She pondered a while, then said, in a slow, deliberate voice, "No, teachers are okay. School is a different matter." I was so anxious to get away from the place I did not ask her why the exception.

I came home sobered by the experience. For days I wondered if indeed someone might be working the voodoo on me. I became so paranoid that not only did I stop writing and reading letters for strangers, I began burning every little scrap of paper with my hand-writing, for fear that it might fall into the wrong hands. Despite doing all that, however, I still had doubts that the witch doctor's prescrip-tion alone would cure me.

So, for peace of mind, I again went to Tembisa Hospital, and was lucky to find a doctor to look at me. He said that there was nothing wrong with my eyes, except that I had strained them by too much reading with too little light. He gave me eyedrops. I used the eye-drops, along with the witch doctor's medicine. My mother bought a paraffin lamp, and I was able to read under more light. My ailment gradually went away. What was responsible for it going away? The answer lies somewhere between witchcraft and Western medicine.

I stopped reading and writing letters for migrant workers, but still helped them in other ways. One day, one of them, Ndlamini, from one of the neighbourhood hostels, asked me to accompany him to the superintendent's office, where he had been summoned to appear for some violation of the Influx Control law.

This is how he had broken the law: because of a persistent drought and crop failure in the tribal reserve, he had brought his family—wife and three children—to live with him in the city. He had rented them a shack, and had just left the hostel to live with them under the same roof, when the summons came.

"I could no longer take it," he said to me, explaining why he did it. "We have been apart for so many years. And they've been suffering all the time alone in the Bantustan, despite the little money I sent them each month. All of it had to go toward paying tribal taxes, making the chief and his *indunas* [surrogates] rich. So I brought them to the city, so we could be together as a family. But that may soon end—because of this." He showed me the summons.

"How can I help?" I asked, looking about the crowded but neat shack. The eyes of his wife and children were riveted upon me as if I were their saviour.

"Every one knows you can talk English and Afrikaans like any white man," Ndlamini said. "Maybe you can talk with the superintendent and tell him that my family and me have to stay together because there's lots of trouble in the Bantustan. My pass is okay, I pay rent, I work hard every day and have never committed a crime— so why can't he please let us live together?"

"I don't know if I can make the superintendent understand your problems," I said.

"But people say you can talk well with white people," Ndlamini said. "They say you even play tennis with them."

"The kinds of white people I play tennis with are very much different from the superintendent," I said.

"If you can't talk to him," Ndlamini said, "then at least come with me to make sure that those black interpreters translate in good faith. Many of them tell the white man the opposite of what you're saying, until, that is, you give them a bribe. Then they will tell the truth. Think of a black man doing that to his own brother." He spat in disgust. "Oh, how the white man has succeeded in turning brother against brother."

"People will do anything to survive," I said. "Even if it be just a day longer than their victims."

The next day Ndlamini and I boarded a bus to the superintendent's office. We arrived there early, and when the office opened, we were the first the lord of Alexandra—a tall, heavyset white man in a brown suit—saw. He was slumped into an easy chair, and a short, black interpreter stood alongside him. As we entered, the latter eyed me suspiciously on account of my school uniform: long grey flannels, white shirt, shiny black shoes, a blue-and-gold blazer with a matching tie.

"Is this your father?" he said, staring at Ndlamini, who, in his shoddy overalls, looked anything but the father of an immaculate schoolboy.

"No, my uncle," I said, secretly winking at Ndlamini.

The superintendent, who had been looking over Ndlamini's dossier, suddenly stared at Ndlamini and said, "Why did you break the law, old man?" The black interpreter translated. I squeezed Ndlamini's hand, an indication that the translation from Afrikaans to Zulu was correct.

"I didn't know I was breaking the law, mei baas," Ndlamini said in a trembling voice.

"You didn't know it's against the law to bring your family to live with you?" the superintendent said incredulously.

"I swear I didn't know, mei baas."

"I find that hard to believe," the superintendent said, shaking his head. "You'll be sending them back to the Bantustan, am I not right?" he asked peremptorily.

"I'll be sending them back, mei baas," Ndlamini said in a defeated voice.

"Good," the superintendent nodded. Removing another piece of paper from the large dossier, he said, "I see here that when your family came over, you immediately left the hostel where the government had put you, and moved into a house without prior permission from this office. That was breaking the law. What made you do it?"

"I couldn't live with my wife and children in a men's hostel, mei baas," Ndlamini said. "And if I had waited to first get permission to move, mei baas, the shack would have long been taken. There were hundreds of people waiting to grab it, mei baas. Strue's God [As true as God exists], I'm telling the truth in every way."

"What's important to you, old man," said the superintendent, "violating the law by moving into a house without permission because others would take it? Or letting them take it, so long as you don't break the law?"

"Not breaking the law is by far the most important, *mei baas*," Ndlamini said.

"Then why did you break the law if you knew it was most important not to?" came the retort.

Ndlamini was tongue-tied. His brow started to sweat. His lips parched. He stared stupidly at the superintendent, then dropped his head, like a victim awaiting sentencing.

"Answer me, old man," the superintendent insisted. "Why did you break the law? Do you know you can be endorsed out?"

I intervened. "My uncle didn't know, sir," I said to the superintendent in impeccable Afrikaans. The black interpreter stared at me coldly, apparently wondering why I dared speak directly to the white man, and call him "sir," instead of the customary *baas*. It seemed as if he thought himself the only one privileged to address the white man as "sir," and I had infringed on that prerogative.

"*Jy praat afrikaans?* [You speak Afrikaans?]" the superintendent asked me, his face lighting up. The tone of his voice suggested that hitherto he had been bored, but that I had, by my unexpected usurpation of the black interpreter's duties, injected some excitement into the otherwise routine job of interrogating and sentencing a black Influx Control offender.

"*Ja, meneer* [Yes, sir]," I replied.

"Do they teach you Afrikaans at school?" he said excitedly. "I mean do they teach it *goed* [well]?"

"*Baie goed, meneer* [Very well, sir]."

"Do all black students like Afrikaans?" he asked. "It's a beautiful language, you know."

The truth was: black students without exception hated the language. But to please him, I said, "*Dit is 'n mooier taal dan Engels, meneer* [We like it better than English, sir]."

His face beamed at the words. Finally, he must have thought, after all these decades, his mother tongue, Afrikaans, was on its way to supplanting English as the language of the land.

"Afrikaans is a bloody beautiful *taal* [language], you know," the superintendent repeated with satisfaction. "All people have to do is take the time to learn it. You know, Afrikaans was invented on the African continent. It isn't a bastardization of Dutch, as some allege. It's a language born on the frontier, born of suffering, when we Afrikaners fought long and hard to conquer the hinterlands. So natural is Afrikaans to South Africa, that scientists say it's the easiest of all languages to learn."

He was lying. The damn language was so difficult to learn that many students wanted it outlawed; so many students each year were forced to repeat classes because they failed Afrikaans. God knows how I ever became competent in it.

"It's very easy to learn indeed, sir," I said.

"The whole world ought to learn it someday, don't you think?" he said. "Instead of the bloody English. It's so simple it would make communications better. People don't understand us and our political system because they don't know Afrikaans. English is dead; the empire has long crumbled. Though the bloody unpatriotic and liberal English in this country still dream that the empire is still intact."

I laughed. "The English don't know reality or the world as you do, sir," I said.

He chortled. "Heh, heh, heh. You're a very smart young chap," he said condescendingly. "You've got potential to become leader of your tribe some day. The future for you is as bright as stars on a cloudless Pretoria night." Turning to Ndlamini, he said, "You must respect the law next time, old man. You can go. Phineas," he addressed the astounded black interpreter, "put the dossier back in the cabinet, and give this poor brother of yours here the forms for him to fill out so his wife and children can remain in Alexandra until conditions in the Bantustan improve."

On the way home, Ndlamini couldn't stop calling me a "miracle worker." "I did nothing extraordinary," I said to him. "I simply told the bastard what he wanted to hear."

41

The Form Three syllabus required more debates. From the nature of the topics it soon became clear why: debates were simply another tool used by the Department of Bantu Education to train us for our "place" in South African life, to define the boundaries of our aspirations. There were no debates on social reform, freedom, equality, political systems and all those other topics that my wayward readings had led me to; topics that stimulated young minds to think, to grapple with the complexities of life and to strive to create a better and more just world.

Despite this lack I still found debates useful in practising English. Almost without exception students hated Afrikaans debates; not only was the language difficult to master, it was the language of our oppressors.

One topic that constantly came up for debate was "Country life is better than town life." Students loved and hated this topic. The ones chosen to defend it, hated it; those chosen to oppose it, loved it. For some reason, teachers always chose the best debaters to be on the affirmative, and I was one of them.

Given my feelings on tribalism, one would assume that I would have made halfhearted efforts to defend a positive view of tribalism. On the contrary, because I believed the opposite, namely, that town life was better than country life, I prepared myself thoroughly, for I knew that if what I believed in was true, then it had to withstand the severest test.

The school library, where I always went with classmates to prepare for debates, had a decent collection of books and encyclopedias, most of them donated by white liberals from Johannesburg's affluent suburbs, and by foundations set up by philanthropists like Harry Oppenheimer.

Despite a decent library, few students had a love for reading. And these were mostly from middle-class black families in which reading was encouraged at an early age. Of course I was the exception. But in a way, I think my mother's and Granny's storytelling had had the same effect upon me when a child, as the reading of books: my mind was stimulated, my creativity encouraged.

To feed my passion for reading, I checked out books at such a rate that the principal said to me, "Are you planning to read every single book in this library?"

I laughed, and said, "I just love reading, sir."

"But you are overdoing it," he said. "Always with a book. Don't you know that man can't live by books alone?"

"I don't read all the time, sir," I said. "I play tennis too."

"And what else?"

There was nothing more; the two were my life.

"Too much reading and too much tennis is not good for you," he said. "Find something else to do with your time."

"That's all I want to do with my time, sir," I said. "Play tennis and read."

"As for the books I see you reading," he said, "they are not what I would expect a black child to want to read. Why do you read them?"

The principal was right; my taste for books had been greatly influenced by the kinds of literature I had seen in the homes of white people. I was under the impression that in the kinds of books they read—poetry, philosophy, classics and so on—there must lie the secret of their power over black people.

"I don't know, sir," I said.

"What's that book you have in your hand?"

I had a copy of *Around the World in Eighty Days*.

"Why are you reading that?"

"Maybe one of these days I'll come to travel around the world too, sir," I said.

"You say it so confidently," he said. "What makes you so sure? What if you never go anywhere outside Alexandra for the rest of your life?"

"I *will* go somewhere, sir. I just have a feeling I will. I don't know why I have that feeling. Maybe I'm just dreaming. But I've had so many dreams come true in my life, that I now look toward dreams for the meaning of my life."

"Okay, philosopher," he said. "May I ask how you plan to travel around the world? Not in a time machine, I hope."

"Tennis will take me places, sir," I said.

"Why is it you want to go places?" he said. "Aren't you happy with the way your life is turning out right here in Alexandra?"

"Even if I were to become the richest man in Alexandra, sir," I said with feeling, "I could never be happy without my freedom. The books I've read have taught me about different ways of life, about places where I can be free to think and feel the way I want, instead of the way apartheid wants. That's something no amount of money can buy. To be honest with you, sir, I see no future for me in South Africa. And if I don't leave—and leave soon—I think I'll go mad or do something crazy, say, kill those who are stripping me of my humanity. My mind is changing, sir, I can feel it changing every day. The books I'm reading are changing the way I see the world, life, reality. I'm beginning to feel like a stranger in my own country."

The principal seemed stunned. He stared at me a while, then said, "I've always had a feeling this would happen to you. It always happens to students as sensitive as you are. Your kind cannot pretend. Maybe it's about time we black people stopped pretending and fooling ourselves that the white man will someday have a change of heart and accept us as equals, and end apartheid. We must start fighting for our rights. I and those of my generation thought we could talk to the white man and he would listen; but we were wrong. The white man listens to nothing but his fears, greed, and mistaken beliefs.

"It's time you young ones took over the struggle. You have what it takes to win. You're impatient, stubborn and willing to sacrifice even your lives for what you believe. All I can say to you is this: keep on reading and playing tennis. That may be your only way out of this nightmare. You're still young, yet already you know a different reality about white people; namely, that they are of two kinds—good and bad. Many black people don't know that. All they know is the racist, abusive and condescending white *baas* and madam. A word of caution, though—be careful, very careful, about the way you handle yourself in this unique position. By that I mean if blacks perceive you as being too closely associated with white people, they may call you a traitor, and do you harm. Always remember that the ghetto is where your home is, where your family is, where your friends are. Your white friends, even without apartheid, can never accept you as one of their own."

"I would never be one of them even if they begged me on their knees," I said. "I'm black and I'm proud, even though in this country, to be black don't seem to mean much. There was a time when I used to hate myself for having been born black, but that time is past. I see things more clearly now."

"I understand what you mean," the principal said. "I, too, once felt that way."

But many black people didn't understand. They interpreted my love for the English language, for poetry, for tennis, as a sign that I was trying to be white. My father constantly levelled this charge against me. He even thought me mad. I did not heed, and kept to my eccentricities, for in them I saw the only hope for the future.

The more books I read, the more I became confident that I could read anything written in English and understand it—as long as I had a dictionary. But when I encountered Shakespeare one cold and overcast day, I knew instantly that my confidence had been premature.

My English teacher, a tall, wiry fellow with a Ph.D. from one of the black universities, gave us *The Merchant of Venice* for a reading assignment.

"This is terrible English," I said to a classmate as we were reading the play.

"I'm never going to understand this," my classmate cried in despair. "If the teacher expects us to, he's mad. We don't have Ph.D.'s like he does."

"Let's try one more time," I said. "Slowly this time. Maybe the words will become familiar to the ear."

But my friend had had enough. I struggled on with the play and, by degrees, began understanding snippets of it. Sensing the difficulty we were having with the play, the teacher issued the following challenge: "Those students who make prose selections from the play, along with explaining what it's all about, will get double marks in exams."

Not one to give up on anything, I chose Portia's "quality of mercy" speech for my presentation. The speech, one of the few sections of the play I could understand, had moved me.

We had several weeks before giving our presentations. One night, as I was practising my oration, Uncle Piet came by and gave me a small transistor radio as a present for doing well in school. Up to then we had had no radio in the house. As I was fiddling with the various stations, I came upon one in the middle of a broadcast of a Shakespearean play—*The Merchant of Venice!* I was mesmerized. Here, I thought, was a way of learning correct pronunciation of all those archaic terms.

After listening to the broadcast, I read the play over several times, each time trying to imitate the voices on the radio. I did that for several days, until I developed an accent.

After I gave my presentation, the teacher said, with a smile, "There's someone who knows how to read Shakespeare. How did you do it, Shiver My Timbers?" He called me "Shiver My Timbers," after the character in *Treasure Island,* because of my habit of dressing in a blazer no matter how hot it was. I did so because my pants had an embarrassing patch right on the buttocks, which I was trying to hide.

I told him about the radio station, and that I had read the play over and over again.

"Listening to Springbok radio is an excellent way of learning how to speak English," he said.

From that day, Springbok radio became my favourite station. Not only did it air plays, but also world news, serialized mystery and high-seas adventure stories and poetry. So spellbinding were the broadcasts of this station, that each time something interesting came on, I would abandon whatever I was doing to listen. Afterward, I would try to read a piece of prose, a poem or a play with the same articulateness and clarity of the station. In this way, my pronunciation and ear for the English language improved.

One day I chanced to hear Dvorak's *New World* Symphony. Up to then I thought the only music was American pop and African vibes. Though I didn't understand the symphony, there was something haunting about it that touched my heart.

Each time I was over at the ranch, working in the bar, I would tune in to classical music. One day, Wilfred walked in and found me listening to a piano concerto.

"Do you understand this kind of music?" he asked.

I said no.

"Then how come you listen to it all the time?"

"I don't know. There's something about this kind of music that soothes."

"I guess you're right," Wilfred said. "One doesn't have to understand something to like it. But, nonetheless, you'll find that understanding classical music will increase your enjoyment of it."

Wilfred then said that I was welcome to listen to his vast collection of classical composers, mostly German, in his living room whenever I wanted to. I began reading their biographies to find out what, if anything, in their lives had influenced their music.

At school, my friends began to taunt me for liking classical music.

"Haven't you anything better to listen to?" they said.

"This is something better to listen to," I said.

"Better than Earth Wind and Fire, Percy Sledge, The Beatles, Abba, The Supremes, Boney M?"

"I do listen to that too," I said, "when I'm in the mood for it."

"Then why do you say classical music is the best?"

"When I'm in the mood for classical music," I said, "classical music is the best music in the world for me. And when I'm in the mood for African vibes or American pop, they too are the best in the world for me."

"Classical music and American pop don't go together," they said.

But they did for me.

My father saw my interest in classical music as another sign that I was trying to be white.

"First it was the books," he said. "Then tennis, then poetry, now it's this rubbish that white people listen to all the time. You really must be going mad. How many black people listen to that rubbish?"

"Many," I said.

"Name me one I know," he said.

I couldn't.

"You see," he said with malignant satisfaction. "You're the only one who's mad."

"I don't care."

"I give up on you, son," he said. "You can never become a man."

After the midyear exams, in which I obtained the highest marks in my class, I was chosen, along with Steve, a student from another class, as the first recipients of new scholarships from Simba Quix, the largest potato-chip-and-rusks company in South Africa. The scholarships were in recognition of our academic excellence in the three years we'd been at the secondary school, and were to help us on to matriculation—paying for everything: books, school fees and uniform.

The awards were made on Parent's Day, before a packed audience in the school courtyard. My mother and all my relatives were there, beaming with pride as the principal read a long list of my academic and athletic achievements. He then called me up to the rostrum to receive a check from Mr. Wilde, a senior manager at Simba Quix.

Mr. Wilde, a tall, broad-shouldered Englishman with a heavy accent and a limp in one leg, said, as he handed me the check, "The idea to award scholarships to achievers like Johannes and Steve, so that they can continue on to matric and university, came up as a result of my company's perception that more young black minds need to be nurtured to assume positions of leadership in our company. Our company does significant business with the black community, and we would like to see that grow. We would have begun this program long ago, had it not been for the laws. But now the laws have been relaxed somewhat, and we hope that Johannes and Steve here are the first of many.

"Not only are we awarding these fine young men scholarships which will pay for every one of their school expenses, but we're also offering them summer employment at our headquarters in Isando. They'll earn very good pocket money, and at the same time, will learn more about the company, for we hope"—here he smiled—"to do everything in our power to have them work for us after they finish school."

After a round of applause for Mr. Wilde's speech, students began putting on dramatic performances for the audience, which included several white people, benefactors of the school in one way or another. Various skits were performed, and I gave a reading of a dozen or so verses from Tennyson's "In Memoriam." A barbecue was held afterward.

42 No one thought it would happen, yet everyone knew it had to happen. All the hate, bitterness, frustration and anger that had crystallized into a powder keg in the minds of black students, waiting for a single igniting spark, found that spark when the Department of Bantu Education suddenly decreed that all black schools had to teach courses in Afrikaans instead of English.

The first spontaneous explosion took place in Soweto on the afternoon of Wednesday, June 16, 1976, where about ten thousand students marched through the dirt streets of Soweto protesting the Afrikaans decree. The immense crowd was orderly and peaceful, and included six- and seven-year-olds, chanting along with older students, who waved placards reading: To Hell with Afrikaans, We Don't Want to Learn the Language of Our Oppressors, Stop Feeding Us a Poisonous Education and We Want Equal Education Not Slave Education.

Unknown to the marchers, along one of the streets leading to Phefeni High School, where a protest rally was to be held, hundreds of policemen, armed with tear gas canisters, rifles, shotguns and *sjamboks*, had formed a barricade across the street. When they reached the barricaded street the marchers stopped, but continued waving placards and chanting:

"AMANDLA! AWETHU! AMANDLA! AWETHU! (POWER IS OURS! POWER IS OURS!)"

While student leaders argued about what to do to diffuse the situation, the police suddenly opened fire. Momentarily the crowd stood dazed, thinking that the bullets were plastic and had been fired into the air. But when several small children began dropping down like swatted flies, their white uniforms soaked in red blood, pandemonium broke out.

The police continued firing into the crowd. Students fled into houses alongside the street; others tripped, fell and were trampled underfoot. Some were so shocked they didn't know what to do except scream and cry. Still others fought bullets with rocks and schoolbags.

One youth saw a thirteen-year-old go down, a bullet having shattered his forehead. He picked the dying boy up, and carried him to a yard nearby. The photo of the two—the lifeless boy in the hands of a youth whose face blazed with anger, hate and defiance—made headlines around the world.

In the school bus from Tembisa, reading the gruesome accounts of what took place in Soweto in the late afternoon edition of the *World*, I felt hate and anger well up inside me. I cried. The entire edition of the *World* was devoted to the story. One of the pictures of the carnage showed a hacked white policeman near an overturned, burnt police car, surrounded by groups of students shouting defiant slogans, fists upraised in the black power salute. I gloated, and wished that more white people had been killed.

The bus was packed, yet silent. Heads were buried inside newspapers. Tears flowed freely down the cheeks of youths returning from school, and men and women returning from work. I again looked at the photo of the two boys, and then and there I knew that my life would never, could never, be the same again.

"They opened fire," mumbled David, who was sitting alongside me, shaking his head with disbelief. "They didn't give any warning. They simply opened fire. Just like that. Just like that," he repeated. "And small children, small defenseless children, dropped down like swatted flies. This is murder, cold-blooded murder."

There was nothing I could say in reply, except stare back. No words could possibly express what I felt. No words could express the hatred I felt for the white race.

"This is the beginning of something too ugly to contemplate," David said. "Our lives can, and should, never be the same after this."

I nodded.

At school assembly the next day, the mood was somber. There was tension in the air. There was a fire, a determination, in students that I had never seen before. The first thing the principal said was, "I guess you've all heard about the tragedy that took place in Soweto yesterday."

"Yes," the crowd of students roared.

"It is indeed a dark moment in our lives," the principal said. "But we here have to go on learning. The government has ordered all other schools to stay open. I'm sure things will settle down and will return to normal soon."

A murmur of disapproval surged through the crowd. One student in the back row shouted, "There can be no school while our brothers and sisters are being murdered in Soweto!"

"Yes, yes, no school, no school!" erupted the rest of the students.

"There will be no demonstrations in this school," the principal said authoritatively. "We've had enough bloodshed in Soweto already."

"The struggle in Soweto is our struggle too," some students clamored. "The Afrikaans decree applies to us as well. We too want an equal education. The bloody Boers should stop force-feeding us slave education. To hell with Afrikaans! To hell with Afrikaans!" The cry infected everybody. Students began organizing into groups to plot strategy for a peaceful rally in solidarity with our brothers and sisters in Soweto. The principal tried to restore order but was ignored. Most teachers helped us with the planning of the rally. "Be peaceful and orderly," one teacher said, "or else you'll have the whole Boer army down your necks in no time."

We painted placards that condemned Bantu Education, Afrikaans and apartheid. We demanded an equal education with whites. We urged the government to stop the killings in Soweto. Student leaders were chosen to lead the march to other schools in the area, where we planned to pick up more students for a rally at a nearby stadium. Within an hour we had filled the street and formed columns. We began marching.

"*AMANDLA! AWETHU! AMANDLA! AWETHU!*" we chanted and waved placards.

From government buildings nearby white people who headed the Tembisa city councils hurriedly stepped out, jumped into cars and zoomed off under police escort. Our ranks swelled with youths who didn't attend school. Black men and women cheered and exhorted us from yards alongside the streets. "TO HELL WITH A FOURTH-CLASS EDUCATION!" "STOP THE GENOCIDE IN SOWETO!" "*AMANDLA! AWETHU! AMANDLA! AWETHU!*" The cries reverberated through the air.

We picked up hundreds of students from other schools and then headed for the stadium. As the river of black faces coursed through the street leading to the stadium, a group of police vans and trucks suddenly appeared from nowhere and barricaded the street.

"Don't panic! Don't panic!" the student leaders yelled at the restless crowd. "Let's remain peaceful and orderly. They'll leave us alone if we don't provoke them."

Policemen with riot gear, rifles, tear gas canisters and *sjamboks* poured out of the trucks and formed a phalanx across the wide street. As in Soweto, most of them were black. From one of the trucks the husky voice of a white man suddenly boomed through a megaphone: "DISPERSE AND RETURN TO YOUR HOMES AND SCHOOLS! OR WE'LL BE FORCED TO USE FORCE!"

A few students started turning back, but the majority stood and waited, chanting defiantly with fists raised in the black power salute. We began singing, *"Nkosi Sikelel'i Afrika"* ("God Bless Africa"), the ANC's anthem:

> *God bless Africa*
> *Raise up our descendants*
> *Hear our prayers.*
> *Come, holy spirit,*
> *Come, holy spirit,*
> *Lord bless us,*
> *Us, your children.*

The police charged. Several shots rang out. Pandemonium broke out. Students fled for cover. It rained tear gas canisters. David and I managed to flee into one of the nearby yards, jumped its fence and ran all the way to school, where teachers told us to go home immediately, for police were raiding schools. The bus stop was a mile or so away. As we made our way through the matchbox-type Tembisa houses, we saw fires and palls of black smoke in the distance. Some beer halls and vehicles had been gutted.

"I hope there's still a bus out of this place," David panted.

We found what turned out to be one of the last buses out of Tembisa, for the police were quarantining the ghetto, barring all company vehicles and public transportation. On our way to Alexandra there was unusual traffic on the highway leading to the Jan Smuts Airport.

"White folks are fleeing by the droves," I remarked.

"They're afraid this whole thing may turn into a revolution," David replied.

Approaching Alexandra, we saw several armoured cars formed into roadblocks, sealing all the roads leading in and out of Alexandra. All vehicles were being stopped and searched. Our bus was stopped, and several soldiers in camouflage uniforms, carrying automatic weapons, ordered us out and lined us up alongside the body of the bus. I shook like a leaf. In the distance, Alexandra resembled a battlefield. Smoke and fire engulfed the area, and from time to time, the sound of gunfire reverberated through the clouds of smoke.

"You'll have to walk home," one of the white soldiers ordered us. "Buses can't go in there. You bloody Kaffirs are burning down everything."

We immediately headed homeward across the veld. From time to time, people glanced nervously over their shoulders, afraid of being shot in the back. When David and I entered Alexandra, we saw several burning government buildings, beer halls, schools, stores belonging to Indians and Chinamen. A bus had been overturned and set afire. People were looting all around, making off with drums of paraffin, bags of mealie meal, carcasses of beef still dripping blood, Primus stoves, boxes of canned goods, loaves of bread and so on. There were power and energy in men, women and children that I had never seen before.

The rebellion had begun in Alexandra.

Over the next few days, it spread to black ghettos in other parts of the country: Pretoria, Springs, Daveyton, Kwa-Thema, Durban, Port Elizabeth, Cape Town. Schools, clinics, government buildings, beer halls, stores belonging to whites, Indians and Chinamen, PUTCO buses, Coca-Cola and other delivery trucks—all went up in flames. Black schooling came to a virtual standstill.

Without schooling the student movement was better able to coordinate its activities. Marches were planned, demonstrations were held, and the black work force was urged to stop working in solidarity with student grievances.

"Our struggle is your struggle," exhorted student leaders. "If we unite and work together, we can and will bring down this evil system. We can defeat the whites. Unity is strength."

At first, black workers were supportive of the students and stayed away from jobs. But gradually, due largely to threats of dismissal from jobs, the need for money to survive and intimidation and beatings by the police, many black men and women returned to work.

The police even succeeded in turning some black workers against the students. In Soweto Zulu migrant workers were reported to have formed vigilantes groups and, with police license, hacked, stabbed and clubbed students to death. To some extent the same thing happened in Alexandra. As black fought against black, Alexandra was sealed off by armoured vehicles and soldiers, to prevent the violence and carnage from spilling into the suburbs, where whites were buying shotguns and rifles. Many were reported leaving the country every day. Each night Prime Minister Vorster and Minister of Police Kruger went on radio to reassure panic-stricken whites that the situation in the ghettos would soon be brought under control.

The death toll mounted. One hundred . . . one hundred and fifty . . . two hundred killed. The more of us they murdered the more bitter and angry we became, and the more we fought on and the more destruction we wreaked. Black schools were ordered closed indefinitely; that is, those that hadn't yet gone up in flames.

Black informers began to mushroom all over the place. In order to stay alive black people sold each other to the white man. The student movement was infiltrated, its leaders arrested in massive pre-dawn raids and detained without trial. New laws went into effect specifically designed to quell black anger. Journalists and teachers and community leaders were arrested along with students. Without leaders the student movement became disorganized.

Each day I found myself in the company of bloodthirsty mobs. I had lost control of myself and seemed possessed by a sinister force, which made me mindless of my safety, which spurred me toward reckless action, unafraid of death.

We had no guns, *sjamboks*, tear gas or armoured vehicles, but we soon learned how to make petrol bombs. The orgy of violence and destruction and killing continued unabated.

One morning I followed a mob that was going about the ghetto, burning and looting stores and butcher shops belonging to Indians and Chinese, whom everyone thought had become rich through cheating and overcharging black peasants. One such Chinese family (the same I had worked for) owned several stores and butcher shops on Twelfth Avenue. The family had fled the first day the riots broke out, and had left three vicious dogs to guard their property behind a high fence. When the mob arrived at the property several out-of-work men and *tsotsis* who were our leaders conferred on what to do with the dogs in order to break into the stores. One of the out-of-work men had apparently worked there after me and he said, "I used to feed and wash these dogs every day. They love meat." A chunk of meat was promptly found and poison spread all over it. It was then thrown over to the dogs, who apparently hadn't eaten anything since their owner fled. They devoured the poisoned meat, much to the jubilation of the crowd. While the dogs groaned and gasped the fence was cut and the mob poured in. Several *tsotsis*, armed with machetes, hacked the dying dogs into bloody pulps.

"I wish the Chinaman was here," one of them said deliriously.

For an instant I became aware of the senselessness of what we were doing. But those misgivings gave way to euphoria as I saw black peasants making off with plundered goods. I joined in. While the mob looted furiously, word came that several army trucks were headed in our direction. Having found little loot thus far, a couple friends and I lingered while the rest of the mob fled.

Moments later we too left, lugging the spoils of our scavenging. On the way home we linked up with another group, mostly girls and women, who had just raided an Indian shop nearby. Everyone was happy. Everyone now had precious food to last a while. Even the destitute could now boast of owning something. I scanned the faces around me and saw the poverty of hate and anger mirrored in them. "These are the makers of a revolution," I said to myself, recalling the movie, *A Tale of Two Cities*. If it had not been for the cordon the army had formed around Alexandra, there would have been a massacre of whites. I could see the guillotine and tribunals of black peasants.

As we headed home people said to one another:

"This paraffin drum will keep the family going for months."

"This bag of mealie meal will last forever."

"I don't know where I'll store this meat," complained someone who was lugging a whole carcass of a sheep over his shoulder. "We don't even have a bathtub where we could put it in some ice."

"Just go to a store that sells bathtubs and take one," came the reply.

"I have enough candles to light up the whole Alexandra."

"I have enough Coca-Cola to drown myself in."

"My little twin sisters won't have to cry all night because I have enough infant formula to replace my mother's dry breasts."

"The rats will wish they had never invaded our house. This bag of Rotex will wipe them off the surface of the earth."

As the crowd of looters made its way down Twelfth Avenue, a cry suddenly went up: "The army is coming! The army is coming!"

Suddenly shots rang out. Tear gas canisters dropped in our midst like hailstones. People abandoned their loot and ran for cover. Several young girls, including two who lived in my yard, ran confusedly about the street, coughing and choking from all the tear gas.

"Run this way! Run this way!" several people screamed at the girls. I was busy soaking my shirt at a nearby communal tap so as to combat the effects of tear gas. More shots rang out. More tear gas. I ran into a tin-and-plastic shack nearby.

"Why are you doing all this?" mumbled the owner of the shack, a grey-haired old man in a threadbare coat, with deformed legs and a bent back. "You know that the police are out to kill all of you."

"It's hunger and hate and anger, *Ntate* [Father]," I said, peeping throught the grimy window at the teargas-enveloped street.

"They'll kill you all," he repeated. "Yeah, that's what white people want to do, kill us all."

"We'll kill some of them too, *Ntate*," I said, still peering through the window.

"What is it you children are fighting for, anyway?" he said, hawking up phlegm and swallowing it.

"To be free, *Ntate*," I said. "We're fighting so that you, me and every black man, woman and child in this country can lead a life of dignity."

"It can never be done," the old man shook his head. The white man will always rule. The freedom struggle is dead."

"It's been reborn in us, *Ntate*," I said. "We'll pick up the flame of liberation and march onward to victory."

"That can never be done," the old man said. "You should not sacrifice your young lives for something that can never be."

"Freedom *will* come to South Africa, *Ntate*," I vowed. "Azania will be born, and we, the young ones, will do it. To die fighting for one's freedom is no sacrifice, for life without freedom isn't worth living. We've been under the white man's yoke for too long, *Ntate;* it's time we tore the chains."

While talking to the old man, I had taken my eyes off the street. Suddenly I saw something that make me start with horror. I said to the old man, in a trembling voice, "Is there any quick way out of this yard beside through the gate?"

"Yes, why?" the old man said.

"I just saw a girl I know being dragged away by the police," I said. "And I think she's dead, but I'm not sure. There was blood all over her dress."

The old man's mouth dropped in horror. "Oh, God! Oh, God!" he cried. "What's the world coming to? What are they doing to us?"

"How do I get out?" I insisted. "I've got to get to her home and tell her parents."

The old man told me there was a small opening in the fence near the lavatories in the back of the yard, which led to Eleventh Avenue; and from there, if I was extremely careful, I could make my way to Thirteenth Avenue in no time.

I reached Mashudu's home only to find her family moaning. Apparently the tragic news had already reached them—the twelve-year-old schoolgirl was indeed dead.

The next day her parents went to the police station to claim the body for burial and were told to pay for it.

She was buried that Sunday, under cloudy skies and an intermittent drizzle. Even though police had banned all gatherings of more than three people, including those of families who wanted to bury their loved ones, hundreds attended Mashudu's funeral, mostly her schoolmates. We carried the small brown coffin shoulder high, intoning African liberation songs. As it was being lowered into the six-foot grave, the preacher, a grey-haired old man with fire in his eyes, said the following eulogy:

"In her, as in hundreds of other black children who have died since this whole nightmare began, had been embodied the hope for a better Africa. Give us strength and courage, O Lord, to triumph over our enemies, our oppressors. Let this child's death, and all the others, be not in vain. Let there come out of all this spilled innocent blood a new South Africa, where we can live in dignity and freedom. As you receive her soul into your bosom, O mighty God, send us the weapons to carry on the struggle against injustice, to carry on till all Africans are liberated. Out of dust we came, back to dust we return. . . ."

As the grave was sealed, it occurred to me that it could easily have been me or any of my siblings in it. I shook with rage and hatred. Why did they kill her, why? I asked myself. She was so young, so full of life and promise. I used to play with her when I was growing up; I had called her "my wife" many times when we played house with other children in the yard. Now she was gone; her life snuffed by a white man's bullet.

Tears streamed down my face. I wondered what direction my life would take now. As the crowd sang *"Nkosi Sikelel'i Afrika,"* I heard Mashudu's brother vow, "They'll pay for this." After the funeral I went back home, shut myself in the bedroom and questioned a belief I had long cherished: that there was a place in South Africa for the teachings of Mahatma Gandhi, that what Martin Luther King, Jr., had done for blacks in America could be done for blacks in South Africa.

No, I was all wrong. The black man's freedom from apartheid could be attained only through the barrel of a gun, amid rivers of blood. The doctrine of nonviolence, of passive resistance, couldn't work against the Boers. To be free, we had to fight the white man, shed his blood, vanquish him on the battlefield. Do I have the courage to kill another human being? I asked myself. My mind refused to answer the question.

43 The rebellion intensified. More black students were killed in clashes with police. Anarchy reigned in the ghettos. The government continued reassuring whites that the situation in the ghettos was under control, that it was only a matter of time before complete order was restored. The government was of the mistaken belief that the student rebellion was ANC-inspired, that students' grievances about the inadequacies of Bantu Education were chimerical, and that as soon as outside Communist agitators had been ferreted out, tried and hanged, blacks would once more be the peaceful, law-abiding, subservient lot whites were used to.

To dramatize the lie Prime Minister Vorster left for Germany for a meeting with the American secretary of state, Henry Kissinger, despite advice by the Progressive party (now Progressive Federal party) that he not go, but remain and talk to authentic black leaders on ways to end the unrest.

Because Alexandra has been cordoned off from the white world by army trucks and soldiers, and only those black men and women who were indispensable to white businesses and homes were allowed in and out, after thorough searches, I hadn't been able to visit the ranch since the outbreak of the rebellion. Out of touch with sane whites, I began to hate all whites. Why weren't liberal whites doing something to stop the slaughter of innocent black children? Why weren't they demanding investigations into the brutal and indiscriminate use of force by police? Why weren't they applying pressure to their representatives in Parliament to force them to enact legislation abolishing Bantu Education and to address a myriad of other black grievances?

The loud silence of the white electorate turned many black moderates into radicals and radicals into revolutionaries. I heard rumours daily that there would soon be an insurrection of black masses throughout the country, that the ANC was secretly organising peasant armies to overthrow the regime, that soon the streets would run red with blood—white people's blood.

Among my friends there was persistent talk of leaving the country and joining the ANC's revolutionary wing, *Umkhonto We Sizwe* (Spear of the Nation), then coming back armed with bazookas and grenades to fight whites to the death. The idea of becoming a freedom fighter appealed to me, now that doubts about the efficacy of nonviolence had been proven true. The more I saw blacks killed by policemen the more revolutionary I became. South Africa will soon be free, I vowed, and I will help set her free.

There was a man named Ngwenya in our yard. He was from Rhodesia (now Zimbabwe), where Robert Mugabe and Joshua Nkomo were fighting a guerilla war to overthrow the white minority rule of Ian Smith. Several of Ngwenya's relatives were freedom fighters in the Patriotic Front, and I visited him one evening to find out more about revolutionary fighting. We had been talking for a while when I finally declared, "I want to become a freedom fighter."

"What kind of freedom fighter?" Ngwenya inquired.

"The one in the bush, with a gun, killing whites," I said.

"To be honest with you," he said, "I can't imagine you with a gun, let alone killing somebody. You love tennis and books too much. One becomes a guerilla fighter when one sacrifices everything for the gun."

"I can do that to bring an end to apartheid."

"Even if you could sacrifice everything," he said, "which I don't doubt you can do, I still think guerilla fighting is not for you."

"It is for me," I said with the impetuosity of youth.

"Can you sacrifice even your tennis and books?" he said with a wry smile. "You know there are no tennis courts or libraries in the jungle, only swamps and thickets. In guerilla fighting you're trained not to make friends with white tennis players but to kill them. When under fire there's no time of dreaming of someday going to America. Can you live such a life?"

"Yes," I said impulsively.

As we talked tear gas began seeping in through a hole in the door and cracks in the windows, and Mrs. Ngwenya, who all along had been sitting by the coal stove, patching her five children's rags, silently stood up, wetted some rags, woke her six-month-old baby up and began dabbing its mouth with the soaked rag to stop it from choking with tear gas.

"This has been happening every night since the riots began," Mr. Ngwenya said bitterly, as he awakened the rest of his children, ranging in age from three to ten. I helped him prepare soaked rags for them. From experience I knew that no one could sleep when the police engulfed the ghetto with tear gas at night to keep blacks off the streets. The method worked, but black families paid a heavy price and children were hardest hit: there had already been several tear gas-related deaths.

Before I left, Mr. Ngwenya said, "There's room for people with your brains in the struggle. Your kind fight on a different front. Teachers and doctors and lawyers are needed to care for the wounded, defend political prisoners and teach the masses about freedom. Writers are also needed to tell the rest of the world what the struggle is all about. So, you see, you don't need only a gun to fight against apartheid. There are many roads that lead to Rome. Think about using your talents in the struggle."

Police power had been so relentlessly and ruthlessly applied that when October rolled around the rebellion had been largely contained. Only a few pockets of sporadic violence remained. Hundreds of black clergymen, journalists, civil rights activists, teachers, lawyers, students and anyone suspected of subversive acts had been detained. Thousands of black students had fled the country to escape arrest. The official death toll in the four months of violence stood at about four hundred; the unofficial figure was twice that.

After a few meetings with puppet black leaders (genuine leaders were languishing in jails under indefinite detention) the government announced that it was no longer mandatory for black schools to teach in Afrikaans. So instead of taking the first step toward improving education in black schools by abolishing the hated language, the government was offered flimsy excuses why in some cases the language had to be learned: "The trend of the future is towards the complete Afrikaanization of South African society, so it will be to everyone's benefit to learn Afrikaans."

After puppet black leaders had ratified the Afrikaans compromise, after the government had crushed with its awesome military might the various black movements that had sought to bring about fundamental reform in Bantu Education, the government ordered black schools reopened. But few school buildings had survived the rebellion. Fewer students returned to classes. Many had been killed, many had fled the country, many were in detention and many were simply afraid to enter a classroom for fear that the police would take them away.

I returned to school but found it impossible to study. After almost six months without schooling, my enthusiasm for learning had been dampened. Besides, I felt, as did many other students, that with Bantu Education, the source of all the violence, still in place, there was no point in learning.

"What did we fight for? What did many of us die for?" was the common feeling among students. Of the few who did return to school, most soon left to seek work. Some girls were forced to leave, for they had become pregnant during the rebellion. Morale among teachers was low. Some became the object of hate for allegedly acting as informers and providing police with lists of student leaders. One teacher offered this flimsy excuse for his treachery: "Because of repeated threats by the police to arrest and kill all students, including innocent ones, we [traitors] provided them with lists of student leaders to prevent a massacre. What's better? A few dozens of you in jail, or all of you dead?"

We would have preferred death.

44 The reopening of schools led to an easing of government restrictions on black travel into white neighbourhoods, and I was able to visit the ranch for the first time in two months. It was an early Tuesday morning, cloudy and windy. The black bus to Pretoria dropped me right in front of the ranch, and as I came up the sloping driveway leading to the clubhouse, I saw Wilfred just leaving the tennis court following a lesson with a short, blonde white woman in a blue-and-white Adidas warm-up. At first Wilfred didn't recognize me, but when he did his eyes behind a pair of gold-rimmed glasses popped out.

"*Mein Gott!*" he cried, as if seeing a ghost. "Look who's here! Mark! So you're still alive!"

I nodded and smiled.

Wilfred and the white woman were standing on a patch of freshly mown grass in front of the first of four all-weather tennis courts, whose surface was strewn with Dunlop tennis balls. Wilfred said something in German to the white woman; she smiled and greeted me in a soft voice with a German accent.

Wilfred, wriggling into his white Adidas sweater, said to me, "Can you please pick up the balls and take them with you to the clubhouse. I'll be with you in a minute." He accompanied the white woman to her car, a snow-white Mercedes Benz of the latest style. I hurriedly picked up the balls and then headed for the clubhouse, where I gulped two large glasses of ginger ale and munched several scones, having left home without eating breakfast, while reading the *Rand Daily Mail*, whose front page was filled with stories of continued violence in ghettos around the country. Minutes later Wilfred entered, a smile on his face.

"So," he said, taking a bottle of Kronebrau beer out of the fridge, "how did you manage to stay alive? You haven't been here in so long that we feared something must have happened to you. The newspapers were full of stories of violence and killings and arrests in the townships. I understand Alexandra was one of the hardest-hit areas."

I said yes and proceeded to recount the nightmare of the past two months. Wilfred listened sullenly.

When I ended he shook his head in disbelief and muttered a curse in German. "But how could the police and army do such things?" he asked angrily.

"I don't know," I sighed.

"You know, we whites have never heard about the atrocities you've just described. What I can't understand is why the bloody government would go on the air each night and say everything was under control, that the few Communists responsible for starting the riots were being efficiently rounded up and black life was returning to normal. When in fact the police and army were shooting down innocent people."

It was clear why news about unrest was censored: the government didn't want whites to panic, or the rest of the world to know about police excesses in dealing with unarmed protesters. While the liberal English papers strove for more detailed coverage despite the censorship, by sending their black reporters into the ghettos, the progovernment Afrikaans papers churned out successive scathing editorials and commentaries deploring the damage to government property, the intimidaton of black workers and the murders of black policemen, mayors and other collaborators with the system.

Claiming that the ghettos were in danger of disintegrating into anarchy instigated by the ANC, the Afrikaans papers urged the government to use maximum force to restore law and order. The ANC, they claimed, was a "terroristic" Communist movement out of touch with the aspirations of blacks, who were perfectly satisfied with the way things were. They then called on all responsible and law-abiding blacks to help the government thwart attempts to turn South Africa —a Christian, civilized, peace-loving multinational democracy—into a Russian satellite. The horrors of African nations under the throes of communism were graphically spelled out: mass starvation, coups and countercoups, mass murders, high infant mortality rates, torture for political dissidents, Draconian laws allowing for any opponent of the system to be arrested without charges and detained without trial.

"Mark," Wilfred said, "everybody will be in the bar tonight. After playing, will you come and tell them the things you've just told me?"

"Wilfred," I said, "you're not offended by the truth because you have an open mind. But many whites are not like you. They don't want to hear the truth, especially how a black man says it. You see, I feel so emotional about what the police and the government are doing to my people that I can't lie for the sake of easing the consciences of white people. The only way I can tell it, is like it is."

"I want you to tell it like it is," Wilfred said. "The truth. Don't worry about how it'll be received. I'll take care of anything that comes up. I give you my word."

I served hundreds of tennis balls and hit more against the wall till about six, then went to the bar. The place was stuffed with animated white faces. Except for two female servants who shuttled between the kitchen and the bar, I was to be the only black. Wilfred stood behind the counter, serving gin, whisky, bourbon, Bloody Marys, and Kronebrau beer. The stereo at the far end of the counter blared popular tunes. White men and women drank, chain-smoked, munched pretzels and other eatables, gossiped eagerly and played darts. As I walked in, damp with sweat, all activity ceased; people drifted toward tables. I sat on a bar stool near the counter facing everybody. Someone bought me a large glass of ginger ale.

From behind the counter Wilfred said, "You all know Mark here.

He's going to tell us the truth about what is going on in the townships, and will answer any question. Go on, Mark."

I held back nothing. The effect was tremendous. White women gasped and sickened; white men shook their heads, some grinned. The questions came.

"But why do you burn your own schools and clinics, and kill your own people?" asked a short, stocky German named Hans. "It's senseless."

"First of all," I said, "it's the police who do most of the killing. Second of all, because the army has sealed off your areas, we can't get at you and kill you. At your property and burn it. We would dearly want to do that. So for the time being, till we devise ways of reaching you, symbols of oppression and collaborators with the system are convenient and necessary targets of our hatred and anger."

Every face stared at me. For a moment I thought I had overstepped my limits. But I felt that if it was the truth they wanted, I had to give it to them in its bleeding nakedness.

"Was Afrikaans the sole cause of the riots?" asked an English liberal named St. Croix.

"What we black students did on June 16 was not riot," I said. "We spontaneously rebelled against an education system designed to make us slaves. And black education is not the only thing that's wrong in this country. Afrikaans was merely the spark that set off a time bomb that's been ticking all these years that we blacks have been living as fourth-class citizens. We black youths feel the same bitterness and anger and hatred that our parents feel. But unlike them we are not prepared to perpetually turn the other cheek, to smile and say, 'Yes, *baas*,' 'Yes, madam,' while our humanity is being trampled to fragments. We've realised that our freedom will not come from a white man's change of heart. We have to fight for our rights."

"What you're saying contradicts what I see and hear every day in my company," said Ziegfried, a tall, bald-headed German who worked as senior manager for a large German electronics company in Johannesburg. "I meet well-educated and happy blacks, who tell me with great warmth and eloquence how conditions are improving in the townships. They show me pictures of beautiful homes with swimming pools, double garages, lawns and flowerbeds. Some of these houses, I must say, are fancier than white people's. So where does all this anger and bitterness come from?"

"You've just described the elite black middle class," I said, "a hopelessly small minority whose aspirations are no different from those of the white man. Many of them make money any way they can so they can live comfortably. The fact of the matter is that the majority of blacks are peasants. They live in shacks and mud houses, they walk barefoot on dirt streets strewn with rocks and broken bottles, their infants often die of malnutrition, their children's growth is stunted, for them education and medical treatment are not free, they live in constant fear of running afoul of the degrading pass laws, of being deported to impoverished tribal reserves. Their lives tell a different story about apartheid and please don't call ghettos townships."

I paused. Across the stuffy bar heads shook. All the time I had been talking, I had been unconscious of myself, of what I was saying. But now reality sunk in. "Did you just say all that to white people?" I asked myself. But something inside me told me that this was probably the only opportunity I'd ever have in this world to tell white South Africans the truth about black life. That gave me courage.

"What is it that black peasants want, then?" asked an Afrikaner with a scruffy red beard, in soiled overalls. He was foreman at the Barretts Tennis-Court Construction Company. His responsibilities included supervising a large pool of cheap black labor.

"Plainly and simply put: we want to be free," I said. "We want to be regarded as human beings in the land of our birth. And the present political system denies us that right."

"So it has to go?" he said with a sinister grin.

"Yes."

"What would take its place?"

"Democracy."

"Don't we have that already?"

"No."

"So you want one man, one vote?"

"Yes."

"To rule over us white people, is that it?" he said. "To make us slaves."

"No," I said, "we blacks are not in the least interested in making slaves out of you. We simply want a country where race and colour don't determine your place in the sun. We want a South Africa where everyone—black, Coloured, white and Indian—is equal before the law. We want to live in peace with everyone as a nation united."

"Since when did blacks want to live peacefully with whites?" he asked. "You're our eternal enemies. God created us that way. Centuries ago we tried to civilize you, to convert you from pagan savages into Christ-loving human beings. And how did you react? You slaughtered us and ate our missionaries. Since the days of Jan Van Riebeeck your bloodthirsty chiefs have sought to exterminate us, 'to drive us back into the sea,' as you're fond of saying. So why shouldn't we defend ourselves? Why shouldn't we fight to preserve our white culture? God had a mission for us when he put us here long before you blacks ever reached here from central Africa. And it is His will that we survive, that we keep alive the flame of Western civilization in this dark continent ruled by religions of the anti-Christ. And God's given us apartheid as a way of ensuring our survival as a pure Christian race. I don't want Coloured grandchildren."

He was getting angry; I could sense it. Were he left alone with me, he would have taught "the cheeky bloody Kaffir" a lesson. Half my mind told me to cool it; to acquiesce to his claims of racial superiority and predestination. I could not. The African in me refused to be told Africa was not my home.

"We blacks haven't the slightest desire to drive you back into the sea," I said, measuring each word carefully. "South Africa is as much our country as it is yours. We can and must learn to live together. We need each other, not as master and servant, but as equals. There's room for everyone in this beloved country."

Murmurs of approval rippled through the dimly lit bar. I gazed through the misty window; night shrouded the place. My eyes darted about the bar and saw confused smiles, smiles that seemed to say, "That's the truth. We agree. But why tell us?"

More questions were asked about black life and the likely future of the country. I answered them without difficulty, with confidence. The barroom crowd dispersed. I was offered a lift all the way to First Avenue by St. Croix.

Hardly a week after black schools reopened, units of the police and the army started raiding classrooms, arresting students. Every student was suspect. It became clear that the safest place to be was anywhere but school. I stopped going. The homes of students were also raided. I began spending entire days at the Barretts Tennis Ranch, playing tennis and reading to keep up with my schoolwork, so that when it finally was safe to return to school, I wouldn't have lagged too far behind.

One Tuesday, at midday, I was reading some poems by Shelley when a beat-up orange Volkswagen stopped in front of the lake near the entrance-gate, where I often had my lunch, and a short, brown-haired bespectacled white man with a barrel chest stepped out. He was flashily dressed in a brand-new Fila tennis outfit, which fitted rather tightly. He held in one arm a stuffed Adidas duffel bag; in the other, three Head tennis rackets, the Arthur Ashe Competition model.

"Hullo," he said with a German accent. "You must be Mark."

"Hi, yes," I said, rising to shake his small, hairy hand.

"I'm Helmut," he smiled, twinkling his eyes. "Wilfred told me a lot about you. He said you're a very good player and practise every day. I've just joined the Ranch, and hope to play everyday too. Maybe sometimes we can play together. I live in Hillbrow. I can sometimes give you a lift home."

"Sure we can play together," I said eagerly. "But I'm not that good a player. Wilfred inflated my tennis abilities." From his clothes, three expensive rackets, mien and well-conditioned body, I took him for a professional player.

We sat down. He told me he was from a small town in Germany, but had been in South Africa a couple months, working for a German company. He had come intending to stay in South Africa, but now had second thoughts, because he had now seen the truth about apartheid.

When he started talking about apartheid, I immediately was on guard. Could he be an undercover agent from BOSS (Bureau of State Security) sent following my speech in the bar?

"When my contract expires," he went on, "I'm going back to Germany. I couldn't live as a white man in this country for as long as those cruel racist laws which oppress your people are still in place."

Somehow he struck me as sincere. I decided to take the risk of talking freely, candidly, about the racial issue. I briefly told him about my life, my convictions, my dreams.

"Keep playing tennis and studying," he urged. "And someday you *will* get to America. If there's anything I can help you with—books, money, anything—just let me know, and we'll talk about it."

Once more I had befriended a white man who didn't fit the stereotype. How many more of his kind were out there? Why were most blacks not meeting them? We agreed to play after lunch. After the first few games, I soon discovered that Helmut was a mere hacker.

He huffed and puffed all over the court, ran around his backhand, double-faulted God knows how many times, cursed himself for missing easy shots. After the match, which he lost 6–0, 6–0, he said, "You're a much better player than I am. Obviously you wouldn't improve much from playing with me. Do you still want us to play together?"

Here was a white man asking me instead of ordering me. Yes, I would play with him.

"And if you like," he said enthusiastically, "we can sometimes play at Ellis Park or other tennis courts in the city."

"But that's against the law," I said.

"To hell with the law," he said angrily. "I do what I want to do. I don't believe in apartheid laws, I told you. You're my friend, just like any other white friend I have. Are you afraid?"

"No."

My friendship with Helmut proved an eye-opener. He followed through with his plans to have us flaunt the law and play on whites-only tennis courts in the city. Each time we did, white people stared at us as if we were aliens from outer space. Racist remarks were thrown at us. We made sure never to play at the same place twice in a row. Each time we drove about the city looking for a court, I thought a car followed us. I told Helmut about my uneasiness.

"Let them follow us," he said nonchalantly. "What's our crime?"

Yes, what was our crime? I became bolder and less worried about what might happen. After each playing session, we would cruise about Hillbrow, searching for restaurants where we could eat together. There were none.

"We don't serve two colours here."

"Kaffirs and white people cannot eat together here."

Such remarks infuriated Helmut, and he would rail at the restaurant owners and call them bigots. The latter would simply smile, quietly pick up the phone and threaten to call the police, and we would leave.

"Someday these bastards are going to get what's coming to them," Helmut would say after each row. "There's going to be a revolution in this country."

"You're a brave German," I said.

"There's no bravery about it," he said. "It's just plain common sense. Whites in this bloody country lack common sense. Can't they accept the fact, the unavoidable reality, that someday you people are going to rule this country? You outnumber them five to one. Why are they so blind, so stubborn? Can't they see that by continuing this barbarism called apartheid they're simply making it impossible for this whole mess to be resolved peacefully? How can you blacks forgive them if this racism goes on much longer? Can't they see, can't they see!" he said with strained hands, as if shaking an invisible foe.

"They refuse to see," I said.

"What utter madness," he cried. "You know"—he clutched my arm anxiously—"this whole thing reminds me of what Hitler did to my country. His madness has left us Germans with a feeling of guilt and shame that can never go away. The very same forces of racial superiority of that idiot and madman I see at work right here. There could yet be another Holocaust in the world."

I didn't know what the Holocaust was.

"I'll tell you all about it when we get back to my flat."

Helmut's apartment was on the fourth floor of a high-rise building overlooking Joubert Park. It was carpeted, handsomely furnished, and had a balcony. Despite my protests about the risks involved in sitting together on a balcony in a crowded section of Johannesburg, Helmut insisted we have our lunch of tuna fish sandwiches and tossed salad there. He began telling me about Hitler's Germany, about the concentration camps, about the ovens and the gas chambers. I felt sick.

"Why could the German people let this happen?" I said. "You say the rest of the world knew; why didn't they stop it?"

"The answer to both your questions is simple and right here," said Helmut. "Doesn't the rest of the world know about the suffering and deaths caused by apartheid? Aren't white South Africans aware of the oppressive nature of the regime they always vote for?"

"You know," I said, with the voice of someone who has just put two and two together. "I think a Holocaust is taking place right now in this country. There are no gas chambers or ovens this time, but black people are dying by the tens of thousands. Just look at the black infant mortality rate. This country has the best medical facilities in the world—Christiaan Barnard performed the first heart transplant right here. It exports food—but just look at the government's homeland policies of breaking up families and carting women and children to deserts where there's no food. And what are homelands if not open-air concentration camps? Just look at the murder rate in the ghettos. Because people aren't allowed to work without permits and passes, they kill each other in order to survive. And finally, just look at what is happening to the black man's mind: lost of self-esteem, apathy, mental illness. What does all that add to? Genocide."

Helmut nodded.

"That's why I can't stay in this country," he said.

Black people often saw me playing tennis with Helmut, or travelling in a car with him while sitting in the front seat, and their suspicions about my being an Uncle Tom mounted. From time to time Helmut drove me home, without a permit.

"They can arrest me if they want," he said.

The more black people saw us together, the more they called me a traitor to the struggle, and vowed to deal with me the same way they dealt with black informants, police and other collaborators with the system: death. I tried to explain that the whites I associated with were sympathetic to the black man's struggle, but was told that there was no such white man in South Africa.

I was in a dilemma. Should I end my association with whites and preserve my life; or should I risk it for what I believed, namely that whites were not monolithic, not all racists to be hated and destroyed? I chose the latter.

My close friendship with Helmut led me to confide in him about my dilemma. He was sympathetic.

"If there's anything I can do to help you," he said one afternoon, "please let me know. I am your friend. I'd even risk my life for you. I know you may not believe me, but I'm serious. I don't see you as a black man but as another human being, with the same needs, feelings and dreams as any white man."

One afternoon, following a morning of fierce rioting in Alexandra, Helmut offered to drive me all the way home. It was his day off, and we had been playing tennis at Ellis Park.

"Don't be silly," I said to him. "They'll kill you."

"Even if I'm with you?"

"Especially if you're with me," I said.

"But it's still daylight."

"It doesn't matter," I said. "People will just watch you being hacked to death and put to flames. Besides, you don't have a permit to enter Alexandra."

"To hell with a permit," he said. "I'm going in with you today."

"You must be mad," I said. "They'll skin you alive."

"I'm going in," he insisted. "My Volkswagen is sturdy and fast. If they come at me I'll race away."

"What if you get stuck?"

"Then I'll die like a true German."

"You're a brave man," I said.

Dusk was creeping in. We drove along an uncrowded street that led from the highway into the northern part of Alexandra. Black children in rags were playing in mud puddles. Helmut drove cautiously. We went into another street teeming with black men and women returning from work. Everywhere people stared at us.

He dropped me right at my door. I told him the shortest way out of the ghetto and wished him luck.

On another day, at about nine in the evening, Helmut dropped me on the outskirts of Alexandra following an afternoon of tennis at the ranch; he would have taken me home, but he had to rush to the airport to meet his girlfriend, who had just arrived from Germany.

"Will you be all right?" he asked. "If not, I'll drive you all the way to Thirteenth Avenue and go to the airport later. My girlfriend will understand."

"Don't worry," I said. "I'll be fine. I know a shortcut home, even in this darkness." During the rioting, just about all of Alexandra's streetlights had been smashed; the authorities hadn't bothered to repair them. The pitch-darkness at night had led to a sharp increase in the murder rate.

Helmut waited, car lights on, until I had disappeared down a narrow, twisting path that led into an unpaved street bordering Alexandra to the north. By keeping to this route, I hoped to reach home in about half the time it normally took on other streets. As I was in my white tennis outfit and sneakers, I jogged briskly down the dark road, praying that I didn't step into any potholes. I was halfway home when I came on a section of the street that still had one or two dim lights. I slowed down to catch a breath. I whistled softly to keep myself company.

Suddenly a group of about ten shadowy figures leaped out of an abandoned building across from the street and surrounded me. Don't panic, I told myself.

One of the shadows spoke. "Back from another meeting with our oppressors, heh, Uncle Tom?" I recognized the owner of the disembodied voice. "What information did you give them this time?"

"I was only playing tennis," I said.

"Playing tennis with whites, huh," Jarvas said. "Aren't there any black tennis players in Alexandra? You think you're better than the rest of us, don't you?"

I didn't answer. I trembled as the circle tightened around me. Since the riots broke out, Jarvas and his gang had increased their reign of terror: they robbed, raped, assaulted and murdered. As I watched them close in on me, I could see that they were armed with knives, tomahawks and machetes. I had to act quickly.

"Listen, Jarvas," I pleaded. "If you want me to stop playing tennis with whites, I'll do so right this minute."

Jarvas laughed fiendishly. "Hear him now," he said. "He's been warned many times, and it's only now that he believes we mean business. Smart guy, heh."

"Let's teach him a lesson," said one of Jarvas' cohorts. "Let's make sure he never plays tennis again."

My mind went into a frenzy. I was completely surrounded; there seemed to be no escape. I could see my life slipping away. I thought of a million things I had done, and a million things I still wanted to do; I prayed. Jarvas and his gang had just about reached me when suddenly down the street a truck with glaring headlights came racing down. Jarvas and his gang jumped to the sides of the street to make way.

I saw salvation. Like a bullet I shot through the opening.

"Get him!" the cry went up. "Don't let him escape." With my speed, I knew that once I made it through the hole, no one on earth could catch me. I was nearly out of the hole when something heavy struck my face; I staggered but regained control. Someone had hit me with brickbat. Pain engulfed my face, but I raced on.

"Get him. Don't let him escape." But I was gone. The truck passed me. Jarvas and his gang were racing after me down the street. Like a well-trained thoroughbred, I steadily pulled away from the pack. Even after the chase had stopped, I continued running, slowing down only when I sighted home. I felt my face; it was bruised and swollen. I spat the blood that had filled my mouth. I noticed that one of my front teeth was missing.

I entered the house and found my mother busy ironing my brother's school pants. Several of my sisters were huddled near the stove doing their homework.

"Good Lord," my mother gasped as she noticed how I looked. "What happened?"

"Nothing," I mumbled between swollen lips.

"Nothing," she exclaimed, coming over to where I stood. "Look at all that blood on your tennis shirt and pants."

"I fell," I said. "I was running and I tripped and fell. The street was full of rocks and potholes."

"Better come up with a better story," my mother said as she poured hot water into the bathtub. I grabbed a rag, immersed it in the hot water, and started dabbing the swollen side of my face.

"Since when did you fall and smash your face up like that?" she asked.

Reluctantly I told her what had happened.

She turned pale and was silent for a long while, deep in thought. She ran her eyes up and down me. "I warned you, child," she said finally, in a sort of broken voice, "that your white friends were going to get you into trouble. Why wouldn't you listen?"

"But what's wrong about having white friends?" I asked. "They're people too, aren't they? Why won't anyone believe me when I say that the white people I play tennis with are not racists. They're on our side, Mama. They believe what we believe. They're fighting for what we're fighting for—an end to apartheid. So why shouldn't we judge them differently from the racist whites?"

"You know the answer to that," my mother said.

"No, I don't," I said brusquely.

"To the black man and woman in the streets all whites are the same. All they know is the white man who's making their lives hell and whom they hate so much they would kill at the first opportunity. Look at your father, he hates all white people. So when you come along and tell blacks like him of 'good white people' they immediately think you're a traitor. So be careful, child; black people are too angry, too desperate."

I woke up at dawn one morning a few weeks following my brush with death, stood with some friends on the veranda of a gutted Chinaman's shop and stared at clouds from burning buildings and vehicles in the distance. There was scattered gunfire; army helicopters whirred above the township; word circulated that armoured police cars had cordoned the ghetto once more.

"It's June sixteenth all over again," someone said.

Everyone nodded. Suddenly from out one of the yards that acted as a shortcut between Twelfth and Thirteenth avenues emerged a group of youths lugging boxes of canned fish, bags of sugar and malt, loaves of brown bread, sacks of flour and maize meal and other eatables. I immediately recognized the stuff as the rations that the authorities, under a new welfare program, gave to elderly persons, many of whom suffered from TB and had no children to look after them.

"Is that stuff from the stadium, man?" one of my friends asked the looters.

"Yes, and there's tons of it, man. Those rooms were loaded."

"How did you guys manage to break down the walls?" The room where the food was stored was as impregnable as a fort. All through the riots people had tried to break in, but the concrete walls and thick iron doors had refused to yield. The stadium also housed the only public library in the township.

"Someone stole a bus and rammed it through the walls."

"Where were the police?"

"The police are trying to put out a fire at the Coloured school." The coloured students in Alexandra had till now refused to participate in the school boycotts, claiming that they were not being taught Bantu Education.

Though Coloured Education was compulsory and slightly better than Bantu Education, it still qualified Coloureds for third-class citizenship, behind whites and Indians. I greeted the news of their gutted school with glee; that was bound to jolt them back to reality, I thought, and convince them that they had no choice but to side with blacks in the struggle.

"What happened to the library?" I asked.

"Who's got time to worry about books when there's plenty of free food?"

"So the books are still there?" I asked, salivating at the thought of finally possessing all those classics I had read on many a visit to the library.

"They're not only there, brother, they're burning," came the reply, punctuated by laughter. "Someone thought it a mighty fine idea to destroy all traces of Bantu Education and white oppression."

"But those books had nothing to do with Bantu Education," I protested. I could picture going up in flames copies of Dickens, Stevenson, Zola, Doyle, Shakespeare and many others—donations by white liberals appalled by the state of black education. In my mind's eye I saw reduced to soot all those wonderful books, which had revealed to me other ways of living, which had sustained me in a world of degradation.

"How long has it been burning?" I asked in a downcast voice.

"Since dawn," was the answer. "When we left the flames were still confined to the west wing of the building."

I raced off to the burning library, thinking I might, if lucky, be in time to salvage a few books. I took shortcuts, crossed dirt streets strewn with charred vehicles, putrid garbage and rotting dogs. A few blocks from the building I met a group of men, women and children lugging loot from the welfare office. As I neared the building, thought of the burning books, I felt angry. Why burn the only things that taught one to believe in the future, to fight for one's right to live in freedom and dignity?

I found the place deserted. The bus was still lodged inside the welfare office's walls, smouldering. A pack of mongrels nearby licked crashed cans of pilchard. A small rag doll covered with what looked like blood was trapped under one of the bus' front wheels. I forced my way through the rubble toward what remained of the library. There the fire had almost died down. Only wisps of greyish-blue smoke floated like ghosts into the hot air. The floor of the charred library was still hot, so I doused my feet in water from a broken pipe nearby, filled a large tin can with water and scattered it in my path as I walked gingerly about the scorched library, overturning metal shelves to see if any books had escaped the flames. I upturned about five shelves: all revealed the charred remains of classic books. My heart sank; I muttered oaths under my breath. I upturned more shelves, found nothing and was about to leave when the urge to turn over all shelves overtook me. By the third of fourth shelf my eyes popped out: books! Underneath were rows of books that not a flame had touched.

Overjoyed, I quickly removed and stacked them in crude piles next to a ditch nearby. While thus engaged I heard a rumble of trucks in the distance. I paid little attention. The rumble came nearer and nearer. I looked up and through a broken window in one of the library's blackened walls I saw two army trucks enter the stadium through a fallen gate. Immediately, camouflaged white soldiers, about a dozen of them, jumped off the back of the trucks, machine guns in hand, and raced every which way. Some headed for the bus, others for the welfare office. Three came straight at me.

"Don't panic," I told myself, "don't panic." I stole into the ditch, taking the piles of books with me. The shadows of clumps of tall reeds alongside the ditch darkened it in spots. I crawled into one. My heart thumped in my throat. A thousand questions flitted across my mind.

"Why did you come here?" I repeatedly asked myself. It seemed ironic that the very love for books that had nourished my dreams of a better life was about to shatter them.

"*Hierdie kaffir kinders is mal* [These Kaffir children are lunatics]," a voice said loudly. "*Kyk net wat doen hulle met boeke, onse geld* [Just look at what they've done to books, our money]."

"I sure hope the government lets them go for years without another library," another voice said in Afrikaans, amid sulfurous oaths. "That'll teach them a lesson, the uncivilized bastards. If they only knew what suffering their black brothers and sisters are going through in the rest of Africa, they would be thankful of what we give them. They're the best-treated blacks in the world."

The voices sounded nearby, but I dared not lift up my head. What if they searched the ditch? I would be killed on the spot, no doubt about that. I wouldn't be the first they had murdered. I would be just another Kaffir "killed while burning and looting government property." I don't know how many times I prayed to God and my ancestors for protection. I hugged one book to my breast. I thought of my family, of all the things I still wanted to do in this world.

I must have been down in the ditch close to half an hour, still as a mouse. At length I heard the trucks leave. I didn't come up immediately, fearing that guards may have been posted about the place. Satisfied there were no unusual sounds above me, I crawled on my stomach along the length of the ditch, which led outside the stadium, on Twelfth Avenue. I left the books behind, planning to pick them up later.

At home I found everyone feasting on Saldanha pilchards and brown bread.

"Did you get the stuff from the welfare office?" I asked my mother.

"Yes," she said. "I was on my way back from Granny's when I saw people breaking into the building. I joined them. Now we have food to last us a while."

"I just came back from there," I said.

She asked me if I had seen the bus.

"Yes."

"A little girl was crushed underneath one of the wheels as she was helping her mother drag a box of canned beans."

I recalled the bloodied rag doll. That afternoon my brother and I went to pick up the books.

45 Despite sporadic unrest in the ghettos, the black Southern Transvaal Lawn Tennis Association announced that trials would be held in Soweto to select a ten-player junior team to take part in the Annual National Junior Tennis Championships in Attredgeville, Pretoria. The announcement came in May; black schools in Tembisa and Alexandra were still closed by government decree. I was able to practise six hours a day at the ranch.

I made the team, but soon thereafter it was announced that the July championships might be scrapped because the government was leery of hundreds of black youths from all over South Africa gathering in Attredgeville, so near to white suburbs of Pretoria. I was disappointed.

I talked the matter over with Scaramouche, who, since I made the team, had been working out with me.

"Don't take it too hard," he said, "there's still a chance that the championships might be held. Even if they're not, there'll be other opportunities for you to compete. There are a few black tournaments coming up, and I'll enter you in singles and we can team up for doubles. Also, it's about time I introduced you to Andre Zietsman, a white friend of mine who is one of the best tennis players in the country. He's a liberal and just returned from America, where he's been on a tennis scholarship. He's a lefty like you, and I think you'll find him helpful."

I looked forward to meeting this Andre Zietsman. Having just returned from America, I thought, he might help me contact universities over there about the possibility of a tennis scholarship.

There was a lull in the unrest. The government gave the go-ahead that the tournament take place. The tennis facilities in Attredgeville were better than in other ghettos, but still distantly inferior to those of whites. The team of five boys and five girls was housed in various homes throughout the township: there wasn't enough sponsorship money to pay for hotel accommodations. There were no hotels in Attredgeville. The level of tennis among us blacks was still appalling, but we had a good time. Often we talked about politics, the protests and the need for black solidarity.

Southern Transvaal again won the team competition. At the same time that the tournament was taking place, thousands of miles away at Wimbledon, England, Arthur Ashe was blazing his way to the finals. His exploits were closely followed in the daily newspapers like the *Star* and *Rand Daily Mail,* which had extensive coverage of Wimbledon. One Sunday morning the entire world awoke to a tennis miracle: Arthur Ashe had won Wimbledon! Pandemonium broke out in the streets of Attredgeville. Blacks everywhere were brandishing newspapers with the headline:

ASHE PAINTS
WIMBLEDON
BLACK

Every black man, woman and child felt proud. We had achieved the ultimate triumph in a white man's sport. We could, if given the opportunity, compete with and beat the best in the world. Everyone at our championship tournament had wanted to become Arthur Ashe. Spectacular matches were played that day.

I became more determined than ever to get to America. At the end of the tournament I returned to Alexandra inspired. I immediately set out to strengthen my ties with white tennis players, intent on using them to improve my game, and to find out more about how a black boy from the ghetto could win a scholarship to an American university. I remained mindless of the dangers of associating with whites.

Schools reopened in August. I enrolled, hoping to complete my first year of matriculation. Luckily, Simba Quix was still willing to underwrite my expenses, and I was able to continue playing tennis each afternoon, instead of being out working to pay my way through school.

My school friends had by now almost all disappeared, victims of arrests and detentions without trial or killings, or they had fled along with the thousands of black youths who were daily fleeing the country since the eruption of June 16, and the police crackdowns that followed. Many of those who fled were reportedly undergoing guerilla training in neighbouring black states under the aegis of *Umkhonto We Sizwe.*

Some of these youths were beginning to infiltrate back into the country in sorties, armed with submachine guns, bombs and other sophisticated weapons. Power stations and various government buildings were blown up. Whites feared the beginning of urban guerilla war. They purchased guns, burglar alarms, rifles and guard dogs in unprecedented quantities. More repressive laws designed to suppress black anger sailed through Parliament with little opposition; more black informants were recruited to report on events in the ghettos. There was talk that one out of every ten blacks in the ghetto was an informant. Armed and camouflaged soldiers would from time to time burst into classrooms, interrupting lessons to read off lists of those suspected of subversive activities, rounding them up in armoured vehicles, headed for unknown destinations. Sometimes plainclothes black policemen from the Special Branch did the rounding up in flashy cars. Students were picked up who to my knowledge had never done anything subversive except call for an end to Bantu Education. Would I be picked up next? I wondered. I became paranoid; my health suffered and learning became impossible; I considered dropping out of school, but my mother begged me to stay.

"God will protect you, child," she said. "I pray for you night and day. You've got to start going to church, too."

Why did God fail to protect innocent students from the police? Nonetheless, I began to go to church on Sundays, not so much to pray but because I felt somewhat safe there. A change gradually came over me; I began to read the Bible more for renewal of strength and courage. I wandered from church to church, listened to the sermons with new ears, and heard pastors begin to preach liberation. Youngsters whose blood was shed in the battle against apartheid were called martyrs. Those who fled and became freedom fighters the government called terrorists; in the churches they were praised as heroes.

Some churches in Soweto and Pretoria sang freedom songs as part of their liturgy, in open defiance of the authorities. Burials for slain youths often turned into political rallies; coffins were borne to the graveyard draped in ANC colours of gold, green and black by young men and women wearing ANC T-shirts, amid chants of "*AMANDLA! AWETHU! AMANDLA! AWETHU!*" and black power salutes. The police countered by dispersing mourners with tear gas, police dogs, rubber bullets and truncheons.

46 I finally met Andre Zietsman, and he proved a dear friend. Blond-haired, well built and as graceful as a cat on the court, Andre was one of South Africa's rising tennis stars. At twenty-four he had already won dozens of prestigious tournaments, and had participated in Wimbledon and the U.S. Open. With his vast experience, he offered to teach me the finer points of the game.

We began meeting clandestinely on Saturday mornings at Ellis Park or some private court in the suburbs, where he gave lessons. We both were aware of the serious risks involved in playing together in a white neighbourhood, but we never dwelled on them.

I came to know Andre rather well; in fact, like Wilfred and his patrons at the ranch, abnormally well considering the type of society we were living in. Gradually we both began feeling comfortable discussing issues that were taboo in meetings between black and white: politics, equality, freedom. In this way Andre (who took no offense to my calling him by his first name) came to tell me about his experiences as a student in America.

"It was very frightening at first," he said, "to see black people and white people living together side by side in New York and Washington, cities as big as Johannesburg and Cape Town. In America there are no laws which keep blacks and whites apart. Blacks vote and get elected to the American parliament, where together with whites they make laws for the benefit of everyone in the country. And these laws say that all people are created equal by God, and therefore should be judged not by their colour but only on merit."

"You mean to tell me," I said incredulously, "that there's not a single apartheid law in America? No Influx Control or Group Areas Act or Immorality Act?"

Though I knew from hearsay and from reading newspapers and books that American society was freer than South African society, somehow my experiences as a black man who had lived all his life under unremitting oppression and racism told me that no country in the world that had blacks and whites living together, and was run by the latter, was without racial segregation of some form.

"Americans have none of those laws," Andre said. "They used to have something similar to apartheid years ago, in what they call the southern states, but Dr. Martin Luther King, Jr., and the others changed most of that." He was driving me to the black bus stop following a practise session; Saturday morning traffic was heavy; he pulled into a parking lot of a Hypermarket to continue his American saga.

"Try imagining," Andre said as he inconspicuously parked the car and I immediately leaped to the backseat so as not to arouse suspicion by being seated in front with him: blacks rarely sat with whites in the front seats of cars. Andre flaunted this unwritten law whenever I was with him, but on this occasion our presence in a parking lot teeming with white faces made me insist on sitting in the back.

"Try imagining," he repeated, rolling up the windows of his Volvo, "the whole of Johannesburg—Soweto, Alexandra and all the other black locations included—as one big city, instead of the racial checkerboard it now is under the Group Areas Act. Imagine that in this new Johannesburg blacks, whites, Coloureds and Indians were allowed to live anyplace they wished, as long as they could afford it. That's how many cities are like in America."

I shook my head; I could not believe, despite his sincerity, what he was telling me. I tried imagining how white South Africans would react to blacks suddenly appearing in their "pure," affluent, silent-as-a-tomb suburbs, not as nannies, garden boys, garden girls, washer-women and maids, but as neighbours. Many whites in South Africa would rather go to war or die than have a black for a neighbour.

"How did you," I asked Andre, "function in such an environment?"

He laughed. "I found it unbelievably confusing at first. Bewildering is the right word. For a long time I felt strangely out of place, as if I were a visitor to another planet, so to speak. I had lived in South Africa all my life, been raised by black nannies and had every black person call me *baas* and master and obey my every desire and whim. I had parents who sent me to the best whites-only schools, where part of my education was how to lord over blacks. They made me take lessons in tennis, music, swimming, cricket, rugby, dance and all other kinds of things, while your parents were debating whether to buy you your first primer and let the family starve. I had a government whose laws provided me with every one of life's comforts, protected my alleged superiority, power and privilege, and made me feel like a king who would live forever in a golden paradise. I never felt guilty about it all. I was told that God wanted us to live that way; that was why he made us white. I was told that you blacks deserved to be our servants because that's God's way of punishing you for the sins committed by your ancestor, Ham.

"All this was my world, my reality. Then suddenly there I was, at eighteen, thrust into a world where all those illusions were shattered. In America blacks attended the same schools with me, sat in the same classes and heard the same teachers, some of whom were blacks. I slept with blacks in the same dormitory, ate meals with them in the same cafeterias. I was shocked and horrified. No one was calling me *baas* and master any longer.

"There was more. I had to use the same libraries as blacks, the same toilets and showers, ride in the same buses, trains and taxis. Everywhere blacks, it seemed, were telling me what to do. The varsity teams had dozens of black players, and boy! what superb athletes. No white man could beat them in basketball, boxing and football." He tried to explain American football, which was different from South African football (soccer).

He paused; we sipped orange juice from a flask. He went on, "But what shocked me the most was that blacks and whites could mix freely at social gatherings and parties. They could even date without the sceptre of being convicted under the Immorality Act hanging over them. Some even intermarried and had children; and the government didn't move in and reclassify everyone as white, black and Coloured."

My head spun as I listened. My mouth was so wide open all through Andre's speech that the police could have flown right in, and I wouldn't have noticed or cared. My mind was feverishly trying to compare American society, the way Andre depicted it, with that of South Africa. There was no comparison whatsoever. The two societies appeared light years apart. America seemed a society moving rapidly toward a greater accommodation of its diverse population; South Africa on the other hand was moving with equal speed, if not more, toward a total separation of all races.

Would I ever see this Promised Land?

47 Andre grew into a close friend. The personality changes he underwent while in America enabled him to accept me as an equal, to respect my opinions and idiosyncrasies as a black man, no matter how abstruse he found them, or how vehemently he disagreed with them, at times. Knowing him convinced me that the white man of South Africa could change his ways of oppression if he wanted to. In refusing to do so he was simply being greedy, intransigent and ruled by unfounded fears and mistaken beliefs.

If four years of attending college in America had awakened Andre to the brutal reality of how wrong his race was in subjugating blacks; if those four years had so racked his conscience that he now realised that there was more underneath a black skin than he was previously prepared to admit, let alone accept; if four years of living in America had taught him that apartheid was wrong, wrong, wrong, then I had hope that some day the rest of his race could similarly awaken—if they wanted to.

My family was again experiencing hard times. My mother had left her job to give birth to another child, her seventh, a pretty, dimpled girl named Linah. We were now two boys and five girls. My father had again been laid off. Starvation stared us in the face; there was no money for police bribes, no diapers or baby food for the infant. I hunted for piece jobs in the suburbs, to no avail. At many places I was considered the "wrong type" of garden boy, messenger, car-washer or dishwasher, simply because I had committed the unpardon-able sin of being educated beyond the limits acceptable to whites who ran the various establishments from which I sought employment.

"There's no place here for natives like you," was the usual reply I received from white people. "You've got too much education. If we hired you, you might cause trouble among our obedient workers. We don't want a mutiny; this is a peaceful country."

In other places, just when I thought I might be hired, I was told to first obtain a permit allowing me to work in a white neighbourhood. I couldn't get a permit because the damn thing had to be stamped on a pass, and I couldn't qualify for a pass because my parents had no legal permit to live in Alexandra.

I discussed the situation with Andre. He promised to seek ways of helping me and the family.

"Why don't you come and work for me at the sports shop?" he said one Saturday afternoon as he was driving me to the black bus stop following a tennis lesson.

"But I don't have a permit," I said.

"I don't care," he said.

I thought for a moment. "It's too risky, Andre," I said. "I don't want to jeopardize the tennis deal we have. Thanks anyway."

One Saturday afternoon, following one of our clandestine tennis lessons, he gave me fifty rands and a bag full of tennis clothes: sweat-ers, shorts, socks, shirts, dresses and warm-ups. He also gave me three Donnay tennis rackets.

"Thanks, Andre," I said, greatly humbled by the gesture. "I'll pay you back the money as soon as I find a job."

"Don't worry about it," he said. "I'm glad to be of some help." He added jokingly, "We whites have everything, and you guys have nothing, you know. So we have to make attempts to equalize things sometimes; otherwise, how could we deal with our consciences?"

How true.

The money bought the family groceries; the infant, diapers, med-icine and formula food until my mother could come out of seclusion and resume work as a "washing girl." I shared the tennis clothes with my brother and sisters.

My tennis game improved tremendously from playing with Andre. I still visited the ranch and played with Helmut during the week, but I learned more from the surreptitious Saturday morning meetings with Andre. I now won many of my matches for the school team with ease, and black players of every level and age in Alexandra became regular victims of my strong net game. I won the Alexandra Open Tennis Championships for the second time.

Despite missing more than half a year of school, I passed Form Four in the top one percent of the class. In January of 1977, three months after my seventeenth birthday, I entered my final year of matriculation. Simba Quix, for which I had worked during the Christmas holidays, renewed my scholarship. I was confident of passing the final exams in December, so I began mapping out my future plans. Mr. Wilde at Simba Quix indicated that whether or not I passed matric, his company was eager to train me as one of its new generation of black salesmen, and that if I did well as a salesmen, I could quickly move up within the company. Simba Quix was doing a lot to open up managerial and supervisory positions to blacks: there were already one or two black district managers in the company.

"And we now pay our black and white managers the same," Mr. Wilde boasted. "We're trying to remove apartheid from our company."

I considered the Simba Quix offer and was tempted to accept it. My mother, grandmother, uncles and aunts for various reasons implored me to do so.

"With your brain," Uncle Piet said, "you'll be paid like a king. And you can then build the family a house like those in Dube, complete with a two-door garage, swimming pool, tennis court, electricity and garden." The minority of blacks who lived in Dube, a posh section of the otherwise squalid Soweto also known as Beverly Hills, were a well-to-do elite. They had the same aspirations as whites. As the upper crust or black middle class, they wielded considerable power in local and national black politics, and the government frequently consulted with them on black issues and appointed them as mayors and town councillors. They were largely conservative, less inclined to embrace revolution as a method of ending apartheid. What they sought was not so much a radical restructuring of South African society as the removal of those features of apartheid that held back black initiative and enterprise. A prominent leader of this elite black middle class was even quoted in a Johannesburg daily as saying that he didn't believe many blacks wanted one person, one vote in South Africa.

Houses like those in Dube were always shown off to foreign tourists during their trips.

"You see how well our natives live?" a government official would proudly tell a bus full of incredulous American, Japanese and European tourists. "Even many of us whites can't afford to live like that."

Then the tourists would wonder what was wrong with apartheid.

Uncle Piet and the rest of my kin yearned to live like those blacks in Dube, and saw me as the only person in the family who could make their yearnings come true.

"Don't you want to end all my misery, child?" implored Granny. "I've been working all these years, and I am tired. You alone can make me happy in the twilight of my life. Take the Simba job when you finish school, child. Promise me you will."

"Taking the job will give meaning to all those years you've spent struggling through school," Aunt Bushy pointed out.

"You know that I've now given my life over to God," said Uncle Cheeks, who had just returned from the penitentiary. "I read the Scriptures every day, and God speaks to me at every waking and sleeping hour. You, He tells me, have been chosen to lead the family out of the land of poverty and destitution. Do not go against God's wish, nephew. Take the job when you finish school, and manna will begin pouring from heaven so we all can eat."

My father insisted that I repay him for bringing me into this world by taking up the job and providing for him.

Any one of these reasons would have compelled me to take up the Simba Quix job after matriculation, but somehow in my heart I knew that I would never be happy until I had breathed and tasted that freedom a society like America could give me. Yes, I could work for Simba Quix, easily rise to the level of manager and get paid oodles of money, with which I could perhaps transform my family and relatives into solid members of the black middle class. Yes, that way I would have accomplished a lot by becoming "somebody" in the black community and being able to bask in the glory of having made it despite apartheid. But would it mean anything for as long as the thought haunted me that despite all my successes I still was not free, that I still was regarded as an alien in the land of my birth, a Kaffir, that I still had to think and feel and act the way apartheid wanted me to, that I still had to carry a pass and watch black men and women brutally denied the right to live in dignity and freedom?

Something inside me told me I would never be happy. I had to leave South Africa somehow, somehow I had to get to America, the Promised Land, where I hoped to find the freedom to use whatever talents I had.

But how does one get from Alexandra to America?

48 On September 12, 1977, newspaper headlines blazed:

STEVEN BIKO
DIES IN
POLICE CUSTODY

The world was shocked. Anger swept the ghettos. The vocal and charismatic leader of the Black Consciousness Movement—a body formed in the late 1960s and made up of black, Coloured and Indian students whose goal was to fight for the ending of apartheid without the assistance of what it called "paternalistic white liberalism"—had been silenced forever by the government.

When he was detained on August 16, under Section Six of the Terrorism Act, he was a robust, thirty-three-year-old black man, full of a passion for living, for giving selflessly of himself in the struggle against apartheid. His mysterious death sixteen days later raised charges by blacks that he had been cold-bloodedly murdered by the South African police. It was rumoured that his head was so bashed during interrogation in a police station in Durban that his brain hemorrhaged. The police then decided that he be taken to an interrogation center in Johannesburg, a distance of about two hundred miles. A white doctor pronounced him fit for the journey. His naked body was then loaded into the back of a van, in the dead of night. He died en route.

The press demanded a full inquiry. Opposition leaders in Parliament demanded the prosecution of those connected with his death. The United States and other Western nations demanded the abolishing of South Africa's Draconian security laws, which allowed for detention without trial. Members of the Black Consciousness Movement vowed to continue the struggle.

The government reacted with savage crackdowns. On October 19 I picked up the paper only to find that the Black Consciousness Movement, the Black Parents' Association, the Black People's Convention, the Black Communities Programmes, the South African Students' Organizations (SASO), the Christian Institute and various other organizations committed to seeking the ending of apartheid through nonviolent means had been banned as Communist fronts hiding under "sweet-sounding names and aims."

The largest black newspaper, the *World*, with a circulation of over two hundred thousand, was shut down, its journalists and editor, Percy Qoboza, detained. Dozens of black leaders were also detained, including several prominent whites opposed to apartheid: Beyers Naude of the Christian Institute, and Donald Woods, editor of the *East London Dispatch* and a friend of Biko's.

In Alexandra army vehicles became a daily sight. The authorities were given additional power over black people, as if they didn't already have absolute power over our lives from birth to death. Gatherings attended by more than three persons, for whatever purpose (even to bury a slain loved one), were banned. Plots to massacre whites were "uncovered," and those involved imprisoned without trial and tortured. Troops were deployed to guard entrances to the white suburbs. The number of black informants in the ghettos was beefed up. Daily I heard stories of friends and kindred betraying one another. Mass paranoia so gripped the ghettos, reminding me of the Reign of Terror during the French Revolution, that I could not even trust my own mother.

I attended meetings where black youths sought ways to get hold of submachine guns and grenades with which to storm white kindergartens and schools and shopping malls in the name of liberation. I was confused, I was desperate, I was angry; yet I lacked the courage to even face the thought of blowing up the kindergarten where Wilfred's son attended. But I had to do something to fight back; I had to find ways of avenging the deaths of hundreds of innocent black children; I had to find ways of dealing with the anger and hate consuming me day by day.

As always I sought refuge in books and tennis. The two somehow restored my sanity. I sensed that, in a way, by reading and playing tennis while my brothers and sisters were dying in the streets, I was shirking my responsibilities in the struggle, I was on the side of apartheid by thinking too much of my own safety and interests.

To relieve my tormented conscience, I convinced myself that it was futile, it was suicidal, to fight bullets and truncheons with stones, armoured vehicles and tear gas with shouts of *"Amandla! Awethu!"* and fists clenched in black power salutes. I led myself to believe that there were other ways of fighting the awesome apartheid machinery besides fleeing the country and joining the ANC as a freedom fighter. As I grappled with my conscience, in me became born a fanatical determination that if I ever left South Africa alive, I would devote every minute of my time, every ounce of my strength, to fighting for the liberation of my countrymen. What my weapons would be I didn't know.

49 My desperate desire to leave South Africa led me to start taking risks, to allow people to use me to my advantage. One Saturday morning, as we were about to leave Ellis Park following a practise session, Helmut said, "Why don't you enter next month's SAB [South African Breweries] Open?"

The tournament was the same one Arthur Ashe nearly won in 1973. Held during the last week of November and first week of December, it consistently attracted top-class players from around the world, thanks to the efforts of Owen Williams, its impresario, renowned in the tennis world as an innovative and astute director. He was supposed to have so successfully directed the world-famous U.S. Open that the Americans entreated him to become permanent director. He declined the offer.

The SAB was regarded as one of the major tournaments in the world, and that year's field, I read in newspapers, promised to be the largest and most illustrious ever, with many of the top American men and women players entered. Since Arthur Ashe and Evonne Goolagong (now Cawley) participated in the tournament, it had been opened to black South African players as well. But the best of us weren't good enough to even win a match in the qualifying round: a sort of minitournament where scores of amateurs and professionals (a majority of them white South Africans) who didn't have enough points to qualify played each other for a handful of slots in the main draw.

I didn't want to become another sacrificial lamb. Moreover, 1977 was a year when S.A.L.T.U. was under pressure from the International Tennis Federation (ITF) to open its doors to blacks or face expulsion. Already several countries had made it a policy to refuse to play against South African teams in the Davis Cup and the Federation Cup; others had even gone to the extent of barring white South African players from tournaments held on their soil. South Africa was also banned from Olympic competition, international track and field, swimming, World Cup soccer, cricket, rugby and a dozen or so other sports.

Black athletes across the country gloated over such isolation. Maybe, we thought, whites will finally remove apartheid from sports. As the isolation increased, and white players began leaving the country and taking up citizenship in America and Britain, the authorities announced a few cosmetic changes in sports apartheid: integrated bleachers, "mixed" professional tournaments and selection of token black players to national teams. Blacks called such meaningless tinkering a sham.

So, aware that white tennis officials were under pressure, black tennis officials refused to release players to take part in the SAB Open, insisting that the former pledge to take immediate steps to integrate tennis at all levels.

"But that can't be done," cried white tennis officials. "Not immediately anyway. That's against the law."

"Then change the law," black tennis officials insisted.

"We are not politicians," countered white tennis officials. "Sports and politics don't mix."

"So don't count on our players showing up to save your hide," retorted black tennis officials.

With the beginning of the tournament fast approaching, and word already out that the ITF would be sending a delegation to investigate how integrated South African tennis was, white tennis officials searched frantically for black token players. One of the officials, Peter Murphy, director of the Ellis Park tennis facility, had often seen Helmut and me play, and he already knew of my involvement with the Barretts Tennis Ranch. Apparently my audacity to break apartheid laws in sports had made me notorious in white tennis circles. Unknown to me, Murphy had talked Helmut into coaxing me to enter the SAB open.

"Enter the SAB Open," I laughed. "You must be joking. Who am I to play against the likes of Stan Smith and Jimmy Connors?"

"There's a way," he said with a mysterious grin, "for you to take part in the qualifying rounds. And if you win, you could find yourself facing Stan Smith in the first round."

Continuing to laugh, I said, "Thanks a lot for the joke."

"I'm serious," Helmut said. "Just say 'yes, I want to play' right this minute, and we'll talk to Peter Murphy about it."

"Who's Peter Murphy?"

He told me.

Remembering the refusal of the Black Tennis Association to send players to the Open, I said, "I don't want to be used by white people."

"But," countered Helmut, "you're always complaining that you lack competition. And what happened to your dream of contacting American universities about tennis scholarships? You would meet a lot of Americans in this tournament if you played, and they might be able to help you. This is a once-in-a-lifetime opportunity. Yes, whites may be using you, but it's all to your advantage."

I was desperate to make contact with American tennis players; the lure of playing in a tournament with some of the best names in tennis was irresistible; I agreed to play.

The tournament was two weeks away. I immediately embarked on a crash program to sharpen my tennis skills and get in shape, physically and mentally. I jogged twice a day—ten miles each time; I skipped rope for an hour each day; I ate food rich in carbohydrates and protein; I served at least a thousand balls each day—topspin, slice, flat; I lifted weights, did push-ups, sit-ups, double-knee jumps and yoga. I worked out with a ball machine, played scores of tough sets against Wilfred and Scaramouche; I pored over dozens of tennis books dealing with strategy and tactics.

Each day I would go to bed exhausted. Throughout the night I would toss and turn, drenched in a cold sweat, unable to sleep. But at the crack of dawn the next day I would be up to catch the first bus to the ranch.

"Are you trying to kill yourself?" my mother said one morning. Throughout the night I had hallucinated and vomited.

"No, Mama," I said, "I'm getting ready for a tennis tournament."

Andre agreed to work out with me in the morning at Ellis Park, twice a week. He too was playing in the tournament.

Word about my decision to play in the tournament reached the S.A.N.L.T.U., and I was ordered to withdraw immediately or be banned for life from black tennis. "Johannes, don't be a fool. Don't push your luck too far. Can't you damn see that the bloody white bastards are using you? Withdraw from the tournament or face dire consequences," read an anonymous letter.

I was in a quandary. I sought advice: Scaramouche told me to go ahead and play.

"But Oom Scary," I said, "each time we play we're slaughtered. It's been four years since Arthur Ashe first came to this country, and how much progress have we made? Where is the next Arthur Ashe? Tennis is still as segregated as ever."

"That may be true," said Scaramouche, sipping Coca-Cola from a mug, "but I believe the attitude of white tennis players and officials is changing. It's only a matter of time before we have true integration in sports."

"What about the argument that there can be no normal sports in an abnormal society?" I asked.

"That's too simple a way of putting it," Scaramouche said. "If you study the history of blacks in America, you'll find that sports were often at the forefront of change."

Scaramouch's argument was persuasive, but my mind was still undecided. I sought my mother's advice.

"Don't push your luck too far, child," my mother said. "This time the death threats may be for real. Why don't you just forget about this tennis, huh? You've got a lot going for you, child, can't you see? Soon you'll be finished with school, and the Simba Chips company will hire you and pay you very well. And you'll be able to build yourself a nice big house, marry a respectable girl and live comfortably. Is that not enough, child?"

"Mama," I said, "I don't think I'll be happy leading that kind of life. Tennis is my life. I want it to take me to America, where I can breathe freedom and do something truly meaningful with my life. Something which will make you and millions of black people proud. Is that not worth more than simply being another slave for white people?"

"Still dreaming of America, I see," my mother said with a sigh of resignation. "But do you for a moment think that such a preposterous dream can ever come true?"

"It will, Mama."

"What black man has ever done what you're hallucinating you'll do?"

"No one," I said with a smile. "I'll be the first."

"My child, I give up on you," my mother sighed. "But I will pray for you. I hope you know what you're getting yourself into."

The matchups for the qualifying round were announced. My first match was against Abe Segal, a former Wimbledon Doubles Champion with Gordon Forbes. Segal had been one of South Africa's premier singles and doubles players during the fifties. Though past his peak, he still played a mean game of singles. So what was I, an inexperienced, star-struck, half-formed black tennis player, going to be to him but fodder? If I needed an excuse for withdrawing, I told myself, this was it; no way should you make a fool of yourself by getting on the same court with a former Wimbledon champion; just pick up the phone and tell Owen Williams to scratch your name. I was alone in the bar; Wilfred was out on the court giving a lesson; I decided to tell him of my decision not to play in the tournament as soon as he finished.

Owen Williams and Peter Murphy had told me that I could withdraw from the tournament at any time I felt my life was in danger. Wilfred came into the bar. I waited until the white man who had had the lesson left.

"Wilfred," I said, as we did the monthly bookkeeping, "I'm thinking of withdrawing from next week's SAB Open."

He looked surprised. "Why?"

"There are too many risks."

"You mean the threats to ban you?"

"Yes, that and the death threats."

"Well," he said, "if that's how you feel, just pick up the phone and call Owen Williams. It's as simple as that."

"What's your opinion on the whole thing, anyway?"

"I think you should go ahead and play," Wilfred said. "It's the best thing you can do for your game. Just being in the tournament will give you a tremendous psychological boost. Also, you may get noticed and get the sponsorship to help you move up in tennis, play more tournaments overseas. Who knows, you may even get a scholarship to America. But that's only my opinion, you may feel differently. It's your life."

I picked up the phone book and slowly dialed Ellis Park and asked to speak to Owen Williams. He was sympathetic to my dilemma, acknowledged the risks I would be taking if I played, but in his opinion thought that I should go ahead and play because the advantages outweighed the risks.

"But I may be killed," I said.

"I don't think so," Owen Williams said. "The death threats are only a bluff."

"And the threat to ban me for life—is that a bluff too?"

"To be honest with you," Owen Williams said, "that may be the best thing that can happen to your tennis. If you're banned, I'll make sure you get into a white club. And you know the difference between black and white tennis, don't you?"

There was a pause. I weighed the risks.

"I'm being used, am I not?" I said.

"Yes, in a way," Owen Williams said bluntly. "But, before you make up your mind, let me tell you this: the future of black tennis lies in the hands of whites, any way you choose to see it. The attitudes of whites have to change. And they are changing, and steps are being taken to bring about nonracial tennis. But you blacks have to do your part too. I'll be the first to admit that much more still needs to be done before tennis is truly nonracial, but we have to start somewhere.

"But instead of helping, what is the Black Tennis Association doing? Using tennis as a political tool. It won't work. You and I know that the government would rather have South Africa isolated from the rest of the world in all sports than see integrated sports overnight, if at all. Things have to be done slowly. Real change is gradual and often painful. Putting pressure on the white man, trying to blackmail him, won't work. You know these Afrikaners, pressure only makes them more stubborn, more fearful of change. It sends them scurrying behind a *laager*.* And this pressure by the Black Tennis Association and the rest of the world is counterproductive. I see their point, but I don't agree with it. All it can do is to make whites less committed to change, make them go it alone. And South Africa has a marvellous record of going it alone. This is not the time for your tennis leaders to turn their back on us. You've got to help us to change."

Owen Williams' argument made sense; but I knew the decision to play or not to play rested on me. I knew that despite his genuine commitment to integrated tennis, he wanted me to play so as to deflect criticism why there weren't any blacks in the tournament. I could hear him say, to the ITF, "He is the only one. Others like him who had wanted to play pulled out at the last minute because of pressure from their leaders. These leaders don't have the best interest of their

---

* A circle of wagons Afrikaner settlers used whenever under attack.

tennis players at heart. They've told us that if we want them to play in our tournaments, then we have to give them the vote first. Fundamental change takes time, but the black man wants everything overnight."

I told Owen Williams that I needed a day to think the matter over and would get back to him; but it was already a foregone conclusion what my final decision would be.

50

The Saturday morning of the most important tennis match of my life was bright and sunny. Wilfred couldn't come with me to Ellis Park because Saturday morning was one of the busiest times at the ranch. But the evening before he gave me a pair of new tennis shoes and ten rands taxi fare, and he and members of the ranch wished me well.

"Remember, don't be nervous," he advised. "Don't rush your strokes. Be prepared to stay out on the court the whole day if that's what it takes to win. Segal is an experienced bugger. He knows you're much younger than he is, so he'll want to end the match quickly. Slow him down, don't play his game, move him around, wear him out. Let him make the mistakes. And watch out, he's a left-hander too."

My family was unable to come see me play. I packed my three rackets and two extra shirts and a pair of shorts in a duffel bag. My mother said a prayer before I left and entreated my ancestors to guide and protect me. My sisters wished me well, and George promised to come to Ellis Park after he had caddied at a golf course in a white suburb nearby. On my way to the bus rank I encountered hostile stares: the papers had carried stories of my decision to enter the tournament, and black people thought me a traitor. Some spat at me.

I avoided taking the bus. The taxi dropped me right at the gate of Ellis Park Tennis Stadium. It was nine o'clock. My match was not until eleven. The stadium was already thronging with people. I noticed that an unusual number of blacks were present, mostly tennis players from Soweto and Pretoria. About three or four officials from the Black Tennis Association were also present. No doubt they had come to see me humiliated. Nobody spoke to me: they only gave me cold stares and muttered "traitor" and "Uncle Tom" under their breaths. It hurt. They have it all wrong, I told myself, I'm not a traitor or an Uncle Tom; if only they knew the true reason why I'm playing.

Abe Segal was well known for his clowning on the tennis court, much in the fashion of the Rumanian, Ilie Nastase. I met him in the locker room just before the match, and he cracked a joke. I laughed, but felt nervous at the same time. When we arrived at one of the main outside courts where we were to play, we found it packed with reporters and white spectators. There was even a television crew. Ironically, none of this unnerved me as much as the group of black spectators in one corner of the grandstand.

There were big names like Stan Smith, Roscoe Tanner, John Newcombe, Bob Hewitt, Frew Macmillan and Bob Lutz entered in the tournament, yet it seemed every spectator wanted to see me play —for a while anyway.

We warmed up. I started play slowly, tentatively. Due to a nervous stomach I had missed breakfast and I felt lightheaded. I had played against left-handers before, but Abe Segal's style of play confused me. He kept spinning the ball, hitting it soft, angling it sharply; he played what is commonly called "junk tennis." I tried to whack the ball down his throat. I became impatient; I hurried my strokes and I made one unforced error after another. He won the first set, 6–2. The crowd, which had been cheering me on, began drifting away. At changeovers, I would glance at the black spectators; many gloated. An elderly white man in a tennis outfit came up to me as I was taking a sip of water. "Run him down," he said, leaning over the fence. "He's got no knees anymore."

"That's what I'm trying to do," I said; "instead, he's the one that's making me run."

My determination, enthusiasm and youth were no match for Segal's vast experience and skill. I lost the second set, 6–3. When we shook hands over the net he patted me on the shoulder and said: "That was a good match. Better luck next time. Don't give up."

I went back to the locker room, drained and depressed. You've let your people down, I told myself. Naked white South African tennis players milled around the locker room, getting ready for matches or about to shower. I was the only black; I felt out of place. "That was a good match," they offered their sympathies.

I didn't shower or change. I went back outside and roamed the tennis courts. Everywhere I went white people smiled at me and said: "That was a good match."

The black people I met laughed at me, as if saying, "Didn't we warn you, fool?" I began to feel guilty. I was convinced that I had played atrociously, that I had been a disgrace to my race. What American university would bother to give a scholarship to such a loser?

At dusk I headed home in a crowded black bus. Though I was out of the tournament, I returned regularly to Ellis Park, dressed in my tennis outfit and carrying my rackets. I was on the prowl for anyone to hit with. I came to practise against professionals like Frew Macmillan, Peter Fleming and Fred McNair. They offered me valuable pointers and urged me to gain more tournament experience. Whenever I practised with American players, I was quick to ask them about tennis scholarships. Many gave me addresses of their former schools to write to, adding that I should feel free to mention that I knew them.

One weekday afternoon on my way home from Ellis Park I bought the paper only to read:

BLACK TENNIS PLAYER
BANNED FOR LIFE

So the die was cast. I was now a tennis player cut off from his roots. I approached Owen Williams, and he told me that my predicament would have to wait until the end of the tournament. Was this his way of reneging on his promise to help me join a white club? I was aware of the fact that our history was littered with the white man's broken promises.

One Tuesday morning, midway through the tournament, I didn't feel like going to Ellis Park. I was down to my last rand. Also, I could no longer bear the pain of meeting with contemptuous stares and oaths from black tennis officials and spectators. But there was nothing to do at home, and I had called the ranch and found that Wilfred had gone to Ellis Park; so I packed my tennis bag and headed for the same.

I wandered about the courts. I was on the lookout for Wilfred and for more American players to hit with. On one of the outside courts I found two of them practising: Stan Smith and Bob Lutz, the number-one doubles team in the world. I sat on a bench overlooking the court, mesmerized by their impeccable styles. Stan Smith, tall, lanky and powerfully built, with blond hair and blue eyes, was one of the world's greatest serve-and-volley players. He moved about the court with the ease and grace of a gazelle. And his well-chiselled face, which from time to time broke into a smile, seemed that of a man at peace with himself and the world.

Bob Lutz was stocky and powerfully built. He was a fine all-around player, with excellent groundstrokes. Both Smith and Lutz were excellent singles players in their own right; Smith was in the quarterfinals of the tournament, and had once been the top player in the world. But it was as a doubles team that he and Lutz were famous the world over. Favoured to win the tournament, they held several doubles records, and watching them play was as exciting as watching a match of singles.

So there I was in the shadow of those two giants of tennis. I found it hard to believe they were made of flesh and blood as I watched them display complete mastery over the racket and the tennis ball. I wondered if even after a lifetime of playing tennis, I could ever be half as good as they. I felt sad that I was growing up in South Africa, where I would probably never get the chance to realise my fullest potential in the game.

From time to time Stan Smith looked at me and smiled. I smiled back. Apparently they had been playing for some time, for Bob Lutz said: "I've had enough, Stan. I think I'll call it a day."

The two then headed for their tennis bags on the side of the court, near where I stood, awed. I had my three rackets with me in a bag slung over my shoulder. I inched nearer to where the two stood, dying for autographs, but shy of asking.

Stan Smith, as he dried his face, looked me up and down, saw that I was in tennis garb and had my racket with me, and said: "Would you like to hit some?"

I couldn't believe my ears. A chance to hit against a Wimbledon champion, my hero! I walked onto the court as if in a dream. Bob Lutz left as Stan and I began playing. I was so nervous I feared I would bumble and make a fool of myself. Anyway, could I return any of those powerful strokes I had seen Stan hit with such ease just moments ago? I did!

I was ecstatic. There was *the* Stan Smith chasing after balls I had hit and missing some of them! I felt such joy I could have died right at that moment and it wouldn't have mattered. Suddenly all the pain I had endured since entering the tournament seemed not in vain.

"Step into the ball," "Follow through," "That's much better, now stay on your toes and move those feet," "Good—good!" "Relax your arm now, don't throttle the racket," "Watch the ball all the way," "Good—good!" The instructions and praise came over the net. Each time I did as Stan suggested, my strokes seemed to improve a thousandfold.

"Try some serves," he said in his mellifluous American accent. He told me what worked and what didn't work with my serve. Some of the pointers he gave me I already knew, but the fact that it was *he* saying them turned them into utterings from an oracle. For about half an hour I played the best tennis of my life, played like a man possessed. A crowd of black and white spectators had gathered about the court, and people were pointing at me and nodding their heads.

Just as we stopped playing I saw a slim, blonde-haired white woman in a white Adidas warm-up, standing near the fence, pocketbook in hand. She was very pretty. I instantly recognized her from photos I had seen in a recent tennis magazine: she was Marjory Gengler, Stan Smith's wife.

Stan, as soon as he finished signing autographs, introduced me to her. She said: "You're quite a good player." A pair of white youngsters in school uniforms leaned over the fence and requested my autograph. I signed the back of their notebooks and their faces beamed. I was soaked with sweat, and Stan, noticing that I had no sweater, gave me one of his. I would frame this sweater and put it on the wall, I thought with joy. Stan and Marjory suggested we have a snack in the Players' Lounge, an exclusive dining area that was off-limits to blacks, not by design, but because mostly South Africa's wealthy went there to mingle with the superstars. There I was, walking side by side with one of the best and most respected tennis players in the world and his wife, chatting with them as if they were bosom friends of mine. If everyone could see me now.

On the way to the Players' Lounge Stan and Marjory asked me about my family, school and where I lived. They seemed so eager to know me. I poured my heart out to them. I drew them vivid pictures of Alexandra, of black life, of the hardships I faced not only as a tennis player and a student, but also as a young man growing up in the ghetto. Much of what I said shocked them. They cared. I suddenly remembered that I had read somewhere that Stan Smith was a graduate of the University of Southern California, where he had studied on a tennis scholarship; and that Marjory had played number one for the Princeton University women's tennis team. Why not tell them about my American dream?

As we entered the Player's Lounge, all eyes were on us. Important people went out of their way to greet Stan and Marjory, and each time they did, I was introduced by the Smiths as a friend. We sat at one of the middle tables and had a sandwich-and-orange-juice snack. Stan and Margie neither drank nor smoked; I didn't either. Stan queried me more about my tennis and what my future plans were. All the time we were talking, Stan and Marjory treated me as an equal, a friend, a human being. Never for a moment did they show signs of condescension. Their attitude toward me made me feel even more at ease, self-confident; it made me bolder in asking personal questions and at the same time reveal my innermost feelings. I wondered if white South African celebrities—including those who regarded themselves as liberal—would have deigned to treat me as an equal in a room full of whites. Yet here were two white persons whom I had known hardly a day, treating me as if we had known each other for years, as if we were brothers and sisters.

Marjory proved the more inquisitive of the two. Baffled by the complexities of apartheid, she asked me to explain why blacks didn't fight to change the system that so dehumanized them. I told her about the sophistication of the apartheid machinery, the battery of Draconian laws used to buttress it, the abject poverty in which a majority of blacks were sunk, leaving them with little energy and will to agitate for their rights. I told her about the indoctrination that took place in black schools under the guise of Bantu Education, the self-hatred that resulted from being constantly told you are less than human and being treated that way. I told her of the anger and hatred pent-up inside millions of blacks, destroying their minds.

I would have gone on to tell Marjory and Stan about the suffering of wives without husbands and children without fathers in impoverished tribal reserves, about the high infant mortality rate among blacks in a country that exported food, and which in 1967 gave the world its first heart transplant. I would have told them about the ragged black boys and girls of seven, eight and nine years who constantly left their homes because of hunger and a disintegrating family life and were making it on their own: by begging along the thoroughfares of Johannesburg; by sleeping in scrapped cars, gutters and in abandoned buildings; by bathing in the diseased Jukskei River; and by eating out of trash cans, sucking festering sores and stealing rotting produce from the Indian traders on First Avenue.

I would have told them about how these orphans of the streets, some of them my friends—their physical, intellectual and emotional growth dwarfed and stunted—had grown up to become prostitutes, unwed mothers and *tsotsis*, littering the ghetto streets with illegitimate children and corpses. I would have told them all this, but I didn't; I feared they would not believe me; I feared upsetting them.

When we parted my soul was uplifted, my hope for the future renewed. At the same time I felt sad. I had fallen in love with the Smiths and did not want to leave them. Never in my life had I met such honest, caring and loving whites. If only South Africa was full of them. I had spent my last rand and had no fare to get home. Stan gave me twenty rands. As we said good-bye to each other, Stan and Marjory asked me if I was planning on coming to Ellis Park the next day.

"I'll be coming to Ellis Park for as long as you two are around," I said eagerly.

"Look Marjory and me up," he said, "and we'll talk some more. If you come early enough we may even hit some. I have a match in the afternoon." I was so happy as I left for the bus stop that on the way I threw a beggar a few coins. I couldn't wait to get home and tell my family about the Smiths.

Next day I rose early and headed for Ellis Park. True to his word, Stan did hit with me before his match. At about noon Marjory and I sat together on the bleachers and watched Stan trounce his opponent. After the match we had lunch in the Players' Lounge. We talked more about South Africa, and Stan and Marjory told me about Agnes and Bremer Hofmeyer, a white Christian couple with whom they were staying for the tournament.

"Agnes and Bremer are very good friends of ours," Stan said. "I hope to introduce you to them before the tournament is over."

I was curious to find out what kinds of individuals the two were because their last name sounded Afrikaner, and I still had yet to meet an Afrikaner who did not believe in apartheid. I asked Stan and Marjory to tell me more about the couple before I met them. What they told me about Agnes was shocking. She and her family used to live in Nairobi, Kenya. During the Mau Mau uprising of the 1950s she and her family refused to build a fence around their home despite warnings that it was dangerous not to do so. The reason Agnes' father refused to build the fence was that he felt that he was on such good terms with the Mau Maus he had nothing to fear. One day, while Agnes was in America, the Mau Maus went on a hunt for a white man to sacrifice to tribal gods. They stormed Agnes' home, killed her mother and hauled her father to a mountaintop, where they buried him alive.

Incredibly, a few years later Agnes returned to the village of those who had murdered her parents, to minister to them of the love of Christ. She told the Mau Maus that she did not harbour any hatred toward them for leaving her an orphan.

I was moved by the story. It reinforced my belief that among white South Africans there was that small minority that really believed in love, freedom and human dignity for all. So why should they be lumped into the same foul den as the racists, and made the object of hate and vengeance? Why couldn't the struggle in South Africa be not one of black against white, but one that pitted those who believed in freedom, justice and equality against those who didn't?

Finally the day neared for Stan and Marjory to return to the United States. We had become such good friends that I cried at the thought of them leaving. Our being together, their understanding of my life and dreams and their encouragement that I remain resolute in my faith that in the end things would work out for the good had filled me with hope for the future, and suddenly it seemed that in leaving they were taking that hope with them. Nothing definite had come up regarding the scholarship, except Stan's promise to pursue the matter diligently upon arrival in the States.

"How long will it be before I hear from the schools?" I asked, with a tinge of impatience. Stan and I had arranged to meet at Ellis Park. "I'll be matriculating soon, and I need to at least have an idea about what lies ahead."

"Well," Stan said, "I can't guarantee that you'll hear from the school, not right away anyway. These things take time. But you'll definitely be hearing from Marjory and me. And please do write and tell us how you're doing."

"Thank you for everything," I said.

"What are your plans now that the tournament will soon be over?" Stan asked.

"I'm banned for life from black tennis as you know," I said, "so I guess I'll have to test the new government policy sanctioning inter-racial sports. I'll apply for membership at one of Johannesburg's whites-only tennis clubs. If I'm refused membership, then I'll just keep practising at the ranch and pray that you come up with something."

"Are there any more tournaments you can play in?" Stan asked.

"Not that I can"—before I could finish the sentence something flashed across my mind. "Oh, you know, Stan," I said excitedly. "There's a series of tournaments called the Sugar Circuit which begin immediately following the SAB Open. They are held in four of five cities along the coast: Durban, Port Elizabeth, East London, Bloemfontein and Cape Town. Before the boycott a few black players took part in one or two of them."

The Sugar Circuit, which Arthur Ashe demanded be integrated in 1973, was regarded as the training ground for many of the world's future tennis professionals.

"How does one enter such tournaments?" Stan asked.

"Owen Williams might know," I said. We found Owen Williams in his office, and he told Stan and me that though the date for accepting entries for some of the tournaments on the Sugar Circuit was already past, he could arrange for me to play in any of them.

"How many would you like to play in?" Stan asked.

"Oh, one or two," I said arbitrarily: I would have liked to play in all of them.

Stan told Owen that he would pay for all my expenses to the tournaments in Port Elizabeth and Cape Town. I was speechless. I wanted to cry, to dance, to fall on my knees and worship Stan. Owen estimated that to play both tournaments would cost about six hundred rands (five hundred dollars). I calculated how long it would take my father, with his salary of ten rands a week, to come up with such an amount: he would have had to work continuously for a year, getting up at four in the morning and coming home at nine in the evening; and we would have to go without food, medical treatment, paying rent, etc. Such a calculation drove home the enormous obstacles facing black boys and girls with dreams of someday becoming Arthur Ashes and Althea Gibsons.

I was awakened from my reverie by Stan saying the following to Owen: " . . . and I think Mark will need rackets, tennis shoes, shirts and shorts." Stan then arranged for me to get three Maxply rackets from a Wilson distributor in downtown Johannesburg. Andre strung them for me for free. Owen got in touch with Abe Segal, who owned a clothing label, and I received a dozen shorts and shirts from him.

Stan and Marjory had promised to apply for permits to visit my family, but because of time constraints—Stan was in the finals of the doubles championship and in the semifinals of the singles competition —and the bureaucracy involved in getting a permit, they could not make it. Stan lost a closely fought semifinal match to the Argentinian, Guillermo Vilas, but he and Lutz handily won the doubles crown.

Stan and Marjory left. Owen handed over the arrangements for my trip to Port Elizabeth and Cape Town to Geoffrey Montsisi, director of the BTF and my only supporter when black tennis officials voted to ban me from black tennis.

All along I had kept my pending trip to the Sugar Circuit a secret even from my family, so when one day I came home with a box full of tennis clothes and new tennis rackets, my mother demanded to know where I had stolen everything.

I told her about Stan sponsoring me. For a few minutes she said nothing, then suddenly tears began streaming down her cheeks. "They're full of God's love, child," she said. "Pray with me that He should bless and protect them all through their lives. They're special human beings."

I kneeled down with my mother, and we prayed.

51 News that Stan had sponsored me to play the Sugar Circuit stunned a lot of people. It infuriated some of the black tennis officials who had banned me, and they began circulating word that Stan had wasted his money on a "traitor" who did not deserve such help; they claimed that there were better black tennis players than I. I knew that this was jealousy, intended to discredit and destroy me as a tennis player, and it bothered me and made me angry.

"Don't pay attention to all this nonsense," scoffed Mr. Montsisi. I was in his office at Cue Promotions to plan the itinerary for my trip.

"They can bark all they want," I said. "Haven't they just banned me from their association, so who the hell are they to decide whether I deserve the sponsorship or not? I'm the one who took the initiative to befriend Stan and Marjory."

"Everything is set for your trip," Mr. Montsisi said, perusing several documents. "You'll be leaving from Jans Smuts Airport. In Port Elizabeth you'll be staying at a hotel right near the tennis courts. It's one of the multinational hotels which don't practise apartheid, not overtly, anyway. And in Cape Town I've made arrangements for you to stay at the home of a Transkeian diplomat who lives right in the middle of Cape Town, about half a mile from the tennis courts. I think you'll love Cape Town."

"You said my host is a Transkeian diplomat. What sort of diplomat?"

"He's head of the Transkeian Consulate. You know the whole homeland business. This man and his family are allowed to live in the posh all-white section of Cape Town."

Transkei, the so-called Xhosa homeland, which Pretoria had prodded to accept an independence so specious no other country in the world would recognize it, had an embassy and consulates throughout what the government called "white South Africa." The most curious thing was that though many of the Transkeian diplomats, including the prime minister himself and his entire cabinet, were regarded as Kaffirs by whites before being granted independence, they now had been given the status of "honorary whites," which meant that technically they were no longer subject to South Africa's dehumanizing racial laws.

Many blacks believed that such arbitrary racial classification was blatant proof that the government had created apartheid not because God so ordained, or that the various races were so radically different they could not coexist as one nation, as white supporters of racial segregation claimed. Apartheid was purely and simply a scheme to perpetuate white dominance, greed and privilege. Surely there is no justification under the sun for regarding a Chinese as a nonwhite and a Japanese as white; a black living in Soweto or Alexandra as a native and a black from America as an "honorary white," and from Zambia or Zimbabwe as a "foreign native."

Despite my detestation of those blacks who went along with the government's policy of homelands—stripping blacks of citizenship in the rich and luscious parts of South Africa and forcing them to become citizens of fragmented deserts—I agreed to stay at the home of the Transkeian diplomat in Cape Town: I wanted to find out his reasons for selling out on his race.

I left for Port Elizabeth on a Sunday, two weeks before Christmas 1977. Throughout the two-hour trip from Jans Smuts Airport to Port Elizabeth I couldn't stop staring out through the window. I was awed by the immense beauty of South Africa, seen from high up in the clouds: rolling hills and plains, meandering rivers and mountain ranges, thick forests, magnificent coastlines, luscious farmland. There's room for everyone, I said to myself, in this beloved country, if only apartheid weren't ruining it for everybody. I was the only black person on the plane and I felt out of place. A middle-aged white woman with a long nose and a fastidiously made-up face was the only other passenger in the row. Each time our eyes met she smiled; I returned a nervous smile. I wished there were other black faces on the plane; people I could talk to, laugh with and tell how nervous and delighted I was on my first plane ride.

Suddenly I felt something inside that horrified me: I wanted to go to the bathroom. Were there any bathrooms for blacks on the plane? We had another hour before reaching Port Elizabeth, and I felt I couldn't hold out that long. I didn't only want to urinate, I wanted to do the other stuff as well. Bizarre thoughts thronged my mind. What would white people do to me if I started smelling like shit? Would they demand that I be thrown off the plane? There were no parachutes, so how could I hope to reach earth alive?

My stomach churned. I finally mustered enough courage to call one of the six stewardesses, all white, who had said to me with a smile when I entered the plane: "Welcome aboard, sir. We hope you have a pleasant flight."

"Excuse me, miss," I said, embarrassed. "I would like to use the bathroom."

"There's one in the back of the plane, sir," she said.

I turned my head and saw two of them, opposite each other. I was about to get up when I saw two white women, one coming out of each. I quickly slumped back into the seat. The stewardess was gone. She came back minutes later.

"Excuse me, miss," I said. "Are those two the only toilets on the plane?"

"Yes."

"The only ones?" I said incredulously.

"Yes. Are they occupied?" she asked innocently.

"I don't know," I said.

She went back to the rear, looked at the doors of the two toilets and came back.

"They're vacant, sir," she said.

"Thank you very much," I said.

The plane came across rough winds, and it shook. I staggered down the aisle, all the time thinking of parachutes.

"The captain requests that, for your safety, you should fasten your seatbelts," a stewardess said. I spun and was about to dive for my seat when one stewardess said: "You can go to the bathroom, sir. That was merely a precaution."

I reached the toilets and glanced at the doors. Each read: Unoccupied. Which one should I go into? I remembered the incident years ago when Granny was bedeviled by the two identical telephone booths. I settled for the one on my left. When I returned to my seat the white woman sitting beside me spoke to me for the first time.

"Are you a tennis player?" she asked in a heavy British accent.

"Yes, ma'am," I said.

"From overseas?"

"No, ma'am," I said. "From this country."

In a surprised voice she said, "Oh, where?"

"Johannesburg."

"You must be good to travel on a plane," she said. "And all those rackets? Are you a professional?"

"No, ma'am, I'm still at school."

"Where? In Soweto?"

"No, Tembisa, near Kempton Park."

We began talking about tennis. She told me she had been to Wimbledon several times, that she was an above-average club player and that all her family was involved with tennis back in England. We discussed some of Britain's top players who had recently played in South Africa: Buster Mottram, Roger Taylor, Virginia Wade, Anne Hobbs, Andrew Jarrett. We then switched to the black tennis situation in South Africa and, in particular, the conspicuous lack of champions of Arthur Ashe's calibre. In an act of pride I told her that I was determined to change all that by becoming the first black South African to win Wimbledon.

"I think you can do it," she said with a smile.

When we arrived in Port Elizabeth it was bright and sunny. I took a taxi to the five-star hotel where I had been booked. A dozen or so white tennis players were staying at the hotel, which was an ornately furnished place. The suite where I stayed was on par with many of the bedrooms of white people I had seen my mother clean. Several things about the place filled me with anger and brought tears to my eyes.

I was treated like a dignitary. Meals were regular and scrumptious, and I had a large colour televison set in my room, whose floor was decked with Persian carpets. I even discovered a bell for room service—all this for 150 rands a week. As I snored in a double bed, back in Alexandra, meantime, my parents most likely were being marched out of their rickety single bed by the police, most likely there wasn't enough food to feed all my siblings, most likely vicious red ants were gnawing at my sisters as they slept on the damp, porous floor. The 150 rands that had been used to pay for my hotel accommodations for a week could have easily kept the family alive for four months. I had wished to live modestly during the trip and send whatever money I saved home, but everything had already been prepaid.

The other thing that made me angry was how grey-haired black men and women—old enough to be my grandparents—insisted on calling me "master" and "sir," despite my begging them to address me as "my son," or "my child."

"If we call you that, sir, word may get back to the *baas* of the hotel, and we will be fired."

"But I'm one of you."

"We want to keep our jobs."

"But I'm from South Africa."

"We want to keep our jobs."

Many South African whites I met during meals in the dining hall thought I was a black American. They were courteous, respectful and treated me as an equal. I played along. There were several American tennis players staying at the same hotel; I introduced myself to them, told them about my friendship with Stan. They were impressed and we began practising together. I drew a bye in the first round of the tournament, so on opening day I had to practise on some courts overlooking the Indian Ocean, only to be frustrated by gusting winds, and I stopped to go sightseeing around Port Elizabeth. Toward afternoon the wind diminished somewhat, but the courts were all taken, and I decided to go down to the beach and lie in the sun and think about my match the following day. I didn't get the chance: the wide beach with fine, golden sand, the calmest waves and the clearest blue water, a few blocks away from the hotel, was reserved for whites. The beach for blacks someone told me, was a strip of rock littered with seaweed and dead crabs some three miles from where I was staying. I was not allowed either to visit the Indian and Coloured beaches, which were somewhat closer and better than the black beach. I spent the evening watching state-controlled television and writing letters home.

In the morning the wind was gusting again. My opponent, a white South African who grew up near Port Elizabeth, was used to playing under windy conditions and he won the match in straight sets. I teamed up with a white South African junior player from Cape Town in doubles; we won our first-round match and lost in three sets in the second. Out of the tournament in both singles and doubles, and unable to visit the black ghettos of Port Elizabeth because of rioting there, I left for Cape Town two days before the week ended. I hoped to use the two days before the tournament began to see as much as possible of what many regarded as the most beautiful city in South Africa, to acclimatize myself to the Cape weather and, most important, to visit the black ghettos of Guguletu and Nyanga, scene of the worst rebellion in the Cape Province during the 1976–77 student protests.

The Transkeian diplomat and his wife met me at the airport. He was a short, dumpy man, and his wife fitted roughly the same description. The two lived with their three young daughters in a penthouse. From their home, on a clear day, one had a breathtaking view of Table Mountain with a thick cloud of fog hovering over Devil's Peak.

Cape Town was known as the home of the Coloureds and was one of the few places in South Africa where blacks were a minority. Given its long miscegenation history—begun when Jan Van Riebeeck and his men, the first whites to settle South Africa, arrived in 1652 without wives—the city was purported to be a most liberal place. But the liberalism, I soon found out, was skin-deep, applying only between Coloureds and whites: blacks were still throttled by the full apartheid machinery.

I hoped to play better in Cape Town, to make up for my poor performance in Port Elizabeth; so the day I arrived I immediately began training by going for a light jog late in the evening. Along one of the streets I stepped into a pothole and severely sprained my ankle. The next day it was so swollen I couldn't even put my foot in a shoe. My first match was two days away. I was determined to play despite the injury. I didn't want to give critics back home ammunition to attack me further. I could hear them saying things like: "He went to Port Elizabeth, how did he fare? He lost in straight sets. Maybe we shouldn't totally fault him for the loss, he may have been extremely nervous and couldn't play his game. He went to Cape Town, how did he do there? He lost again. Doesn't that prove he's not good enough? That he's a token player shoved into the limelight for effect."

I hobbled my way to a 6–0, 6–1 loss. The injury forced me to scratch out of the doubles competition. I was miserable. Why me?

Why me? I had so much to prove by playing my best. I could see Stan receiving an anonymous missive detailing my humiliating defeats, ending with the statement: don't waste your time on him. I could see Stan abandoning all efforts to help me obtain a tennis scholarship. I could see myself remaining in South Africa, an outcast, rejected by the Black Tennis Association and not accepted by the white tennis association because of apartheid. I could see myself leaving tennis. What would my life be without the game?

I snapped out of my depression and began making arrangements to visit Guguletu and Nyanga and conduct some tennis clinics there. I solicited old rackets and tennis balls from the players and the tournament organizers. I managed to get a few things. Guguletu and Nyanga were other Alexandras, hovels of poverty. The two tennis courts were run down and buried under weeds. I got youngsters to help me clear some of the weeds. The tennis clinic was a success, dozens of eager black boys and girls showed up. Many had talent. I knew that if they couldn't continue receiving the coaching, they would simply give up and drift into gangs and other vices. So I wrote the Black Tennis Foundation and told Mr. Montsisi about them.

The diplomat regarded himself as a staunch opponent of apartheid. When I asked him why then was he part of the "homeland lie" he told me that the best way to destroy the system was from within. I told him that I respected his views but didn't agree with them. One day he took me to the Crossroads Squatters Camp. What I saw there made me cry.

The place was worse than any ghetto I had ever seen. The shacks were made of plastic, tin and cardboard and stood near clumps of blue gum trees, whose branches screamed like ghosts in the icy Cape wind. There was no running water, sewerage system, streetlights or privacy. Malnourished children ran around half-naked, with distended bellies and large heads full of sores. Here and there a mangy dog licked the bloody feces of a child with dysentery. Here and there a rasping cough of someone with tuberculosis issued from a shack. Women washed their rags in leaky, rusted washtubs.

"Every single day," the diplomat said, "these people have to wake up at dawn, dismantle their shacks and hide them in the bush because the authorities raid the place each morning with tear gas launchers, bulldozers and crowbars. The authorities have decreed that Crossroads should go."

I had heard about that decree. Since "independence" was foisted on the Transkei, the tens of thousands of Xhosas living in Crossroads were to be stripped of their South African citizenship and deported to the tribal reserve. But in the Transkei, as in all the other poverty-stricken homelands, blacks could not eke out a living. That was the main reason why many flocked to the cities to seek work.

The Pretoria government paid no attention to such facts in its mad pursuit of its homeland nightmare. So black families were forcibly torn apart, with men remaining in single-sex barracks to work in the cities, and women and children deported to starve and suffer in homelands ruled by Pretoria-anointed dictators whose brutality against their own kind often surpassed that of the South African government. The motive of apartheid was clear: divide and rule; pit brother against brother, sister against sister.

When I returned from Cape Town I started working part-time for the BTF. It was a nonpaying job. I took it not only because I wanted to help boys and girls learn the game and, I hoped, stay out of trouble, but also because I didn't know what to do with my life. The matric results hadn't come out, and I hadn't received word from Stan.

I had learned a lot from my stint on the Sugar Circuit, one being that there was no way I was ever going to improve my game to any respectable level if I didn't constantly play against whites who were more skilled and experienced. Now that I was banned from black tennis it was easier on my mind whether to decide to seek membership at a white club. I talked the matter over with Wilfred, Andre and Scaramouche, and all three supported my intention.

I decided to seek membership at the Wanderers Club—one of the finest, most prestigious and most exclusive of clubs in South Africa.

It was a bright and sunny Monday morning when I took the black bus to Rosebank, where the Wanderers Tennis Club was located, about a mile or so from where the Smiths used to live.

"The Wanderers Club please," I said, handing the driver fifteen cents. He gave me a used ticket, which was against the PUTCO company policy. I stared at the ticket.

"We have to make money somehow, brother," he said. "The white man isn't paying us enough."

"I understand, brother," I said, making my way into the bus. We stopped at Bramley, and the bus immediately filled with black women in maid uniforms, returning to work after their day off Sunday visiting their children or husbands or relatives in the ghetto.

"Take my seat," I said to an old woman who was standing alongside waiting for the little boy next to me to offer her a seat. The little boy pretended to be asleep.

"Thank you, my son," the old woman said. "May God make you live to a ripe old age, and His blessings follow you wherever you go."

"Thank you, Grandma," I replied.

I arrived at the Wanderers Club in an unusually happy mood, feeling that it was my lucky day. There was a tribal superstition I clung to, which said that if one did others a good turn, things would go right for that one day. The Wanderers Club parking lot was filled with expensive cars: Mercedes Benzes, Volvos, Jaguars and Rolls-Royces.

What am I doing in such circles? Can I really hope to be accepted? As I walked toward the administrative building, I saw a couple of white schoolboys heading for a vast cricket field that was part of the Wanderers Club; minutes later I met a couple of young black school-age boys dressed in rags, lugging huge golf bags to the eighteen-hole course nearby.

I entered the palatial building through the front door and walked confidently down the corridor decorated from wall to wall by trophies and plaques honoring winners of Wanderers tournaments since the club was founded. I didn't bother reading any of the names on the trophies or plaques, for I knew none of them belonged to a black person. Maybe someday my children would walk down the same aisle and read my name among those, I dreamed. I was abruptly awakened from my reverie by a snarling black guard:

"What do you want here, boy, are you lost?" he said in Zulu.

"No, I'm looking for Mr. Ferguson."

"You have any message for the *baas*?"

"I want to talk to him."

He eyed me suspiciously, then said: "The *baas* is not around, boy."

"Can I leave him a message at his office?"

"Give me the message," the guard demanded. "I'll deliver it."

"I'd rather do it personally, if you don't mind," I said.

"The *baas* is not here, now get out."

The club in his hand made me leave. I tried another entrance. Along a different corridor I met a young white woman in tennis attire.

"Can you please tell me where Mr. Ferguson's office is?"

"Certainly. Just around the corner to your left."

I came to a door with a sign: Mr. Ferguson, President of the Wanderers Lawn Tennis Association. I knocked.

"Come in," said a rich male voice.

I paused a short while, then went in.

"What can I do for you?"

"I'm the one who plays at the Barretts Tennis Ranch," I said. "I believe Owen Williams told you about me."

"Oh, yes. You're the young man who took part in the SAB Open. Sit down, please. How was your trip to the circuit? Stan is a nice person, isn't he? How is your tennis coming along?"

I answered all questions.

"So I hear you're thinking of applying for membership at our club?"

"Yes, sir, I need the competition."

"You understand now that you are the first black person ever to apply for membership."

"Yes, sir. I hope I'm qualified."

"There's no doubt as to your qualifications. You are a fine tennis player, well mannered and able to speak English, rather well, I must say."

I smiled.

"I personally would like to see you become a member," he said. "It's about time we allowed hardworking players like you in. But the decision is not mine alone. I wish it were. I have to present your case to the full committee at our next meeting. I have no doubt the committee would be sympathetic, but as I see it, even if they vote to accept you, there are several serious obstacles which can't be overcome overnight. I wish they could."

"What are they, sir?" I said.

He proceeded to tell me a nauseatingly familiar story, one I had expected to hear. The government's multiracial sports policy mandated that if blacks were accepted to any white clubs, separate showers, locker rooms, restaurants and bathrooms had to be created for them. It seemed unlikely, Mr. Ferguson said, that the trustees of the club would approve the spending of thousands of rands for the creation of facilities to serve one black tennis player.

"It may take time for the law to be changed," Mr. Ferguson said. "But white sports officials across the country are working around the clock to get the government to act fast."

"I understand, sir."

"One thing which may be possible is for you to play in our tournaments. I don't think there'll be any problems with that. All you'll have to do would be to use the servants' bathrooms, and eat where they eat."

"I'll think of it, sir."

I left. So this was the white man's version of integrated sports. I was an outcast from the black tennis world, and the white tennis world wasn't ready to accept me, so where did I belong, what should I do? Was this the end? The only way I saw out was if I obtained a tennis scholarship to America. Could I? I hadn't heard anything from Stan; it was now the middle of January, nearly a month and a half since Stan and Marjory left for the United States. Had they forgotten about me? Had they received the letter I wrote them thanking them for all their help? The results of the matriculation exams were due in a few days. I had no doubt I had passed, despite the difficulties of the past school year; but what would I do with a matriculation certificate? I had two options: go on to university or seek work. I could not see myself going to any of the inferior tribal universities run by white apartheid ideologues; it would simply mean more intellectual stunting, anger, frustration and hatred. After all the changes my personality had undergone, all those battles I had fought for the right to undergo those changes and the price I had paid to feel and think and act like a human being, I could not see myself reverting back to the "yes, *baas*" mentality.

52 "It can't be! It's not true! It can't be!" I muttered to myself over and over, clutching a copy of the *World*. The matriculation exams had come out, and my name wasn't in the paper, which could mean only one thing: I had failed. That was inconceivable; all my thirteen years in school I only had to worry about whether I was going to come out number one or two in class, not if I was going to pass or fail. Yet here it was, in black and white, the possibility that I might have failed.

It was late afternoon, and there was no way I could take the bus to Tembisa to confront the principal about what surely must be a mistake. Wasn't I one of the best students in school? Then how could I have failed?

"There must be a mistake, child," my mother said in a shaking voice. "How could you have failed?"

"My name is not in the paper, Mama," I said.

"I still believe there's a mistake," she said.

"I'll find out tomorrow," I said.

I took the first school bus to Tembisa. I found many of my class-mates thronging the principal's office, copies of yesterday's news-papers in their hands. They too had come to protest the results.

"We too are baffled about the results," the principal, flanked by several matriculation teachers, addressed us. "We expected many of you to do well based on your performance over the two years. But when the results came from Pretoria, we found that many of you had failed."

"They deliberately failed us, the bloody Boers!" shouted a stu-dent. "They don't want us to go on to university because they know we'll carry on the struggle there."

I managed to see the principal alone, and he showed me the com-puter printouts from Pretoria: yes, I had obtained a third-class pass because I had failed my mother tongue! I had obtained A's and B's in all the other subjects, but because I had failed Tsonga, which carried more weight, I had failed.

"But, sir," I said, "even without my mother tongue, my average comes out higher than a second-class pass. So how could I have failed?"

"Beats me, too," he said. "That's why we have lodged a protest with the Department of Bantu Education. We think that the com-puter must have made a mistake. We hope to hear from them in a week or two."

I went back home in a daze. What would I do with a third-class pass? I wouldn't be allowed to enter even a black South African university with that, so how could I hope to enter an American one if I was to be awarded a tennis scholarship? Why did I have to fail now? Did the government know of my intention to study in America, and was this an effort to stop me? My future appeared blotted out. I sunk into depression. I couldn't eat or play tennis; I couldn't think of anything but the matriculation results and what they meant. I pinned my hopes on the thought that a mistake had definitely been made by the Department of Bantu Education, as would be shown when the principal's inquiry was answered.

The reply came back, along with the certificates: I had failed my mother tongue, no doubt about that; but on going over my exam transcripts and finding I had passed every other subject with high marks, the Department of Bantu Education's Advisory Board had decided to award me a second-class instead of a third-class pass. But still I couldn't enter any tribal university because I had failed my mother tongue.

That week a letter arrived from Stan:

Dear Mark,

Margie and I arrived home safely and are doing fine. We received your letter some time ago, and are glad you had a relatively good time on the Sugar Circuit. Sorry about the injury, but that often happens in the game. Hope you've fully recovered and are back on the court.

I did manage to get in touch with George Toley, my coach at U.S.C., and he's indicated a willingness to help. The NCAA tournament will be taking place in Georgia shortly, and he intends to approach the coaches of the various schools on your behalf. He might be writing you directly as soon as he has anything. I'll be away on the tour; in case you need to get hold of me, write to my Washington address.

Keep in touch. Margie sends her love. We're expecting our first child sometime in July. Take care.

Your friend
Stanley R. Smith

The letter was a welcome relief; it took my mind off my brooding over the second-class pass. I immediately sat down to reply. I told Stan and Marjory that I had passed matriculation, but omitted mentioning that it was with a second-class certificate. My mother asked me one morning what I planned to do now that I had completed school.

"Are you going to take that job from the Simba Chips company?" she asked.

"No," I said.

"What are you going to do?" she said. "You can't go to university with a second-class pass, can you?"

"Yes."

"So what are you going to do?"

"I'm going to wait till I hear news from America."

"You still dreaming about going to America!" my mother sighed. "How can you go to America with a second-class pass?"

"They'll take me," I said.

"If I were you I'd stop dreaming and start working."

"I don't have a pass," I offered as an excuse.

"Then go get one."

"We don't have a permit allowing us to be in Alexandra," I said, "and our other papers are not in order, so how can the authorities give me a pass?"

"They'll give you one," she said.

I wasn't hopeful of getting a pass. Besides, I didn't want one: it represented too much emotional pain; I knew that once I had one, supposing I could get one, the system would have succeeded in shackling my being with a chain I would never be able to unloose.

It was now February, and I still had no job. I spent my days playing tennis at the ranch, hoping for a letter from Stan or George Toley telling me that some university in America had decided to award me a tennis scholarship. Then I would have no need for a pass or a job. I would finally be free to pursue my life's dream: to become a professional tennis player.

But everyone thought I was hallucinating in thinking I could become a professional tennis player, let alone get to America. Scaramouche and Wilfred thought I had a remote chance of getting to America, but they both urged me to get a job, preferably one that would allow me time to practise and play in tournaments. Despite being refused membership to white clubs, I was now allowed to take part in their tournaments. I had played in three of them, and done rather well. The authorities knew that I was playing in white tournaments, but they did nothing to stop me: they probably thought that those blacks who saw me as a traitor for mixing with whites would soon get rid of me.

By playing in white tennis tournaments I got to meet Keith Brebnor, coach of one of South Africa's crack junior tennis squads. Some of the players who had trained under him had gone on to win scholarships to prestigious American universities and later became world-class tennis stars—players like Johan Kriek, Kevin Curren, Rosalyn Fairbanks, Robbie Venter, Derek Segal, Illana Kloss, Derek Tarr, Christo Steyn, Rory Chappel. Andre arranged with Keith for me to join the squad.

"Stan Smith is trying to get him a scholarship to America," Andre told Keith. "So practising with your team will prepare him for the rigors of American collegiate tennis, should he get the scholarship."

I became the first black allowed on the squad. Every Saturday morning for eight weeks, I would take a bus to Ellis Park, where the team trained. I couldn't believe how sophisticated and exciting tennis training could be—provided one had the proper facilities and qualified coaches. The squad of a dozen or so boys and girls—among the cream of the crop in South African junior tennis—was drilled by Keith and his assistants on the ways to hit forehands, backhands, volleys, drop shots, serves, lobs, etc., with power and precision; we had lessons on "court coverage," percentage tennis, mental attitude for winning tennis and strategy and tactics. None of these things were taught, as far as I could tell, in black tennis circles. If they were, definitely not with as much clarity and depth as among whites.

As the only black player on the squad, I was overly self-conscious at first and performed below par. Gradually, however, as the white players began opening up to me, talking, laughing and even joking, I began feeling comfortable in their midst, with the result that I was soon playing at their level. The improvement I would have made in years of playing tennis in the ghetto would not have equalled the improvement I made in those eight weeks with the squad.

Some of the white players on the squad started inviting me to their homes during the week, where they had floodlit courts. Through such interaction I learned a lot about white people, their unfounded fears, the difficulties they faced in trying to figure out who the black man really was, what it was he wanted, why he hated whites, why there was such tension among the races. I would be asked: "How can we live with you people when you hate us so much?"

I would reply that for as long as meaningful contact between the races was forbidden by law, the stereotypes each race had of the other would persist. Blacks would continue being suspicious of the motives of whites; and whites would continue being suspicious of the motives of blacks; blacks would continue hating whites; and whites would continue fearing blacks. Everything blacks said was good for the country, whites would say was bad, and vice versa.

"Apartheid," I said, "thrived on the enmity and fear between black and white."

At the end of the eighth week Keith took me aside following practise and gave me an evaluation of my game.

"You've made tremendous progress. But I think it's important that you keep on playing against stiff competition; that way you won't lose the gains you've already made. Tennis is like a muscle, it atrophies when not exercised and nourished. And the exercise and nourishment your game needs is to play more tournaments and practise against good players. The level of competition among American universities is very high, so you'll need to be ready."

"Will any of the players on the squad be around even after we disband?" I asked.

"No," said Keith. "Many of them are leaving to play junior tournaments in America and Europe."

"Can I go?" I said in jest.

He smiled. "Do you have three thousand rands?"

I did not have that kind of money.

"Do the players pay for the trip themselves?"

"Yes, their parents do."

It would have taken my father almost five years to come up with the money to finance the summer-long trip. So this was what I was up against as a black tennis player. I just somehow had to get to America.

53 One day I was arrested for being in a white neighbourhood after the ten o'clock evening curfew, and for being without a pass. I told the arresting officers, one black and one white, that I was a student. Luckily I was in the habit of carrying several books with the name of my former school on them. They let me go with the warning to get a pass.

"You're eighteen years old now," said the black officer. "You should have got one two years ago."

I began making plans to go apply for one, even though I detested the idea of carrying a pass. At the pass office I was interrogated by a young black man in a checkered suit who appeared to enjoy the job he was doing: putting his own folks through hell.

"I have come to apply for a pass," I said. I was dressed in my Sunday best.

"What's your name?" he said, placing his shiny shoes across the table and leaning back on the swivel chair, twirling a silver pen. He had copied every mannerism of his *baas*.

I told him my name.

"How old are you?"

"Eighteen."

"Who are your parents?"

I told him.

"Where do they live?"
I told him.
"What tribe are they from?"
I told him. He jotted everything down on a pad.
"What schools did you attend?"
I told him.
"Who were your principals?"
I told him. I was getting irritated with each question.
"Have you been arrested before?"
"No."
"How long have your parents been living in Alexandra?"
"Twenty-five years."
"Continuously in the same place?"
"We moved a couple times."
"Where does your father work?"
"Germiston."
"For how long has he been working there?"
I told him.
"Where does your mother work?"
"Ferndale."
"What does she do?"
I told him.
"How were they married?"
I asked him what he meant.
"I mean were they married in the Marriage Court, *lobola* or what?"
"My father paid several cattle for my mother, and later the two got a certificate at the Marriage Court."
"*Lobola*, that's what it is," the interrogator said, writing everything down. He stood up, told me go to wait outside, and he would call me back. I waited for half an hour.
"You have serious problems," he said, perusing a stack of papers on the table.
"What problems?"
"Your parents' files here show that they don't have a permit to live in Alexandra," he said with a important tone.
"But my parents have been living together for over twenty years. And I have a brother and five sisters."
"That doesn't mean anything. They are still living here illegally."
"So what does that mean?"

"It means we can't start the pass process."

"What do you want?" I demanded. "What more papers can I bring you?"

I had notes from my principals, my birth certificate, my mother's and father's passes, rent receipts, my baptismal certificate (I was told I needed one before I could qualify for a pass) and other miscellaneous papers.

"Your parents have to get a permit."

"But this office refuses to give them one!"

"Your parents have to come with you."

"My mother can come, but my father dare not miss a day. He'll be fired."

"He's got to come."

"But he'll be fired."

"Then bring your mother."

"Is that all?"

"That's all," he said. "Oh, don't forget to bring the necessary papers."

"Which ones?" I thought I had brought all necessary papers.

"The necessary ones," he said impatiently.

"Which ones?" I insisted.

"Don't be bloody cheeky, boy," he raged. "You know that you don't have a letter from your employer."

"But I'm not working," I said.

"Then what do you need a pass for?"

"I need one to look for work."

"You first find a job and then you apply for a pass."

"But I can't hunt for a job without a pass!"

"That's your own problem," he said, standing up and heading for the door. "Next," he called out to the long queue of pass applicants.

Where could I begin to look for a job? Did I want a job? I didn't want to work for Simba Quix: Isando was too far; besides, I might be told that my parents had to be residents of Tembisa for me to be eligible to work in Tsando. One feature of the Influx Control law stated that blacks could not seek employment in cities other than those they lived in; if you lived in Johannesburg, you had to be employed in Johannesburg; to work in Pretoria you had to get a special permit which was rarely granted.

One of the reasons why I didn't want to work outside Johannesburg was that the time I would spend travelling to and from work (to

Isando was something like five hours round trip) would mean I had to stop playing tennis during the week, and I couldn't afford to do that.

How anxiously I awaited news from America. I instructed George and my sisters to watch for the mailman each day for fear that because all the twenty households in the yard had a common postbox, someone might be filching my letters: no word arrived from Stan or George Toley. I began to despair. Maybe going to America was just a dream that would fizzle away; after all, who was I to think that I could go to America? Being kicked out of black tennis had left me with few friends; it seemed people went out of their way to dissociate themselves from me. And the threats from the militants to stop associating with white people hadn't ceased. Each day I expected to be crippled or killed. My relationship with my father once more became strained; he couldn't understand why I wasn't working.

"You mean your mother and I have fed you all these years for you to end up a loafer?" he said one day. "What did we starve ourselves to send you to school for? Find a job or else get out of my house. I can't go on feeding a bearded child."

One day I returned home from tennis to find that my father, in his rage for my not working, had destroyed several of my books.

"What he was looking for were your tennis rackets," my brother told me.

There was no use in arguing with my father over why he did what he did. He was right, I had to get a job.

"Why don't you get a job and help me keep your brothers and sisters in school, my child?" my mother said to me one evening.

I looked at her. She appeared exhausted, no doubt from being worked like a mule by white people: she washed and ironed for them, cleaned their homes, weeded their gardens, washed and fed their children and catered to their every whim. Even when she was ill she had hobbled to work, even when any of my siblings was ill she had gone to work, reluctantly. We had to eat, she would say, we had to have books and school fees, we had to pay rent, we had to have bribes for the policemen. She had recently been diagnosed a diabetic, and told to watch her diet, not to worry too much, not to work too hard. But she continued working too hard and worrying too much. There was no doubt she was suffering, yet she remained upbeat, downplaying everything with a shrug and saying, "Any caring mother would do all that and more for her children."

I began to feel guilty for being selfish, for thinking too much of myself and tennis. If I got a job, I could help tremendously. I could take the burden off my mother's shoulders and repay her for all she had done for me by making the rest of her life comfortable.

During a visit to Andre's sport shop to have my racket strung, I told him that I was looking for a job.

"Business isn't exactly roaring," he said, "but I could use some help." He paused, then suddenly said, "Wait a minute. I know of a job that will pay you five times what I can possibly pay you. My father is on the executive board of Barclays Bank. I can talk to him about your getting a job in one of the branches in Johannesburg. You have your matric certificate, right! Excellent, there won't be any problem, then. My father tells me that Barclays Bank is planning on expanding its services to the black townships and with your brains, you can become a manager of one of the branches in no time. And you know how much managers make! Over five hundred rands a month, the same as whites. Do you want me to talk to my father?"

"Yes," I said gratefully.

"Barclays Bank has a policy of nondiscrimination. You work in the same offices as whites, sit in the same lounge, and get the same fringe benefits. I tell you you may find working there so rewarding you may not even want to go to America," he laughed.

I told him about my pass problem.

"Don't worry about that," he said.

A few weeks later I took copies of my matric certificate and letters of recommendation from my principal and teachers and went for an interview at the Barclays Bank's headquarters in Johannesburg. Mr. Dandridge, the personnel officer, was highly impressed with my credentials, especially my command of the English language.

"That's a definite plus in the company," he said. "And the fact that you are articulate in Afrikaans and good in mathematics makes you a highly qualified applicant. Barclays Bank has a new program in place, to train qualified blacks for managerial positions in all areas of banking. With your talent there's no limit to what you can achieve. I think banking is an excellent career choice."

I don't know how much of this was public relations, how much of it was Andre's father's influence and how much of it was my merit. But I was pleased: finally I had a job, a job with a company that professed not to discriminate on the basis of colour or race. At least in this job I would not be subjected to the indignities and racism that blacks faced in the workplace; and at the same time I would be earning more than I had ever dreamed of (I had been promised a starting salary of nearly three hundred rands a month) and be able to help my parents and siblings at school. Maybe Andre was right; working for Barclays Bank could turn out to be better than going to America.

Mr. Dandridge gave me a letter to take along with other necessary documents to the pass offices of the West Rand Board. The young black man in the checkered suit, after reading the letter, grudgingly gave me papers indicating that I was now qualified to apply for a pass. I was fingerprinted the same day, and a specimen of my fingerprints sent to government computers in Pretoria to check, among other things, if I had committed any crimes (the same computers were also used to monitor the movement of millions of blacks with passes). I was then given more papers to take with me to the main post office on Albert Street, a run-down section of Johannesburg. There I experienced the worst degradation of my life.

The offices opened at ten, but I arrived at six in the morning. Already, hundreds of black men and women thronged outside its gates. Many were there for passes and permits to enable them to live and work in urban areas, to marry or move to another ghetto. Some in the multitude had been waiting in the queue for days, hoping that white madams and *baas*es who daily came to the offices seeking cheap black labor would throw them a job as a garden boy or maid: they dared not leave the offices without a job, for if arrested they would be instantly deported to the tribal reserves.

There was fear, desperation and hopelessness in the eyes of many. People, angry and hostile, jostled each other to be first in line before the offices opened. Arrogant black policemen kept the multitude away from the gates with vulgar language and *sjambok* stabs.

The offices opened. The queue moved at a snail's pace; I struck up a conversation with an unemployed man in a dark suit. His name was Bra Modise, and he was from Soweto. He had been coming to the offices for over a month without success. A high school dropout, he used to work for a landscaping company; it went out of business, and he had to come to the offices to request a permit to hunt for another job.

He began talking about what went on inside the building. "There are scores of tables inside," he said. "And brother, you have to go through every one of them. God help you if you don't understand Afrikaans, for the tables are manned by stubborn Afrikaners who believe very much in apartheid. They'll make that clear in their treatment of you. They'll humiliate you to the point where you feel you are not human. They'll strip you of your dignity, and there's not a damn thing you can do about it. You'll get angry, yes, you'll hate, yes, but there's not a damn thing you can do. After all, they know they hold your fate in their hands: you, not they, need the 'passport to existence.' "

He paused, lit an already half-smoked cigarette, took long draws and blew the smoke heavenward in a dreamy sort of way, creating a cloud above his head. Meanwhile the queue had moved to the point where we were about to enter the building. Bra Modise's pass problems required him to go to some office at the end of the building. I had to go to the tables.

The tables were manned by white and black clerks, but they both acted the same. From table to table I was asked all sort of intimate details about my life and the lives of my parents. All information was entered onto forms, to be fed into a computer later. Several men and women in the queue who fumbled were summarily flung out of the building by black guards. In order not to appear fumbling, people said, "Yes, *baas*," "Yes, madam" to everything the white clerks said; thus, with the stroke of a pen, a man's future was determined, his destiny altered. Black man after black man, black woman after black woman were sent back for more papers, more receipts, more certificates, more of everything that would satisfy the whims of bureaucrats who revelled at the sight of a grovelling black man or woman. Fortunately I had all the papers required, a fact which annoyed some of the black clerks, who took perverse pleasure in throwing out of the building men and women who lacked this or that paper, this or that stamp. All the time these black clerks were on the lookout for bribes.

I finished with the tables and was told to go down to several rooms at the end of the building for a physical. A black man walking alongside me said, "This place is hell, brother, just pray you only come here once. Never, never lose your stinker [pass]. People have been known to go mad, to commit suicide, rather than come here again."

For the physical I was herded into a large room along with thirty or so black men, mostly migrant workers. We were ordered to strip down to the waist and line up facing the wall, waiting our turn at the X-ray machine. Our clothes lay in random bundles about the floor. There was talk from the white and black clerks carrying out the physical that some of the migrant workers had lice and needed to be fumigated. My senses were numb with anger; I moved about as in a nightmare, obeying every order. A black man in a white coat came up to me, jerked my right arm, and smeared it above the elbow with an acid ointment.

"Next!" the black man in the white coat shouted. I moved on to a white man in a white coat standing nearby, a needle in his hand. He jabbed the needle, recklessly, into the spot dabbed with the ointment. Pain shot through my arm as dark blood oozed from the needle's point of entry. My arm felt limp. I moved on to the X-ray machine. A black man in a white coat shoved me onto a platform and snapped: "Breathe in!"

My chest was X-rayed. I was ordered to pick up my bundle of clothes and proceed down the hall, to where a white man and a black man, both dressed in white coats, sat. As I wondered what the examination this time was I saw a muscular black man stand in front of the white man as if waiting for some command.

"*Vula!* [Open!]" the black man shouted.

The migrant worker unzipped his fly and exposed his intimates. The white man stared at them for a couple moments, then said: "Okay, next!" My turn came. I was okay. Veneral disease disqualified you for a pass.

The ordeal lasted the entire day, at the end of which I seethed with hatred and anger; I wanted to kill somebody. I can't take this degradation anymore, I told myself as I headed for the black bus stop, new passbook in hand: it contained my picture, fingerprints, address, employer's address, age, colour of hair and eyes, height, tribal affiliation—it contained every detail of my life necessary for the police to know my life history upon demand, and I was supposed to carry the damn thing with me every hour of the day and night.

But how could we blacks allow whites to do this to us—to degrade us, to trample on our dignity—without fighting back? The fact that for the rest of my life I was doomed to carry the odious thing—a reminder of my inferior station in South African life—filled me with outrage and revived my determination to get to America. Not even a job at Barclays Bank was worth my freedom. If the scholarship offer came I would leave.

No offer came. I began working at the Elloff Street branch of Barclays Bank. The branch manager was a soft-spoken liberal Afrikaner. On welcoming me aboard he told me that I was first to work in the bookkeeping section, sorting and filing checks according to some intricate accounting system.

Indian and Coloured women manned the department, and one of

them was assigned to teach me the basics. I was a quick learner. Within a few days I was quite adept at the machine. The bank closed at three, and we in bookkeeping worked until four, so I was able to occasionally bring my tennis rackets and outfit to work, and instead of heading home afterward, I would go down to Ellis Park for a training session with Andre or one of the young white players I had befriended.

At the end of the month I got my first paycheck: a whopping 295 rands! I couldn't believe that I was actually making almost three times what my parents together were making. I immediately opened a savings account and a checking account, and bought myself a new suit. I paid George's and my sisters' school fees, bought them books and still was left with half my wages. We began eating nourishing meals, and my mother talked about getting some new furniture.

"I'm not making a million rands, Mama," I said, laughing. "We'll get all that eventually, but first I have to save enough."

"We'll buy everything on layaway, child," she said excitedly. "Oh, praise to the Lord for giving you this job. Now your father and I can look forward to a new home someday, where we can live out the rest of our lives. I'm so happy child, I truly am. This is the happiest day of my life. Now all your sisters and brother can go to university and become doctors and teachers."

The bank manager told me that I was making so much progress I was to be sent to the bank's training headquarters to take several tests to determine my potential for advancement within the bank. I scored impressively on all the tests. I was told "a great banking career" lay ahead of me. My salary was increased by 40 rands. My mother urged me to start tithing as a way of thanking God for all the good luck. More to please her than anything else, I began to tithe. George and my sisters no longer went about in rags; we now could even afford a Christmas tree. There was talk of applying for a permit to move to decent matchbox houses the government was building for blacks in Tembisa. I was against moving to Tembisa for two reasons: I would be farther away from Johannesburg and the tennis facilities; and the matchbox houses were rented out along tribal lines, a further attempt by the authorities to divide and rule.

"But the Tembisa houses are better than what we have here," my mother argued.

"I don't mind helping you settle in Tembisa," I said. "But I'm staying in Alexandra."

"But Alexandra is being demolished."

"It'll take them a long time to destroy it completely."

"But the family has to stay together, child."

"I'll still visit you."

I continued playing in white tennis tournaments on weekends, and my game kept on improving. A Grand Prix professional tournament was to be played at Ellis Park during a long weekend in April, and I entered. Players like Bjorn Borg, Roscoe Tanner, Guillermo Vilas, and Yannick Noah were also entered. I read about how Arthur Ashe, during a goodwill tour of West Africa, "discovered" Yannick Noah (then eleven years old) in Yaoundé, Cameroon; he then contacted the French Tennis Federation, which arranged for Noah's passage to France, where he enrolled in a prestigious tennis program in Nice. In a few years he became the brightest new star on the tennis scene. Could the same happen with me if Stan managed to get me to America? I wondered.

Playing in the tournament was another milestone in my career as a tennis player. Though I lost early in the qualifying round to a white South African, I participated in a clinic with Lennart Bergelin, Bjorn Borg's coach. On another day I was in the locker room when the Argentinian, Guillermo Vilas, walked in from a practise session. I introduced myself. I had read somewhere that he was a fine poet, and as I also had begun writing poetry, and had my poetry book with me, I took it out and asked his opinion of several poems I had lately written.

He wasn't particularly fluent in English, but he liked them.

"I can see a lot of anger in them," he said.

"They reflect the life I and my people lead," I said.

He autographed the book and told me to keep writing.

The tournament over, I returned to work and continued hoping for word from Stan or George Toley. One evening in early May I returned home from work and found my two youngest sisters waiting for me by the gate. The minute they saw me they rushed toward me, jumping up and down with jubilation: "The mailman gave us two letters for you," they cried. "They are from America. Mama has them."

I was so happy I gave them fifty cents each. Indeed there were two letters awaiting me: one was a regular letter from George Toley; the other was a thick, yellow package from Princeton University. George Toley's letter read:

Dear Mark,

Stan told me about you and your intention to obtain a tennis scholarship to an American university. Unfortunately U.S.C. has already given out all of its tennis scholarships. But I'm in Georgia now, at the NCAA tennis championships, and I have contacted coaches from various schools across the country on your behalf. Many have indicated they'll be getting in touch with you as soon as the tournament is over.

Please let me know if I can be of further help. Good luck. . . .

With trembling hands and pounding heart I opened the fat package from Princeton University. It contained several brochures about the university—the loveliest school I had ever seen—a lengthy application form and a hand-written letter from Dick Benjamin, the school's tennis coach. For about five minutes I gaped at the pictures of the university campus: the buildings were many, large and of fine architecture; there were trees and flower gardens all over campus; there were huge laboratories, theatres, and dormitories; the gym had an Olympic-size swimming pool and a weight room. The tennis brochure showed the Princeton tennis team (made up of whites) practising in first-class indoor and outdoor courts; the tennis schedule was long and took the team to tournaments all over the United States.

What I found hardest to believe was that there were pictures of classrooms with black and white students; pictures of these same students walking side by side about the campus. So this is what Andre had told me about.

"So," my mother awakened me from my reverie. "What do the letters say?"

"I'll find out in a minute." I started reading Dick Benjamin's letter.

Dear Mark,

I met George Toley during the NCAA Tournament, and he told me about you. You sound like an interesting young man. I have enclosed an application form for you to complete and return to me before the deadline marked on it. Princeton doesn't give out athletic scholarships, but many of our tennis players receive financial aid based on need.

It is possible for Princeton to underwrite all your expenses at the school if you qualify. So please send me all the necessary information as promptly as you can. . . .

I read the letter over three times to make sure I wasn't dreaming. It was all true. I sat down immediately and wrote the two personal essays required as part of the application. I gave a detailed statement of my parents assets: we owned no land, no car, nor our shack. The total value of our furniture was something like 200 rands ($150); my parents' combined income averaged 700 rands ($600) a year, and tuition alone at Princeton was nearly $10,000.

The next day at work I called my former principals at Tembisa and Alexandra Secondary School and requested letters of recommendation. I also requested the same from Wilfred and Owen Williams. I mailed Stan a letter asking him to please send a letter of recommendation to Princeton. I waited.

In the following weeks I received more letters from universities in Illinois, New York, Louisiana, Indiana, Wisconsin, Florida, South Carolina, Georgia, Washington, California, Texas and a dozen other American states. All the letters contained brochures about the school, an application form and a personal letter from the tennis coach. I was dazed. I knew that I could not possibly answer all the letters—there were over forty—and I had to select a dozen or so to write to. But how would I go about doing it? What sort of universities were those? How did they differ from each other, if they did at all?

I finally chose the schools to apply to according to the sound of their names, the beauty of their brochures, the personality of the coach's letter, and the nature of their curriculum. In the meantime I awaited the reply from Princeton. I wrote Stan a letter telling him all about the universities I had heard from. I kept the news of the schools a secret, and instructed my mother and siblings to do the same, for fear that someone might hear of it and tell the authorities, whom I knew did not like the idea of blacks leaving the country to study overseas.

I had no doubt that I would leave my job as soon as I was offered a scholarship. I began thinking about passports and plane fare. The government would undoubtedly try to make it impossible for me to get a passport, especially following my involvement in the student protests: many blacks had been refused passports for various reasons, most of them trumped up.

One of the reasons the South African government was reluctant to grant passports to blacks, I believe, had to do with the nature of the American government. President Carter came into office in 1976, just a few months after the violent student protests in Soweto. He had vowed to make human rights a major part of his foreign policy and therefore vigorously condemned the South African government for the killing of hundreds of blacks during the protests, and the imprisonment, banishment, detention without trial and torture of hundreds of others. He had even threatened to impose economic sanctions to pressure Pretoria to end apartheid. And his appointment of Andrew Young as U.N. ambassador brought tremendous joy and hope to blacks and infuriated and frightened the government and its supporters. Some whites were said to have called for his assassination.

The attitude of the Carter administration toward South Africa yielded results. There was a drop in the number of those detained without trial and of deaths of political prisoners while under police custody. In its frenzy to win American friendship and support, the South African government instituted cosmetic changes such as multiracial sports, allowed the Sullivan Code—a set of principles calling for equality between black and whites in the workplace—to be practised by American companies doing business in South Africa and reduced a number of forced resettlements.

Despite all this effort to placate the American government, however, pressure for fundamental change continued from Washington. Americans continued to welcome and listen to black South Africans (among whom were those who fled during the 1976–77 crackdowns) who could provide firsthand accounts of black life under apartheid, instead of the South African government and its huge propaganda machine being the sole purveyor of such information.

There was a possibility that if I did get a scholarship to an American university I would be refused a passport. I began making plans to inform some of my influential white friends about the likelihood of my getting a scholarship to America, so that if the government tried to make it impossible for me to get a passport, I could turn to them for help. Accordingly I talked the matter over with Wilfred, Owen Williams, Andre and others. I also made sure to inform Stan about the proceedings every step of the way.

About a month after I had mailed the application form to Princeton University, a reply came.

Dear Mark,

Princeton has received your application. It's almost certain that if you decide to attend Princeton, the university will pay your tuition, room and board for the length of your stay as an undergraduate, beginning in the fall of 1979. Please complete the enclosed forms and return them to me as soon as you can. . . .

I couldn't believe my eyes. I finally had my ticket to America. I danced around the shack, hugged everybody, sent my brother to the store to buy two liters of Coca-Cola and a packet of Tennis biscuits.

"So you finally got your dream," my mother said, with a mixture of joy and sadness. "So when will you be leaving us?"

"The letter says I won't begin school until 1979," I said. "So that's a little over six months away." It was May, the letter had said "fall of 1979," and I took it to mean January of 1979, largely because I didn't know "fall" meant "autumn," and I also didn't know that American universities began their term in September instead of January.

"So who'll help me keep your brother and sisters in school?" my mother asked.

"Come on, Mama, I'll be working for the next six months," I said, "and I'll put away enough money to be able to see them through school. Besides, I'll be only gone for four years. I'll come back a tennis star, and I'll be able to help not only you but every black person in this country," I said dreamily.

One of my sisters—despite my insistence that everything be kept secret—told one of her friends that "her brother would soon be going to America," and soon all Alexandra knew. I began to receive threats that everything would be done to stop me from going. Each time I went to play tennis in a white neighbourhood, I thought I was being followed. The police began stopping me in the streets and demanding my papers: luckily my pass was in order. I began wishing that I were leaving the next day, instead of in a year's time. Anything could happen in a year.

I couldn't afford to cut off my relationship with white tennis players, which probably would have placated the militants, and not give the police the excuse to lock me up; if I did that, how would I prepare myself to face the rigors of American collegiate tennis? I continued with my life as before, and hoped for the best.

More brochures, application forms and letters from tennis coaches from various American universities continued to come. I got an average of two letters a week. One day in June a letter came from a tennis coach from a college named Limestone in Gaffney, South Carolina.

The coach's name was Professor Killion, and the letter was short and to the point:

Dear Mark,

George Toley told me about you. I'm interested in you joining my tennis team this fall (September). I'm offering you a full tennis scholarship, which includes tuition, room and board and books. The package is worth about $6,000 a year. All you have to do is sign the enclosed contract (if you accept the scholarship) and begin making preparations to be here by September 18. We are an NAIA (National Association of Intercollegiate Athletics) school, but we have a very tough schedule. Several of my players are ranked in the state, so you'll find plenty of competition. . . .

My head spun. Could it be true, could it be true? I asked myself over and over again. Could it be true that in just over two months I could be on my way to the Promised Land? I kept the news of my scholarship award a secret for several days, still doubtful that it was all true.

"What is it, Mark?" my coworkers at the bank asked. "You seem so happy one would think you've discovered gold in your backyard."

"Nothing," I would say. "I'm just happy, that's all."

The day I informed my family (my father was still at work) everyone screamed with joy. My sisters hugged and kissed me and sang me ditties of praise. My mother thanked God so many times that I thought He or She would surely appear and say: "That's no miracle. I do this all the time."

When I told Wilfred the news he was beside himself with joy. He told every one of his patrons, and I became the toast of the ranch. Even those whites who had kept at a distance from me came over to congratulate me. Many expressed disbelief over the fact that I had obtained the scholarship. I wished so much to share the good news with my friends in the ghetto and with my former teachers and principals, but my mother warned me against it.

"This is not the time," she said. "They may do something to you. Wait until the last minute, when you know for sure you are leaving."

I agreed to the scholarship offer from Limestone.

I told Mr. Montsisi over at the Black Tennis Foundation, and he promised to keep the news secret.

"I always knew you would end up going to America," he said.

"Is that so?"

"You're an unusual type," he said. "You believe in yourself.

That's what we blacks as a nation need. Faith in ourselves. We believe too much of what the white man tells us about ourselves, and the results of that have been disastrous: whites are running our country."

When Owen and Jennifer Williams heard that I had been awarded the scholarship they were delighted, and pledged to help in any way they could. I told them about my concern about getting a passport, and they told me not to worry. They assigned Mr. Montsisi to assist me in making preparations for the trip. It was decided that I should leave a week before September 18 so that I would have some time to get used to America.

"It's another world," said Owen, chomping his large cigar, a habit of his. "There there is no apartheid. I don't think you will have much difficulty adjusting, though, because of your experiences at the ranch and at white tournaments. Even with that, if I were you I would start reading as much as I can on American society. There's plenty of literature over at the American consulate in Johannesburg."

The consulate was a few blocks from where I worked. At lunchtime and immediately after work, I would go there to read pamphlets, books and magazines about American society. I read for the first time the American Constitution and the Declaration of Independence and was so moved by the preamble that I copied it down and read it over and over again as one would read a favourite poem or passage from the Bible. How I wished that in South Africa we had a document containing the noble words: "We hold these truths to be self-evident, that all men are created equal, that they are endowed by their Creator with certain unalienable Rights, that among these are Life, Liberty and the pursuit of Happiness. . . ." Instead we had documents that denied us the vote and considered us inferior to the white man. How much would my life change under the freedom in America? How much would I achieve when finally I could dream and create without restraint? The future appeared full of endless possibilities.

Toward the end of June, I received a package from Limestone College: it contained a letter of admission from the college, a letter from the Bethel Baptist Church in Gaffney welcoming me to the community there and promising to do everything to "make me feel at home" and also a letter of congratulations from the tennis coach. A few days later I received another letter of congratulations, this time from Stan Smith: Professor Killion had informed him about my scholarship award. Stan offered to help me obtain a visa. Armed with the admission letter, the church letter and several other letters from my former schools and other influential whites I had come to know, Mr. Montsisi and I went to the Department of the Interior in Pretoria to apply for a passport.

I was interrogated for almost two hours by a white man who had in front of him a dossier containing every fact of my life.

"Why do you want to go study in America?" he asked. "Aren't there any universities in this country?"

I replied that there were no "tennis universities."

"I never heard of tennis universities," he said icily.

I didn't reply.

"You're using this tennis thing as an excuse, aren't you, boy?" he said, looking me straight in the eyes. "I know you blacks. You leave the country and start telling Americans lies about how bad things are here. Is apartheid a bad system, boy?"

"No, sir."

"Do you like living in South Africa?"

"I like it very much."

"Then why are you leaving?"

"It's the tennis, sir," I said. "If there were black tennis universities I would stay."

"After your studies, will you be coming back?" he said.

"I wouldn't want to live in another place, sir," I said. "South Africa is my home. When I finish my studies I'm coming back to work among my people."

"Do you know that a passport takes a long time to get?"

I nodded.

"We can't possibly issue you one until November. There's a lot of information you still have to provide us with."

"But school starts in September, sir," I said.

"I know that," he said, "but we have laws here and they must be obeyed."

"Can I go and talk with the man I came with?" I asked. Mr. Montsisi had been told he couldn't be present when I was being "interviewed."

"Sure," he said, "in fact, tell him to come in. I'll explain to both of you how these things work."

It was evident that the South African government didn't want me to leave the country. Why? What did they have against me? Did they know about my involvement in the students protests? Did they know about my breaking the law by playing tennis with whites? Mr.

Montsisi came back with me and was told about how long it took to get a passport. He pleaded that an exception be made in my case, but the white man was adamant. We left and went back to the Black Tennis Foundation, where we told Owen what had happened. He made a few calls, including one to Stan Smith in America. Stan suggested that we get in touch with the American embassy in Pretoria. The embassy requested that I come for an interview in a couple days. The interview resulted in my being issued a visa—before I even got my passport.

Mr. Montsisi and I went back to the Department of the Interior, armed with the visa and other papers from the embassy. The same passport official now began raising other obstacles. Did I have the sum needed as deposit for the passport? What about my plane ticket? Mr. Montsisi, who now talked on my behalf, told the official that the deposit and the plane ticket would be taken care of.

I didn't have the four hundred rands' deposit, nor the sixteen hundred rands for the plane ticket. Mr. Montsisi approached several members of the Black Tennis Foundation board of trustees, requesting that they help. One of them, a white multimillionaire industrialist named Alf Chalmers, offered twelve hundred rands: I purchased a plane ticket. Mr. Montsisi and I then went back to the department, where no more questions were asked. We were told to come pick up the passport in two weeks. Indeed, two weeks later, on the fifteenth of August, I had my passport. I quit my job at the bank the same week, with the intention of devoting the rest of my days in South Africa to practising tennis, preparing for the journey and saying goodbye to family and friends.

54 At four o'clock in the morning, September 16, 1978, everyone in the family was up—my mother, father, brother and five sisters—watching me as I packed my last bags. All was ready. After eighteen years of living life as a fourth-class citizen, a slave, in the land of apartheid, I was at last leaving for another world, a different way of life, a better existence, away from bondage.

In a few hours, I would be flying through clouds, across vast oceans, on my way to the Promised Land, where I hoped to find the freedom and opportunity to realise my dreams, my fullest potential as a human being. Little was I aware as I packed that last bag that I was soon to become the first black boy ever to leave South Africa on a tennis scholarship, one more vital link the oppressed of South Africa had with the outside world.

The bags packed, I cast my eyes about the crowded kitchen, dimly lit by a flickering, half-burnt candle. I tried to avoid looking at the faces surrounding me; I could not bear the expression of fear and anguish written on them, as they realised that yes, I was leaving. Their faces told me that they thought my imminent departure a dream from which they would surely awaken, and find I was going nowhere. To many blacks in Alexandra, in Soweto and in the whole of South Africa for that matter, the fact that I was leaving for America, to study and to play tennis, was unprecedented, beyond belief, a miracle. It simply didn't happen that way for black children in South Africa.

I glanced at my wristwatch; it read half-past five. It was time to say farewell to everybody. I kissed my mother, forty-four years old, a born survivor. Tears began forming in her big eyes, and slowly rolled down her cheeks, onto her nightgown. She made no effort to dry them.

"Don't cry, Mama," I said, fighting back my own tears. "Please don't cry. I'll be back soon. I'm only going away for four years."

"These are tears of joy, my child," she said. "I'm very happy that God has given you this opportunity to make something of yourself, of your life. Don't waste it, child."

"I won't, Mama," I said. "I promise I won't."

I then turned and kissed my brother, George, standing near my mother. He too began crying. I then kissed each of my five sisters, and they too began crying. I too started crying. My father emerged from the bedroom and stood by the wall, behind everybody. I went over and kissed his gaunt face; he didn't resist the kiss. He was getting old now. His hairline was receding rapidly; his face was beginning to resemble an ancient topographical map of Africa.

Impassively he stood there against the wall, in the shadow of the flickering candle, seemingly trying to awaken himself from some bad dream, some nightmare. I could tell from the look on his face that he found the fact that I was leaving hard to believe: I, his son, his firstborn, his own flesh and blood, the son he had watched grow, the son whom he had wanted so much to be like him, but who had grown up to be so much different, was about to leave him suffering, gaunt, aging, helpless, hopeless, fearful of the future.

As I kissed him again, and embraced his emaciated body, a tear and a twinkle came to his eyes: he understood that despite my fanatical opposition to his way of life, despite all the shocks of childhood he had subjected me to, I still loved him, dearly.

"Take care of yourself, son," he said softly.

"I will, Papa."

Tears began streaming down his hollow cheeks. My father was crying. After eighteen years of my knowing him, he was, for the first time, crying. He's human after all; he loves me.

Tears began streaming down my face too. I pitied him, myself, my family, the rest of black South Africa. Why does apartheid do this to us? Why does it refuse us the right to lead normal lives? Why had it created within my father's heart a granite wall, which had prevented him from expressing feelings of love, care, compassion and understanding? But the wall had been shattered. My leaving had broken down the barrier which for eighteen years had barred me from reaching into my father and sharing with him the love and understanding of fathers and sons.

"Write to us always," my father said. He couldn't control his feelings, so he went back to the bedroom to don his overalls and go face the whims of white folks.

"I will, Papa," my voice trailed after him, reminding him that I was still his son; and he, still my father.

My mother left where she was standing and came over to where I was stashing my passport and other documents into a totebag. She embraced me tightly and kissed me again, saying:

"Wherever you go in this world, child, always believe in yourself. Always have hope. Always have faith. Always believe in the power of God and never forsake Him. Trust in Him, always, with all your heart and all your strength, and He'll guide you in all your ways. He made it all happen."

I nodded. Dawn was starting to break outside. Soon the car that was to take me to Jans Smuts Airport would be here. I again embraced and kissed my brother and sisters. I was overcome with grief at the thought of leaving them behind. They had become so much a part of me. They had become me in a way. I embraced them more tightly this time, aware that, possibly, I wouldn't be seeing them in a long time, perhaps for many years. How much would I have changed? How much would they have changed? How much would South Africa have changed?

I shuddered to think what life in Alexandra, in Johannesburg, in South Africa, in apartheid country, in the land of slavery, held for them. Did they have a future? Would the family remain together long enough for them to finish school, to grow up? Or would the authorities tear them from each other, deport some to the tribal reserves, arrest some, killing some? They were so young and unknowing; the same storms of life that had battered my life, warped my character and had stunted my growth they still had to face. Would they survive such storms? Would they live long enough to swim safely to the other shore? Which shore?

My mind raced back to the few happy times, and the many troubled times, we had shared together. I had watched them grow, had tried to protect them, sometimes in vain, but always unhesitatingly, from the harsh elements of black life—violence, hate, poverty, hunger, ignorance, suffering, death. When I began work at the bank I knew that much of their suffering would be ameliorated. But now I was leaving them, to venture alone into the unknown, to cast adrift my ship in search of freedom and liberty in a new land. A quest for a new life, different from the nightmare I had been living for eighteen years. A quest for a life whose ultimate goal, I hoped, would be the betterment of my life, my family's and that of the black people of South Africa.

I felt the responsibilities piling on my conscience. By going to America I felt that I owed the duty to my race and country to use my life in a meaningful way, to see my successes and failures as the successes and failure of the black race. Would I, in whatever endeavors I ended up undertaking in America, succeed, and would I do so nobly?

Yet deep within me I knew that I could never really leave South Africa or Alexandra. I was Alexandra, I was South Africa, I was part of what Alan Paton described as "a tragically beautiful land."

Suddenly there was a loud knock at the door. It wasn't the police this time, though it could easily have been. It was the man from down the street, who had offered to take me to the airport. He had declined to be paid. He had said it would be an "honour" for him to take me there. He had never been to the airport. He didn't even know how to get there, yet he had assured me that I would get there on time. He had a map of the route. He had faith. Few black people, he had told me the night before, had ever been to an airport, and fewer still had ever seen a plane on the ground, let alone climbed aboard one.

"How could we bother about flying birds when so few of us own cars?" he had said. "As for me, I would like to see the flying bird with my own two eyes before I die. They say it flies, it's huge. I don't believe it."

The man's car was too small to fit my family in, so they could not come with me to the airport.

"I hope you understand," the man said to my mother in an apologetic voice.

"We understand," my mother said. "We'll stay behind, *murena* [sir]. He's in God's hands now. Please do stay until his plane takes off. You'll be our eyes."

"I'll stay," the man promised.

George and my sisters began crying, sensing that the time had finally come for us to be parted.

"Come now," I said, fighting to hold back my own tears. "You're big boys and girls now," I said, forcing a smile. "No tears. You know that I'll be back soon. I'm only going away for four years. I'll write you and send you postcards of New York, Los Angeles, San Francisco, St. Louis and Chicago."

Write them I would, but would they get my letters? Someone had warned me about "the system" that made letters to loved ones disappear mysteriously if a black person who went overseas got "naughty." I did not know if "the system" truly existed, but I had heard so many black people talk about "it" that emotionally "it" existed. I began wondering whether it was worth it, going to America, if it meant being unable to communicate with my family.

Was American worth leaving my family behind, suffering?

Deep inside me something told me: "Yes, go." I could sense that my family, too, knew that I had to go, wanted me to go, though they didn't understand why I had to go. They would understand in time. Time, so slow yet so fast. Time, so permanent yet so fleeting. Time, so personal yet belonging to no one. Time, as she had done to me for the past eighteen years, will provide them also with the half-baked answers to the surreal life I was about to sever myself from.

"Hurry now," the man said. "I have the bags in the car. We don't know the way, you know."

I kissed my brother and sisters for the third time—the last time. Two of my youngest sisters clung to me and didn't want to let go. My mother and Florah took them away. I didn't kiss my mother; it was a hard thing to do; I don't know why. I stared a couple of moments at my brother, now twelve years old. In him I could see myself. I wished

I could somehow take him with me, take everyone with me, but particularly him, for I shuddered to think how he would react to, how he would combat the nightmarish life I had undergone that now lay before him. How would he deal with the fear, the frustration, the hate, the anger that were the lot of every black child? Would he stay out of trouble long enough to become a man, to realise his dreams, whatever they might be?

As I left for the car I told him to be brave, to believe in himself, to set goals, to have faith, to strive doggedly to realise those goals. I told him never to let the white man define his manhood. I told him to be a fighter, to be resilient, to have patience, to have hope, to take care of our ailing mother, our sisters and our father, whom I sensed he was beginning to hate just as I had done when his age. Déjà vu.

"Forgive Papa," I told him. "He's a good and loving father inside. Learn to understand him and his ways. Learn to understand the pain of his life."

I got into the car. My youngest sister wanted to climb aboard but my mother held her back. She began hollering.

"He'll be back soon," my mother said, quieting her.

Soon? I wondered.

As the car left the yard and went up the potholed street, I turned my head for a last look at my family, standing in a row in front of the shack, waving sadly in the pale morning mist. I wanted to tell the man to turn back, but I didn't. I followed destiny.

INDEX

Aesop's Fables, 171
African National Congress (ANC), 229–30, 268, 269, 289
Alexandra, 3–5
  rebellion in, 261–68, 283–86
Alexandra Health Clinic, 140, 246
Alexandra Open Tennis Championships, 241, 294
Alexandra Secondary School, 225, 339
Ali, Mohammad, 151–52, 154, 234
Anderson, Marian, 234
Anglo-Boer War, 204
Apartheid, 309–10, 314
  and ANC, 230
  pervasiveness, 201–2
  rebellion against, 259–68, 270–71
  reign of terror, 296–98
  and segregated buses, 198–200
  and separation of families, 181
  two worlds of, 93–94
Armstrong, Louis, 234
Around the World in Eighty Days, 254
Ashe, Arthur, 208, 210, 228–34, 235–40, 287–88, 298, 312

Babalazi (blue Monday hangover), 30
Baldwin, James, 234
Bantu Affairs Department (BAD), 35
Bantu Education, 193, 268, 271, 289
Bantu Education Department, 252, 259, 324
Barclays Bank, 180, 332–33, 335

Barnard, Christiaan, 279
Barretts Tennis-Court Construction Company, 275
Barretts Tennis Ranch, 227, 231, 236, 276, 322
Batman and Robin comic book, 170
Begging for food, 97–99
Belafonte, Harry, 234
Benjamin, Dick, 338
Bergelin, Lennart, 337
Bethel Baptist Church, 343
Biko, Steven, 296
Birth certificate, obtaining, 108–19
Black Beauty, 192
Black Communities Programmes, 297
Black Consciousness Movement, 296
Black Parents' Association, 297
Black spot, 91
Black Tennis Association, 300, 303, 304, 319
Black Tennis Foundation (BTF), 240, 319, 342, 345
Blood, boiled as soup, 63–64
Book burning, 284–86
Bophuthatswana, 5
Borg, Bjorn, 337
Bovet Community School, 136
Boxing match, black vs. white, 231
Brebnor, Keith, 326–28
Bunche, Ralph, 234
Buses, segregated, 198–200

Carter, Jimmy, 339
Carver, George Washington, 234
Chalmers, Alf, 345
Chappel, Rory, 326
Charcoal brazier, and poison gas, 80–82
Christian Institute, 297
Christianity, 55–62
  of expediency, 76–77
Circumcision school, 222–23
Cleaver, Eldridge, 234
Cole, Nat (King), 234
Coloureds, 210–11
  in Alexandra, 4
Connors, Jimmy, 239, 299
Crossroads Squatters Camp, 319–20
Cry, the Beloved Country (Paton), 209
Curren, Kevin, 326

Dagga (marijuana), 53
David Copperfield, 192
Davis, Sammy, Jr., 234
Davis Cup, 299
Debates, 252–53
Dennis the Menace comic book, 170
Diviner, 246–48
Douglass, Frederick, 234
Dubois, W. E. B., 234
Dvorak, Antonin, 257

East London Dispatch, 297
Ellington, Duke, 234
Ellis Park Tennis Stadium, 232–33,
  235, 280, 304, 306
English, learning to speak, 194, 256–57
Evangelists, 55–60
Eyewitness to murder, 162–66

Fah-fee (numbers game), 30
Fairbanks, Rosalyn, 326
The Fantastic Four comic book, 170
Federation Cup, 299
Fitzgerald, Ella, 234
Fleming, Peter, 306
Forbes, Gordon, 302
Foster, Bob, 231–32
French Tennis Federation, 337
Full Gospel Apostles of God, 76–77
Full Gospel Church of God, 77, 216

Gandhi, Mahatma, 230
Garvey, Marcus, 234

Gazankulu, 5
Gengler (Smith), Marjory, 308–13,
  325
Goolagong, Evonne, 298
Group Areas Act, 211, 291
Guguletu, 319

Halfway House, 227
Hebelungu (nutrition program), 140
Hewitt, Bob, 305
Hobbs, Anne, 316
Hofmeyer, Agnes, 310
Hofmeyer, Bremer, 310
Holocaust, 279
Horn, Norma, 227
Horn, Wilfred, 227–28, 231, 237, 245,
  257, 271–74, 302, 306, 326, 339,
  342
Horne, Lena, 234
Hughes, Langston, 234
The Hunchback of Notre Dame, 192

Impis (Zulu warriors), 70–74, 79
The Incredible Hulk comic book, 170
Indians in Alexandra, 4
Influx Control laws, 16, 181, 249
"In Memoriam" (Tennyson), 259
International Tennis Federation (ITF),
  298

Jackson, Jesse, 234
Jarrett, Andrew, 316
Johannesburg Zoo, 202–4
The Justice League of America comic
  book, 170

Killion, Professor, 342, 343
King, Martin Luther, Jr., 156–57, 234,
  290
King's Bioscope movie house, 53, 159
Kissinger, Henry, 268
Kloss, Illana, 326
Kriek, Johan, 326
Kruger, Minister of Police, 264

Lenglen, Suzanne, 215
Limestone College, 341, 343
Livingstone, Dr., 59
Lobola (bride price), 132, 329
Locusts, gathered for food, 62–
  63

Louis, Joe, 234
Lutz, Bob, 305, 306, 307, 313

Macmillan, Frew, 305, 306
Magabulela (hand-me-downs), 184
Malcolm X, 234
Mandela, Nelson, 230
Marshall, Thurgood, 234
Matanyula (prostitution of young boys), 68–74
Mau Maus, 310–11
Mbeki, Gouan, 230
McNair, Fred, 306
The Merchant of Venice, 255–56
Mfundis (preacher), 219–21
Modderbee (penitentiary), 29, 35
Modise, Bra, 333–34
Montsisi, Geoffrey, 313, 319, 342–43, 344–45
Moore, Ray, 236
Mottram, Buster, 316
Movies, impressions of whites gained from, 53–54
Mphephu, Miss, 137–39
Mphephu, Patrick, 5
Mugabe, Robert, 269
Munyama, Mrs., 75
Murder, eyewitness to, 162–66
Murogo (weeds) served as food, 63
Murphy, Peter, 300, 302

Nastase, Ilie, 304
National Association of Intercollegiate Athletics (NAIA), 342
National Junior Tennis Championships, 287
National Tennis Tournament, 245
Naude, Beyers, 297
Newcombe, John, 305
New World Symphony (Dvorak), 257
Ngwenya, 269–70
Nkomo, Joshua, 269
Noah, Yannick, 337
Number Four (prison for blacks), 23, 29
Nyanga, 319

Okker, Tom, 239
Operation Clean-up Month, 16
Oppenheimer, Harry, 253
Owens, Jesse, 234

Pass laws, 5
Paton, Alan, 209
Peri-Urban Police, 8–25, 27–30
Phefeni High School, 259
Pinocchio, 171
Poitier, Sidney, 234
Police raids, 8–25, 27–30, 75
Princeton University, 308, 337, 340
Prostitution, young boys, 68–74

Qoboza, Percy, 297

Rand Daily Mail, 202, 272, 287
Rebellion against apartheid, 259–68, 270–71
Richie Rich comic book, 170
Robeson, Paul, 234
Robinson, Jackie, 234
Robinson Crusoe, 192

Scaramouche, 210–11, 215, 226, 240, 287, 300, 326
School
 black, 127–29, 135–43, 145–47
 dropouts, 225
 registering for, 123–134
 white, 187
Segal, Abe, 302, 304–5, 312
Segal, Derek, 326
Sharpeville, 5, 158
Sherlock Holmes Mysteries comic book, 170
Shit men, 83–85
Simba Quix, 258, 288, 294, 295, 330
Sisulu, Walter, 230
Sjambok (animal-hide whip), 8
Smith, Ian, 269
Smith, Stan, 299, 305, 306–13, 325–26, 337, 343
Sobukwe, Robert, 230
Sonjas (worms) eaten as food, 63
South African Breweries (SAB) Open, 298, 299
South African Lawn Tennis Union (S.A.L.T.U.), 215, 298
South African National Lawn Tennis Union (S.A.N.L.T.U.), 215, 300
South African Students' Organizations (SASO), 297
Southern Transvaal Lawn Tennis Association, 287

Soweto, 91
  rebellion in, 259–60, 263
Spiderman comic book, 170
St. Croix, 274, 276
Star, 202, 287
Stevenson, Robert Louis, 193
Stewart, Sherwood, 233
Steyn, Christo, 326
Stockvel, 174–75, 179
Sugar Circuit, 312–13
Sullivan Code, 340
Sunday Express, 202
Sunday Times, 202
Superman comic book, 170
The Swiss Family Robinson, 192

A Tale of Two Cities, 192
Tanner, Roscoe, 305, 336
Tarr, Derek, 326
Tarzan of the Apes comic book, 170
Taylor, Roger, 316
Tembisa, 91–92, 336
Tembisa Hospital, 246, 248
Tennis
  Ashe plays in South Africa, 228–33,
    235–40
  at Barretts, 227, 231, 236, 276, 322
  introduction to, 208–11
  in school, 226–27
  Sugar Circuit, 312–13
  tournament play, 241, 245, 287–88,
    294, 298–305, 317–18
Thor—God of Thunder comic book, 170
The Three Musketeers, 192
Tilden, Bill, 215
Toley, George, 325, 337, 342
Tom Sawyer, 192
Transkei, 5, 313–14, 319–20
Treasure Island (Stevenson), 192, 193,
    256
Tribal folklore, 78–80, 100–103
Tribalism, 207–8
Tribal laws and rituals, 31–34

Tsongas, 5, 79
Tsotsis, 27, 53, 196–97
  murder by, 163–64
Tutu, Desmond, 3
Twelve Apostle Church of God, 242

Umkhonto We Sizwe (Speak of the
    Nation), 269, 288
University of Southern California, 308
Up from Slavery (Washington), 197

Venda, 5, 34
  tribal reserve, visit to, 86–91
Venter, Robbie, 326
Vermin, in and around houses, 94–
    96
Verwoerd, Dr., 193
Vilas, Guillermo, 313, 337
Voodoo, 74–75
Vorster, Prime Minister, 264, 268

Wade, Virginia, 316
Wanderers Lawn Tennis Association,
    322
Wanderers Tennis Club, 320–21
Washington, Booker T., 197, 234
West Rand Board, 333
Wilde, Mr., 258, 294
Williams, Jennifer, 343
Williams, Owen, 240, 298, 302–4, 306,
    312, 322, 339, 340, 343
Witchcraft, 74–75
Witch doctor, 76, 88–90, 246–48
Witwatersrand, 4
Woods, Donald, 297
World, 260, 297, 323
Wright, Richard, 234
Writing, upside down, 197–98

Young, Andrew, 340

Zietsman, Andre, 287, 289–92, 293,
    326, 332–33